P9-CCC-009

STATE AND LOCAL GOVERNMENT

THE ESSENTIALS

Second Edition

Ann O'M. Bowman

University of South Carolina

Richard C. Kearney

East Carolina University

HOUGHTON MIFFLIN COMPANY   Boston   New York

To those who do, from those who teach.
And especially for Rachel, Roxanne,
Carson, Joel, Laura, Nicole, and Andrew.

Editor in Chief: Jean Woy
Sponsoring Editor: Katherine Meisenheimer
Senior Project Editor: Kathryn Dinovo
Senior Manufacturing Coordinator: Jane Spelman
Marketing Manager: Nicola Poser
Marketing Assistant: Laura McGinn

Cover image: © Frank Whitney/The Image Bank

Chapter opening image: Getty Images

Copyright © 2003 by Houghton Mifflin Company. All rights reserved.

No part of this work may be reproduced or transmitted in any form or by any means, electronic or mechanical, including photocopying and recording, or by any information storage or retrieval system without the prior written permission of Houghton Mifflin Company unless such copying is expressly permitted by federal copyright law. Address inquiries to College Permissions, Houghton Mifflin Company, 222 Berkeley Street, Boston, MA 02116-3764.

Printed in the U.S.A.

Library of Congress Control Number: 2001135724

ISBN: 0-618-21459-3

3 4 5 6 7 8 9-QWF-07 06 05 04 03

CONTENTS

PREFACE   xiii

1 New Directions for State and Local Government   1

The Study of State and Local Government   2
From Sewers to Science: The Functions of State and
Local Governments   2
Our Approach   3
State and Local Government Capacity   5
How States and Localities Increased Their Capacity   6
What Increased Capacity Has Meant   7
Problems Facing State and Local Governments   11
The People: Designers and Consumers of Government   13
Ethnic-Racial Composition   13
Population Growth and Migration   14
Political Culture   16
Linking Capacity to Results   18
Chapter Recap   19
Key Terms   19
Surfing the Net   19

2 Federalism and the States   20

The Concept of Federalism   22
Unitary, Confederate, and Federal Systems   22
The Advantages and Disadvantages of Federalism   23
The History of U.S. Federalism   24
Early History   24
The Move Toward Federalism   25
State-Centered Federalism   27
The Growth of National Power Through the Constitution
and the Judiciary   28
The Growth of National Power Through Congress   30
A New Era of State Resurgence?   32
Intergovernmental Relations   33
Interstate Cooperation   33
Tribal Governments   34
Intergovernmental Financial Relations   35

Models of Federalism   36
Dual Federalism (1787–1932)   **36**
Cooperative Federalism (1933–1964)   **36**
Contemporary Variations on Cooperative Federalism
(Since 1964)   **37**
Federal Purse Strings   39
The Importance of Federal Funds   **39**
Here's the Check and Here's What to Do with It: Mandates,
Preemptions, Set-asides, and Cost Ceilings   **41**
The Future of Federalism   43
Chapter Recap   45
Key Terms   46
Surfing the Net   46

3 State Constitutions   47

The Evolution of State Constitutions   49
The First State Constitutions   **49**
Legislative Supremacy   **51**
The Growth of Executive Power   **51**
Weaknesses of Constitutions   52
Excessive Length   **52**
Problems of Substance   **55**
Constitutional Reform   56
The Model State Constitution   **57**
Constitutions Today   **60**
Methods for Constitutional Change   60
Informal Constitutional Change   **61**
Formal Constitutional Change   **61**
State Responsiveness and Constitutional Reform   66
Chapter Recap   67
Key Terms   67
Surfing the Net   67

4 Citizen Participation and Elections   68

Participation   69
Why and How People Participate   **69**
Nonparticipation   **70**
The Struggle for the Right to Vote   **71**
Voting Patterns   **72**

Elections   75
Primaries   **75**
Runoff Elections   **76**
General Elections   **77**
Recent State Elections   **78**
Nonpartisan Elections   **79**
Election-Day Lawmaking   80
The Initiative   **81**
The Recall   **83**
Citizen Access to Government   84
Open Meeting Laws   **84**
Administrative Procedure Acts   **85**
Advisory Committees   **85**
Citizen Surveys   **86**
E-Government   **86**
Volunteerism   87
The Effects of Citizen Participation   88
Chapter Recap   89
Key Terms   90
Surfing the Net   90

5 *Political Parties, Interest Groups, and Campaigns*   **91**

Political Parties   91
Political Parties in Theory and in Reality   **92**
Party Organization   **94**
The Two-Party System   **96**
Is the Party Over?   **98**
Interest Groups   98
Types of Interest Groups   **99**
Interest Groups in the States   **101**
Techniques Used by Interest Groups   **103**
Local-Level Interest Groups   **107**
Political Campaigns   107
A New Era of Campaigns   **108**
Campaign Finance   **110**
Chapter Recap   113
Key Terms   114
Surfing the Net   114

6 State Legislatures   115

The Essence of Legislatures   116
Legislative Dynamics   117
The Senate and the House   118
Legislative Districts   119
Legislative Compensation   121
Legislative Leadership   122
Legislative Committees   123
Legislative Behavior   125
Legislative Norms   125
Legislative Cue Taking   126
How a Bill Becomes Law (or Not)   127
Legislative Reform and Capacity   130
The Ideal Legislature   130
The Effects of Reform   131
Term Limits   132
Relationship with the Executive Branch   135
Dealing with the Governor   136
Overseeing the Bureaucracy   137
Legislatures and Capacity   139
Chapter Recap   140
Key Terms   140
Surfing the Net   140

7 Governors   141

The Office of Governor   142
History of the Office   142
Today's Governors   143
Getting There: Gubernatorial Campaigns   145
The Roles of the Governor: Duties and Responsibilities   146
Policymaker   146
Chief Legislator   147
Chief Administrator   149
Ceremonial Leader   151
Intergovernmental Coordinator   151
Economic Development Promoter   152
Party Leader   153
Formal Powers of the Governor   154
Tenure   154

Appointment Power   **155**
Veto Power   **158**
Budgetary Power   **160**
Reorganization Power   **161**
Staffing Power   **162**
The Relevance of the Formal Powers   **163**
Informal Powers   164
Tools of Persuasion and Leadership   **164**
Characteristics of a Successful Governor   **166**
Removal from Office   167
Other Executive Branch Officials   168
Attorney General   **168**
Lieutenant Governor   **168**
Treasurer   **169**
Secretary of State   **170**
The Vigor of U.S. Governors   170
Chapter Recap   170
Key Terms   171
Surfing the Net   171

8 Public Administration: Budgeting and Service Delivery   172

Public Employees in State and Local Governments:
Who They Are, What They Do   175
Budgeting in State and Local Government   176
The Budget Cycle   **176**
The Actors in Budgeting   **179**
Pervasive Incrementalism   **181**
Types of Budgets   **181**
Personnel Policy in State and Local Government:
From Patronage to Merit   183
The Merit System   **183**
State and Local Advances   **184**
Merit-System Controversies   **185**
The Politics of Bureaucracy   192
Joining Administration and Politics   **192**
Professionals in State and Local Government   **193**
Reinventing Government   194
Total Quality Management   **195**
Privatization   **196**

E-Government **197**
The Quality of Public Administration 198
Chapter Recap 200
Key Terms 201
Surfing the Net 201

9 *The Judiciary* **202**

The Structure of State Court Systems 204
The Two Tiers of Courts **204**
Structural Reforms **206**
How Judges Are Selected 208
Legislative Election **208**
Partisan Popular Election **208**
Nonpartisan Popular Election **210**
Merit Plan **211**
Gubernatorial Appointment **213**
Which Selection Plan Is Best? **214**
Removal of Judges **214**
Judicial Decisionmaking 215
In and Out of the Trial Court **215**
Inside the Appellate Court **217**
Influence of the Legal System **217**
Personal Values, Attitudes, and Characteristics of Judges **219**
New Judicial Federalism 220
Judicial Activism in the States **220**
Current Trends in State Courts **221**
State Court Reform 222
Financial Improvements **222**
Dealing with Growing Caseloads **223**
Compensating the Judges **224**
State Courts Enter the 2000s **225**
Crime and Criminal Justice 225
Chapter Recap 227
Key Terms 228
Surfing the Net 228

10 *State-Local Relations* **229**

The Distribution of Authority 230
The Amount and Type of Authority **230**

A State-Local Tug of War 231
State Mandates 232
An Uneasy Relationship 233
What Local Governments Want from the States 234
State-Local Organizations 235
Metropolitics: A New Challenge for State Government 237
Smart Growth versus Urban Sprawl 239
Regional Governance 242
States and Their Rural Communities 245
The Interaction of States and Localities 246
Chapter Recap 246
Key Terms 247
Surfing the Net 247

11 *Local Government: Structure and Leadership* **248**

Five Types of Local Governments 249
Counties 250
Municipalities 253
Towns and Townships 257
Special Districts 258
School Districts 260
Leadership in Local Government 262
Mayors and Managers 263
City Councils 266
The Issue of Governance 270
Chapter Recap 271
Key Terms 271
Surfing the Net 271

12 *Taxing and Spending* **273**

The Principles of Finance 274
Interdependence 274
Diversity 275
Revenues 276
Criteria for Evaluating Taxes 276
Major State and Local Taxes 280
User Fees 286
Severance Tax 287
Gambling: Lotteries and Casinos 287

The Political Economy of Taxation   289
Spending   **289**
Tax Revolt   **291**
Fiscal Stress   **292**
Limited Discretion   **294**
Borrowing and Debt   295
Estimating Revenues   **295**
Rainy Day Funds   **296**
Other Financial Management Practices   **296**
Where All the Money Goes: State and Local Spending   298
Economic Development   **298**
Education Policy   **300**
Social Welfare and Health Care Policy   **300**
State and Local Finance in the 2000s   302
Chapter Recap   303
Key Terms   304
Surfing the Net   304

REFERENCES   305

INDEX   325

PREFACE

This book is unabashedly pro-government—state and local government, that is. Despite the drumbeat of criticism of government and public officials in the mass media, we like politics and public service. We believe that government can be a force for good in society. We do acknowledge some of the concerns voiced by critics of government. Yes, there continue to be inefficiencies, and sure, there are some politicians who, once elected, seem to forget the interests of the people back home, not to mention what their parents taught them. But by and large, state and local governments work well. On a daily basis, they tackle some of the toughest problems imaginable. And in the face of their critics, they design and implement creative and successful solutions to problems ranging from serious felonies to street paving.

The full-length edition of *State and Local Government* will continue to appear at regular intervals. But some instructors prefer to assign a briefer paperback text in order to accommodate the demands of a quarter system, to leave time for other readings, and for many other reasons. In this abbreviated version of our text, we attempt to capture the essentials of state and local government in all their immediacy and vitality. A major goal is to foster continuing student interest and involvement in state and local politics, policy, and public service. Many of the students who read this text will work in state and local government. Some will run successfully for public office. We want our readers to know that state and local government is a place where one person can still make a difference and serve a cause. For students who go on to graduate study in political science, public administration, or related fields, states and localities are fertile fields for research. And for those who are taking this course because they "have to" and who claim to dislike politics and government, we hope they will keep an open mind as they explore the contemporary world of politics at the grass roots.

The Theme of *State and Local Government: The Essentials*

This book revolves around a central theme: the increased capacity and responsiveness of state and local governments. In a way, this is yesterday's news. It has been decades since these levels of government were routinely dismissed as outmoded and ineffective. But state and local governments continue to be proactive, expanding their capacity to address effectively the myriad problems confronting their citizens. And from Alaska to Wyoming, they are increasingly more responsive to their rapidly changing environment and the demands of the populace.

Our confidence in these governments does not blind us, however, to the varying capabilities of the 50 states and more than 87,000 units of local government. Some are better equipped to operate effectively than others. Many state and local governments benefit from talented leadership, a problem-solving focus, and an engaged citizenry. Others do not fare so well. (Recall, for example, the dismal performance of some Florida counties in administering the 2000 presidential election.) The important point is that, as a group, states and localities are the driving forces—the prime movers—in the American federal system. Even those perennially clustered at the lower end of various ratings scales have made quantum leaps in their capability and responsiveness.

Major Changes in the Second Edition

The political landscape of state and local government is forever changing. As a result, the second edition incorporates many new topics and emerging issues, without sacrificing the central theme of increased governmental capacity and responsiveness. Among the fresh items are the growing importance of tribal governments, the rethinking of legislative term limits, the enthusiastic embrace of e-government, the challenges of urban sprawl, and the pressures of fiscal stress, to name but a few. In exploring these topics and issues, we emphasize the differences across states and localities. In the second edition, coverage of local governments has been expanded and more examples of policymaking have been added. An additional feature of the second edition is a Chapter Recap section that lists the major points of each chapter. Finally, we have made numerous updates to the tables and figures in the book, which yield opportunities for students to conduct their own web-based research.

Structure and Content Updates

This book provides basic and up-to-date coverage of state and local institutions, processes, and policies. It can be used as a "standalone" text or in conjunction with supplementary readings.

In Chapter 1, we introduce the functions of nonnational governments and explore the theme of capacity and responsiveness. The central importance of federalism and intergovernmental relations is recognized in Chapter 2, which traces the twists and turns of the federal system from the scribblings of the framers to the Supreme Court's latest pronouncements on the Tenth Amendment. This chapter also includes a new section on tribal governments and discussion of the slowed pace of devolution. The evolution and modern reform of the fundamental legal underpinnings of state governments—their constitutions—are discussed in Chapter 3. Chapter 4 explores citizen participation and elections, focusing on the increased access of citizens and the demands they are making on government. Chapter 5, "Political Parties, Interest Groups, and Campaigns," includes essential material on party organization and interparty competition. Types and techniques of interest groups and the "new era" of political campaigns also receive attention.

Coverage of the three branches of government—legislative, executive, and judicial—includes results of the 2002 elections. Legislative dynamics, behavior, processes, and capacity are illustrated in Chapter 6. The roles, responsibilities, and powers of governors are examined in Chapter 7, with illustrations from today's chief executives. Chapter 8 offers coverage of public administration, budgeting, and personnel policy, along with the politics of bureaucracy and the privatization, "reinventing government," and e-government movements. In Chapter 9, judicial selection and decisionmaking are considered within the context of judicial federalism and state court reform. A section on crime and criminal justice illustrates the importance of the state judiciary.

Local governments, although still considered to be creatures of the state, are not treated as afterthoughts in this book. Most of the chapters provide a local dimension, whether political processes or governmental institutions. In addition, two chapters focus solely on the localities. Chapter 10 is devoted to state-local relations, including the distribution of authority between the two levels of government, and the all-important issue of urban sprawl and smart growth. Chapter 11 focuses on the multiple types and structures of local government and on leadership and governance in these jurisdictions. Finally, in Chapter 12, the principles and political economy of taxing and spending are explained, along with the fiscal crisis that struck nearly all the states in 2002.

Throughout the text, policy examples are used to illustrate key concepts and critical points. Policymaking is, after all, a central function of government, regardless of level. Special attention is given to education, criminal justice, economic development, social welfare, and environmental protection policy.

Those who prefer a more comprehensive and detailed treatment of state and local government, including separate policy chapters, are invited to examine the fifth edition of *State and Local Government* by the same authors (Houghton Mifflin, ©2002, ISBN 0-618-13207-4).

Features of the Text

Much effort has been invested in making this book accessible to students. Examples throughout the chapters showcase the innovative, the unusual, and the insightful in state and local politics. Thoroughly updated photographs provide visual images to bring the current world of state and local government to life for the reader. Maps, tables, and figures provide recent information in an engaging format. A glossary of key terms is located in the margins of the text. At the end of each chapter, major points are bulleted in a Chapter Recap section. References to websites, which can be accessed through the book's website, encourage student curiosity, engagement, and individual research.

In addition to the chapter-by-chapter links, the companion website makes a number of other resources available to students and instructors. An interactive U.S. map explores the similarities and differences among the states. Our "Evolution of Devolution" time line illustrates how the capacity and responsibilities of state and local governments have fluctuated over time. On-line chapter quizzes allow students to test their understanding of important concepts. The site is accessible through the Houghton Mifflin College Division's Political Science home page at http://politicalscience.college.hmco.com.

A very helpful Instructor's Resource Manual with Test Items, written by Professor Jeffrey Greene of the University of Montana, is available to the instructor. The manual features learning objectives, chapter overviews, suggested readings and lecture topics, multiple-choice questions, terms for identification, and essays.

Acknowledgments

First, we would like to thank our colleagues who reviewed both editions of the Essentials version. They provided us with many thoughtful observations and examples, which, whenever possible, we have incorporated. These include Walter Huber, Muskingum College; William E. Kelly, Auburn University; James L. McDowell, Indiana State University; John H. Portz, Northeastern University; Donald Roy, Ferris State University; Loran B. Smith, Washburn University; Mark Somma, California State University, Fresno; and Nelson Wikstrom, Virginia Commonwealth University.

We also extend our appreciation to the good folks at Houghton Mifflin, especially Katherine Meisenheimer, Michael Kerns, and Kathryn Dinovo, and to Nancy Benjamin of Books By Design, who coordinated production and copyediting. Research assistance at the University of South Carolina was provided by Margaret Fu. At East Carolina University, Nichole Icenogle assisted with various aspects of the book. Kathy Morgan compiled the index. Finally, Carson, Blease, Kathy, Joel, and Laura contributed in many special ways to the final product, as usual. We assure them that they are not taken for granted.

A.O'M.B.
R.C.K.

NEW DIRECTIONS FOR STATE AND LOCAL GOVERNMENT

The Study of State and Local Government
From Sewers to Science: The Functions of State and Local Governments » Our Approach

State and Local Government Capacity
How States and Localities Increased Their Capacity » What Increased Capacity Has Meant » Problems Facing State and Local Governments

The People: Designers and Consumers of Government
Ethnic-Racial Composition » Population Growth and Migration » Political Culture

Linking Capacity to Results

With appropriate oratorical flourishes, the governor of Wisconsin, Scott McCallum, delivered his 2002 State of the State message to the people of the Badger State. Although parts of the speech were specific to the state—the references to the Green Bay Packers, for example—many of the themes resonated beyond Wisconsin's borders. Economic growth, environmental protection, and educational improvement were topics in countless gubernatorial addresses throughout the country. Governor McCallum's themes were universal; his upbeat "we can do it together" exhortations have been echoed in one state capitol after another. In the governor's words: "I am pleased to report that the state of our state reflects the will of our people . . . and like the state of our state . . . our will is strong. Our fellow citizens are looking to the future with courage, confidence and hope. And I am optimistic that what we do in the coming year will move Wisconsin toward an even brighter tomorrow."[1] In Wisconsin and elsewhere, state and local governments are indeed leading the country into the future.

The Study of State and Local Government

The study of state and local government has typically received short shrift in the survey of U.S. politics.[2] Scholars and journalists tend to focus on glamorous and imperial presidents, a rancorous and gridlocked Congress, and an independent and powerful Supreme Court. National and international issues capture the lion's share of attention. Yet state and local politics are fascinating precisely because of their up-close-and-personal nature. True, a governor seldom gets involved in an international peace conference; state legislatures rarely debate global warming. But the actors and institutions of states and localities are directly involved in our day-to-day lives. Education, welfare, health care, and crime are among the many concerns of state and local governments. These issues affect all of us as well.

From Sewers to Science: The Functions of State and Local Governments

State and local governments are busy. They exist, in large measure, to provide services to the public. This is no easy task. States and localities must offer services efficiently, effectively, and fairly, and they must do so with limited financial resources. The high costs of inefficient government lead to higher taxes and thus to greater citizen displeasure with government, which in turn can lead to tax revolts and taxpayer exodus. A government performs effectively if it accomplishes what it sets out to do. In addition, a government is expected to function fairly, delivering its services in an equitable manner. It is no wonder, then, that state and local governments constantly experiment with new programs and new systems for delivering services, all the while seeking efficiency, effectiveness, and equity. For instance, the massive restructuring of Wyoming's state government was intended, according to the governor, to produce "a better method of delivering services from the state government to the citizens."[3]

Each year, the Ford Foundation sponsors "Innovations in American Government" awards to recognize the creativity that abounds in governments throughout the nation. More than one thousand jurisdictions compete for the prestigious and lucrative prize. The criteria for the awards are that the government's innovation be original, successful, and easily replicated by other jurisdictions. The 2001 winners and their innovations included:

- Oklahoma's "OK-FIRST" program, which provides real-time weather data to local public safety officials.
- California's educational program, "Mathematics, Engineering, Science Achievement" (MESA), which helps disadvantaged students excel in math and science.
- Toledo (Ohio) Public Schools' "Toledo Plan," a peer-review concept that uses tough performance standards and union-management collaboration to redesign school governance.

■ The Winnebago Tribe of Nebraska's economic development corporation, Ho-Chunk, Inc., which performs the business functions of the tribe.[4]

Although the winning innovations vary in terms of their policy focus, they reflect a willingness on the part of government to try something new.

Our Approach

capacity
The ability of government to respond effectively to change, make decisions efficiently and responsively, and manage conflict.

jurisdiction
The territorial range of government authority; sometimes used as a synonym for "city" or "town."

The argument of this book is that states and localities have the capacity to play central roles in the U.S. federal system. **Capacity** refers to a government's ability to respond effectively to change, make decisions efficiently and responsively, and manage conflict.[5] Capacity, then, is tied to governmental capability and performance. In short, states and communities with capacity work better than do those without it.

But what factors make one government more capable than another? Governmental institutions such as the bureaucracy matter. The fiscal resources of a **jurisdiction** and the quality of its leadership make a difference. Much of the research on capacity has focused on the administrative dimension of government performance, evaluating items such as financial management, information technology, and strategic planning. In a recent study of state government performance, the highest overall scores went to Michigan, Utah, and Washington.[6] Among the thirty-five cities examined, Austin, Texas, and Phoenix, Arizona, were at the top of the list. Other things being equal, we would expect high-scoring states and cities to produce "better" government than low-scoring jurisdictions.

Table 1.1 compares the states on three indicators that are associated with capacity: gross state product (the value of goods and services produced in the state), average salary of state and local government employees, and the level of state spending for technology. The table ranks the states from highest to lowest on the three measures. It is important to remember that rankings, although easy to compare across categories, do not display actual values. Thus the gap between the state ranked first and the state ranked fiftieth may be modest, or it may be substantial. Arguably, the higher a state ranks on these indicators, the greater its capacity. A strong economy, a bureaucracy staffed with well-paid employees, and high levels of spending on technology enhance capacity. It is interesting to note that California, Massachusetts, and New York rank among the top ten in each category.

A 1999 survey in Iowa showed another side to governance and capacity. When asked about the characteristics of good government, Iowans put trustworthiness, ethics, financial responsibility, and accountability at the top of the list.[7] Bottom line: We want our institutions and leaders to govern honestly and wisely. As political scientist David Hedge reminds us, better government is found in jurisdictions that are responsible and democratic.[8] But states and localities face significant challenges as they govern. Complex, often contradictory forces test the most capable of governments. State and local governments need all the capacity they can muster and maybe even a little bit of luck to meet those challenges.

TABLE 1.1   State Rankings on Three Indicators

STATE	GROSS STATE PRODUCT (per capita)	STATE AND LOCAL GOVERNMENT EMPLOYEE AVERAGE SALARY	STATE TECHNOLOGY SPENDING
Alabama	45	45	27
Alaska	3	5	41
Arizona	32	23	23
Arkansas	47	49	30
California	9	1	1
Colorado	8	16	26
Connecticut	1	4	28
Delaware	2	18	42
Florida	38	22	5
Georgia	15	30	11
Hawaii	17	20	39
Idaho	43	43	43
Illinois	11	14	8
Indiana	30	27	20
Iowa	33	24	31
Kansas	31	40	35
Kentucky	40	44	22
Louisiana	35	47	21
Maine	42	36	37
Maryland	20	10	17
Massachusetts	4	9	10
Michigan	27	11	4
Minnesota	14	15	15
Mississippi	49	50	33
Missouri	28	33	16
Montana	48	38	46
Nebraska	23	35	38
Nevada	7	6	40
New Hampshire	10	25	45
New Jersey	6	2	13
New Mexico	37	37	34
New York	5	3	2
North Carolina	19	26	9
North Dakota	44	32	47
Ohio	24	19	6

STATE	GROSS STATE PRODUCT (per capita)	STATE AND LOCAL GOVERNMENT EMPLOYEE AVERAGE SALARY	STATE TECHNOLOGY SPENDING
Oklahoma	46	46	32
Oregon	21	17	24
Pennsylvania	25	12	7
Rhode Island	22	7	44
South Carolina	41	42	25
South Dakota	34	48	49
Tennessee	29	34	19
Texas	18	29	3
Utah	36	31	29
Vermont	39	28	48
Virginia	16	21	12
Washington	13	8	14
West Virginia	50	39	36
Wisconsin	26	13	18
Wyoming	12	41	50

SOURCE: *Governing's State and Local Sourcebook 2002*, pp. 3, 49, 99. Supplement to *Governing* (2002). Reprinted with permission of *Governing Magazine*. Copyright © 2002.

federalism
A system of government in which powers are divided between a central (national) government and regional (state) governments.

Federalism, with its overlapping spheres of authority, provides the context for state and local action. Intervention by the national government in the affairs of a state or local government is defensible, even desirable in clear instances. For example, in the mid-1990s, unprecedented flooding in the Red River Valley area of North Dakota and Minnesota overwhelmed local jurisdictions. Federal disaster relief to the devastated communities saved the day. Our approach takes into account intergovernmental relations (that is, the relationships among the three levels of government)—particularly the possibilities for cooperation and conflict. Jurisdictions (national, state, or local) possess policymaking authority over specific territory. Yet they confront innumerable situations in which boundaries blur and they must work together to accomplish an objective. This point was brought home most vividly in the wake of the September 11, 2001, terrorist attacks on the United States. Local governments were the first to respond, but before long, federal and state governments were heavily involved. Indeed, the characteristics of cooperation and conflict define the U.S. federal system.

State and Local Government Capacity

With notable exceptions, states and their local governments in the 1950s and 1960s were havens of traditionalism and inactivity. Many states were characterized by unrepresentative legislatures, glad-handing governors, and a hodge-podge court system. Public policy tended to reflect the interests of the elite; delivery of services was frequently inefficient and ineffective. According to former North Carolina governor Terry Sanford, the states "had lost their confidence, and people their faith in the states."[9] No wonder that, by comparison, the federal government appeared to be the answer, regardless of the question. In fact, political scientist Luther Gulick proclaimed, "It is a matter of brutal record. The American State is finished. I do not predict that the states will go, but affirm that they have gone."[10]

Those days are as outmoded as a black-and-white television set. States and their local governments have proved themselves capable of designing and implementing "an explosion of innovations and initiatives."[11] As a result, even many national leaders have embraced the roles of states and localities as laboratories for policy experimentation.[12]

The blossoming of state governments in the 1980s—their transformation from weak links in the federal chain to viable and progressive political units—resulted from a number of actions and circumstances.[13] In turn, the resurgence of state governments has generated a host of positive outcomes. During the 1990s, states and localities honed their capacity in an effort to become **proactive** rather than reactive. They squarely faced hard choices and creatively crafted new directions. Still, a word of caution is necessary. As Table 1.1 suggests, not all states enjoy the same level of capacity.

proactive
An anticipatory condition, as opposed to a reactive one.

How States and Localities Increased Their Capacity

Among the factors that contributed to the resurgence of the states, two stand out: the reform of state constitutions and institutions, and the presence of state and local lobbyists at the national level.

State Reform   State governments quietly and methodically reformed themselves by modernizing their constitutions and restructuring their institutions. During the past three decades, more than three-quarters of the states have ratified new constitutions or substantially amended existing ones. Formerly thought of as the "drag anchors of state programs" and as "protectors of special interests,"[14] these documents have been streamlined and made more workable. Even in states without wide-scale constitutional reform, tinkering with constitutions is almost endless, thanks to the amendment process. Virtually every state general election finds constitutional issues on the ballot.

States have also undertaken a variety of internal adjustments intended to improve the operations of state governments.[15] Modernized constitutions and statutory changes have strengthened the powers of governors by increasing appointment and removal powers and by permitting longer terms, consecutive succession, larger staffs, enhanced budget authority, and reorganization of the executive branch.[16] Throughout the country, state agencies are staffed by skilled administrators.[17] The bureaucracy itself is increasingly more demographically representative of the public.[18] Annual rather than biennial sessions, more-efficient rules and procedures, additional staff, and higher salaries have helped make reapportioned state legislatures more professional, capable, and effective.[19] State judicial systems have been the targets of reform as well; examples include the establishment of unified court systems, the hiring of court administrators, and the creation of additional layers of courts.[20]

State and Local Presence in Washington, D.C. Nonnational governments have energized their lobbying efforts in the nation's capital. The three major state-level organizations are the National Governors Association, the National Conference of State Legislatures, and the Council of State Governments. Major players for local governments are the National League of Cities, the National Association of Counties, the U.S. Conference of Mayors, and the International City/County Management Association. Beyond the "Big Seven," as they are known in Washington, D.C., are myriad others representing a variety of state and local officials—for example, the Association of State Highway and Transportation Officials and the National Association of State Development Agencies. In addition, most states and a few of the largest cities have their own liaison offices in Washington.[21]

The intergovernmental lobbies serve an important function in guarding the interests of their members in the nation's capital. Congress regularly solicits these organizations for information and advice on proposed legislation; and through the State and Local Legal Center, nonnational governments are increasing their impact on the federal judiciary. Furthermore, these groups provide a forum in which jurisdictions can learn from one another.

What Increased Capacity Has Meant

In combination, the forces discussed in the preceding section have enhanced state and local government capacity and led to a resurgence that has generated a variety of positive outcomes. These outcomes reinforce the performance of states and localities.

Improved Revenue Systems The recession of the early 1980s and the wave of popularly sponsored taxation and expenditure limitations at state and local levels caused states to implement new revenue-raising strategies in order to maintain existing service levels. States also granted local governments more flexibility in their revenue systems. South Carolina, for example, now allows counties the option of providing property-tax relief to residents while increasing the local sales tax.

State governments first increased user charges, gasoline taxes, and so-called sin taxes on alcohol and tobacco; only then did they reluctantly raise sales and income taxes. Revenue structures were redesigned to make them more diversified and more equitable. State "rainy day funds," legalized gambling through state-run lotteries and pari-mutuels, and extension of the sales tax to services are examples of diversification strategies. Exemptions of food and medicine from consumer sales taxes and the enactment of property-tax breaks for poor and elderly people characterize efforts at tax equity.

States constantly tinker with their revenue-raising schemes. One successful foray into creative revenue raising has been the specialty license plate. Maryland, for example, has raised millions of dollars with its "Treasure the Chesapeake" plate.[22] Monies generated by the plates are earmarked for special programs—in this case, water-quality monitoring and erosion control in the Chesapeake Bay. More than thirty states now offer specialty plates. In fact, many states responded to the events of September 11, 2001, by marketing patriotic license plates. Michigan charged $35 for its patriotic plate, with monies designated for the Salvation Army and the American Red Cross. One of the latest efforts of enterprising cities is to sell merchandise. Los Angeles County has marketed coroner toe tags as key chains; Portland and Tampa rent the entire outside surfaces of their buses to advertisers.[23] New York City, which loses thousands of street signs (Wall Street is especially popular) to souvenir-stealing tourists, now sells replicas. Baseball fans could purchase bricks ($19.95 each) from the old Comiskey Park at the City of Chicago Store. And in Seattle, gardeners welcome the opportunity to purchase "ZooDoo" for their shrubs and flowers, from which the city takes in an extra $20,000 a year.[24] As these examples show, states and localities are willing to experiment when it comes to revenue enhancement.

Expanding the Scope of State Operations   Unlike the national government, which has shed functions like unwanted pounds, state governments are adding functions. In some instances, states are filling in the gap left by the national government's de-emphasis of an activity. Provision of state-sponsored low-income housing is one good example of this behavior; increased state regulation of the trucking industry is another. Before the U.S. Congress reversed itself and enacted family-leave legislation giving workers unpaid leave to care for newborn babies and ailing relatives, many states had already done so.[25] Among the states enacting family-leave measures were California, Hawaii, and Oregon; all passed laws in 1991, two years ahead of the federal government. In other cases, states have taken the initiative in ongoing intergovernmental programs by creatively using programmatic authority and resources. States, for example, led the way in welfare reform, establishing workfare programs and imposing time limits on the receipt of welfare benefits. Carving out a major role for itself was the state of Wisconsin, whose plans to withdraw from the federal welfare system and create its own plan for public relief hastened federal welfare reform. States were also at the forefront of health care reform long before it splashed onto the national scene. In fact, proponents of national health care reform borrowed heavily from the approaches used by Hawaii, Minnesota, and Florida.[26]

The innovative behavior continues. As public outcry grew over the escalating cost of prescription drugs, Maine took action in 2000 and became the first state to adopt legislation placing price controls on medications sold there. Seeking alternatives to parental tax credits and daycare, Minnesota developed a program that subsidizes low-income parents who stay at home during their child's first year. Moreover, many governors now travel overseas to pitch their states' exports and suitability for foreign investment. In short, states are taking on the role of policy innovators and experimenters in the U.S. federal system—and in so doing, they are creating a climate for local-government creativity and inventiveness.

Faster Diffusion of Innovations   Among states and localities, there have always been leaders and followers. Now that nonnational governments are doing more policymaking, they are looking more frequently to their neighbors for advice, information, and models.[27] As a result, successful solutions spread from one jurisdiction to another. For example, as states searched for ways to deal with problems associated with AIDS, they looked to New York, California, and Massachusetts, the early leaders in the field. New York was the first state to take legislative action, creating a multifunctional AIDS Institute; California and Massachusetts quickly followed suit. These states were the first to address tough problems such as testing for the disease, providing counseling to high-risk groups, and developing new anti-AIDS drugs. Other states have led the way in different areas. Pennsylvania, for example, began the modernization of workers' compensation laws in the early 1990s. Within five years, forty other states had enacted similar "business-friendly" provisions in their statutes.[28] Another fast-moving innovation was a Florida law that allowed consumers to stop telephone solicitations. By 1999, five more states had passed laws letting residents put their names on a "do-not-call" list for telemarketers. Seven additional states adopted similar legislation over the next two years.[29]

Local-level innovations spread quickly, too. In 1991, attention shifted to Dade County, Florida, where, in a controversial experiment, a private company was hired to run a public elementary school.[30] Other school districts, notably Baltimore and Minneapolis, have followed the same example. Initial experiments in privatization of public schools have spawned other innovations. Charter schools, designed in Minnesota, spread rapidly; by 2002, close to 2,500 were in operation around the country.[31]

In short, state and local governments learn from one another. Communication links are increasingly varied and frequently used. A state might turn to nearby states when searching for policy solutions. Regional consultation and emulation is logical: Similar problems beset jurisdictions in the same region, a program used in a neighboring state is politically more acceptable than one from a distant state, and organizational affiliations bring state and local administrators together with their colleagues from nearby areas.

Interjurisdictional Cooperation   Accompanying the quickening flow of innovations has been an increase in interjurisdictional cooperation. States are choosing to confront and resolve their immediate problems jointly. Many local governments have forged regional organizations to develop areawide solutions to pressing problems. Such collaboration takes many forms, including informal consultations and agreements, interstate committees, legal contracts, reciprocal legislation, and interstate compacts. For example, twenty-three states have a mutual agreement to aid one another when natural disasters such as hurricanes, earthquakes, and forest fires strike. Five states—Mississippi, Minnesota, West Virginia, Florida, and Massachusetts—were among the first to band together to share information and design tactics in their lawsuits against tobacco companies in the mid-1990s; by 1998, thirty-seven other states had joined in the effort to recover the Medicaid costs of treating tobacco-caused diseases.[32] In the same year, twenty states filed an antitrust lawsuit against Microsoft Corporation, claiming that the firm illegally stifled competition, harmed consumers, and undercut innovation in the computer software industry. In 2000, twenty-eight states went after the world's five largest record labels and three largest music retailers, accusing them of fixing the prices of compact discs.[33] The states sought hundreds of millions of dollars in damages on behalf of consumers. An effort to craft an interstate agreement on the simplification of sales and use taxes had attracted more than twenty-five states by 2002.[34] The goal is to make it easier for states to collect taxes on items purchased online through the Internet. In each of these instances, the states worked together because they could see some benefit from cooperation.

Increased jurisdictional cooperation fosters a healthy climate for joint problem solving. In addition, when state and local governments solve their own problems, they protect their power and authority within the federal system. All in all, it appears that states are becoming more comfortable working with one another. Research shows that at the beginning of the twenty-first century, states were engaged in more cooperative actions than ever before.[35]

Increased National-State Conflict   An inevitable byproduct of more capable state and local governments is intensified conflict with the national government. One source of this trouble has been federal laws and grant requirements that supersede state policy; another is the movement of states onto the national government's turf. National-state conflict is primarily a cyclical phenomenon, but contention has increased in recent years. The issue of unfunded mandates—the costly requirements that federal legislation imposes on states and localities—has been particularly troublesome.[36] In an effort to increase the visibility of the mandates issue, several national organizations of state and local officials sponsored a "National Unfunded Mandate Day" in both 1993 and 1994. Making a strong case against mandates, then-governor George Voinovich of Ohio stated: "Unfunded mandates devastate our budgets, inhibit flexibility and innovation in implementing new programs, preempt important state initiatives, and deprive states of their responsibility to set priorities."[37] Congress responded in 1995 by passing a mandate relief bill that requires cost-benefit analyses of proposed mandates.

Conflict between the national government and the states characterizes a variety of policy areas: the removal of the exemption of local governments from federal antitrust laws (laws against business monopolies), disagreement over energy and water resources, the minimum drinking age, the speed limit on interstate highways, air- and water-quality standards, interstate trucking, severance taxes (fees imposed on the extraction of natural resources such as petroleum), registration and taxation of state and municipal bonds, offshore oil drilling, land management and reclamation, and the storage and disposal of hazardous chemical wastes. Some of the disputes pit a single state against the national government, as in Nevada's fight to block the U.S. Energy Department's plan to build a nuclear fuel waste storage facility 100 miles northwest of Las Vegas. In other conflicts, the national government finds itself besieged by a coordinated, multistate effort. For instance, state governments banded together in 2002 to push for major improvements in the federal food stamp program.

National-state conflicts are resolved (and sometimes made worse) by the federal judicial system. Cases dealing with alleged violations of the U.S. Constitution by state and local governments are heard in federal courts and decided by federal judges. Sometimes the rulings take the federal government into spheres long considered the purview of state and local governments. In Kansas City, Missouri, for instance, a federal district judge forced the local school board to increase taxes to pay for a court-ordered magnet plan.[38]

According to a recent study, state and local governments won a higher proportion of cases before the U.S. Supreme Court during the period 1981–1989 than during the 1950s and 1960s.[39] However, in cases involving the national government, the success rates for states and localities remained relatively low: Of the forty-four federalism cases decided by the Court from 1981 to 1989, state and local governments prevailed almost 40 percent of the time, a success rate similar to that of earlier decades. This percentage has been exceeded in the 1990s, but only slightly. One of the big wins for states and localities was the 1997 decision invalidating part of the federal Brady Handgun Violence Protection Act. Others included the 1995 ruling in the *Lopez* case and the 2000 decision in the *Morrison* case, both of which limited Congress's ability to use the interstate commerce clause.[40]

Problems Facing State and Local Governments

Increased capacity does not mean that all state and local problems have been solved. Two tough challenges face nonnational governments today: fiscal stress and interjurisdictional conflict.

Fiscal Stress   One of the most intractable problems involves money. Given the cyclical peaks and troughs in the national economy as well as the frequent fundamental changes in public finance, state and local finances remain vulnerable.

As the 1990s dawned, recessionary clouds hovered over the financial horizon. Policymakers in affected states searched furiously for solutions in an effort that one pundit labeled "a new kind of big game hunt for state budget entrepreneurs."[41] New York faced a budget shortfall of close to $1 billion; California, a whopping $9 billion. By the fall of 1991, thirty-one states had raised taxes by a combined $16.2 billion, and twenty-nine states had cut spending by $7.5 billion.[42] The situation was severe enough that some Floridians and Texans swallowed hard and began talking about the imposition of a personal income tax in their states.

By the mid-1990s, however, the recession was over, the economy had improved, and most states were enjoying revenue boomlets. By the end of the decade, states were amassing huge surpluses. Total year-end balances for 2001 reached nearly $30 billion.[43] Cutting taxes, eliminating surcharges, and funding new programs had become top legislative priorities. Even as legislators licked their chops over the surplus revenues, the national economy cooled down in 2002, meaning that state officials once again faced hard choices. For example, during the darkest days of the earlier recession, California worked to regain fiscal balance by **downsizing** state agencies. Although the state was successful in paring its work force, much of the savings was wiped out by unplanned but necessary spending in areas such as corrections. The operation of state and local governments, even the leanest of the lean, requires dollars—lots of them. Fiscal stress is a very real concern.

downsizing
Reducing the size and cost of something, especially government.

Increased Interjurisdictional Conflict   Tension is inherent in a federal system because each of the entities has its own set of interests, as well as a share of the national interest. When one state's pursuit of its interests negatively affects another state, conflict occurs. Such conflict can become destructive, threatening the continuation of state resurgence. In effect, states end up wasting their energies and resources on counterproductive battles among themselves.

Interjurisdictional conflict is particularly common in two policy areas very dear to state and local governments: natural resources and economic development. States rich in natural resources want to use these resources in a manner that will yield the greatest return. Oil-producing states, for instance, levy severance taxes that raise the price of oil. And states with abundant water supplies resist efforts by arid states to tap into the supply. The most serious disputes often occur among neighboring states. In 2000, Georgia was fending off attacks from Alabama and Florida over the effect downstream of increased water consumption in metropolitan Atlanta.[44] In short, the essential question revolves around a state's right to control a resource that occurs naturally and that is highly desired by other states. Resource-poor states argue that resources are in fact national and should rightfully be shared among states. The result is a series of seemingly endless battles played out in the federal courts.

In the area of economic development, conflict is extensive because all jurisdictions want healthy economies. Toward this end, states try to make themselves attractive to business and industry through tax breaks and regulatory relaxation. Conflict arises when states get involved in bidding wars—that is, when an enterprise is so highly valued that actions taken by one state are matched and exceeded by another. Suppose, for example, that an automobile manufacturer is considering shutting down an existing facility and relocating. States hungry for manufacturing activity will assemble a package of incentives such as below-cost land, tax concessions, and subsidized job training in an attempt to attract the manufacturer. The state that wants to keep the manufacturer will try to match these inducements. In the long run, economic activity is simply relocated from one state to another. The big winner is the manufacturer. For instance, a division of the Eastman Kodak Company chose to locate its new facility in Pennsylvania rather than Maryland. The Keystone State's incentive package was one factor in the location decision.

The pressure is great, even among jurisdictions that have agreed to forgo competitive behavior. Several years ago, the states of Connecticut and New Jersey, along with New York City, agreed not to engage in bidding wars over each other's businesses. However, the relocation of an international bank from the Big Apple to Connecticut unraveled the agreement. After one city official labeled the move "a shameless raid," New York City launched an advertising blitz in the Connecticut media aimed at nixing the deal.[45] Unsuccessful at that, the city announced a new policy of offering incentives for Connecticut firms interested in relocating to New York City. So much for neighborliness.

The People: Designers and Consumers of Government

A book on state and local government is not only about places and governments; it is also about people—the public and assorted officeholders—and the institutions they create, the processes they engage in, and the policies they adopt. Thus this volume contains chapters on institutions, such as legislatures, and on processes, such as elections; and it discusses policies, such as those pertaining to education. In each case, however, people are the ultimate focus: A legislature is composed of lawmakers and staff members who deal with constituents; elections involve candidates, campaign workers, and voters (as well as nonvoters); and education essentially involves students, teachers, administrators, parents, and taxpayers. In short, the word *people* encompasses an array of individuals and roles in the political system.

Ethnic-Racial Composition

More than 281 million people live in this country. Some can trace their heritage back to the *Mayflower*, whereas others look back only as far as a recent naturalization ceremony. Very few can claim indigenous (native) American ancestry. Instead, most Americans owe their nationality to some forebear who came here in search of a better life or—in the case of a significant minority, the descendants of slaves—to ancestors who made the journey to this country not out of choice but due to physical coercion. The appeal of the United States to economic and political refugees from other countries continues, with Central Americans and Southeast Asians among the most recent arrivals. News photographs of Haitians and Cubans crowded aboard rickety boats in a desperate attempt to gain asylum in the United States remind us of the strength of the attraction.

The United States is a nation of immigrants. This gives it ethnic richness and cultural diversity. Current U.S. Census figures put the Anglo population at 75 percent, the African-American population at 12 percent, the Latino population at 12 percent, and the Asian population at 4 percent. (The percentages total more than 100 percent because of some double-counting.) Large cities, in which immigrants have found economic opportunity, often have distinct ethnic enclaves—Greektown, Little Italy, Koreatown. Miami, for instance, has become a stronghold for refugees from Latin America and the Caribbean. Some people continue to celebrate their ethnic background, referring to themselves as Polish Americans or Irish Americans. Use of the term "African American" in recognition of the cultural heritage of blacks has become the norm. Ethnicity and culture still matter, despite the image of America as a melting pot. Researchers have found that a state's racial and ethnic diversity goes a long way in explaining its politics.[46] Looking toward the future, census projections for the year 2050 estimate an Anglo population at 52 percent, an African-American population at 16 percent, a Latino population at 22 percent, and an Asian population at 10 percent. If the trends hold, state policy in the twenty-first century will be mightily affected.

Illegal immigration is putting the Statue of Liberty's welcoming words (about "your poor, your huddled masses") to a severe test. Immigrants' demands for public services such as health care, education, and welfare have hit states like California and Florida hard. The governors of those states sued the federal government in 1994, arguing that it had failed to protect the nation's borders. Californians, with their penchant for taking government into their own hands, went a step further: In a state election, they overwhelmingly approved an anti–illegal immigration measure—"Save Our State"—that would deny illegal immigrants access to education and to nonemergency medical services. In addition, public employees would be required to report any "apparent" illegal immigrants they encounter. Once passed, "Save Our State" immediately met with legal challenges in the courts, and in 1999, California dropped its effort to implement the law.

At the same time, states with aging work forces and slow population growth are encouraging immigration as a way to ward off economic decline. Iowa, for example, recently enacted a series of immigrant-friendly policies, hoping to attract workers for its meatpacking plants. But the politics of immigration remain dicey. Even as the state government took these actions, polls showed that 54 percent of Iowans opposed increasing immigration.[47]

Population Growth and Migration

The 2000 census figures showed several trends. Reflecting the pattern of the previous decade, high rates of growth occurred in the western states; substantially slower growth rates characterized the Northeast and Midwest. (State population changes for 1990–2000 are shown in Figure 1.1.) Nevada and Arizona continued to outpace the other states, with growth rates a phenomenal 66.3 percent and 40.0 percent, respectively. A strong labor market and an attractive, inexpensive lifestyle are among those states' features. None of the fifty states lost population during the 1990s; however, two states had growth rates of less than 1 percent: North Dakota and West Virginia.[48] In percentage terms, Florida relinquished its role as the South's growth leader; Georgia grew at a faster clip. California appeared to have recaptured its appeal, as a population exodus from the state was reversed toward the end of the 1990s. The Census Bureau's projections for the year 2025 show Nevada, California, Arizona, and New Mexico with the largest population gains. In those four states, international immigration is expected to propel much of the growth.

For cities, the population trends are equally compelling. In general, cities in the **Sunbelt** region enjoyed higher rates of growth than did cities in the **Frostbelt** region. Nevertheless, within these overall patterns is some variation, as the

Sunbelt
An unofficial region of the United States, generally comprising the South and the West.

Frostbelt
An unofficial region of the United States, generally consisting of the Northeast and the Midwest.

| **FIGURE 1.1** | **Percent Change in State Population, 1990–2000** |

SOURCE: www.census.gov/population/cen2000.

figures for the twenty largest cities show (Table 1.2). Among Sunbelt cities, Austin and Phoenix grew the most (more than 34 percent during the decade), while Los Angeles and Memphis had the lowest percentage growth (6 percent and 6.5 percent, respectively). The Frostbelt cities of Baltimore (−11.5 percent) and Detroit (−7.5 percent) were hit hard by population loss, while their regional counterpart, Columbus, Ohio, experienced a growth rate of 12.4 percent. Notice too, in Table 1.2, that eight of the twenty largest cities are located in two states: California and Texas, each with four.

Population growth and migration carry economic and political consequences for state and local governments. As a general rule, power and influence follow population. A state's representation in the U.S. Congress and its votes in the Electoral College are at stake. In 2000, Utah missed out on a new congressional seat by only 856 people. The seat went to North Carolina instead. In response, Utah filed a lawsuit in federal court over the way the U.S. Bureau of the Census counts state residents living overseas.[49] Utah's judicial challenge was rejected and the Tar Heel state kept its new congressional seat. The stakes are high for local governments, too. As a central city's population size is eclipsed by its suburban population, a loss in the city's political clout results. Aware of the impor-

TABLE 1.2	**Population Size and Change for the Twenty Largest Cities**

CITY AND STATE	2000 POPULATION	PERCENTAGE CHANGE, 1990–2000
New York, NY	8,008,278	9.4
Los Angeles, CA	3,694,820	6.0
Chicago, IL	2,896,016	4.0
Houston, TX	1,953,631	19.8
Philadelphia, PA	1,517,550	−4.3
Phoenix, AZ	1,321,045	34.3
San Diego, CA	1,223,400	10.2
Dallas, TX	1,188,580	18.0
San Antonio, TX	1,144,646	22.3
Detroit, MI	951,270	−7.5
San Jose, CA	894,943	14.4
Indianapolis, IN	791,926	6.7
San Francisco, CA	776,733	7.3
Jacksonville, FL	735,617	15.8
Columbus, OH	711,470	12.4
Austin, TX	656,562	41.0
Baltimore, MD	651,154	−11.5
Memphis, TN	650,100	6.5
Milwaukee, WI	596,974	−5.0
Boston, MA	589,141	2.6

SOURCE: U.S. Census Bureau, "Incorporated Places of 100,000 or More, Ranked by Population: 2000." *Census 2000 PHC-T-5 Ranking Tables for Incorporated Places of 100,000 or More: 1900 and 2000,* Table 2. www.census.gov, April 2001.

tance of "the count," many cities spent thousands of dollars on media advertisements encouraging residents to mail in their census forms.

Political Culture

political culture
The attitudes, values, and beliefs that people hold toward government.

One of the phrases that a new arrival in town may hear from longtime residents is "We don't do things that way here." Visitors to California, for example, might have been confused by the absence of numbered exits on the state's freeways—after all, in the other forty-nine states, freeway exits are numbered. But California preferred to use names, many of them evocative (El Camino Real, Monterrey Park, Santa Clarita), despite the inconvenience to motorists. It was not until 2002 that the state gave way to convention and began numbering its 5,800 freeway exits.[50] **Political culture**—the attitudes, values, and beliefs that people hold toward government—is the conceptual equivalent of simply saying "It's *our* thing."[51] As developed by political scientist Daniel Elazar in the 1960s, the term refers to the way in which people think about their government and the manner in which the political system operates. Political culture is a soft concept—one that is difficult to measure—yet it has remained quite useful in explaining state politics and policy.[52]

According to Elazar, the United States is an amalgam of three major political cultures, each of which has distinctive characteristics. In an individualistic political culture, politics is a kind of open marketplace in which people participate because of essentially private motivations. In a moralistic political culture, politics is an effort to establish a good and just society. Citizens are expected to be active in public affairs. In a traditionalistic political culture, politics functions to maintain the existing order, and political participation is confined to social elites. These differing conceptions about the purpose of government and the role of politics lead to different behaviors.

Political culture is a factor in the differences (and similarities) in state policy. Research has found that moralistic states demonstrate the greatest tendency toward policy innovation, whereas traditionalistic states exhibit the least.[53] In economic development policy, for example, political culture has been shown to influence a state's willingness to offer tax breaks to businesses.[54] Other research has linked political culture to state environmental policy and state expenditures on AIDS programs.[55]

Today, few states are characterized by pure forms of these cultures. The mass media have had a homogenizing effect on cultural differences; migration has diversified cultural enclaves. This process of cultural erosion and synthesis has produced hybrid political cultures. For example, Florida, once considered a traditionalistic state, now has many areas in which an individualistic culture prevails, and even a moralistic community or two. In an effort to extend Elazar's pioneering work, researcher Joel Lieske has used race, ethnicity, and religion to identify contemporary subcultures.[56] With counties as the building blocks and statistical analysis as the method, he identified ten distinctive regional subcultures. A state like Pennsylvania, which Elazar characterized as individualistic, becomes a mix of "heartland," Germanic, ethnic, and "rurban" counties in Lieske's formulation. Very few states are dominated by a single subculture, as are Utah by a Mormon subculture and New Hampshire and Vermont by an Anglo-French subculture.

Political culture is not the only explanation for why states do what they do, however. Socioeconomic characteristics (income and education levels, for example) and political structural factors (the amount of competition between political parties) also contribute to states' and communities' actions. In fact, sorting out the cause-and-effect relationships among these variables is a daunting job.[57] For example, why do some states pass more laws to regulate handguns than other states do? Emily Van Dunk's study found that several factors were important, although, surprisingly, the crime rate and partisanship were not among them.[58] States with nontraditional political cultures adopt more handgun regulations, as do states with more women in the legislature and those with populations that are more urbanized and nonwhite. In general, political factors, socioeconomic characteristics, and the particulars of a specific problem combine to produce government action.

Linking Capacity to Results

State and local governments have become the new heroes of American federalism. Their ability to solve pressing problems is one of the reasons why this has occurred. The interaction of three unique characteristics of our fifty-state system—diversity, competitiveness, and resiliency—makes it easier.[59] Consider the diversity of the United States. States and their communities have different fiscal capacities (some are rich, some are poor) and different voter preferences for public services and taxes (some are liberal, some are conservative). Along with the national government's reluctance to equalize intergovernmental fiscal disparities, these differences perpetuate diversity. As a result, citizens and businesses are offered real choices in taxation and expenditure policies across different jurisdictions.

Diversity is tempered, however, by the natural competitiveness of a federal system. No state can afford to be too far out of line with the prevailing thinking on appropriate levels of taxes and expenditures. During the 1970s, Massachusetts, a high-tax state, was labeled "Taxachusetts"; a poor-service state—Mississippi, for example—was stigmatized as "backward." Neither state could flourish by being at the extreme end of the scale. States with lower taxes became more attractive than Massachusetts; states with better services became more inviting than Mississippi. Eventually, the workings of government, through an attentive public and enlightened opinion leaders, brought Massachusetts's tax levels and Mississippi's service levels back into line with prevailing thinking. Such competition over taxes and expenditures stabilizes the federal system.

The third characteristic, resiliency, captures the ability of state governments to recover from adversity. States are survivors. For example, to find innovative policy ideas these days, look at the state level, which has witnessed a veritable burst of activism in policy initiatives. Resiliency is the key.

It is unlikely that the days of unfettered national dominance will return. The federal government is mired in its own problems, among them the national debt and international conflicts. As one astute observer of the U.S. governmental scene has commented, "Over the past decade, without ever quite admitting it, we have ceased to rely on Congress (or the federal government, for that matter) to deal with our most serious public problems. . . . [T]he states have been accepting the challenge of dealing with problems that no other level of government is handling."[60]

As the twentieth century ended, it was not surprising that polls showed high levels of public trust and confidence in government—state government, that is.[61] Return to the first page of this chapter and re-read Governor McCallum's inspirational words. The twenty-first century has begun, and nonnational governments are taking charge. Years of increased capacity are producing results.

Chapter Recap

➤ State and local governments are directly involved in our daily lives.

➤ During the past two decades, the story of states and localities has been one of transformation. They have shed their backward ways, reformed their institutions, and emerged as capable and proactive.

➤ The United States is becoming more racially and ethnically diverse. The increase in population in Sunbelt states such as Nevada and Arizona outpaces the rest of the nation. Meanwhile, states like North Dakota and West Virginia show negligible population growth.

➤ As a whole, the fifty states are diverse, competitive, and resilient. With increased capacity to govern effectively, they are producing results.

Key Terms

capacity *(p. 3)*

jurisdiction *(p. 3)*

federalism *(p. 5)*

proactive *(p. 6)*

downsizing *(p. 12)*

Sunbelt *(p. 14)*

Frostbelt *(p. 14)*

political culture *(p. 16)*

Surfing the Net

A website that contains links to a wealth of policy information about the fifty states is **www.stateline.org,** a publication of the Pew Center on the States. Not only is there material about key issues, there are links to multistate organizations, national organizations of state officials, and state-based think tanks. Another useful site for comparative information about the states is **www.statescape.com.** To learn what's happening in the states, politically and otherwise, check out the Washington Post's "News from the States," **www.washingtonpost.com/wp-srv/national/longterm/50states/front.htm.** If you want up-to-date, insightful discussions of issues in states and localities, try *Governing* magazine at **www.governing.com.** If you need data about states and localities, the official source is the U.S. Bureau of the Census at **www.census.gov.** States and localities were originally assigned domain names that used their two-letter abbreviation and ended with .us. For example, the official home page for the state of Iowa is found at **www.state.ia.us.** Some states have added simpler addresses such as Utah's new **www.utah.gov.**

2

FEDERALISM AND THE STATES

The Concept of Federalism
Unitary, Confederate, and Federal Systems » The Advantages and Disadvantages of Federalism

The History of U.S. Federalism
Early History » The Move Toward Federalism » State-Centered Federalism » The Growth of National Power Through the Constitution and the Judiciary » The Growth of National Power Through Congress » A New Era of State Resurgence?

Intergovernmental Relations
Interstate Cooperation » Tribal Governments » Intergovernmental Financial Relations

Models of Federalism
Dual Federalism (1787–1932) » Cooperative Federalism (1933–1964) » Contemporary Variations on Cooperative Federalism (Since 1964)

Federal Purse Strings
The Importance of Federal Funds » Here's the Check and Here's What to Do with It: Mandates, Preemptions, Set-asides, and Cost Ceilings

The Future of Federalism

A single broad and enduring issue in American federalism transcends all others: What is the proper balance of power and responsibility between the national government and the states? The debate over this profound question was first joined by the Founders in preconstitutional days and argued between the Federalists and the Anti-Federalists. It continues today in the halls of Congress, the U.S. Supreme Court, and the state and local governments, sometimes over what appear to be mundane issues.

The immediate aftermath of the September 11, 2001, terrorist attack on the World Trade Center towers provided stark evidence of the undisputed duties and responsibilities of state and local governments. As corporate workers fled the towers for their lives, New York City police and firefighters mounted the stairways into the burning buildings. State and local emergency agencies quickly coordinated the on-the-scene response. National political leaders, for their part, focused on international relations, intelligence gathering, and military responses.

More typically, role confusion reigns. For instance, which level of government should have the power to determine the right to die? Under Oregon's Death with Dignity Act, a terminally ill person, upon receiving the agreement of two physicians, may ingest lethal drugs to end his life. In a 1996 referendum, Oregon voters reaffirmed the controversial 1994 law by a 60 percent majority. Approximately ninety people had committed suicide under the law through November 6, 2001, when U.S. Attorney General John Ashcroft authorized the U.S. Drug Enforcement Administration to revoke the license of any physician who prescribed the suicide drugs. Oregon quickly obtained a stay of Ashcroft's order in federal court and promised to sue Ashcroft, a social and religious conservative, in federal court. The critical issue: Did Ashcroft brazenly usurp state

Supporters of Oregon's Death with Dignity Act hold a press conference following voters' decision to uphold the controversial law. (AP/Wide World Photos)

sovereignty and trample on states' rights, or can the Oregon-established legal right of a terminally ill person to choose the time and means of her own death be denied by the national government?

The Oregon case is the type of conflict that defines U.S. federalism. As a system for organizing government, federalism has important consequences that often affect our political and personal lives, in ways both direct and hidden.

The Concept of Federalism

In a nation—a large group of people organized under a single, sovereign government and sharing historical, cultural, and other values—powers and responsibilities can be divided among different levels of government in three ways: through a unitary government, a confederacy, or a federal system. To understand our federal system, we must know how it differs from the other forms of government.

Unitary, Confederate, and Federal Systems

unitary system
One in which all authority is derived from a central authority.

The great majority of countries (more than 90 percent) have a **unitary system** in which most, if not all, legal power is located in the central government. The central government may create or abolish regional or local governments as it sees fit. These subgovernments can exercise only those powers and responsibilities granted to them by the central government. In France, the United Kingdom, Argentina, Egypt, and the many other countries with unitary systems, the central government is strong and the regional or local jurisdictions are weak.

confederacy
A league of sovereign states in which a limited central government exercises few independent powers.

A **confederacy** is the opposite of a unitary system. In a confederacy, the central government is weak and regional governments are powerful. The regional jurisdictions establish a central government to deal with areas of mutual concern, such as national defense and a common currency, but they severely restrict the central government's authority in other areas. If they see fit, they may change or even abolish the central government. The United States began as a confederacy, and the southern states formed one following secession in 1861.

federal system
A means of dividing the power and functions of government between a central government and a specified number of geographically defined regional jurisdictions.

A **federal system** falls somewhere between the unitary and confederate forms in the way it divides powers among levels of government. This system has a minimum of two governmental levels, each of which derives its powers directly from the people, and each of which can act directly on the people within its jurisdiction without permission from any other authority. Each level of government is supreme in the powers assigned to it, and each is protected by a constitution from being destroyed by the other.[1] Thus federalism is a means of dividing the power and functions of government between a central government and a specified number of geographically defined regional jurisdictions. In effect, people hold dual citizenship, in the national government and in their regional government.

In the U.S. federal system, the regional governments are called states. In other federal systems, such as that of Canada, regional governments are known as provinces. Altogether there are approximately twenty federal systems in the world.

The Advantages and Disadvantages of Federalism

Federalism as it has evolved in the United States is a reasonably effective system of government. But it is not perfect; nor is it well suited to the circumstances of most other nations. Ironically, federalism's weaknesses are closely related to its strengths.

The advantages of federalism are as follows:

1. *A federal system helps manage social and political conflict.* It broadly disperses political power within and among governments. For example, the U.S. Senate represents the geographical diversity of the states, with two senators for each territorial unit, and the House of Representatives is apportioned on the basis of population. This system enables national as well as subregional concerns to reach the central government. Local interests are expressed in state capitols through state legislatures and, of course, in city and county councils and other local legislative bodies. Many potential places exist for resolving conflicts before they reach the crisis stage. Also, federalism achieves unity through diversity. Ethnicity, color, language, religious preference, and other differences are not distributed randomly in the population; rather, people who share certain traits tend to cluster together spatially. And state and local governments represent such groups. For example, the large and growing Hispanic population of Texas is increasingly gaining representation in the state legislature and in mayoral and city council offices.

2. *Federalism promotes administrative efficiency.* The wide variety of services that citizens demand are delivered more efficiently without a large central bureaucracy. From public elementary education to garbage collection, the government closest to the problem seems to work most efficiently and effectively in adapting public programs to local needs.

3. *Federalism encourages innovation.* States and localities can customize their policies to accommodate diverse demands and needs—and, indeed, such heterogeneity flourishes. New policies are constantly being tested by the more than 88,000 government "laboratories" that exist throughout the country, thus further encouraging experimentation and flexibility.

4. *A federal system maximizes political participation in government.* Citizens have opportunities to participate at all three levels of government through elections, public hearings, and other means. The local and state governments serve as political training camps for aspiring leaders who can test the waters in a school board or county council election and, if successful, move on to higher electoral prizes in the state or national arena. The great majority of presidents and U.S. senators and representatives got their start in state or local politics. Through almost one million offices regularly filled in elections, citizens can have a meaningful say in decisions that affect their lives.

5. *A federal system helps protect individual freedom.* Federalism provides numerous potential points of opposition to national government policies and political ideology. James Madison argued that the numerous checks inherent in a

factions
Any groups of citizens or interests united in a cause or action that can threaten the rights or interests of the larger community.

federal system would control the effects of **factions,** making "it less probable that a majority of the whole will have a motive to invade the rights of other citizens."[2] Thus the states serve as defenders of democracy by ensuring that no national ideological juggernaut can sweep over the entire nation, menacing the rights of individual citizens.

Now we turn to a list of disadvantages:

1. *Federalism may facilitate the management of conflict in some settings, but in others it makes conflict more dangerous.* Federal experiments in Canada and the former Yugoslavia bear out this point. In Canada, the ethnically French province of Quebec fueled a secessionist movement during the 1970s that has yet to burn out. Violent ethnic conflict in Nigeria is another example of the failure of federalism.

2. *Although provision of services through governments that are close to the people can promote effectiveness and efficiency, federalism can also hinder progress.* It is extraordinarily difficult, if not impossible, to coordinate the efforts of all state and local governments. Picture trying to get 88,000 squawking and flapping chickens to move in the same direction at once. Business interests level this criticism when they encounter government regulations on products and services that vary widely across the United States.

3. *Not surprisingly, so many governments lead to duplication and confusion.* For example, fifty sets of law on business regulation can make doing business across state lines tough for a firm.

4. *Federalism may promote state and local innovation, but it can also hinder national programs and priorities.* These many points of involvement can encourage obstruction and delay and result in an ineffective national government. An obvious example is the successful opposition of the southern states to voting rights for African Americans for more than a hundred years.

5. *Broad opportunity for political participation is highly desirable in a democracy, but it may encourage local biases that damage the national interest.* For example, hazardous, radioactive, and solid wastes must be disposed of somewhere, but local officials and citizens are quick to protest: "Not in my back yard!"

The History of U.S. Federalism

The men who met in Philadelphia during the hot summer of 1787 to draw up the U.S. Constitution were not wild-eyed optimists, nor were they revolutionaries. In fact, as we'll see in this section, they were consummate pragmatists whose beliefs shaped the new republic and created both the strengths and weaknesses of our federal system.

Early History

The Framers of the Constitution held to the belief of English political philosopher Thomas Hobbes that human beings are contentious and selfish. Some of them openly disdained the masses. Most of the Framers agreed that their goal in

Philadelphia was to find a means of controlling lower forms of human behavior while still allowing citizens to have a voice in making the laws they were compelled to obey. As noted earlier, the "philosopher of the Constitution," James Madison, formulated the problem in terms of factions, groups that pursue their own interests without concern for the interests of society as a whole. Political differences and self-interest, Madison felt, led to the formation of factions, and the Framers' duty was to identify "constitutional devices that would force various interests to check and control one another."[3]

Three practical devices to control factions were placed in the U.S. Constitution. The first was a system of representative government in which citizens would elect individuals who would filter and refine the views of the masses. The second was the division of government into three branches: executive, legislative, and judicial. The legislative body was divided into two houses, each with a check on the activities of the other. Equal in power would be a strong chief executive with the authority to veto legislative acts, and an independent judiciary. Finally, the government was structured as a federal system in which the most dangerous faction of all—a majority—would be controlled by the sovereign states. Madison's ultimate hope was that the new Constitution would "check interest with interest, class with class, faction with faction, and one branch of government with another in a harmonious system of mutual frustration."[4]

Sometimes today there appears to be more frustration than harmony, but Madison's dream did come true. The U.S. federal system is the longest-lived constitutional government on earth. Its dimensions and activities are vastly different from what the Framers envisioned, but it remains a dynamic, adaptable, responsive, and usually effective system for conducting the affairs of government.

The Move Toward Federalism

The drive for independence by the thirteen American colonies was, according to the Declaration of Independence, in large measure a reaction to "a history of repeated injuries and usurpations" under a British unitary system of government. The Declaration proudly proclaimed the colonies' liberation from the "absolute tyranny" exercised over them by the English Crown.

The struggle for independence dominated political debate in the colonies, and there was little time to develop a consensus on the form of government best suited to the future needs of American society. Hence the move toward federalism was gradual. It is interesting that the first independent government established in America was a confederacy; thus Americans tested two types of government—unitary and confederate—before deciding permanently on the third.

The Articles of Confederation   During the War for Independence, the colonies, now called states, agreed to establish a confederation. A unicameral (one-house) Congress was created to exercise the authority of the new national government. Its powers were limited to the authority to wage war, make peace, enter into treaties and alliances, appoint and receive ambassadors, regulate Indian affairs, and create a postal system. The states held all powers not expressly granted to the Congress. The governing document was the Articles of Confederation (effective from 1776 to 1787).

The inherent weaknesses of the confederacy quickly became apparent. The central government had to rely on the good will of the states for all of its revenues and, therefore, often could not honor its financial obligations. Bankruptcy was a chronic concern. Furthermore, the lack of national authority to regulate either domestic or international commerce led to discriminatory trade practices by the states, particularly through the use of protective tariffs. These and many other defects were important concerns. But the key event that brought together representatives of the states to draft a constitution for a new type of government was Shays's Rebellion. In 1787, Daniel Shays, a Revolutionary War officer, led an armed revolt of New England farmers who were fighting mad about debt and taxes. The weak central government had difficulty helping Massachusetts put down the rebellion.

The Constitutional Convention   How did the Framers create a long-lasting and successful system of government that seems to have the best features of both unitary and confederate forms? Above all they were pragmatists; they developed a practical compromise on the key issues of the day, including the proper role of the national government and the states. The reconciliation of the interests and powers of the states with the need for a strong national government is the United States' most distinctive political invention.

The constitutional convention turned on the self-interest of both large states and small states. The large states supported the Virginia Plan, which proposed a strong central government spearheaded by a powerful bicameral Congress. Because representation in both chambers was to be based on population, larger states would be favored. The smaller states countered with the New Jersey Plan, which put forward a one-house legislature composed of an equal number of representatives from each state.

The New Jersey Plan was defeated by a vote of 7 to 3, but the smaller states refused to give in. Finally, Connecticut moved that the lower house (the House of Representatives) be based on the population of each state and the upper house (the Senate) on equal state membership. This Great Compromise was approved, ensuring that a faction of large states would not dominate the small ones.

The Framers reached another important compromise by specifying the powers of the new central government. Those seventeen powers, to be exercised through Congress, included taxation, regulation of commerce, operation of post offices, establishment of a national court system, declaration of war, conduct of foreign affairs, and administration of military forces.

A third key compromise reached by the Framers concerned the question of who should resolve disputes between the national government and the states: Congress, the state courts, or the Supreme Court? The importance of the decision that the Supreme Court would be the final arbiter was understood only years later, when the Court established the supremacy of the national government over the states through several critical rulings.

State-Centered Federalism

nation-centered federalism
A theory holding that the national government is dominant over the states.

state-centered federalism
A theory holding that the national government represents a voluntary compact or agreement between the states, which retain a dominant position.

reserved powers
Those powers residing with the states by virtue of the Tenth Amendment.

Tenth Amendment
The amendment to the Constitution, ratified in 1791, reserving powers to the state.

enumerated (delegated) powers
Those powers expressly given to the national government in Article I, Section 8, of the Constitution.

compact theory
A theory of federalism that became the foundation for states' rights arguments.

Despite the fact that the new Constitution made the national government much stronger than it had been under the Articles of Confederation, the sovereign power of the states was still important.[5] As James Madison wrote, "The powers delegated by the proposed Constitution to the federal government are few and defined. Those which are to remain in the State governments are numerous and infinite."[6]

The first decades under the new Constitution witnessed a clash between profoundly different views on governing. George Washington, John Adams, and their fellow "Federalists" favored national supremacy, or **nation-centered federalism.** Opposed to them were Thomas Jefferson and the Republicans, who preferred **state-centered federalism.** Much of the debate then, as today, concerned the meaning of the **reserved powers** clause of the **Tenth Amendment** to the Constitution. Ratified in 1791, the Tenth Amendment gave support to the states by openly acknowledging that "the powers not delegated to the United States by the Constitution, nor prohibited by it to the States, are reserved to the States respectively, or to the people." But, in fact, the Tenth Amendment was an early omen of the eventual triumph of nation-centered federalism. As pointed out by constitutional scholar Walter Berns, if the states were intended to be the dominant federal actors, they would not have needed the Tenth Amendment to remind them.[7]

Those who defended the power of the states under the Constitution—that is, state-centered federalism—saw the Constitution as a *compact,* an agreement, among the sovereign states that maintained their sovereignty, or the right of self-governance. The powers of the national government listed in the Constitution—the **enumerated (delegated) powers**—were to be interpreted narrowly, and the states were obliged to resist any unconstitutional efforts by the national government to extend its authority.[8]

This **compact theory** of federalism became the foundation for states' rights arguments. In particular, it became central to the fight of the southern states against what they considered discrimination by the North. During the 1820s, a national tariff seriously damaged the economy of the southern states. The slave-based agricultural economy of the South had already begun a protracted period of decline while the North prospered. The tariff, which placed high taxes on imported manufactured goods from Europe, hit the South hard, for the South produced few manufactured goods. Rightly or wrongly, southerners blamed the "tariff of abominations" for many of their economic problems.

In 1828, Vice President John C. Calhoun of South Carolina asserted that the United States was composed of sovereign states united in a central government through a compact. The powers of the national government had been entrusted to it by the states, not permanently handed over. Calhoun claimed that the states thus had complete authority to reinterpret or even *nullify* (reject) the compact at any time. Most important, Calhoun declared that if a large majority of the states sided with the national government, the nullifying state had the right to *secede*, or withdraw from the Union.

In 1832, after an additional tariff was enacted by the national government, South Carolina nullified it. President Andrew Jackson and the Congress threatened military action to force the state to comply with the law, and Jackson even threatened to hang Calhoun, who by this time had resigned from the vice presidency.[9]

Ultimately, eleven southern states (led by South Carolina) did secede from the Union, at which point they formed the Confederate States of America. The long conflict between state sovereignty and national supremacy was definitively resolved by five years of carnage in such places as Manassas, Shiloh, and Gettysburg, followed by the eventual readmittance of the renegade states to the Union. The Civil War, often referred to in the South as The War Between the States, remains the single most violent episode in American history, resulting in more than 620,000 deaths (more than in all our other wars combined).

The Growth of National Power Through the Constitution and the Judiciary

After the Civil War, a nation-centered concept of federalism evolved. For the most part, the national government has become the primary governing force, with the states and localities generally following its lead. Recently the states have been more inclined to act independently, but they are restrained by the history of the Supreme Court's interpretations of key sections of the Constitution.

The National Supremacy Clause   The Judiciary Act of 1789 created the U.S. Supreme Court and various lower courts. It also established the supremacy of national law and the Constitution, and made the U.S. Supreme Court the final arbiter of any legal disputes between the national government and the states. This act was constitutionally grounded in the **national supremacy clause** (Article VI, Section 2), which provides that the national laws and the Constitution are the supreme laws of the land.

national supremacy clause
Article VI of the Constitution, which makes national laws superior to state laws.

The Necessary and Proper Clause   The fourth chief justice of the United States, John Marshall, was the architect of the federal judiciary during his thirty-four years on the bench. Almost single-handedly, he made it a coequal branch of government. Several of his rulings laid the groundwork for the expansion of national governmental power. In the case of *McCulloch* v. *Maryland* (1819), two issues were before the bench: the right of the national government to establish a national bank, and the right of the state of Maryland to tax that bank, once it was established.[10]

The crux of the issue was how to interpret the **necessary and proper clause.** The final power delegated to Congress under Article I, Section 8, is the power "to make all laws which shall be *necessary and proper* for carrying into execution the foregoing powers, and all other powers vested by this Constitution in the Government of the United States" (emphasis added). Thomas Jefferson argued that necessary meant "indispensable," whereas Alexander Hamilton asserted that it meant merely "convenient." Hamilton argued that in addition to the

necessary and proper clause
Portion of Article I, Section 8, of the Constitution that authorizes Congress to enact all laws "necessary and proper" to carry out its responsibilities.

implied powers
Those powers that are not expressly granted by the Constitution but inferred from the enumerated powers.

enumerated powers, Congress possessed **implied powers.** In the case of the national bank, valid congressional action was implied through the powers of taxation, borrowing, and currency found in Article I, Section 8.

The bank dispute was eventually heard by Chief Justice Marshall. Marshall was persuaded by the Hamiltonian point of view. He pointed out that the Constitution nowhere stipulates that the only powers that may be carried out are those expressly described in Article I, Section 8. Thus he ruled that Congress had the implied power to establish the bank and that Maryland had no right to tax it. Significantly, *McCulloch* v. *Maryland* meant that the national government had an almost unlimited right to decide how to exercise its delegated powers. Over the years, Congress has enacted a great many laws that are only vaguely, if at all, associated with the enumerated powers and that stretch the phrase *necessary and proper* beyond its logical limits.

interstate commerce clause
Article I, Section 8, of the U.S. Constitution, which permits Congress to regulate trade with foreign countries and among the states.

The Interstate Commerce Clause   Another important ruling of the Marshall Court extended national power through an expansive interpretation of the **interstate commerce clause** of Article I, Section 8. The commerce clause gives Congress the power "to regulate commerce with foreign nations, and among the several states, and with the Indian tribes." In *Gibbons* v. *Ogden* (1824),[11] two important questions were addressed by Marshall: What is commerce? And how broadly should Congress's power to regulate commerce be interpreted?

The United States was just developing a national economy as the Industrial Revolution expanded. National oversight was needed, along with regulation of emerging transportation networks and of state activities related to the passage of goods across state lines (interstate commerce). The immediate question was whether New York could grant a monopoly to run a steamship service between New York and New Jersey. Marshall's answer? No, it could not. He defined commerce very broadly and held that Congress's power to regulate commerce applied not only to traffic across state boundaries but, in some cases, also to traffic of goods, merchandise, and people within a state.

general welfare clause
The portion of Article I, Section 8, of the Constitution that provides for the general welfare of the United States.

The General Welfare Clause   The **general welfare clause** of Article I, Section 8, states that "the Congress shall have power to lay and collect taxes, duties, imposts, and excises to pay the debts and provide for the common defense and *general welfare* of the United States" (emphasis added). Before the Great Depression of the 1930s, it was believed that poor people were responsible for their own plight and that it was up to private charity and state and local governments to provide limited assistance. The Great Depression inflicted massive unemployment and poverty throughout the country and made necessary a major change in the national government's attitude. Despite their best efforts, the states and localities were staggered by the tremendous loss of tax revenues and by the need to help poor and displaced persons obtain food and shelter. Franklin D. Roosevelt, who won the presidency in 1932, set in motion numerous "New Deal" programs that completely redefined federal responsibility for the general welfare.

**Fourteenth
Amendment**
Enacted in 1868 to
protect the rights of
freed slaves, an
amendment that
contains due process
and equal rights
provisions that now
apply to all citizens.

The Fourteenth Amendment   Ratified by the states in 1868, the **Fourteenth Amendment** gave former slaves official status as citizens of the United States and of the state in which they lived. It included two other very important principles as well—*due process* and *equal protection* of the laws. The federal courts have used the Fourteenth Amendment to increase national power over the states in several critical fields, especially with respect to civil rights, criminal law, and election practices.

The Growth of National Power Through Congress

The U.S. Supreme Court has not been the only force behind nation-centered federalism; Congress has worked hand in hand with the judiciary. The interstate commerce clause represents a good example. Given the simple authority to control or eliminate state barriers to trade across state lines, Congress now regulates commercial activities within a state's boundaries as well, as long as these activities purportedly have substantial national consequences (examples include banking and business fraud). Congress has also used the authority of the interstate commerce clause to expand national power into fields only vaguely related to commerce, such as protecting endangered species. The states have made hundreds of legal challenges to such exercise of the commerce power, but until very recently almost all of these were resolved by the U.S. Supreme Court in favor of the national government.

Sixteenth Amendment
Enacted in 1913, an
amendment that
grants the national
government the
power to levy income
taxes.

Taxing and Spending Power   Probably the most controversial source of the rise in national power in recent years has been the use of the *taxing and spending power* by Congress to extend its influence over the state and local governments. Under Article I, Section 8, Congress holds the power to tax and spend to provide for the common defense and general welfare. But the **Sixteenth Amendment,** which grants Congress the power to tax the income of individuals and corporations, moved the center of financial power from the states to Washington, D.C. Through the income tax, the national government raises huge amounts of money. Much of this money is sent to the states and localities. Because Congress insists on some sort of accountability in how state and local governments spend these funds, attached to federal grants are a variety of conditions to which the recipients must adhere if they are to receive the money. The federal government also imposes mandates and regulations related to the purposes of the individual grant. For example, in 2000 Congress set a blood-alcohol standard of .08 for drunk driving; noncomplying states face the loss of significant federal transportation dollars.

federal preemption
The principle that
national laws take
precedence over state
laws.

Federal Preemption   The national government has also seized power through the process known as **federal preemption.** The legal basis for preemption is Article VI of the Constitution, the national supremacy clause. Whenever a state law conflicts with a national law, the national law is dominant.

Some federal preemption concerns the requirements attached to grants. The minimum drinking age is a case in point; any state failing to enforce a minimum drinking age of twenty-one risks losing substantial sums of federal highway funds. Congressional passage of a national law that supersedes existing state legislation is directly preemptive. One such federal law is the Air Quality Act, which replaced state standards on permissible levels of air pollutants with minimum national standards. An extreme case of preemption is the Voting Rights Act of 1965, which enables the U.S. Justice Department to exercise an advance veto over changes in election procedures and jurisdictions in specified states and localities.

Smothering (Then Resuscitating) the Tenth Amendment   Actions by the Congress and the federal courts have gradually undermined the Tenth Amendment, which reserves to the states all powers not specifically granted to the national government or prohibited to the states. In fact, it is very difficult to identify any field of state activity not intruded on by the national government today.

The Supreme Court has sent mixed signals on the relevance of the Tenth Amendment. Following forty years of case law that essentially relegated the Tenth Amendment to the basement of federalism, the Court surprisingly ruled in favor of state and local governments in the 1976 case of *National League of Cities* v. *Usery*. At issue was the constitutionality under the interstate commerce clause of the 1974 amendments to the Fair Labor Standards Act (FLSA), which extended federal minimum wage and maximum hour requirements to state and local employees. In this case, the Court said that Congress did not have the constitutional right to impose wage and hour requirements on employees carrying out basic—or integral—functions, such as law enforcement or firefighting.[12]

But just nine years later, the Court reversed itself in *Garcia* v. *San Antonio Metropolitan Transit Authority*. A spate of litigation had not been able to resolve the issue of just which state and local activities are "integral." So the Court expressly overturned its findings in *Usery* and once again applied federal wage and hour laws to nonnational governments—in this specific instance, to a mass transit system run by the city of San Antonio.[13] What really offended the states was the written opinion of the Court, in which it excused itself from such future controversies involving state claims against congressional power exercised under the commerce clause. Now Congress alone, with little or no judicial oversight, would be allowed to determine, through the political process, how extensively it would intrude on what had been state and local prerogatives. One dissenting Supreme Court justice wrote that "all that stands between the remaining essentials of state sovereignty and Congress is the latter's underdeveloped capacity for self-restraint."[14] In the view of some critics, the states were relegated to the status of any other special-interest group and the Tenth Amendment was irrelevant. Other critics more optimistically observed that the narrow 5-to-4 decision could be revisited by a more conservative Supreme Court at a later date.[15]

Sure enough, in 1995 the Court seemingly reaffirmed the Tenth Amendment in *U.S.* v. *Lopez* by recognizing a limit to Congress's power over interstate commerce. Ironically, this case also involved San Antonio, where a high school student, Alfonso Lopez, was arrested for bringing a handgun to school. He was charged with violating the Gun Free School Zones Act of 1990, which banned the possession of a firearm within 1,000 feet of a school. In another 5-to-4 decision, the Court ruled that in this instance Congress had unconstitutionally extended its power to regulate commerce because there was no connection between the gun law and interstate commerce.[16] In 1999, the Court revisited *Garcia* and *Lopez,* ruling that the state and local governments could ignore FLSA requirements that they pay their employees the federal minimum wage and time and one-half pay for overtime work. A 2000 Supreme Court ruling further restricted Congress's power to regulate interstate commerce by finding that female rape victims cannot sue their attackers in federal court under the Violence Against Women Act. Instead, they must pursue their claims in state court.[17]

The Court has continued to recalibrate the scales of power in favor of the states in a series of rulings beginning in 1997. First, the Court gave states the authority to incarcerate convicted sexual predators in mental institutions once their criminal sentences have ended.[18] Next, the Court ruled that Congress offended "the very principle of separate state sovereignty" by requiring local police to conduct background checks on people who want to purchase handguns (although they may do so voluntarily). Thus, a major section of the so-called Brady Bill was declared unconstitutional.[19] The Court then let stand a lower-court ruling that upheld the constitutionality of California's Proposition 209, which banned race- or sex-based hiring preferences in college admissions, hiring decisions, and government contracting.[20] The Court also upheld Oregon's Death with Dignity Act, which permitted doctor-assisted suicides,[21] and granted states the freedom to restrict antiabortion demonstrations outside health clinics.[22]

Recent rulings based on the Eleventh Amendment have revived the notion of the sovereign immunity of the states. According to this doctrine, which dates back to the Middle Ages, a king (the state) cannot be sued without his (its) consent (the Eleventh Amendment protects states from lawsuits by citizens of other states or foreign nations). Supreme Court decisions have upheld the sovereign immunity of the states from being sued in federal courts in cases involving lawsuits by Indian tribes,[23] patent infringement when a state ventures into commercial activities,[24] and discrimination against older employees.[25] The Court also protected the states from private complaints before federal agencies.[26]

A New Era of State Resurgence?

The Rehnquist Court has clearly and undeniably positioned itself on the side of the states in most conflicts with the national government. However, the Supreme Court does not decide unilaterally in favor of the states in all cases. For example, in 2000 the Court asserted that the states cannot infringe on the president's foreign policymaking role, declaring unconstitutional a Massachusetts law that restricted state purchases from firms doing business with the country of Myanmar[27] and overturning a state law in Nebraska (and, by implication, in thirty-one other states) banning partial-term abortions.[28] In 2001, the Court limited the authority of the states to regulate tobacco advertising near playgrounds and schools.[29] Finally, the Court's willingness to overturn the Florida Supreme

Court's decisions in issues concerning the ballot counting in the 2000 presidential race indicates that ideology and partisanship sometimes trump federalism.

Federal intrusions into the affairs of state and local governments continue to be burdensome and unwelcome. For now, the Tenth and Eleventh Amendments are useful weapons for fending off federal encroachments on the power of state and local officials, but their power can be shattered by a single justice's change of heart or the next Supreme Court vacancy.[30]

Intergovernmental Relations

States, local governments, and the federal government are tied together in a complex web of relationships that is constantly being respun.

Interstate Cooperation

Cooperation Under the Constitution   There are four formal provisions for cooperation among the states.

1. The *full faith and credit clause* of the Constitution binds every citizen of every state to the laws and policies of other states. Crossing a state boundary does not alter a legal obligation. The courts have interpreted full faith and credit to apply to contracts, wills, divorces, and many other legalities. The clause does not, however, extend to criminal judgments.
2. The *interstate rendition clause* begins where full faith and credit leaves off, covering persons convicted of criminal violations. Governors are required to extradite (return) fugitives to the state in which they were found guilty or are under indictment (although in certain cases they may refuse).
3. The *privileges and immunities clause* states that "the citizens of each state shall be entitled to all privileges and immunities of citizens in the several states." This clause was intended by the Framers to prevent any state from discriminating against citizens of another state who happen to be traveling or temporarily dwelling outside their own state's borders. Of course, states do discriminate against nonresidents in such matters as out-of-state tuition, hunting and fishing license fees, and residency requirements for voting. The Supreme Court has upheld these and other minor discrepancies, so long as the "fundamental rights" of nonresidents are not violated.
4. Finally, the *interstate compact clause* authorizes the states to negotiate compacts. Early interstate compacts were used to settle boundary disputes. More than 120 are in effect today in a variety of areas, including shared water resources, pest control, riverboat gambling, and education.

Informal Cooperation Among the States   Interstate cooperation can be facilitated through a variety of informal methods. One example is the establishment of regional interstate commissions, such as the Appalachian Regional Commission (ARC), which was created by national legislation in 1965 to attack poverty in the states of Appalachia.

In addition, states have developed uniform laws to help manage common problems ranging from child support to welfare cheating. Interstate cooperation also occurs through information sharing among elected and appointed officials and the organizations to which they belong, such as the National Governors Association (NGA) and the National Conference of State Legislatures. It may take place in legal actions, as demonstrated by the state attorneys general who recently joined together to sue the tobacco companies for driving up medical costs. Or, one state may contract with another for a service, as Hawaii does with Arizona for a medical management information system.

Of course, interstate relations do not always go well; occasionally, the states get into serious conflicts and disagreements. Those that the states cannot settle themselves are taken directly to the U.S. Supreme Court for resolution. One conflict recently resolved by the Court involves which state owns Ellis Island, where millions of immigrants landed just offshore from New York City between 1892 and 1954. Originally the Island comprised only three acres, but landfill projects expanded it to 27.5 acres. In 1998, after some two hundred years of dispute, the Court decided that New York retained sovereignty over the original three acres, while New Jersey gained control of the landfill area. With a nod to the biblical king Solomon, the Court divided the Great Hall, where some 12 million immigrants were processed, equally between the two states.[31]

Tribal Governments

With the arrival of the Europeans, the number of the estimated 7 to 10 million people who lived in what is now the continental United States soon was severely depleted by warfare, disease, and famine. Hundreds of treaties, statutes, and other agreements notwithstanding, the Native Americans were eventually deprived of their traditional lands and isolated on reservations. Today, some 2.5 million people identify themselves as Native American. About one third of them continue to live on tribal reservations, mostly in the western portion of the United States. The Navajo Nation, for instance, has a population of more than 250,000 and covers some 17 million acres, extending from northwest New Mexico to northeast Arizona and southeast Utah.

Tribes are semisovereign nations exercising self-government on their reservations. They are under the authority and supervision of Congress, but their legal relationship with the states is complex. Tribal governments are permitted to adopt constitutions, regulate their internal affairs, hold elections, and enforce their own laws. States are prevented from taxing or regulating tribes, or extending judicial power over them. Off the reservation, however, Native Americans are subject to the same legalities as any other state residents.

Occasionally, interactions between tribal governments, the state, and nearby local governments are testy. Actions concerning tribal land use may conflict with local zoning or state environmental policy. The tax-free sale of gasoline and alcohol and tobacco products on the reservation diminishes sales tax revenues. Tribes seek to recover ancestral lands from present occupants. And tribal casinos sometimes offer games that are prohibited under state law. When conflicts arise,

revenues
Monies raised by governments from taxes, fees, enterprises, and payments from other levels of government.

expenditures
Allocations of government monies.

grant-in-aid
An intergovernmental transfer of funds or other assets, subject to conditions.

revenue sharing
A "no-strings" form of financial aid from one level of government to another.

categorical grant
A form of financial aid from one level of government to another to be used for a narrowly defined purpose.

block grant
A form of financial aid from one level of government to another for use in a broad area.

formula grant
A funding mechanism that automatically allocates monies based on conditions in the recipient government.

project grant
A funding mechanism that awards monies based on the strength of an applicant government's proposal.

states and tribal governments may sort out their differences through compacts. Otherwise, Congress may be asked to enter the fray.

Intergovernmental Financial Relations

Revenues are the funds that governments have at their disposal. They are derived from taxes, fees and charges, and transfers from other levels of government. **Expenditures** are the ways in which the governmental revenues are disbursed. Governments spend money to operate programs, to build public facilities, and to pay off debts.

The **grant-in-aid** is the primary mechanism for transferring money from the national to the state and local governments. The national government makes grants available for a number of reasons: to redistribute wealth, to establish minimum policy standards, and to achieve national goals. But grants are primarily designed to help meet the needs of state and local governments, including environmental protection, transportation, community and regional development, education, and health care. Federal grant outlays total nearly $300 billion a year.

Discretion of Recipients   There are two major variations in grants: the amount of discretion (independence) the recipient has in determining how to spend the money, and the conditions under which the grant is awarded. Imagine a spectrum running from maximum discretion to minimum discretion. The grant labels that correspond to these endpoints are **revenue sharing** and **categorical grants,** respectively. Under revenue sharing, states and communities are allocated funds that they may use for any purpose. A categorical grant, in contrast, can be used by the recipient government only for a narrowly defined purpose, such as removing asbestos from school buildings or acquiring land for outdoor recreation.

Located between revenue sharing and categorical grants on the discretion spectrum are block grants. **Block grants** are *broad-based grants;* that is, they can be used anywhere within a functional area such as transportation or health care. The difference between categorical and block grants is that the recipient government decides how block grants will be spent. For instance, a local school system can decide whether the purchase of personal computers is more important than buying microscopes for the science laboratory. Today there are about 660 grants in existence, including 24 block grants. Block grants give nonnational governments considerable flexibility in responding to pressing needs and preferred goals. These grant mechanisms assume that state and local governments can make rational choices among competing claims.

Conditions for Grants   Grants also vary in the manner in which they are awarded. A **formula grant** makes funding available automatically, based on state and local conditions such as poverty level or unemployment rate. A **project grant** is awarded to selected applicants, based on administrative assessments of the strength of competing proposals. Block grants are distributed on a formula basis; categorical grants can be either formula- or project-based.

Recognition of these two characteristics—the amount of discretion enjoyed by the recipient jurisdiction and the manner in which the grant is awarded—is important for understanding the grant system. Another, less prominent factor also affects intergovernmental financial relations: the existence of *matching requirements*. Most federal grants require that the recipient government use its own resources to pay a certain percentage of program costs. This arrangement is designed to stimulate state and local spending on programs deemed to be in the national interest and to discourage nonnational governments from participating in a program simply because money is available.

Models of Federalism

Perceptions of the role of the states in the federal system have shifted from time to time throughout our history. Those who study the federal system have generally described these perceptions through various models or metaphors that attempt to present federalism's complexity in a readily understandable form. Such models have been used both to enhance understanding and, when opportunities arise, to pursue ideological and partisan objectives.[32]

Dual Federalism (1787–1932)

dual federalism
A model of federalism in which the responsibilities and activities of the national and state governments are separate and distinct.

The model of **dual federalism** holds that the national and state governments are sovereign and equal within their respective spheres of authority as set forth in the Constitution. The national government exercises those powers specifically designated to it, and the remainder are reserved for the states. The metaphor is that of a layer cake, with two separate colored layers one on top of the other.

Dual federalism, which has its roots in the compact theory, was dominant for the first 145 years of U.S. federalism, although the Civil War and other events led to substantial modifications of the model.[33] Until 1860, the functions of the national government remained largely restricted to the delegated powers. Federal financial assistance to the states was very limited. The states had the dominant influence on the everyday lives of their citizens. After the Civil War shattered the doctrines of nullification and secession and dealt the compact theory of state-centered federalism a deathblow, the nation-centered view became paramount.

Cooperative Federalism (1933–1964)

The selection of a specific date for the demise of dual federalism is rather subjective, but 1933, when Franklin D. Roosevelt became president, is a reasonable estimate. Roosevelt's New Deal buried dual federalism by expanding national authority over commerce, taxation, and the economy.

cooperative federalism
A model of federalism that stresses the linkages and joint arrangements among the three levels of government.

Cooperative federalism recognizes the sharing of responsibilities and financing by all levels of government. Beginning with the Great Depression, the national government increasingly cooperated with states and localities to provide jobs and social welfare, to develop the nation's infrastructure, and to promote economic development.

The cooperative aspects of this era were measured in governmental finances. The national government spent huge amounts of money to alleviate the ravages of the Great Depression and to get the U.S. economic machinery back into gear. Total federal expenditures rose from 2.5 percent of the gross national product (GNP) in 1929 to 18.7 percent just thirty years later, far surpassing the growth in state and local spending during the same period. The number of federal grants-in-aid rose from twelve in 1932, with a value of $193 million, to twenty-six in 1937, with a value of $2.66 billion. A substantial amount of the federal aid was sent directly to local governments, particularly counties and school districts. The variety of grant programs also exploded, with disbursements for maternal and child health care, aid to the blind, treatment of venereal disease, public housing, road and bridge construction, and wildlife conservation.

Contemporary Variations on Cooperative Federalism (Since 1964)

The broad theme of cooperative federalism has many variations. All of them stress intergovernmental sharing. Among these variations are creative federalism and new federalism.

creative federalism
A model of cooperative federalism in which many new grants-in-aid, including direct national-local financial arrangements, are made.

Creative federalism was devised by President Lyndon B. Johnson to promote his dream of a "Great Society." Johnson sought to build the Great Society through a massive, grant-funded attack on the most serious problems facing the nation: poverty, crime, poor health care, and inadequate education, among others. More than two hundred new grants were put into place during the five years of Johnson's presidency. The major "creativity" in Johnson's policy of vast government spending involved bypassing the states in distributing funds for some seventy of the new programs. Federal disbursements went directly to cities and counties rather than through the states. Understandably, the states did not appreciate losing influence over how localities could spend their national dollars.

new federalism
A model that represents a return of powers and responsibilities to the states.

New federalism is a model that has been employed with distinct but related meanings in five different presidencies, beginning with that of Richard M. Nixon.

Nixon's Federalism   The new federalism initiated by Richard Nixon was intended to restore power to the states and localities and to improve intergovernmental arrangements for delivering services. Among the major policy changes were the establishment of ten regional councils to coordinate national program administration across the country and the implementation of revenue sharing to give states and localities greater flexibility in program spending and decisionmaking.

Reagan's New Federalism   Ronald Reagan's brand of new federalism, like Nixon's version, sought to give more power and program authority to states and localities, at least in theory. However, Reagan's main goal—to shrink the size of the national government—soon became obvious.

Reagan's new-federalism initiative won congressional approval to merge fifty-seven categorical grants into nine new block grants and to eliminate another sixty categorical grants. The states got more authority, but the funding for the new block grants decreased almost 25 percent from the previous year's allocation for the separate categorical grants.[34] The Reagan administration contended that state and local governments needed less money because the block grants would reduce paperwork.

Reagan and his allies also terminated revenue sharing in 1986. Called *general revenue sharing* (GRS) when enacted during the Nixon administration, this program was highly popular with state and local officials. GRS provided funds, with no strings attached, to state and general-purpose local governments. It was discontinued largely because of the mounting national budget deficit; another factor was Congress's desire to exert greater control over, and take more credit for, how federal monies were spent.

Bush's New Federalism   The Reagan legacy lived on when George Bush (senior) entered the White House in 1988. Although the style was different—in the view of many state and local officials, the Bush administration was more sympathetic—the substance remained the same.[35] The Bush administration continued emphasizing the sorting out of national, state, and local responsibilities in such areas as transportation and education. President Bush, like Reagan, also proposed a variety of "turnovers" of federal programs to the states, but congressional debate over the merits of the various plans was inconclusive.

President Clinton, the Republican Congress, and the "Devolution Revolution"
The arrival in the White House of former Arkansas governor Bill Clinton was greeted by state and local officials with high hopes. In the words of an Arizona legislator, "Bill Clinton had been with us in the state government trenches for years. It simply was natural to believe he would not forget just because he changed 'residences.'"[36]

By 1994, with the election of Republican majorities in the U.S. House and Senate as well as the election of many new Republican governors, new federalism came back in style with impressive force. The New Federalists, whose ranks included many Democrats, sought once again to sort out intergovernmental responsibilities. For the first time in recent memory, the states and localities were basically united and working together through a coalition of government interest groups, including the National Governors' Association and the National League of Cities, to design smaller, more efficient government with greater program and policy flexibility for the states and localities.

This planned delegating of power from the federal to state and local governments is termed **devolution**. The constellation of supporters for devolution is impressive. The governors, acting as individuals and through the National Governors' Association, have never been more active in Washington than they are now. They have found a Supreme Court increasingly likely to rule in favor of state authority. Moreover, public opinion is solidly in favor of greater state and local government authority. Public opinion polls consistently show that citizens believe state and local governments do a better job than the national government in spending money and delivering services.[37] Together, these powerful forces for devolution are gradually reversing more than a century of centralizing tendencies in U.S. federalism. This trend has been so striking that it has been called the "devolution revolution."

devolution
The delegating of power and programs from the federal to state and local governments.

The principal tool for devolving federal financial and programmatic authority and responsibility to the states has been the block grant. In 1996, the sixty-one-year-old entitlement program Aid to Families with Dependent Children (AFDC) was converted to a block grant to the states. As one of the turnbacks supported by several previous presidents, the Personal Responsibility and Work Opportunity Reconciliation Act made AFDC a state responsibility.

Although such steps are encouraging to states and localities, the federal government seems always to be standing by to jerk the rug out from under their feet. Serious discussion about additional turnbacks and innovations lost steam in 1998 as conservative moralistic forces in Congress sought to usurp state authority over property rights, electric utility deregulation, and blood-alcohol limits, among other issues.

George W. Bush and New Federalism   The views of the latest president Bush (like Clinton, a former governor) have not yet been clearly articulated, but legislative initiatives of his administration and of Republican supporters in Congress sought to preempt state authority over school testing systems, override forty state laws that guarantee patient rights, obstruct state laws that permit the medical use of marijuana, and impose new homeland security requirements on the states. The predominance of business interests in Washington, D.C., appears to have stanched devolution in what one writer calls "the law of political physics—that for every flurry of state and local business regulations, there is an equal and opposite" effort by business to counter it in the nation's capitol.[38] In fairness, it must be noted that the events of September 11, 2001, and the subsequent war on terrorism consumed the Bush administration during late 2001 and throughout 2002.

Federal Purse Strings

Federalism today turns less on theory and more on money. The distribution of intergovernmental monies and the conditions attached to them define the distribution of governmental power and authority. Federalism is a matter not only of which level of government will do what, but of which level will pay for it. Some have called this a period of "fend-for-yourself federalism," with each jurisdiction essentially on its own in a Darwinian struggle for financial survival.

The Importance of Federal Funds

Figure 2.1 provides a historical look at national grant-in-aid expenditures. It is important to remember that the figures in this table have not been adjusted for inflation; the $24.1 billion spent in 1970 was worth vastly more than it would be today. Furthermore, the amounts do not take into account the increase in population since 1970. The second set of bars in Figure 2.1 documents the recently growing proportion of national dollars in the expenditures of state and local governments, reflecting the fact that aid to states and localities still consumes a relatively small share of the federal government's budget.

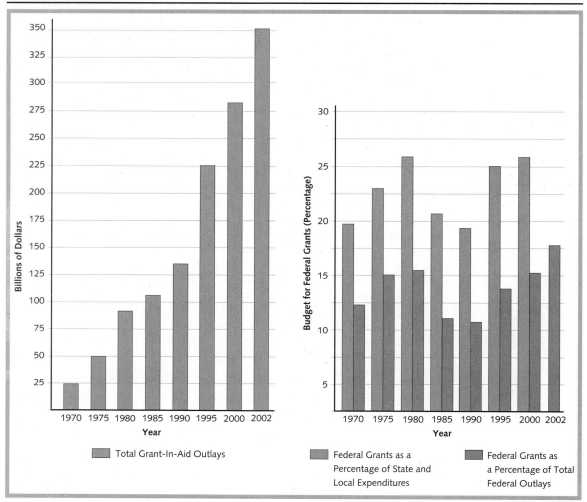

FIGURE 2.1   Historical Trends in Federal Grant-in-Aid Outlays

NOTE: Figures for 2002 are estimates. Data for 2002 Federal Grants as a Percentage of State and Local Expenditures were not available at the time of printing.

SOURCE: U.S. Office of Management and Budget, The Budget of the United States Government, Fiscal Year 2000, Historical Tables, and www.access.gpo.gov/usbudget/fy2001/pdf/hist.pdf.

Although the Washington-funded portion of state and local government expenditures is only around 26 percent, it represents an important source of revenue for nonnational governments. Grants to state and local governments averaged approximately $1,035 per person in fiscal year 2001. However, the funds were not spread evenly across the country (see Table 2.1). Alaska and New York received the most per capita. Federal grants poured into these states at the rate of $1,985 and $1,502, respectively. In last place is Virginia, where federal grant monies averaged just $569 per person.

States battle in Congress over their share of grant allocations, which are affected by such factors as the existence of military installations in the state and social welfare needs. The states attempt to influence competitive project grant awards and lobby Congress to adjust the weighing of certain factors in formula grants in their favor. State and local influence is wielded by the representatives sitting in Congress and through various actions by elected state and local officials and their Washington lobbyists.[39] But national expenditures in nongrant forms also affect state and local economies substantially. In the nongrant category are payments to individuals (representing 63 percent of total federal grants today, up from 36 percent in the 1980s), notably through the Social Security system; purchases by the national government; and wages and salaries of federal workers, most of whom work outside of Washington, D.C. In this sense, federal expenditures emphasize people more than places.

Here's the Check and Here's What to Do with It: Mandates, Preemptions, Set-asides, and Cost Ceilings

Although many voices are crying, "Let the states and localities do it," Congress continues to impose mandates and preempt the states. In addition, Congress includes set-asides and cost ceilings in block grants. Old habits die hard, and one of Congress's oldest habits is to place requirements and conditions on the states. Washington-based politicians may claim to support state power in principle, but when it conflicts with other priorities, devolution takes a back seat.

federal mandate
A requirement that a state or local government undertake a specific activity or provide a particular service as a condition of funding.

Federal mandates are especially burdensome when they are unfunded—that is, when the national government requires the states and localities to take action but does not pay for it. Who does pay? The states and localities do. Recent federal mandates have required mandatory HIV testing of newborn babies if voluntary testing does not reduce transmission rates from infected mothers; established mandatory standards for drinking water and clean air; and required that every child in grades 3–8 be tested in math and reading annually. The total cost of these "mandate millstones" hanging round the necks of states and localities runs up to $5 billion annually.[40] Mounting opposition to mandates without money finally convinced Congress to enact the Unfunded Mandate Reform Act of 1995, which provides that any bill imposing a mandate of more than $50 million on a state or local government must include a cost estimate. If passed, the

| TABLE 2.1 | Federal Grants to State and Local Governments, 2000, in Rank Order | | |

ENTITY	GRANT PER CAPITA	ENTITY	GRANT PER CAPITA
1. Alaska	$1,985	26. Nebraska	884
2. New York	1,502	27. Idaho	875
3. Wyoming	1,335	28. Michigan	873
4. West Virginia	1,319	28. Oklahoma	873
5. Rhode Island	1,312	30. Hawaii	866
6. North Dakota	1,276	31. North Carolina	852
7. Vermont	1,269	32. Washington	842
8. Montana	1,254	33. Wisconsin	839
9. New Mexico	1,233	34. Ohio	838
10. Maine	1,230	35. New Jersey	826
11. Mississippi	1,102	36. Georgia	825
12. South Dakota	1,089	37. Minnesota	807
13. Louisiana	1,078	38. Iowa	806
14. Kentucky	1,053	39. New Hampshire	786
15. Connecticut	1,005	40. Illinois	784
16. Tennessee	994	41. Texas	777
17. Massachusetts	984	41. Arizona	777
18. Pennsylvania	979	43. Kansas	773
19. Arkansas	973	44. Utah	754
20. Delaware	924	45. Indiana	750
21. California	920	46. Maryland	729
22. South Carolina	919	47. Florida	688
23. Missouri	902	48. Colorado	628
24. Oregon	899	49. Nevada	571
25. Alabama	898	50. Virginia	569

NOTE: For information on the dollar amounts of federal grants to the states and Washington, D.C., in 2000, see the table at our website at **www.hmco.com/college.**

SOURCE: Calculated from *Budget Information for States, FY 2002* (Washington, D.C.: U.S. Government Printing Office, 2001), p. 3.

legislation must include sufficient funds to pay for the mandate. Indications are that proposed laws containing unfunded mandates are facing much tougher scrutiny in Congress than before and that Congress is taking a more consultative approach with state and local officials. However, members are always threatening to revert to their mandating ways.

As noted earlier, *preemption* represents another intrusion of the national government into the state sphere. It takes two forms: *total* preemption, whereby the national government seizes all regulatory authority for a given function from states and localities; and *partial* preemption, whereby the national government establishes minimum national standards for state-implemented programs. Both forms prevent states from doing what they want to do. One example of a totally preemptive action is the Americans with Disabilities Act, which requires states and localities to make physical and occupational accommodation for disabled persons. Many partial preemptions involve environmental protection, whereby states may regulate pollution emissions so long as state standards are at least as stringent as those of the federal government. The terms of the 1994 General Agreement on Tariffs and Trade (GATT), which permits foreign corporations to challenge state laws that may unfairly discriminate against them, has raised new concerns.

Thus, when mandates and preemptions are taken into consideration, a less optimistic picture of intergovernmental relations emerges. To the states and localities it seems that the country has shifted from cooperative federalism to coercive federalism or, in the words of Governor Ben Nelson of Nebraska, demoted states from significant policymakers to branch managers "of a behemoth central "government."[41]

set-asides

Requirements in block grants that assign a certain percentage expenditure for a particular activity.

Set-asides offer an alternative mechanism through which policymakers in Washington, D.C., can influence the behavior of distant governments. Set-asides are provisions in block grants that designate a certain minimum percentage expenditure on a particular activity. For example, the Alcohol, Drug Abuse, and Mental Health Block Grant contains requirements that states spend at least 50 percent of the funds on services to intravenous (IV) drug users. The Congress reasoned that the sharing of hypodermic needles among addicts was contributing to the spread of the AIDS virus and that states were not doing enough to address the problem. But state leaders, though they admitted AIDS was a national priority, argued that the problem was not uniformly spread around the country. Why should Montana spend the same proportion of its funds on IV drug users as New York? Perhaps Montana should spend its drug abuse funds on adolescent alcohol abusers. In any case, the issue is clear: Who should decide how federal funds are to be spent—the government allocating the funds or the one implementing the program?

The Future of Federalism

For the states and localities, a decade of national policy gridlock has meant a golden opportunity to reverse more than a century of centralizing forces. They have taken up the slack in the federal system and are busily innovating, developing and implementing policies in a great variety of fields, from social welfare and health care to education and economic development. As laboratories of democracy, states have experimented with and designed numerous policies that later have served as models for other states and for Congress. For instance, states have recently pioneered policy initiatives on children's issues, unwanted telemarketing calls, health insurance for the poor, a patients' bill of rights, campaign finance reform, and welfare reform, among many other fields.

Some states, including Massachusetts, Minnesota, Oregon, Washington, and Wisconsin, consistently rank high as policy initiators. But others predictably bring up the rear. Counting as policy laggards are Alabama, Mississippi, and South Carolina.[43] Why are some states more innovative than others? A host of factors come into play, including political culture, the presence of policy entrepreneurs, levels of population and population growth, urbanization, and state wealth. And while all states achieve positive policy breakthroughs at one time or another, most are also guilty of occasional boneheaded decisions.

California made a huge mess of electricity deregulation in 2000–2001 that resulted in rolling brownouts and shockingly high utility bills. Arizona's offer of a tax-incentive program designed to take old, fuel-wasting vehicles off the roads and replace them with cleaner-burning vehicles turned into a $483 million headache when the response was more enthusiastic than anticipated. Of course, on the positive side, one state learns from another's mistakes.

Sentiment continues to build that Washington is not the best location for addressing all the nation's complex policy problems. As one observer puts it, Washington, D.C., represents a "mainframe government in a PC "world."[44] Whereas centrally designing and implementing policies and programs once was believed to be the best approach, today it implies wasteful and ineffective one-size-fits-all government. The clear trend in government, as well as in business, is to decentralize decisionmaking to the lowest feasible level of the organization. For the U.S. federal system, that means sending decisionmaking to the states and localities and even, in some instances, to nonprofit organizations and citizens' groups.

Unfortunately, at the very time that state and local governments are most needed as policy leaders and problem solvers, certain social and economic forces seriously threaten state and local government capability. The economic recession that began in late 2001 severely reduced state and local revenues. The breakdown of the traditional family and high rates of births to unmarried women and teenage girls have left millions of children in poverty. Illegal drugs and gang activity, homelessness, and a flood of immigrants present seemingly impossible challenges for the cities. Finally, the growing disparity of wealth and income threatens our great reservoir of political and social stability, the middle class.

For its part, the federal government is provoking growing criticism for tying the hands of the states and localities with mandates, preemptions, and confused and conflicting policy directives. Most state and local governments *want* to become more creative, but they are also being *forced* to do so to figure out how to implement and pay for federally mandated requirements. This conflicted, ambiguous federalism is something less than empowerment.[45] When the president or members of Congress take actions to squash innovative programs such as legalization of medical marijuana in California or assisted suicide in Oregon, they profess to do so for purposes of the national interest or high moral principles. But some see the issue as also being about money and power and, perhaps at the most basic level, about the need for Congress to justify its existence in an increasingly state and local political world.

States and localities are demanding cooperative relationships and flexible or facilitative federalism in which the national government helps them through selective funding for technical assistance—a federalism in which they are treated as partners in governance, not as just another self-absorbed interest group. What states want, in a word, is empowerment.

The states are determined to oppose further federal preemptions of their powers and responsibilities. They have fought to protect the health, safety, and physical environment of their citizens, often with standards and a level of commitment that far exceed those of the federal government. They have continued to serve as political laboratories for experiments in service delivery and other fields, despite severe reductions in federal financial support and expensive government-spending requirements. As the burdens of governing nearly 300 million Americans have grown, the limitations of the national government have become evident. Effective federalism in the United States today demands a cooperative partnership among nation, states, and localities.

The question of the balance of power and responsibility in U.S. federalism is no less important now than it was two hundred years ago. The focus of the debate has shifted, however, to a pragmatic interest in how the responsibility of governing should be sorted out among the three levels of government. As pointed out by Samuel H. Beer, an insightful observer of U.S. government, "The American federal system has never been static. It has changed radically over the years, as tides of centralization and decentralization have altered the balance of power and the allocation of functions among the different levels of "government."[46] The pendulum marking the balance has swung to and fro over the two centuries of U.S. federalism. Today it swings in the direction of the state and local governments.

Chapter Recap

➤ U.S. federalism is an ongoing experiment in governance.

➤ A fundamental question is: What is the proper balance of power and responsibility between the national government and the states?

➤ Until recently, the trend has been generally in the direction of a stronger national government. But beginning in the early 1980s, there has been a resurgence of the state and local governments as political and policy actors.

➤ The power relationships among the three levels of government are described by various models, including dual and cooperative federalism. The operative model is cooperative federalism, under the variant known as new federalism.

➤ A key ingredient of federalism is intergovernmental relations, particularly those concerning finance.

➤ The national government imposes certain controversial requirements on grants-in-aid, including mandates, preemptions, and set-asides.

Key Terms

unitary system (*p. 22*)
confederacy (*p. 22*)
federal system (*p. 22*)
factions (*p. 24*)
nation-centered federalism (*p. 27*)
state-centered federalism (*p. 27*)
reserved powers (*p. 27*)
Tenth Amendment (*p. 27*)
enumerated (delegated)
   powers (*p. 27*)
compact theory (*p. 27*)
national supremacy clause (*p. 28*)
necessary and proper clause (*p. 28*)
implied powers (*p. 29*)
interstate commerce clause (*p. 29*)
general welfare clause (*p. 29*)
Fourteenth Amendment (*p. 30*)

Sixteenth Amendment (*p. 30*)
federal preemption (*p. 30*)
revenues (*p. 35*)
expenditures (*p. 35*)
grant-in-aid (*p. 35*)
revenue sharing (*p. 35*)
categorical grant (*p. 35*)
block grant (*p. 35*)
formula grant (*p. 35*)
project grant (*p. 35*)
dual federalism (*p. 36*)
cooperative federalism (*p. 36*)
creative federalism (*p. 37*)
new federalism (*p. 37*)
devolution (*p. 38*)
federal mandate (*p. 41*)
set-asides (*p. 43*)

Surfing the Net

Examples of unfunded mandates are found on a Heritage Foundation webpage at **www.regulation.org/states.html.** Federalism decisions of the U.S. Supreme Court and other federalism topics may be reviewed at The Council of State Governments' website at **www.statesnews.org.** or **www.csg.org.** Other websites that often feature federalism news and issues are **www.governing.com** and **www.stateline.org.**

3

STATE CONSTITUTIONS

The Evolution of State Constitutions
 The First State Constitutions » Legislative Supremacy » The
 Growth of Executive Power

Weaknesses of Constitutions
 Excessive Length » Problems of Substance

Constitutional Reform
 The Model State Constitution » Constitutions Today

Methods for Constitutional Change
 Informal Constitutional Change » Formal Constitutional Change

State Responsiveness and Constitutional Reform

Can two men—or two women—be legally married? Congress and more than thirty states have enacted laws denying recognition to same-sex marriages. But in *Baker* v. *Vermont,* the Vermont Supreme Court determined that under the common benefits clause of the state constitution, same-sex couples should have the same legal rights as conventional couples. The court instructed the state legislature to pass a law implementing this ruling. In March 2000, Green Mountain State gays were granted the statutory right to obtain a "civil union" license, with which they are free to partake of all the rights and benefits of a traditional marriage. Anti–civil union sentiment brought record numbers to the polls that November and delivered control of the state house to the Republicans for the first time in more than a decade, but Governor Howard Dean, who had signed the bill, was reelected. Thus, civil unions survived their first challenge at the ballot box in Vermont.[1]

The *Baker* case illustrates *judicial federalism,* whereby state supreme courts are increasingly grounding their rulings on the language of their state—rather than the national—constitution. It also reflects the fact that state constitutions are once again becoming the guardians of civil liberties, as they were throughout the early history of the United States.

All state constitutions both distribute and constrain political power among groups and regions. They set forth the basic framework and operating rules for government, allocate power to the three branches, establish the scope of state and local governmental authority, and protect individual rights.[2] Constitutions represent the *fundamental law* of a state, superior to statutory law. They provide a set of rules for the game of state government, and those who master the regulations and procedures have a distinct advantage over novices. Everything that a state government does and represents is rooted in its constitution. Constitutions do not describe the full reality of a political system, but they do provide a window through which to perceive its reality. Only the federal Constitution and federal statutes take priority over state constitutions. This is why the constitution is called the *fundamental law.*

To most people, however, constitutional law still means the federal document. State constitutions are often neglected in secondary school and college courses in history and political science. Astonishingly, one national survey discovered that 51 percent of Americans were not aware that their state had its own constitution.[3]

In the U.S. system of *dual constitutionalism,* in which there are both national and state constitutions, the national government is supreme within the spheres of authority specifically delegated to it, by the states, in the U.S. Constitution. Powers granted to the national government are denied to the states. But the national Constitution is incomplete. It leaves many key constitutional issues to the states, including those pertaining to local finance, public education, and the organization of state and local government.[4] In theory, state constitutions are supreme for all matters not expressly within the national government's jurisdiction or preempted by federal constitutional or statutory law. In practice, however, congressional actions and federal court interpretations have expanded the powers of the national government and, in some fields, eroded the powers of the states. And, in reality, many powers, such as taxing, spending, and protecting citizens' health and safety, are shared by all levels of government.

The earliest state constitutions were simple documents reflecting an agrarian economy, single-owner businesses, and horse-and-buggy transportation. As American society and the economy changed, the rules of state government also required transformation. Some reforms have reflected changing political fortunes: Newly powerful groups have pressed to revise the state constitution to reflect their interests, or one or another political party has gained control of state government and sought to solidify its power. Constitutional reforms have promoted different views of politics and the public interest, as when Progressive reformers rallied for honest and efficient government in the late nineteenth and early twentieth centuries.[5] Since the 1960s, constitutional revisions have concentrated power in the governor's office, unified court systems, and generally sought to make state government more efficient, effective, and responsive to shifting social and economic forces. The fact that constitutions are subject to change also recognizes that human judgment is not infallible, nor human understanding perfect.[6] In 2000, for instance, Alabama voters finally removed a prohibition against miscegenation (mixed-race marriage). Through constitutional reform, states can elevate their role as democratic laboratories by responding to the changing needs and opinions of citizens. This is in sharp contrast to the seldom-amended federal Constitution.

The Evolution of State Constitutions

When the states won their independence from Great Britain more than two hundred years ago, there was no precedent for writing constitutions. There was a preexisting constitution of the Five Nations of the Iroquois called the Great Binding Law, but it was oral and not particularly relevant to the people in the colonies.[7] The thirteen colonial charters provided the foundation for the new state constitutions. These were brief documents (around five pages each) that the Crown had granted to trading companies and individuals to govern settlements in the new territories. As the settlements became full colonies, the charters were expanded to incorporate the "rights of Englishmen"—political and civil rights first enumerated by the Magna Carta in 1215. For distant territories too remote from their native country to be governed by its laws, these charters also laid down some basic principles of colonial government.[8]

In what was to become Connecticut, early settlers escaping the oppressive rule of the Massachusetts Bay Colony took matters of governance into their own hands. Under the leadership of Thomas Hooker, these ambitious farmers established an independent government free from references to the British Crown. The Fundamental Orders of 1639 contended that "the choice of the public magistrates belongs unto the people by God's own allowance. The privilege of election belongs to the people . . . it is in their power, also, to set the bounds and limitations of the power [of elected officials]."[9] Years later, a representative of King James II was sent to take possession of the Fundamental Orders and unite the New England colonies under the Crown. In a night meeting, as the Orders were laid out on a table before the king's men, the candles suddenly were extinguished. When they were rekindled, the document had disappeared. According to legend, a patriot had hidden it in a nearby hollow tree, later to be known as the Charter Oak. Infuriated, the king's men dissolved the colony's government and imposed autocratic rule that lasted many years. But they never found the Fundamental Orders, which essentially governed Connecticut until the Constitution of 1818 was adopted.[10]

The First State Constitutions

Following the War of Independence, the former colonies drafted their first constitutions in special revolutionary conventions or in legislative assemblies. With the exception of Massachusetts, the new states put their constitutions into effect immediately, without popular ratification. The making of the first state constitutions was not a casual or simple affair. Critical questions had to be answered in constitutional conventions, including those concerning how the new government would be structured, how and when elections would be held, and how land once owned by the Crown would be distributed. Territorial integrity was not well defined. For example, in what is now known as Kentucky, people frustrated with Virginia's rule met in 1784 and petitioned the Congress for statehood. It took six years and nine constitutional conventions before Kentucky became a state. Complicating factors causing delay involved the "necessity of communicating across the mountains, the change from the Articles of Confederation to the Constitution of the United States, Indian attacks, [and] the revelation of a plot to have Kentucky secure independence and join Spain."[11]

In content, most of these documents simply extended the colonial charters, removing references to the king and inserting a bill of rights. All incorporated the principles of limited government: a weak executive branch, the separation of powers, checks and balances, a bill of rights to protect the people and their property from arbitrary government actions, and (except for Pennsylvania) a bicameral legislature.[12] The earliest constitutions were not truly democratic. Essentially, they called for government by an aristocracy. Officeholding and voting, for instance, were restricted to white males of wealth and property.[13]

Only one of the thirteen original state constitutions, that of Massachusetts, survives (although it has been amended 118 times). It is the oldest active constitution in the world. Its longevity can be attributed in large part to the foresight of its drafter, John Adams, who grounded the document in extensive

This painting illustrates the signing of the Massachusetts state constitution, which is the oldest living active constitution in the world. (Photo courtesy of the Massachusetts Archives)

research of governments that took him all the way back to the Magna Carta. Even after many amendments, the Massachusetts constitution reflects a composite of the wisdom of the foremost political philosophers of the eighteenth century: John Locke, Jean-Jacques Rousseau, and the Baron de Montesquieu.[14] In its constitution, Massachusetts establishes itself as a commonwealth (from the words *common weal,* meaning "general well-being"), on the principle that its citizens have a right to protect and manage their collective interests. (Kentucky, Pennsylvania, and Virginia are also commonwealths.)

Legislative Supremacy

legislative supremacy
The legislature's dominance of the other two branches of government.

The first state constitutions reflected their framers' fear and distrust of the executive—a result of their experiences with the colonial governors. The governors were not all tyrants; but because they represented the British Crown and Parliament, they became a symbol of oppression to the colonists. As a result, the guiding principle of the new constitutional governments was **legislative supremacy,** and the legislatures were given overwhelming power at the expense of governors. Most governors were to be elected by the legislature, not the people, and were restricted to a single term of office. State judiciaries also were limited in authorized powers; and judges, like governors, were to be elected by the legislature.

The Growth of Executive Power

Disillusionment with the legislatures soon developed, spreading rapidly through the states during the early 1800s. There were many reasons for disenchantment, including the legislatures' failure to address problems caused by rapid population growth and the Industrial Revolution; the growing amount of legislation that favored private interests; and a mounting load of state indebtedness, which led nine states to default on their bonds in a single two-year period.

Gradually the executive branch began to accumulate more power and stature through constitutional amendments that provided for popular election of governors, who were also given longer terms and the authority to veto legislative bills. The constitutions of states admitted to the Union during the early 1800s established stronger executive powers at the outset. This trend toward centralization of power in the executive branch continued during the 1830s and 1840s, the so-called Jacksonian era; however, the Jacksonian principle of popular elections to fill most government offices resulted in a fragmented state executive branch. The governor now had to share authority with a lieutenant governor, an attorney general, a treasurer, and other popularly elected officials, as well as with numerous agency heads appointed by the legislature.

As executive power grew, public confidence in state legislatures continued to erode. This circumstance was reflected in the process of constitutional revision. One delegate at Kentucky's 1890 constitutional convention proclaimed that "the principal, if not the sole purpose of this constitution which we are here to frame, is to restrain the legislature's will and restrict its authority."[15] Also affecting constitutional change were broader social and economic forces in the

United States, such as the extension of suffrage and popular participation in government, the rise of a corporate economy, the Civil War and Reconstruction, the growth of industry and commerce, the process of urbanization, and a growing movement for government reform. States rapidly replaced and amended their constitutions from the early 1800s to 1920 in response to these and other forces. For example, the decade of the Civil War saw the highest level of constitutional activity in U.S. history, much of it in the southern states; between 1860 and 1870, twenty-seven constitutions were replaced or thoroughly revised as Confederate states ratified new documents after secession, then redrew the documents after Union victory to incorporate certain conditions of readmission to the United States.

Constitutional change after Reconstruction was driven by the Populist and Progressive reform movements. During the late 1800s, the Populists championed the causes of the "little man," including farmers and laborers. They sought to open the political process to the people through such constitutional devices as the initiative, the referendum, and the recall (see Chapter 4). The Progressives, who made their mark during the 1890–1920 period, were kindred spirits whose favorite targets were concentrated wealth, inefficiencies in government, machine politics, corruption, and boss rule in the cities. Reformers in both groups successfully promoted constitutional reforms such as regulation of campaign spending and party activities, replacement of party conventions with direct primary elections, and selection of judges through nonpartisan elections.

Weaknesses of Constitutions

Despite the numerous constitutional amendments and replacements enacted during the nineteenth and early twentieth centuries, by 1950 the states were buffeted by a rising chorus criticizing their fundamental laws. Ironically, many states were victims of past constitutional change, which left them with documents that were extravagantly long, frustratingly inflexible, and distressingly detailed. In general, state constitutions still provided for a feeble executive branch, granting limited administrative authority to the governor, permitting the popular election of numerous other executive branch officials, and organizing the executive into a hodgepodge of semiautonomous agencies, boards, and commissions. State judiciaries remained uncoordinated and overly complex, whereas legislatures suffered from archaic structures and procedures. Statutory detail, out-of-date language, local amendments (those that apply only to designated local governments), and other problems contaminated the documents and straitjacketed state government.

Excessive Length

From the first constitutions, which averaged 5,000 words, state documents had expanded into enormous tracts of verbiage averaging 27,000 words by 1967. (The U.S. Constitution contains 7,800 words.) Some of this growth resulted from increasing social and economic complexity, as well as from a perceived need to be very specific about what the legislatures could and could not do. The states did have to delineate their residual powers (those powers not delegated to the national government), identify the scope of their responsibility, and define the powers of local governments. In addition, state constitutions are much easier to amend than the federal Constitution. However, some constitutions went too far. Louisiana's exceeded 253,000 words. If local provisions were counted, Georgia's contained around 583,500 words, surpassing Tolstoy's *War and Peace* in length. Even today, the constitution of South Carolina limits local government indebtedness but then lists seventeen pages of exceptions. Maryland's constitution devotes an article to off-street parking in Baltimore. Oklahoma's sets the flash point for kerosene at 115 degrees for purposes of illumination,[16] and California's addresses a compelling issue of our time—the length of wrestling matches. The dubious prize for most verbose constitution today (Georgia's was replaced with a much briefer version) goes to Alabama's 310,296-word document. Table 3.1 provides an overview of the fifty state constitutions, including each one's length.

Not surprisingly, lengthy state constitutions tend to be plagued by contradictions and meaningless clauses. Some even address problems that are no longer with us, such as the regulation of steamboats[17] or the need to teach livestock feeding in Oklahoma public schools.

Verbose constitutions, such as those of Alabama, Oklahoma, and Texas, fail to distinguish between fundamental law and issues that properly should be decided by the state legislature.[18] Excessive detail leads to litigation, as the courts must rule on conflicting provisions and challenges to constitutionality; hence the courts are often unnecessarily burdened with decisions that should be made by the legislature. Once incorporated into a constitution, a decision becomes as close to permanent as anything can be in politics. In contrast to a statute, which can be changed by a simple legislative majority, constitutional change requires an extraordinary majority, usually two-thirds or three-fourths of the legislature. This requirement hampers the legislature's ability to confront problems quickly and makes policy change more difficult. Of course, enshrining a principle in the constitution can be a deliberate strategy to protect special interests. Too many amendments may also deprive local governments of needed flexibility to cope with their own problems. Indeed, too much detail generates confusion, not only for legislatures and courts but also for the general public. It encourages political subterfuge to get around archaic or irrelevant provisions and breeds disrespect or even contempt for government.

State constitutions are political documents and, contrary to the admonitions of reformers, may sometimes be used to address some of the most controversial issues in politics, such as abortion rights, gay rights, and even smokers' rights. Many detailed provisions explicitly favor or protect special interests, including public utilities, farmers, timber companies, religious groups, and others.

There is enormous variance in the length of state constitutions (see Table 3.1). What accounts for such disparity? Studies by political scientists find, not surprisingly, that interest groups play an important role. In states with only one strong political party, where legislative outcomes tend to be unpredictable because of dissension among members of the majority party, interest groups try to

| | | TABLE 3.1 | State Constitutions | | |

STATE	NUMBER OF CONSTITUTIONS	EFFECTIVE DATE OF PRESENT CONSTITUTION	ESTIMATED NUMBER OF WORDS	NUMBER OF AMENDMENTS Submitted to Voters	Adopted
Alabama	6	Nov. 28, 1901	310,296	913	664
Alaska	1	Jan. 3, 1959	15,988	37	28
Arizona	1	Feb. 14, 1912	28,876	227	125
Arkansas	5	Oct. 30, 1874	40,720	179	85
California	2	July 4, 1879	54,645	834	500
Colorado	1	Aug. 1, 1876	45,679	282	135
Connecticut	4	Dec. 30, 1965	16,608	30	29
Delaware	4	June 10, 1897	19,000	*	132
Florida	6	Jan. 7, 1969	38,000	116	86
Georgia	10	July 1, 1983	37,849	68	51
Hawaii	1	Aug. 21, 1959	20,774	113	95
Idaho	1	July 3, 1890	23,442	202	115
Illinois	4	July 1, 1971	13,700	17	11
Indiana	2	Nov. 1, 1851	10,315	74	42
Iowa	2	Sept. 3, 1857	12,616	57	52
Kansas	1	Jan. 29, 1861	12,616	120	91
Kentucky	4	Sept. 28, 1891	23,911	70	36
Louisiana	11	Jan. 1, 1975	54,112	153	107
Maine	1	March 15, 1820	13,500	198	168
Maryland	4	Oct. 5, 1867	41,349	249	214
Massachusetts	1	Oct. 25, 1780	36,700	146	118
Michigan	4	Jan. 1, 1964	25,530	57	23
Minnesota	1	May 11, 1858	11,547	213	118
Mississippi	4	Nov. 1, 1890	24,323	155	121
Missouri	4	March 30, 1945	42,000	156	99
Montana	2	July 1, 1973	13,726	43	23
Nebraska	2	Oct. 12, 1875	20,048	319	213
Nevada	1	Oct. 31, 1864	20,770	206	128
New Hampshire	2	June 2, 1784	9,200	282	143
New Jersey	3	Jan. 1, 1948	17,800	65	52
New Mexico	1	Jan. 6, 1912	27,200	264	139
New York	4	Jan. 1, 1895	51,700	287	217
North Carolina	3	July 1, 1971	11,000	38	30
North Dakota	1	Nov. 2, 1889	20,564	249	137

STATE	NUMBER OF CONSTITUTIONS	EFFECTIVE DATE OF PRESENT CONSTITUTION	ESTIMATED NUMBER OF WORDS	NUMBER OF AMENDMENTS Submitted to Voters	Adopted
Ohio	2	Sept. 1, 1851	36,900	263	159
Oklahoma	1	Nov. 16, 1907	79,153	314	161
Oregon	1	Feb. 14, 1859	49,326	434	220
Pennsylvania	5	1968	27,503	32	26
Rhode Island	2	May 2, 1843	10,233	105	59
South Carolina	7	Jan. 1, 1896	22,500	665	480
South Dakota	1	Nov. 2, 1889	25,315	206	105
Tennessee	3	Feb. 23, 1870	15,300	57	34
Texas	5	Feb. 15, 1876	80,806	564	390
Utah	1	Jan. 4, 1896	11,000	146	96
Vermont	3	July 9, 1793	8,295	210	52
Virginia	6	July 1, 1971	21,092	42	34
Washington	1	Nov. 11, 1889	50,237	163	92
West Virginia	2	April 9, 1872	26,000	116	67
Wisconsin	1	May 29, 1848	14,392	181	133
Wyoming	1	July 10, 1890	31,800	111	68

*Proposed amendments are not submitted to the voters in Delaware.

NOTE: The information in this table is current through January 1, 2000. The constitutions referred to include those Civil War documents customarily listed by the individual states.

SOURCE: Copyright © 2000 The Council of State Governments. Reprinted with permission from *The Book of the States.*

insulate their "pet" agencies and programs from uncertainty by seeking protective provisions for them in the constitution.[19] Also, research indicates that long, detailed documents tend to become even longer because their very complexity encourages further amendment, until they finally grow so cumbersome that political support develops for a simpler version. By 2002, for example, momentum was rapidly building to rewrite Alabama's ponderous constitution. Finally, the easier it is to amend a constitution, the higher the amendment rate.[20]

Problems of Substance

In addition to the contradictions, anachronisms, wordiness, and grants of special privilege found in state constitutions, their *substance* has drawn criticism. Specific concerns voiced by reformers include the following:

- *The long ballot.* As elected executive branch officials are not beholden to the governor for their jobs, the governor has little or no formal influence on their decisions and activities. Reformers who seek to maximize the governor's powers would restrict the executive branch to only two elected leaders: the governor and the lieutenant governor.

- *A glut of executive boards and commissions.* This Jacksonian-era reform product was intended to expand opportunities for public participation in state government and to limit the powers of the governor. Today, it leads to fragmentation and a lack of policy coordination in the executive branch.

- *A swamp of local governments.* There are more than 88,000 municipalities, counties, and special-purpose districts in the states. Sometimes they work at cross-purposes, and nearly always they suffer from overlapping responsibilities and an absence of coordination.

- *Restrictions on local government authority.* Localities in some states have to obtain explicit permission from the state legislature before providing a new service, tapping a new source of revenue, or exercising any other authority not specifically granted them by the state.

- *Unequal treatment of racial minorities and women.* Even today, constitutional language sometimes discriminates against African Americans, Latinos, women, and other groups by denying them certain rights guaranteed to white males. (Arizona's constitutional provision requiring that statewide executive officers be male had to be deleted in 1988 when Rose Mofford became governor.)

Constitutional Reform

Shortly after World War II, problems of constitutional substance began to generate increasing commentary on the sorry condition of state constitutions. One of the most influential voices came in 1955 from the U.S. Advisory Commission on Intergovernmental Relations, popularly known as the Kestnbaum Commission. In its final report to the president, the Commission stated that

> the Constitution prepared by the Founding Fathers, with its broad grants of authority and avoidance of legislative detail, has withstood the test of time far better than the constitutions later adopted by the States. The Commission believes that most states would benefit from a fundamental review of their constitution to make sure that they provide for vigorous and responsible government, not forbid it.[21]

Model State Constitution
An ideal of the structure and contents of a state constitution.

Another important voice for constitutional reform was the National Municipal League, which developed a **Model State Constitution** in 1921 that is now in its sixth version.[22]

Thomas Jefferson believed that each generation has the right to choose for itself its own form of government. He suggested that a new constitution every nineteen or twenty years would be appropriate. Between 1960 and 1980, it would appear that the states took his remarks to heart. Every state altered its fundamental law in some respect during this period, and new or substantially revised constitutions were put into operation in more than half the states. During the 1970s alone, ten states held conventions to consider changing or replacing their constitution. One of these was Louisiana, which set a record by adopting its eleventh constitution; Georgia is in second place with ten.

positive-law tradition
A state constitutional tradition based on detailed provisions and procedures.

higher-law tradition
A state constitutional tradition based on basic and enduring principles that reach beyond statutory law.

Two state constitutional traditions are evident today.[23] The newer **positive-law tradition** is represented by the detailed and lengthy documents of states such as Alabama, New York, and Texas. Detailed provisions tend to usurp the lawmaking powers of state legislatures by locking in rigid procedures and policies that typically favor strong political or economic interests. The original **higher-law tradition** is represented by the U.S. Constitution and the National Municipal League's Model State Constitution. It is embodied in brief documents that put forward basic, enduring principles and processes of government, and that view public policy choices as the proper responsibility of legislatures. Of course, no constitutional formula can be suitable for all the states because they differ too much in history, society, economics, and political culture. The best constitutions strike a balance between the need for stability and the requirement for enough flexibility to deal with emerging problems. Today, the higher-law tradition is once again in favor. State constitutions are briefer, more readable, and simple enough for the average citizen to understand.

The Model State Constitution

The Model State Constitution has twelve basic articles that are embodied to a greater or lesser extent in the various state constitutions in existence today. The following list provides a brief description of each article and the ways in which its contents are changing.

Bill of Rights   Individual rights and liberties were first protected in state constitutions. They closely resemble, and in some cases are identical to, those delineated in the first eight amendments to the U.S. Constitution. State constitutions and courts were the principal guardians of civil liberties until 1868, when the adoption of the Fourteenth Amendment extended the protective umbrella of the national courts over the states.[24] U.S. Supreme Court rulings also applied the U.S. Bill of Rights to the states, especially during the Warren Court beginning in 1953. Some states had failed to uphold their trust, particularly those that perpetuated the unequal treatment of women and minorities.

In the 1980s, however, activist states began to reassert guarantees of individual rights under state constitutions. At a minimum, all state constitutions must protect and guarantee those rights found in the U.S. Bill of Rights. But state constitutional provisions may guarantee additional or more extensive rights to citizens. Seventeen states now have equal rights amendments that guarantee sexual equality and prohibit sex-based discrimination. The U.S. Constitution does not guarantee a right to privacy, but ten states do so. And thirteen states give constitutional rights to crime victims. Some constitutional provisions border on the exotic. Californians possess the right to fish, residents of New Hampshire hold the right to revolution, and all Massachusetts citizens enjoy freedom from excessive noise.

The major reason for the rebirth of state activism in protecting civil liberties and rights has been the conservatism of the U.S. Supreme Court. One commentator accused the Supreme Court of having abdicated its role as "keeper of the nation's "conscience."[25] The states' power to write and interpret their constitutions differently from the U.S. Constitution's provisions in the area of protecting civil rights and liberties has been upheld by the Supreme Court, as long as the state provisions have "adequate and independent" grounds.[26] Increasingly, civil rights and liberties cases are being filed by plaintiffs in state rather than federal courts, based on state bill of rights protections.

Power of the State   This very brief article states simply that the enumerated powers are not the only ones held by the state—that, indeed, the state has all powers not denied to it by the state or national constitutions.

Suffrage and Election   This article provides for the legal registration of voters and for election procedures. Recent extensions of voting rights and alterations in election procedures have been made in response to U.S. Supreme Court decisions and to national constitutional and statutory changes. Generally, states have improved election administration; liberalized registration, voting, and officeholding requirements; and shortened residency requirements. Some states have amended this article to provide for public financing of election campaigns; others have adopted provisions designed to count ballots more accurately.

The Legislative Branch   This article sets forth the powers, procedures, and organizing principles of the legislature. In a pair of decisions in the 1960s, the U.S. Supreme Court ordered that state legislatures be apportioned on the basis of one person, one vote. That is, legislators must represent approximately the same number of constituents—House members the same as other House members and senators the same as other senators. District lines must be redrawn every ten years, after the national census has revealed population changes. Quite a few states have placed term limits on their elected officials in this article.

On the basis of this article, states have taken numerous actions to approach greater conformity with the Model State Constitution, including increasing the length and frequency of legislative sessions, streamlining rules and procedures, and authorizing special sessions. Instead of stipulating specific dollar amounts for legislators' pay and fringe benefits (which are soon rendered inappropriate by inflation), most state constitutions now establish a procedure to determine and occasionally adjust the compensation of legislators. Specific pay levels are implemented through statute.

Interestingly, the model constitution for many years recommended a unicameral legislature as a means to overcome complexity, delay, and confusion. In its most recent revision, the National Municipal League tacitly recognized the refusal of the states to follow this suggestion (only Nebraska has a single-house general assembly) by providing recommendations appropriate for a bicameral body.

The Executive Branch   The powers and organization of the executive branch, which are outlined in this article, have seen many notable modifications. Essentially, executive power continues to be centralized in the office of the governor. Governors have won longer terms and the right to run for reelection. Line-item vetoes, shorter ballots, the authority to make appointments within the executive branch, and the ability to reorganize the state bureaucracy have also increased gubernatorial powers. A number of states have opted for team election of the governor and lieutenant governor. And several states have recently limited the terms of officers within the executive branch.

The Judicial Branch   All states have substantially revised not only their courts' organization and procedures but also the election of judges. Moreover, a large majority have unified their court systems under a single authority, usually the state supreme court. Many states now select judges through a merit plan rather than by gubernatorial appointment, legislative election, or popular election. The states have also established commissions to investigate charges against judges and to recommend discipline or removal from the bench when necessary.

Finance   This article consists of provisions relating to taxation, debt, and expenditures for state and local government, including tax and spending limitations. In many states, tax relief has been granted to senior citizens, veterans, and disabled people.

Local   Here, the authority of municipalities, counties, and other local governments is recognized. Most states have increased local authority through home rule provisions, which give localities more discretion in providing services. Local taxing authority has been extended. In addition, mechanisms for improved intergovernmental cooperation, such as consolidated city and county governments and regional districts to provide services, have been created.

Public Education   On the basis of this article, the states establish and maintain free public schools for all children. Higher-education institutions, including technical schools, colleges, and universities, are commonly established in this section.

Civil Service   The Model State Constitution sets forth a *merit system* of personnel administration for state government under which civil servants are to be hired, promoted, paid, evaluated, and retained on the basis of competence, fitness, and performance instead of political party affiliation or other such criteria.

Intergovernmental Relations   As recommended by the Model State Constitution, some states stipulate specific devices for cooperation among various state entities, among local jurisdictions, or between a state and its localities. They may detail methods for sharing in the provision of certain services, or they may list cost-sharing mechanisms such as local option sales taxes.

Constitutional Revision   In this article the methods for revising, amending, and replacing the constitution are described. Generally, the trend has been to make it easier for the voters, the legislature, or both to change the constitution. For example, several states have enabled voters to implement revisions through citizen-initiative petitions.

Constitutions Today

In general, state constitutions today conform more closely to the higher-law tradition and the Model State Constitution than those of the past did. They are shorter, more concise, and simpler, and they contain fewer errors, anachronisms, and contradictions. They give the state legislatures more responsibility for determining public policy through statute rather than through constitutional amendment. The two newest states, Alaska and Hawaii, have constitutional documents that follow the model constitution quite closely.

However, much work remains to be done. Some state constitutions are still riddled with unnecessary detail because new amendments have continually been added to the old documents, and obsolete provisions and other relics can still be found. But there are more important deficiencies as well—deficiencies that demand the attention of legislators and citizens in states whose constitutions inhibit the operations of state government and obstruct the ability to adapt to change. In some jurisdictions, the governor's formal powers remain weak; a plethora of boards and commissions makes any thought of executive management and coordination a pipe dream; local governments chafe under the tight leash of state authority; and many other problems persist. Constitutional revision must be an ongoing process if the states are to be capable of coping with the changing contours of American society and of staying in the vanguard of innovation and change.

Methods for Constitutional Change

There are only two methods for altering the U.S. Constitution. The first is the constitutional convention, wherein delegates representing the states assemble to consider modifying or replacing the Constitution. Despite periodic calls for a national constitutional convention, only one has taken place—in Philadelphia, more than two hundred years ago. Two-thirds of the states must agree to call a convention; three-fourths are required to ratify any changes in the Constitution.

The second means of amending the U.S. Constitution is through congressional initiative, wherein Congress, by a two-thirds vote of both houses, agrees to send one or more proposed changes to the states. Again, three-fourths of the states must ratify the proposals.

Both methods of revision are very difficult to bring to a successful conclusion. Since 1787, more than one thousand amendments have been submitted to the states by Congress. Only twenty-seven have been approved (the most recent one, in 1992, limits the ability of members of Congress to increase their pay), and the first ten of these were appended to the Constitution as a condition by several states for ratification. Note that neither method for amending the U.S. Constitution provides for popular participation by voters, in sharp contrast to the citizen-participation requirements for state constitutional change, as we shall see in the next section.

Informal Constitutional Change

interpretation

An informal means of revising constitutions whereby members of the executive, legislative, or judicial branch apply constitutional principles and law to the everyday affairs of governing.

One informal and four formal methods for amending state constitutions exist. The informal route is **interpretation** of constitutional meaning by the state legislature, executive branch, courts, or attorneys general, or through usage and custom. Courts and attorneys general may issue advisory opinions on meanings of specific provisions. The force of habit can be a powerful influence, specific constitutional provisions notwithstanding. It is a good bet that one or more antiquated or unrealistic constitutional provisions are ignored in every state. A common example is the requirement that all bills be read, in their entirety, three times in each house for enactment. Another is the list of conditions for holding political office, such as a belief in God.

judicial review

The power of the U.S. Supreme Court or state supreme courts to declare unconstitutional not only actions of the executive and legislative branches but also decisions of lower courts.

State supreme courts play the most direct role in changing constitutions through interpretation. In large measure, a constitution is what the judges say it is in their decisions from the bench. Judicial interpretation of constitutions may be based on a variety of standards, including strict attention to the express language of the document and to the original intent of the framers or authors of amendments, deference to legislative enactments on executive actions, precedent, policy considerations, and individual or minority rights. The power of the state supreme courts to review executive actions, legislative actions, and decisions of lower courts is known as **judicial review.** This power evolved in the states much as it did on the national level—through the courts' own insistence that they hold this authority. During recent years, as the U.S. Supreme Court has become more conservative and less activist in its interpretations of the law, some state courts have moved in the opposite direction and earned reputations as judicial activists.

Formal Constitutional Change

The four formal procedures for constitutional change are legislative proposal, initiative, constitutional convention, and constitutional commission. All of them involve two basic steps: initiation and **ratification.** The state legislature, or in some cases the voters, propose (initiate) a constitutional change. Then the proposed amendment is submitted to the voters for approval (ratification).

ratification

The formal approval of a constitution or constitutional amendment by a majority of the voters of a state.

Legislative Proposal   Historically, **legislative proposal** is the most common road taken to revision; more than 90 percent of all changes in state constitutions have come through this method, which is permitted in all fifty states.

legislative proposal

The most common means of amending a state constitution, wherein the legislature proposes a revision, usually by a two-thirds majority.

The specifics of legislative proposal techniques vary, but most states require either two-thirds or three-fifths of the members of each house to approve a proposal before it is sent to the voters for ratification. Twelve states require two consecutive legislative sessions to consider and pass a proposed amendment. The procedure can become quite complicated. For instance, South Carolina's legislative proposal must be passed by two-thirds of the members of each house; it is then sent to the people during the next general election. If a majority of voters show approval, the proposal returns to the next legislative session, in which a majority of legislators have to concur.

Almost all states accept a simple majority for voter ratification of a proposed revision. In New Hampshire, however, two-thirds of the voters must approve of the proposal. And Tennessee requires approval by a majority of the number of citizens who cast a vote for governor.

Legislative proposal is probably best suited to revisions that are relatively narrow in scope. However, some legislatures, such as South Carolina's, have presented a series of proposals to the voters over a period of years and thereby have significantly revised the constitution. The disadvantage to such a strategy is that it tends to result in a patchwork of amendments that can conflict or overlap with other constitutional provisions.

Initiative   Eighteen states permit their citizens to initiate and ratify changes in the constitution on their own, bypassing the legislature (see Table 3.2). Only five of these initiative states are east of the Mississippi River, reflecting the fact that the initiative was a product of the Progressive reform movement of the early 1900s. Most of the territories admitted as states during this period chose to permit the **initiative** (known as constitutional initiative in some states). Twenty-three states also authorize the initiative for enacting statutory change. The initiative is used much less often than legislative proposal in amending constitutions.

initiative
A proposed law or constitutional amendment that is placed on the ballot by citizen petition.

The number of signatures needed for the initiative petition to be valid varies widely: Arizona requires 15 percent of total votes cast in the last gubernatorial election, whereas Massachusetts requires merely 3 percent. Moreover, to ensure that an initiative favoring one region does not become embodied in the constitution, eight states specify that the petition signatures must be collected widely throughout the state.

In general, a petition for constitutional amendment is sent to the office of the secretary of state for verification that the required number of registered voters have signed their names. Then the question is placed on a statewide ballot in the next general election. Ratification requires a majority vote of the people in most states.

direct initiative
A procedure by which the voters of a jurisdiction propose the passage of constitutional amendments, state laws, or local ordinances, bypassing the legislative body.

It is usually easy enough to collect the required number of signatures to place a proposed amendment on a statewide ballot. But actual passage of the initiative is much more difficult once it receives a close public examination and opposing interests are activated. If the legislature is circumvented altogether and propositions are placed directly on the general-election ballot by citizens, the procedure is called a **direct initiative.** If a legislature participates by voting on the citizen proposal, as in Massachusetts and Mississippi, the procedure is known as an **indirect initiative.**

indirect initiative
Similar to the direct initiative, except that the voter-initiated proposal must be submitted to the legislature before going on the ballot for voter approval.

The initiative is useful in making limited changes to the state constitution and, in recent years, has addressed some controversial issues that state legislatures have been loath to confront. Colorado voters, for example, adopted an initiative to prohibit the use of public funds for abortions. In 1998, a California

TABLE 3.2	States Authorizing Constitutional Amendment by Citizen Initiative
STATE	**NUMBER OF SIGNATURES REQUIRED ON INITIATIVE PETITION**
Arizona	15% of total votes cast for all candidates for governor at last election
Arkansas	10% of voters for governor at last election
California	8% of total voters for all candidates for governor at last election
Colorado	5% of total legal votes for all candidates for secretary of state at last general election
Florida	8% of total votes cast in the state in the last election for presidential electors
Illinois[a]	8% of total votes cast for candidates for governor at last election
Massachusetts[b]	3% of total votes cast for governor at preceding biennial state election (not fewer than 25,000 qualified voters)
Michigan	10% of total voters for all candidates at the gubernatorial election
Mississippi	12% of total votes for all candidates for governor at last election
Missouri	8% of legal voters for all candidates for governor at last election
Montana	10% of qualified electors, the number of qualified electors to be determined by number of votes cast for governor in preceding general election
Nebraska	10% of of total votes for governor at last election
Nevada	10% of voters who voted in entire state in last general election
North Dakota	4% of population of the state
Ohio	10% of total number of electors who voted for governor in last election
Oklahoma	15% of legal voters for state office receiving highest number of voters at last general state election
Oregon	8% of total votes for all candidates for governor at last election of which governor was elected for four-year term
South Dakota	10% of total votes for governor in last election

[a]Only Article IV, the Legislature, may be amended by initiative petition.

[b]Before being submitted to the electorate for ratification, initiative measures must be approved at two sessions of a successively elected legislature by not less than one-fourth of all members elected, sitting in joint session.

SOURCE: Adapted by permission from *The Book of States*, p. 7. Copyright © 2000. Used with the permission of The Council of State Governments.

initiative dismantled bilingual public education. Other controversial proposals have included those for legalized gambling, gun control, prayer in the public schools, and medical use of marijuana.

A major advantage of the initiative is that it permits the people's will to counter a despotic or inertia-ridden legislature. For instance, Illinois voters in 1978 reduced the size of the House of Representatives from 177 to 118 after the legislature voted itself a huge pay raise during a period of economic hardship. Another advantage is that this method appears to enhance citizen interest and participation in government.

However, the initiative can also be abused by special interest groups with self-ish motives who seek to gain privileges, and under crisis conditions it can result in ill-conceived, radical changes to the constitution. Indeed, the initiative can result in just the kind of excessive detail and poorly drafted verbiage that is so widely condemned by constitutional scholars and reformers.[28] It can also make doing routine business extremely difficult. In California, for example, an initiative prevents local governments from hiking taxes without two-thirds approval of the electorate.

Constitutional Convention   Legislative proposals and initiatives are quite specific about the type of constitutional change that is sought. Only those questions that actually appear on the ballot are considered. In contrast, a **constitutional convention** assembles delegates who suggest revisions or even an entirely new document; the proposed changes are then submitted to the voters for ratification. The convention is especially well suited for considering far-reaching constitutional changes or a new fundamental law.

constitutional convention

An assembly of delegates chosen by popular election or appointed by the legislature or the governor to revise an existing constitution or to create a new one.

The convention is the oldest method for constitutional change in the states and is available in all fifty of them. The process begins when the electorate or the legislature decides to call for a constitutional convention. In fourteen states, the question of calling a convention must be regularly voted on by the electorate, as Thomas Jefferson once proposed. Alaskans and Iowans hold an "automatic convention call" every ten years; in New York and Maryland, the convention issue is submitted to the voters every twenty years. Except in Delaware, where the legislature can take direct action, proposals emerging from the convention must be ratified by the voters before they become part of the constitution.

Delegates to a convention are usually elected by the voters from state house or senate districts. Most delegates are elected on a nonpartisan basis, although some states provide for partisan ballots. Conventions are usually dominated by middle-aged and elderly white males with high levels of formal education.[29] Many are professionals; the proportion of lawyers alone typically ranges from 25 to 50 percent. There is normally a substantial number of educators and business people, as well as a smattering of retirees and homemakers.[30] This delegate composition is not surprising, since convention calls are strongly supported by higher socioeconomic groups in urban areas.[31] Recent conventions have been more representative of state population characteristics, however.

The characteristics of a delegate pool are important for several reasons. First, the delegates need knowledge of and experience in state government and politics if they are to contribute meaningfully to the debate and drafting of proposed amendments. It is usually not too difficult to attract qualified people for service; the experience is important and unique, and many consider it a privilege. Second, the delegates should represent a cross-section of the state's population insofar as possible. If the delegate pool does not reflect gender, racial, regional, ethnic, and other salient characteristics of the population, the fruit of its labor may lack legitimacy in the eyes of substantial numbers of voters. Finally, partisanship should be avoided where possible. Partisan differences can wreck consensus on major issues and destroy the prospects for voter ratification of suggested amendments that emerge from the convention.

Voter approval of convention proposals is problematic. If partisan, racial, regional, or other disagreements dominate media reports on the convention, voter approval is difficult to obtain. People naturally tend to be skeptical of suggestions for sweeping changes in the basic structures and procedures of government. Furthermore, if they have not been regularly involved with and informed of the progress of the convention, they may be reluctant to give their approval to the recommendations.

Delegates usually understand these dynamics and are sensitive to how their proposed changes may affect the general public. They must, for example, carefully consider how to present the proposed amendments for ratification. There are two choices: the all-or-nothing strategy of consolidating all changes in a single vote, and the piecemeal strategy of offering each proposal as a separate ballot decision. In recent years, voters have tended to reject inclusive packages. Each suggested change is certain to offend some minority, and when all the offended minorities coalesce, they may well constitute a majority of voters.[32] In 1968, for example, Maryland voters soundly rejected a new constitution, but separate amendments later submitted to the people were approved.

However, separate proposals do not ensure victory. Texas's eight constitutional amendments each met defeat in 1975 for several reasons, including conflicts among the delegates, popular discontent with the legislature (which had formulated the proposals and organized *itself* as the convention), and a general perception that since the state had a large budget surplus and low taxes, there was no pressing need for change. The Texas convention proposed a new constitution of only 17,500 words, to replace a badly written 63,000-word document with more than 200 amendments. Amazingly, after spending some $4 million and many months in debate, the Texas convention became the first in history to reject its own proposals. The next year the legislature, under virulent public criticism and pressure, reorganized the rejected document into eight constitutional amendments and submitted them to the voters in the general election. All were voted down by margins of 2.5 to 1 or greater.[33]

constitutional commission
A meeting of delegates appointed by the governor or legislature to study constitutional problems and propose solutions.

Constitutional Commission   Often called a *study commission,* the **constitutional commission** is usually established to study the existing document and to recommend changes to the legislature or to the voters. Depending on the mandate, the constitutional commission may examine the entire constitution with a view toward replacement or change, focus on one or more specific articles or provisions, or be given the freedom to decide its own scope of activity. Commission recommendations to the legislature and/or governor are only advisory, thus helping to account for this method's popularity with elected officials, who sometimes prefer to study a problem to death rather than engage it head on. Some or all of the recommendations may be submitted to the voters; others may be completely ignored. Only in Florida can a commission send its proposals directly to voters.[34]

Constitutional commissions were operating from 1998 to 2000 in Florida and Utah. Service on a constitutional commission can be a thankless task, as legislators sometimes ignore the commission's recommendations or employ them as a symbolic device for relieving political pressure. For example, Kentucky's 1987–1988 Revision Commission recommended seventy-seven changes to the constitution, but only one was referred by the legislature to the voters as a proposed amendment.[35] When used properly, however, commissions can furnish high-quality research both inexpensively and relatively quickly.

State Responsiveness and Constitutional Reform

Each state's constitution is designed specifically to meet the needs of that state. The rich political culture, history, economics, values, and ideals of the state's community are reflected in state constitutional language. Through their constitutions, the states experiment with different governmental institutions and processes. As super-patriot Thomas Paine observed more than two hundred years ago, "It is in the interest of all the states, that the constitution of each should be somewhat diversified from each other. We are a people founded upon experiments, and have the happy opportunity of trying variety in order to discover the "best."[36]

State constitutions were the original guardians of individual rights and liberties, with their own bills of rights preceding that of the U.S. Constitution by many years. They are reassuming their rightful position in American government today as independent state constitutional law develops further. Yet few tasks in government are more difficult than modernizing a constitution. The process requires "sustained, dedicated, organized effort; vigorous, aggressive and imaginative leadership; bipartisan political support; education of the electorate on the issues; judicious selection of the means; and seemingly endless "patience."[37] In the words of constitutional scholar W. Brooke Graves, "The advocate of constitutional reform in an American state should be endowed with the patience of Job and the sense of time of a geologist."[38] The solemn duty of framing the original state constitutions, so effectively discharged by our predecessors, must be matched by the continuous oversight of present and future generations. Changes are necessary to adjust state governments to the vagaries of the future.

The constitutional changes enacted in the states during the four and one-half decades since the Kestnbaum Commission report have generally resulted in documents in the higher-law tradition, documents that "are shorter, more clearly written, modernized, less encumbered with restrictions, more basic in content and have more reasonable amending processes. They also establish improved governmental structures and contain substantive provisions assuring greater openness, accountability and equity."[39] The states have made a great deal of progress in modernizing their governments. As state constitutional scholar Richard Leach has put it, "There are not many constitutional horrors left."[40]

Recent constitutional amendments have responded to, and indeed caused, profound changes in state government and politics. Since the genesis of modern reform in the mid-1960s, some forty states have adopted new constitutions or substantially amended existing ones. Problems persist, and future constitutional tinkering and replacements will be necessary. But in most states, the constitutional landscape is much cleaner and more functional than it was thirty years ago.

Chapter Recap

➤ The constitution is the fundamental law of a state, superior to statutory law.

➤ State constitutions evolved from the original colonial charters. Shifting from an original basis of legislative supremacy, they have gradually increased executive power.

➤ Some constitutions continue to suffer from excessive length and substantive problems.

➤ Constitutional reform has modernized the documents and made them conform more closely to present challenges of governance.

➤ Methods for changing constitutions include interpretation, judicial review, legislative proposal, initiative, constitutional convention, and constitutional commission.

Key Terms

legislative supremacy (*p. 51*)
Model State Constitution (*p. 56*)
positive-law tradition (*p. 57*)
higher-law tradition (*p. 57*)
interpretation (*p. 61*)
judicial review (*p. 61*)
ratification (*p. 61*)

legislative proposal (*p. 61*)
initiative (*p. 62*)
direct initiative (*p. 62*)
indirect initiative (*p. 62*)
constitutional convention (*p. 64*)
constitutional commission (*p. 65*)

Surfing the Net

For full texts of state statutes and constitutions, see individual state websites (for example, **www.state.fl.us**). State constitutions can also be accessed through **www.law.cornell.edu/statutes.html, www.findlaw.com/11stategov/index const.html,** or **www.constitution.org.** The Alaska constitution draws heavily on the Model State Constitution. It is located in the state of Alaska Documents Library at **www.law.state.ak.us.**

4

CITIZEN PARTICIPATION AND ELECTIONS

Participation
> Why and How People Participate » Nonparticipation »
> The Struggle for the Right to Vote » Voting Patterns

Elections
> Primaries » Runoff Elections » General Elections » Recent State
> Elections » Nonpartisan Elections

Election-Day Lawmaking
> The Initiative » The Recall

Citizen Access to Government
> Open Meeting Laws » Administrative Procedure Acts » Advisory
> Committees » Citizen Surveys » E-Government

Volunteerism

The Effects of Citizen Participation

Throughout the country, communities are casting about for ways to increase citizen participation in governance. Some of their efforts catch fire; however, many attempts simply fizzle because they do not effectively engage the public. Philadelphia offers an example of a successful venture in rekindling the citizen-government link. An experiment in political conversation, called Citizen Voices, created a series of dialogues in which citizens identified and discussed issues that mattered to them. In Philadelphia, five issues repeatedly surfaced: schools and education, quality of life, jobs, government reform, and crime. As Citizen Voices gained momentum, candidates for local office tossed aside their canned speeches, joining instead in unscripted conversations with citizens. Once the election was over, participants in the project got together and crafted an agenda for the city of Philadelphia—a "to-do" list that was presented to the new mayor and city council when they took office in 2000.[1] It was *citizens* who were setting the agenda.

Participation

participation
Actions through which ordinary members of a political system attempt to influence outcomes.

Democracy assumes citizen **participation**—acting to influence government. In contemporary America, there is persistent evidence that citizens are not much interested in participation. We have grown accustomed to reports of low voter turnout and public hearings that no public attends. On the surface, government works just fine with limited participation: The interests of the active become translated into public policy, and those who are inactive can be safely ignored because they do not vote. If, however, some traditional nonvoters (such as low-income, less-educated citizens) went to the polls, then vote-seeking candidates might be forced to pay more attention to their interests, and public policy might be nudged in a different direction. In this light, it is important to understand both why many people do participate and why others do not. This chapter addresses individual citizen involvement in government; Chapter 5 takes up collective participation (that is, participation by political parties and interest groups).

Why and How People Participate

In a representative democracy, voting is the most common form of participation. For many citizens, it is a matter of civic responsibility. It is a fundamental facet of citizenship—after all, it is called "the right to vote." Citizens go to the polls to elect the officials who will govern them. But there are other methods of participation. Consider the citizen who is unhappy because the property taxes on her home have increased substantially from one year to the next. What options are available to her besides voting against incumbent officeholders at the next election? As shown in Figure 4.1, she can be either active or passive; and her actions, either constructive or destructive. Basically, she has four potential responses: loyalty, voice, exit, and neglect.[2]

According to this formulation, voting is an example of loyalty, a passive but constructive response to government action. Specifically, this response reflects the irate taxpayer's underlying support for her community despite her displeasure with particular tax policies. An active constructive response is voice: The aggrieved property owner could contact officials, work in the campaign of a candidate who promises to lower tax assessments, or (assuming that others in the community share her sentiments) participate in antitax groups and organize demonstrations.

Destructive responses (those that undermine the citizen-government relationship) are similarly passive or active. If the citizen simply shrugs and concludes that "you can't fight city hall," she is exhibiting a response termed neglect. She has virtually given up on the community and does not participate. A more active version of giving up is to exit—that is, to leave the community al-

FIGURE 4.1   **Possible Responses to Dissatisfaction in the Community**

Each of these participatory options affects public policy decisions in a community. Citizens who choose the voice *option frequently find themselves in the thick of things.*

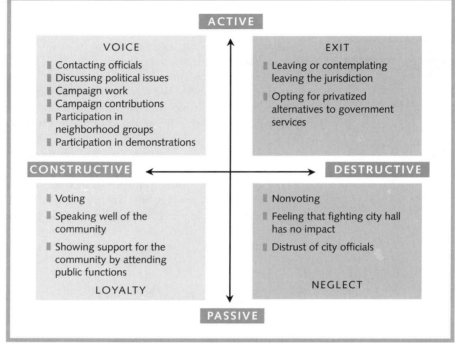

SOURCE: From "The Organization of Political Space and Citizen Responses to Dissatisfaction in Urban Communities," by William Lyons and David Lowery, from *Journal of Politics,* 48:2, pp. 321–346. Copyright © 1986 by the University of Texas Press. All rights reserved.

together (a response often referred to as "voting with your feet"). The unhappy citizen will relocate in a community that is more in line with her tax preferences.

Every citizen confronts these participatory options. It is much healthier for the political system if citizens engage in the constructive responses, but some individuals are likely to conclude that constructive participation is of little value to them and opt for neglect or, in more extreme cases, exit.

Nonparticipation

What explains the citizens who choose neglect as their best option? One explanation for nonparticipation in politics is socioeconomic status. Individuals with lower levels of income and education tend to participate less than wealthier, more educated individuals do.[3] Tied closely to income and education levels is occupational status. Unskilled workers and hourly wage earners do not participate in politics to the same degree that white-collar workers and professionals do. Individuals of lower socioeconomic status may not have the time, resources, or civic skills required to become actively involved in politics.

Other explanations for nonparticipation have included age (younger people have participated less than middle-aged individuals), race (blacks have participated less than whites), and gender (women have participated less than men). However, of these factors, only age has continued to affect political activity levels. African-American political participation actually surpasses that of whites when socioeconomic status is taken into consideration,[4] and the gender gap in the types and levels of political participation has actually reversed.[5] America's youth, however, remain less likely to frequent polling places. A study of state elections in the mid-1990s showed that persons between eighteen and twenty-nine years of age constituted only 6 percent of the voting public but 38 percent of the nonvoters.[6] Alarmed by these statistics, groups such as Kids Voting USA have developed programs to socialize children to political affairs.[7] The underlying assumption is that children who get into the habit of citizen participation at an early age will be more politically active as adults.

The explanation for nonparticipation does not rest solely with the individual. Institutional features—the way the political system is designed—may suppress participation. For example, local governments that have instituted nonpartisan elections, in which candidates run without party affiliation, have removed an important mobilizing factor for voters. Voter turnout tends to be lower in these elections than in partisan contests. Moreover, some state governments still have not modernized their voter registration procedures to make the process quick and easy, thus discouraging potential registrants. City council meetings scheduled at 10:00 A.M. put a tremendous strain on workers who must take time off from their jobs if they want to attend; consequently, attendance is low. And local governments in which it is difficult for citizens to contact the appropriate official with a service request or complaint are not doing much to facilitate participation. Features like these play an often unrecognized role in dampening participation.

Nonparticipants typically have lower levels of interest in politics and tend to be weakly connected to their communities.[8] In many communities, the media have launched efforts to boost participation in civic life. Television stations convene forums and town meetings on the issues of the day, and local newspapers report the views of ordinary citizens on current events. Called public or civic journalism, the idea is to reconnect people with the democratic process and, in doing so, to make them active participants in public life.

The Struggle for the Right to Vote

State constitutions in the eighteenth and early nineteenth centuries entrusted only propertied white males with the vote. They did not encourage public involvement in government, and the eventual softening of restrictions on suffrage did not occur without a struggle. Restrictions based on property ownership and wealth were eventually dropped, but women, blacks, and Native Americans were still denied the right to vote.

In an effort to attract women to its rugged territory, Wyoming enfranchised women in 1869. The suffragists—women who were actively fighting for the right to vote—scored a victory when Colorado extended the vote to women in 1893. Gradually, other states began enfranchising women. In 1920 the Nineteenth Amendment to the U.S. Constitution, forbidding states to deny the right to vote "on account of sex," was ratified.

Even after the Fifteenth Amendment (1870) extended the vote to blacks, some southern states clung defiantly to traditional ways that denied blacks and poor people their rights. Poll taxes and literacy tests prevented the poor and uneducated, regardless of race, from voting. Furthermore, southern Democrats designed the "white primary" to limit black political influence. In the one-party South, the Democratic primary elections, in which candidates for the general election were chosen, were the scene of the important contests. The general election amounted to little more than ratification of the Democratic party's choices because so few elections were contested by the Republicans. Thus blacks were still barred from effective participation because they could not vote in the primaries. In *Smith* v. *Allwright* (1944), the U.S. Supreme Court ruled that since primaries were part of the machinery that chose officials, they were subject to the same nondiscriminatory standards as general elections, and the days of the white primary came to an end.

Although most states expanded the franchise, segregationists in the South continued to erect elaborate barriers to participation.[9] The number of black voters increased steadily during the mid–twentieth century, yet substantial discrimination remained. The outlawing of the white primary forced racists to resort to more informal methods—including physical intimidation—of keeping blacks from the polls. Blacks gained access to the polls primarily through national enactments such as the Civil Rights Act of 1964 and the Twenty-Fourth Amendment (1964), which made poll taxes unconstitutional.

> **Voting Rights Act of 1965**
>
> The law that effectively enfranchised racial minorities by giving the national government the power to decide whether individuals are qualified to vote and to intercede in state and local electoral operations when necessary.

The **Voting Rights Act of 1965** finally broke the back of the segregationists' efforts. Under its provisions, federal poll watchers and registrars were dispatched to particular counties to investigate voter discrimination. To this day, counties covered under the Voting Rights Act (all of nine southern states and parts of seven other states) must submit to the U.S. Department of Justice any changes in election laws, such as new precinct lines or new polling places. Over time, judicial interpretations, congressional actions, and Justice Department rules have modified the Voting Rights Act. One of the most important modifications has been to substitute an "effects" test for the original "intent" test. In other words, if a governmental action has the effect of discouraging minority voting, whether intentionally or not, the action must be rejected. Civil rights activists welcomed this change because proving the intent of an action is much more difficult than demonstrating its effect.

Voting Patterns

In the 1990s, both voter registration and voter turnout increased slightly from the previous decade. The media played a large part in stimulating public interest in elections and voting; even MTV repeatedly ran advertisements urging its viewers to vote. Voter turnout is affected by several factors. First, it varies according to the type of election. A presidential race usually attracts a higher proportion of eligible voters than a state or local election does. In 2000, voter turnout was at 51.2 percent of the voting-age population; in 1998, when there was no presidential election on the ballot—but many governors' races—turnout was only 36.4 percent.[10] As Table 4.1 shows, 1970 was the last time that turnout in a non–presidential election year exceeded 40 percent of the voting-age population. Second, popular candidates running a close race seem to increase voter interest. When each candidate has a chance to win, voters sense that their vote will matter more than in a race with a sure winner. Third, not only partisan competition but party ideology affects voter turnout.[11] When parties take distinctive ideological stances in competitive elections, the incentive for party-identifiers to vote increases.

There are noteworthy differences among states in terms of the proportions of both voting-age population registered and voter turnout. Nationally, more than 76 percent of the voting-age population was registered to vote in 2000. But when we look at the figures for individual states, wide variation appears. Compare two states with very similar voting-age populations: Maine, with 882,000, and Nevada, with 898,000. Ninety-two percent of the voting-age population in Maine were registered; in Nevada, the comparable figure was 64.6 percent.[12] Registration matters because people who are registered tend to vote. And votes translate into political power. Recognition of this fact led the Council of American-Islamic Relations to launch a major effort in 2002 designed to increase registration of Muslims.[13]

States can also be differentiated according to voter turnout rates (see Figure 4.2). In 2000, the highest turnout rates were recorded in Minnesota, where 68.75 percent of the voting-age population voted, and Maine, with 67.34 percent voting. Hawaii, with 40.5 percent voting, garnered the dubious distinction of being the state with the lowest voter turnout in 2000.[14] States with moralistic political cultures typically experience higher voter turnout than do states with traditionalistic political cultures. For example, Oregon voters turn out for state

| **TABLE 4.1** | **Voter Turnout in Off-Year Elections** |

YEAR	VOTER TURNOUT
2000	39.0%
1998	36.4
1994	38.8
1990	36.5
1986	36.4
1982	39.8
1978	37.2
1974	38.2
1970	46.6
1966	48.4
1962	47.3

SOURCE: The Learning Network, "National Voter Turnout," www.infoplease.com. Updated by the authors.

FIGURE 4.2 State Voter Turnout, 2000

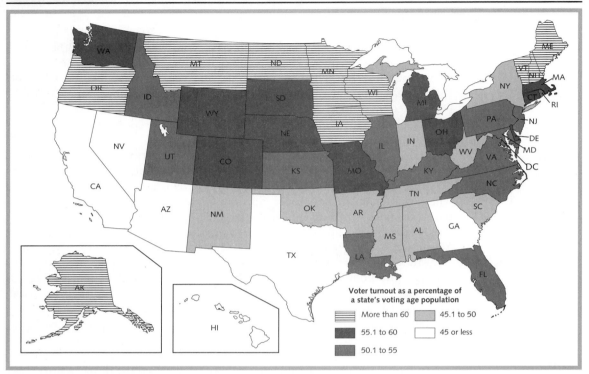

Voter turnout as a percentage of a state's voting age population

More than 60	45.1 to 50
55.1 to 60	45 or less
50.1 to 55	

SOURCE: U.S. Federal Election Commission, "Voter Registration and Turnout 2000," www.fec.gov.

elections at about twice the rate of Mississippi voters. States with competitive political parties tend to turn out a higher proportion of voters; each party needs to mobilize individuals who identify with it in order to win. Finally, the states can affect turnout by the way in which they administer the elections: Is voting a convenient exercise, or is it an arduous task marked by long lines at the polling places and confusing ballots once inside the voting booth?

Registering to vote is getting easier. All states but two permit voters to register by mail.[15] Passage of the National Voter Registration Act in 1993 means that individuals can register to vote when they apply for a driver's license or register their automobile. Many states, such as Florida, have taken another step by allowing on-line voter registration; any computer terminal can be a registration site. And some states have moved the closing date for registration nearer to the actual date of the election, giving potential voters more time to register. This factor is important because campaigns tend to heighten the public's interest in the election. Most states now close their registration books fewer than thirty days before an election, and Idaho, Maine, Minnesota, New Hampshire, Wisconsin, and Wyoming allow registration on election day.[16] North Dakota is the only state in the nation that does not require voter registration.

Absentee balloting has also been made easier than it was in the past. Most states still require a voter applying for an absentee ballot to supply an acceptable reason, such as being away on business or in school, but some have lifted these restrictions and allow any voter to vote in absentia. Arizona, California, Colorado, Iowa, Nevada, Tennessee, and Texas are among the states that allow early voting. Voters can cast "in-person absentee ballots" before election day at satellite polling stations.[17] Sixteen states have statutes authorizing mail ballot elections under certain conditions, such as special elections and nonpartisan elections.[18] Oregon conducted its 2000 general election almost entirely by mail. Analysis of the Beaver State's elections shows that vote-by-mail elections can increase the turnout rate by as much as 15 percent.[19] In short, the notion of election *day* is gradually giving way.

Elections

Elections are central to a representative democracy. Voters choose governors and legislators, and in most states, lieutenant governors, attorneys general, secretaries of state, and state treasurers; in some, they also choose the heads of the agriculture and education departments, judges, and the public utility commissioners. At the local level, the list of elected officials includes mayors and council members, county commissioners, county judges, sheriffs, tax assessors, and school board members. If state and local governments are to function effectively, elections must provide talented, capable leaders. But elections are not just about outcomes; they are also about the process itself. Florida's troubles with ballot design, voting machines, and recount rules in the 2000 presidential election underscored the need for elections to be administered fairly and transparently.

Primaries

In order for a party to choose a nominee for the general-election ballot, a winnowing of potential candidates must occur. In the pre-Jacksonian era, party nominees were chosen by a legislative caucus—that is, a conference of the party's legislators. Caucuses gave way to the mechanism of state party conventions, which were similar to national presidential nomination conventions but without most of the spectacle; popularly elected delegates from across a state convened to select the party's nominees. Then the Progressive movement sought to open up the nomination process and make it more democratic. Political parties adopted the **primary system,** whereby voters directly choose among several candidates, to select the party's nominees for the general election. The use of primaries has effectively diminished the organizational power of political parties.

primary system
The electoral mechanism for selecting party nominees to compete in the general election.

Thirteen states still allow for party conventions in particular instances, such as nominations for lieutenant governor and supreme court justices (Michigan) and selection of a slate of nominees by third parties (Kansas). Connecticut, the last state to adopt primaries, operates a unique challenge system whereby party nominees for various state offices are selected at a convention; but if a contest develops at the convention and a second candidate receives as much as 15 percent of the votes, the convention's nominee and the challenger square off in a primary.[20]

Primaries can be divided into two types: closed and open. The only voters who can participate in a **closed primary** for a particular party are those who are registered in that party. An **open primary** does not require party membership; any voter who is qualified to vote in the general election can participate in the party's primary. However, even this basic distinction lends itself to some variation. States differ, for example, in terms of the ease with which voters can change party affiliation and participate in the closed primary of the other party. In eleven states, a voter is an enrolled member of one party (or is an Independent and may or may not be eligible to vote in either party's primary) and can change that affiliation only well in advance of the primary election.[21] Arizona and Pennsylvania are two of the states that conduct completely closed primaries. Fifteen other closed-primary states—Iowa and Wyoming are examples—allow more flexibility to accommodate shifts in voters' loyalties.

Open primaries account for (and perhaps contribute to) fleeting partisan loyalties among the public. The key difference among states with open primaries is whether a voter is required to identify publicly which party's primary he is participating in. Ten states, including Alabama and Indiana, require voters to request a specific party's ballot at the polling place. Eleven other open-primary states make no such demand; voters secretly select the ballot of the party in which they wish to participate. Idaho and Wisconsin are examples of states in which primaries are truly open.

A few states fall outside the strict closed or open classification. Two western states, Alaska and Washington, use what is referred to as a **blanket primary.** Under this system, voters can vote in the primaries of both parties in a single election. In other words, voters may cross over from one party's primary ballot to the other's. A voter could select from among Democratic candidates for governor and among Republican candidates for the legislature, in effect participating in both primaries. In a sense, this is the ultimate open primary.

The other variation on the closed- versus open-primary pattern is found in Louisiana, which uses a single nonpartisan primary for its statewide and congressional races. Voters can choose from among any of the candidates, regardless of party affiliation. If no one candidate receives a majority of the votes in a race, the top two vote getters face each other in a runoff election. The nonpartisan primary is particularly disruptive to political party power.

Runoff Elections

A **runoff election** is a second election that is held if no one candidate for a state office receives a majority of votes in the primary. Runoffs have become a controversial topic because of the contention that different people win than would win in a system without runoffs.

The use of primary election runoffs has a distinct regional flavor. Runoffs, sometimes called second primaries, take place in nine states: Alabama, Arkansas, Florida, Georgia, Mississippi, North Carolina, Oklahoma, South Carolina, and

---

closed primary
A primary in which only voters registered in the party are allowed to participate.

open primary
A primary in which voters may vote for either party's candidates.

blanket primary
A primary in which a voter is allowed to vote for candidates of both parties in a single election.

runoff election
A second election pitting the top two vote getters from a first election in which no candidate received a majority of the votes cast.

Texas. (Kentucky and South Dakota use primary runoffs but only in certain instances.) Traditionally southern states were one-party (Democratic) states, so the greatest amount of competition for an office occurred in the Democratic party's primaries, in which as many as ten candidates might enter a race. In these states, a candidate must receive more than 50 percent of the votes in the primary to become the party's nominee. (North Carolina recently lowered the winning primary percentage to 40 percent.) When many candidates compete, it is quite probable that no one will be able to amass a majority of the votes, so the top two vote getters face each other in a runoff election. This process ensures that the party's nominee is preferred by a majority of the primary voters. In the past, Democratic nominees in runoff states typically faced only nominal, if any, Republican opposition in the general election, so winning the Democratic primary was tantamount to being elected to office. The general election was a virtual formality.

Theoretically, the rationale for the runoff primary is majority rule. But political circumstances have changed since several southern states adopted the runoff primary system in the 1920s, and the Democratic party is no longer unchallenged in the region. The growth of Republicanism has produced an increasing number of meaningfully contested general elections since the 1970s. Has the runoff primary outlived its usefulness? Does it systematically disadvantage the political party using it? In other words, do runoffs generate such divisiveness within the party that its nominee is weakened in the general election?

One study of this issue supports the speculation that candidates who emerge from a bloody intraparty runoff are systematically disadvantaged in the general election.[22] Being involved in a runoff costs Democratic gubernatorial candidates in the South approximately 4.56 votes per 100 votes cast, on average, in the subsequent general election. (Incumbency tends to restore some of the deficit, however.) The reasons for this are complex, but they seem to reflect the factionalized majority party's inability to overcome the rancor that the two-primary structure produces. The increasing competitiveness of the Republican party in the South has led to more crowded Republican primaries and, hence, to greater use of runoffs. Thus, the Republicans may eventually be susceptible to the kind of divisiveness that afflicts the Democrats.

General Elections

Primaries and runoffs culminate in the general election, through which winning candidates become officeholders. Virtually all states hold general elections in November of even-numbered years. However, a few states—Kentucky, New Jersey, and Virginia among them—schedule their gubernatorial and legislative elections in odd-numbered years.

General elections typically pit candidates of the two parties against one another. The winner is the candidate who receives a majority of the votes cast. In a race where more than two candidates compete (which occurs when an Independent or a third-party candidate enters a race), the leading vote getter is less likely to receive a majority of the votes cast. Instead, the candidate with the most votes—a **plurality**—wins. A few states allow candidates to run under the label

plurality
The number of votes (though not necessarily a majority) cast for the winning candidate in an election with more than two candidates.

fusion
A state-election
provision that allows
multiparty candidates.

of more than one party. The term for this is **fusion.** New York is a prime example. In 1994, George Pataki was the candidate for governor of the Republican, Conservative, and Tax Cut Now parties.

Political parties have traditionally been active in general elections, mobilizing voters in support of their candidates. Over time, however, their role has changed, as general-election campaigns have become more candidate centered and geared to the candidate's own organization.[23] One new twist in the past two decades has been the emergence of legislative party caucuses as major factors in general elections. In large states with professionalized legislatures, the funds distributed to their party's nominees by legislative party caucuses run into the millions of dollars. For example, Vern Riffe, who was speaker of the Ohio house of representatives for twenty years, hosted an annual "birthday party" to raise campaign funds for house Democrats.[24] Attendance at the event came at a high price: $500 per ticket. With lobbyists and political action committees purchasing blocs of tickets, the speaker was able to raise a substantial campaign war chest to distribute among Democratic candidates. In addition to funding, legislative party caucuses provide other types of election assistance, such as seminars on issues and on campaign management. In some states, the formal state party organization has given way to the legislative party caucus.

Recent State Elections

Most states schedule their elections in "off-years"—that is, in years in which no presidential election is held. Only eleven states elected governors during the presidential election year of 2000; forty-one held their statewide races in other years. (The number sums to fifty-two because New Hampshire and Vermont limit their governors to two-year terms, thereby holding gubernatorial elections in both "off" and "on" years.) Off-year elections prevent the presidential race from diverting attention from state races and also minimize the possible **coattail effect,** by which a presidential candidate can affect the fortunes of state candidates of the same party. By holding elections in off-years, races for governor may serve as referenda on the president's performance. Generally, however, the health of a state's economy is a critical issue in gubernatorial elections.[25]

coattail effect
The tendency of a
winning (or losing)
presidential candidate
to carry state candidates of the same
party into (or out of)
office.

The decade of the 1990s opened with Democrats dominating both governors' offices and state legislatures throughout the country. The 1994 elections produced tremendous partisan change, with Republicans gaining control of thirty governorships and half of the legislative chambers. Since that time, Republican gubernatorial fortunes have ebbed slightly as Democrats staged a comeback; by 2002, the lineup featured twenty-seven Republicans, twenty-one Democrats, and two Independents. In the legislative branch, the partisan balance triggered by the 1994 elections has been maintained. In 2002, Democrats controlled both houses in seventeen states, Republicans controlled both houses in seventeen states, and in fifteen states, partisan control of the houses was split.[26] (The remaining state, Nebraska, has a nonpartisan, unicameral legislature.)

The stakes were high for the 2002 state elections, with thirty-six governors' seats on the ballots. Republicans, holding seven of the governorships in the ten largest states, wanted to keep them—and, if possible, win the biggest prize: the governorship of California. Democrats, buoyed by their victories in the only two governors' races held in 2001 (New Jersey and Virginia), wanted to extend their winning streak. The changing demographics of the nation, especially the increase in the Latino population, and the economic slowdown following the September 11, 2001, terrorist attacks, factored heavily in campaign strategies.

The results of the 2002 gubernatorial elections left both Democrats and Republicans smiling. The Democratic party was able to increase its share of governors' seats, but not enough to gain a majority of them. The Democrats retained the governorship of California, and for the first time in many years, counted Arizona, Illinois, Michigan, Pennsylvania, and Wisconsin in their column. Republicans relished their incumbents' victories in Texas, New York, Florida, and Ohio. Further, GOP gubernatorial candidates were successful in some traditionally Democratic states such as Georgia, Hawaii, Maryland, and Massachusetts. Alabama provided a reminder that every vote does matter: the margin of victory in the disputed governor's race was less than half of a percentage point. The results were mixed for women gubernatorial candidates. Carrying a major party's banner in nine states, women were successful in four of them: Arizona, Hawaii, Kansas, and Michigan.

Nonpartisan Elections

nonpartisan election
An election without party labels.

A **nonpartisan election** removes the political party identification from candidates in an effort to "depoliticize" the electoral campaign. Elections that have been made nonpartisan include those for many judicial offices and local-level positions. The special task of judges—adjudicating guilt or innocence, determining right and wrong—does not lend itself to partisan interpretation. (Judicial selection is discussed in depth in Chapter 9.) The job of local governments—delivering public services—has also traditionally been considered nonideological. Nonpartisan local elections are likely to be found in municipalities, as well as in school districts and special districts.

Under a nonpartisan election system, all candidates for an office compete in a first election and, if there's no majority winner, the top two vote getters run in a second election (runoff). (Even states without party primary runoffs for state offices may allow runoffs in local elections.) The occurrence of nonpartisan local elections is largely a function of region. Although nationally 73 percent of cities use nonpartisan elections, according to a recent survey, the regional figures range from 94 percent in the West to 21 percent in the Northeast.[27] Large cities are no more likely to conduct partisan elections than smaller ones are; however, those that do, such as New York City and Chicago, tend to attract attention.

Most studies have concluded that nonpartisanship depresses turnout in municipal elections that are held independent of state and national elections. The figures are not dramatic, but in what are already low-turnout elections, the difference can run as high as 10 percent of municipal voters.[28] Nonpartisan elections seem to produce a more socioeconomically elite city council and a greater number of officeholders who consider themselves Republicans.

What does it take to get elected? In the absence of political parties, candidates are forced to create their own organizations in order to run for office. They raise and spend money (much of it their own), and they seek the support of business

slating groups

Nonpartisan political organizations that endorse and promote a slate of candidates.

and citizen groups. Money matters; and according to new studies of city elections in Atlanta and St. Louis, so do incumbency and newspaper endorsements.[29] In some communities, **slating groups** function as unofficial parties by recruiting candidates and financing their campaigns.[30] Citizens' groups can also be an important factor in local elections.

Election-Day Lawmaking

What happens when the government does not respond to the messages that the people are sending? More and more, the answer is to transform the messages into ballot propositions and let the citizens make their own laws. As explained in Chapter 3, *initiatives* are proposed laws or constitutional amendments that are placed on the ballot by citizen petition, to be approved or rejected by popular vote. An initiative lets citizens enact their own laws, bypassing the state legislature. This mechanism for legislation by popular vote was one of several reforms of the Progressive era, which lasted roughly from 1890 to 1920. Other Progressive reforms included the popular referendum and the recall. The **popular referendum** allows citizens to petition to vote on actions taken by legislative bodies. It provides a means by which the public can overturn a legislative enactment. (A popular referendum is different from a general **referendum**—a proposition put on the ballot by the legislature that requires voter approval before it can take effect. Constitutional amendments and bond issues are examples of general referenda.) The **recall** election, another citizen-initiated process, requires elected officials to stand for a vote on their removal before their term has expired. Recall provides the public with an opportunity to force an official out of office.

popular referendum

A special type of referendum whereby citizens can petition to vote on actions taken by legislative bodies.

referendum

A procedure whereby a governing body submits proposed laws, constitutional amendments, or bond issues to the voters for ratification.

recall

A procedure that allows citizens to vote elected officials out of office before their term has expired.

The key characteristic shared by initiative, popular referendum, and recall is that they are actions begun by citizens. The Progressives advocated these mechanisms to expand the role of citizens and to restrict the power of intermediary institutions such as legislatures, political parties, and elected officials.[31] Their efforts were particularly successful in the western part of the United States, probably owing to the difficulty of amending existing state constitutions in the East and to an elitist fear of the working class (namely, the industrialized immigrants in the Northeast and the rural black sharecroppers in the South). The newer western states, in contrast, were quite open, both procedurally and socially. In 1898, South Dakota became the first state to adopt the initiative process. And the initiative was actually used for the first time in Oregon in 1902, when citizens successfully petitioned for ballot questions on mandatory political party primaries and local-option liquor sales. Both of the initiatives were approved.

Today, twenty-four states allow the initiative for constitutional amendments, statutes, or both; Mississippi is the most recent addition, having adopted it in 1992. A few of these states use the indirect initiative, which gives the legislature an opportunity to consider the proposed measure. If the legislature fails to act, or if it rejects the measure, the proposal is put before the voters at the next election. Popular referendum is provided for in twenty-five states, and recall of state officials in seventeen. These figures understate the use of such mechanisms throughout the country, however, because many states without statewide initiative, popular referendum, and recall allow their use at the local government level.[32]

The Initiative

The first step in the initiative process is the petition. A draft of the proposed law (or constitutional amendment) is circulated along with a petition for citizens to sign. The petition signature requirement varies by state but usually falls between 5 and 10 percent of the number of votes cast in the preceding statewide election. To ensure that a matter is of statewide concern and that signatures have been gathered beyond a single area, some states set geographic distributional requirements. In Montana, for example, signature requirements must be met in at least one-third of the legislative districts; in Nebraska, in two-fifths of the counties. Door-to-door canvassing is one way to gather signatures; another method involves dispatching supporters to shopping malls and sporting events. Increasingly, initiative organizers are relying on direct mail: Petition forms are simply mailed to a preselected, computer-generated list of likely signers.

The Return of Initiatives Initiatives emerged as a potent force in the 1970s, thanks primarily to the activism of three types of groups: environmental activists, consumer advocates, and tax-limitation organizations. One of the most influential modern initiatives was California's Proposition 13 (1978), which rolled back property taxes in the state and spawned an immediate wave of tax-reduction propositions across the land. The increased popularity of initiatives has at least two explanations: (1) Some observers believe that wavering public confidence in government has led citizens to take matters into their own hands. The attitude seems to be "if government can't be trusted to do the right thing, we'll do it ourselves." (2) New methods of signature collection have brought the initiative process within the reach of virtually any well-financed group with a grievance or concern. An example from Massachusetts makes the point. When then Governor Paul Cellucci could not get the legislature to pass his tax-cut proposals, he took the issue straight to the voters. Using donations from supporters, he paid a company to collect sufficient signatures on petitions, and he got his issue on the 2000 ballot.[33] Massachusetts voters approved it.

Recent Initiatives If ballot questions are any indication of the public's mood, then the public has had quite an attitude lately. In 2000, a record number of education initiatives appeared on state ballots, further indication of just how serious the public has become about schools. The specific topics included vouchers for private schools, the creation of charter schools, teacher salaries, bilingual education, and instruction about homosexuality. Several states took up animal protection, such as Massachusetts's initiative banning dog racing, Oklahoma's banning cockfighting, and the measures in Oregon and Washington to prohibit the use of certain kinds of traps and poisons. Legalizing the medical use of marijuana returned to the ballot, as did authorizing physician-assisted suicide and prohibiting same-sex marriages. Yet, as is typically the case, more initiatives went

Citizens make their voices heard—enthusiastically—on a ballot question. (Gregg Mancuso/Stock, Boston, LLC)

down to defeat than passed. Historically, the approval rate for initiatives is approximately one-third.[34]

Possible Overuse of Initiatives   In the 2000 elections, there were sixty-nine citizen-initiated questions on the ballots in seventeen states—and 2000 was not a particularly busy year. Oregon led the way, with nineteen statewide issues on the ballot; Colorado and Washington had six each. The Oregon situation raises troubling questions about the use of initiatives in particular and the wisdom of direct democracy more generally. By resorting to initiatives, citizens can bypass (or, in the case of indirect initiatives, prod) an obstructionist legislature. And initiatives can be positive or negative; that is, they can be used in the absence of legislative action or they can be used to repudiate actions taken by the legislature. But is the initiative process appropriate for resolving tough public problems? Seldom are issues so simple that a yes-or-no ballot question can adequately reflect appropriate options and alternatives. A legislative setting, in contrast, fosters the negotiation and compromise that produce workable solutions. Legislatures are deliberative bodies, not instant problem solvers.

Related to this concern is the question of whether the public is too ill informed to make intelligent choices or falls prey to emotional appeals. Ballot questions are considered low-information elections: Facing little information or conflicting claims, voters respond to readily available cues.[35] Well-financed business and religious groups have used the initiative process to their advantage. A political scientist who has studied the initiative process contends that "it is a political tool that has been discovered by interest groups."[36] Advocates and opponents of the Indian Gaming Initiative in California in 1998 spent a total of $92 million to influence voters.[37] Claiming that the potential for mischief is great, some initiative states have enacted laws requiring clear identification of financial sponsors of initiatives.

Legislators are of two minds when it comes to direct citizen involvement in policymaking. On the one hand, having the public decide a controversial issue such as abortion or school prayer helps legislators out of tight spots. On the other hand, increased citizen lawmaking intrudes on the central function of the legislature and usurps legislative power.[38] Given the popularity of initiatives, legislators must proceed cautiously with actions that would make them more difficult to use. So far, efforts to increase the signature requirements or to limit the kinds of topics an initiative may address have been unsuccessful. A citizenry accustomed to the initiative process does not look kindly on its dismantling.

The Recall

Recalls, too, were once a little-used mechanism in state and local governments. Only seventeen states provide for recall of state officials; and in seven of them, judicial officers are exempt. City and county government charters, even in states without recall provisions, typically include mechanisms for recall of local elected officials. In fact, the first known recall was aimed at a Los Angeles city council member in 1904.[39] Recalls have a much higher petition signature requirement than initiatives do; it is common to require a signature minimum of 25 percent of the votes cast in the last election for the office of the official sought to be recalled. (Kansas, for example, requires a 40 percent minimum.)

Recall efforts usually involve a public perception of official misconduct. On occasion, however, simply running afoul of citizen preferences is enough to trigger a recall, as former state senator George Petak of Wisconsin discovered. Petak, a Republican, had promised his constituents that he would vote against a regional sales tax to fund a new stadium for the Milwaukee Brewers.[40] However, in the heat of legislative debate and partisan pressure, he voted for the tax. That was all it took. A successful petition drive put him into a recall election in 1996, which he lost. (The recall had further implications: Because a Democrat defeated Petak, Republicans lost their one-seat control of the senate.)

In a few states, such as Wisconsin, the recall ballot resembles an election ballot. The name of the official who is the subject of the recall appears on the ballot, as do the names of challengers. To continue in office, the official must receive the most votes. In other states, the ballot includes no candidates but contains wording such as "Should Official X be recalled on the following charges?" (A brief statement of the charges would follow.) A majority vote is required to remove an official, and the vacancy created by a successful recall is filled by a subsequent special election or by appointment.

The rationale for the recall process is straightforward: Public officials should be subject to continuous voter control.[41] As the organizer of the successful campaign to recall a mayor stated, "We've shown you can fight city hall."[42] Whether it is used or not, the power to recall public officials is valued by the public. A recent national survey indicated that two-thirds of those polled favored amending the U.S. Constitution to permit the recall of members of Congress.[43]

Initiatives and recalls have helped open up state and local government to the public. Yet, ironically, increased citizen participation can also jam up the machinery of government, thus making its operation more cumbersome. Advocates of greater citizen activism, however, would gladly trade a little efficiency to achieve their goal.

Citizen Access to Government

Citizens have opportunities to participate in government in ways that do not involve voting. Because state and local governments have undertaken extensive measures to open themselves to public scrutiny and stimulate public input, citizen access to government has been increased. Many of these measures are directly connected with the policymaking process. At the very least, they enable government and the citizenry to exchange information, and thus they contribute to the growing capacity of state and local governments. At most, they may alter political power patterns and resource allocations.[44]

Many of the accessibility measures adopted by state and local governments are the direct result of public demands that government be more accountable. Others have resulted from an official effort to involve the public in the ongoing work of government. Five types of official access are discussed in the following sections.

Open Meeting Laws

open-meeting laws
Statutes that open the meetings of government bodies to the public.

Florida's 1967 "sunshine law" is credited with sparking a surge of interest in openness in government, and today **open meeting laws** are on the books in all fifty states. These laws do just what the name implies: They open meetings of government bodies to the public, or, in Florida's terminology, they bring government "into the sunshine." Open meeting laws apply to both the state and local levels and affect the executive branch as well as the legislative branch. Basic open meeting laws have been supplemented by additional requirements in many states. More than forty states require advance public notice of meetings, thirty-seven insist that minutes be taken, thirty-five levy penalties against officials who violate the law, and thirty-one void actions taken in meetings held contrary to sunshine provisions.[45]

Some states remain relatively resistant to the sun's rays. In 1997, Rhode Island failed to adopt a package of tougher open meeting laws despite extensive media attention and public pressure. That same year, North Dakota legislators strengthened the state's open meeting law but exempted themselves from most of the provisions.[46] In general, however, the trend is toward more openness. For example, the advent of electronic mail—making cyberspace meetings possible—led Colorado to expand its open records laws. Now, the stored e-mail files of the state's politicians are open to the public.

Administrative Procedure Acts

After state legislation is passed or a local ordinance is adopted, an administrative agency typically is responsible for implementation. This process involves the establishment of rules and regulations and, hence, constitutes a powerful responsibility. In practice, agencies often have wide latitude in translating legislative intent into action. For example, if a new state law creates annual automobile safety inspections, it is the responsibility of the state's Department of Motor Vehicles to make it work. Bureaucrats might determine the items to be covered in the safety inspection, the number and location of inspection stations, and the fee to be charged. These decisions are just as important as the original enactment.

To ensure public access to this critical rule-making process, states have adopted **administrative procedure acts**, which usually require public notice of the proposed rule and an opportunity for citizen comment. Virtually all states provide for this "notification and comment" process, as it is known. In addition, some states give citizens the right to petition an administrative agency for an adjustment in the rules.

> **administrative procedure acts**
> Acts that standardize administrative agency operations as a means of safeguarding clients and the general public.

Advisory Committees

Another arena for citizen participation that is popular in state and especially local governments is the **advisory committee,** in the form of citizen task forces, commissions, and panels. Regardless of name, these organizations are designed to study a problem and to offer advice, usually in the form of recommendations. People chosen to serve on an advisory committee tend to have expertise as well as interest in the issue and, in most cases, political connections. But not always. In 1991, Oregon's governor Barbara Roberts invited a random cross-section of Oregonians to attend interactive, televised meetings at one of thirty sites. The governor went live (on cable television) to each of the sites to ask citizens to assess the performance of their governments. She got an earful. But she also received invaluable input.[47]

> **advisory committee**
> An organization created by government to involve members of the public in studying and recommending solutions to public problems.

Citizen advisory committees provide a formal arena for citizen input. If officials heed public preferences, citizen advice can become the basis for public policy. Citizen advisory organizations also provide elected officials with a "safe" course of action. In a politically explosive situation, a governor can say, "I've appointed a citizen task force to study the issue and report back to me with recommendations for action." The governor thus buys time, with the hope that the issue will gradually cool down. Another benefit of these organizations is that they ease citizen acceptance of subsequent policy decisions, since the governor can note that an action "was recommended by an impartial panel of citizens." This is not to suggest that citizen advisory committees are merely tools for manipulation by politicians, but they do have uses beyond citizen participation.

Citizen Surveys

One effective way of determining what is on the public's mind is to ask people, and this can be done in a systematic manner through citizen surveys. By sampling the population, government officials can obtain a reading of the public's policy preferences and its evaluation of governmental performance. Technological advances such as computer-aided telephone interviewing make it easier to scientifically sample public opinion in a state. In the midst of a budget crunch, Texas installed a toll-free hotline so that citizens could call in with money-saving suggestions. The telephone rang off the hook—more than four thousand calls were received in the first twenty days.

For local governments, citizen surveys have provided information on the effectiveness and quality of public services.[48] Surveys supplement the more traditional approach of relying on complaints to identify problems. But even the complaint process has become more sophisticated as cities adopt CRM—customer relationship management—to track complaints and provide information. Houston was one of the first localities to use a 3-1-1 nonemergency service number as part of a CRM system.[49]

An important feature of citizen surveys is that they can counteract some of the bias that clouds most avenues of participation. As noted at the beginning of this chapter, political participation is generally an activity undertaken by those of middle to upper socioeconomic status. Nonparticipants seldom transmit their opinions to government. But in a carefully designed citizen survey, one that gives all residents an opportunity to participate, those whose opinions are often muted have a better chance to be heard.

E-Government

The Internet has the potential to bring state and local government into citizens' homes in a way earlier technology could not. States and localities have already incorporated electronic communications into their daily operations. Websites abound; e-mails proliferate. People can click on a city's homepage and find an array of useful information, such as the agenda for the next city council meeting, the minutes of previous council sessions, the city budget, the comprehensive plan, and the like. States have created elaborate websites that link the user to vast databases and information resources. In a clever twist, Pennsylvania decided to promote its web address by emblazoning it across the bottom border of its vehicle license plates.

Now states and localities are expanding their use of the Internet in dealing with the public. It started with the downloading of public reports and generic forms and has moved into more highly individualized interaction such as filing of taxes, applying for licenses and permits, and accessing personal information. Voting online began in 2000 with a small set of experiments by Alaska, Arizona, and Washington in their presidential primaries. Shaken by Florida's problems with voting machines in the 2000 presidential election, several states moved quickly to embrace new elections technology for the 2002 elections. In some states, electronic voting devices that use ATM-like touchscreens replaced optical-scan ballots and punch-card machines.[50]

One of the major concerns as the push toward e-government grows is that the so-called technology have-nots will be left behind. Low-income Americans lag far behind middle- and upper-income groups in their access to the Internet. This "digital divide" has led many communities to install personal computers in libraries, as well as in government information kiosks located in shopping malls and transit stations. In an effort to get its rural communities wired, North Dakota spent more than $3 million to connect some sixty communities to a broadband network.[51]

Volunteerism

volunteerism

A form of participation in which individuals or groups donate time or money to a public purpose.

Voluntary action is participatory activity unrelated to the ballot box. People and organizations donate their time and talents to supplement or even replace government activity. **Volunteerism** is a means of bringing fresh ideas and energy, whether physical or financial, into government while relieving some of the service burden. One highly visible example of volunteerism is the "Adopt a Highway" program. Over the past ten years, the number of local businesses and civic clubs willing to pick up litter along designated stretches of state highways has skyrocketed. You have probably noticed the "Adopt a Highway" signs with the names of volunteering groups listed underneath. The state saves money, the roadsides stay cleaner, and the volunteering groups have good feelings and free advertising to go along with their sore backs. Washington created the first statewide volunteerism office in 1969, and almost all states have followed suit. One of the most ambitious efforts has been "Volunteer for Minnesota," which assists local communities in the design of a program, including the actual recruitment, training, and placement of volunteers.[52]

Local governments use volunteers in a variety of ways. Generally, volunteerism is most successful when citizens can develop the required job skills quickly or participate in activities they enjoy, such as library work, recreation programs, or fire protection.[53] In addition to providing services to others, volunteers can be utilized for self-help; that is, they can engage in activities in which they are the primary beneficiaries. For example, some New York City neighborhoods take responsibility for the security and maintenance of nearby parks. Residential crime-watch programs are another variety of self-help. In both of these instances, the volunteers and their neighborhoods benefit. Overall, studies show, volunteerism is especially successful in rural areas and small towns.[54]

The Effects of Citizen Participation

Consider again the four quadrants of Figure 4.1. Constructive participatory behaviors, whether active or passive, invigorate government. The capacity of state and local governments depends on a number of factors, one of which is citizen participation. Underlying this argument is the implicit but strongly held belief shared by most observers of democracies that an accessible, responsive government is a legitimate government.

A mobilized public can generate systemwide change. Public policy tends to reflect the interests of active citizens. The mobilization of lower-class voters, for instance, is linked to more generous state welfare policies.[55] From the perspective of government officials and institutions, citizen participation can be a nuisance because it may disrupt established routines. The challenge is to incorporate citizen participation into ongoing operations. A noteworthy example is Dayton, Ohio, where neighborhood-based "priority boards" shape city services and policies. As a Dayton official noted, "Citizen participation in this city is just a way of life."[56] Citizen involvement may not be easy or efficient, but, in a democracy, it is the ultimate test of the legitimacy of that government.

Recent research raises the stakes for citizen participation. Political scientists Tom Rice and Alexander Sumberg developed measures to reflect the civic culture of each state, looking at, among other things, the level of citizen involvement and the amount of political equality.[57] Vermont and Massachusetts were found to be the most civic states, Mississippi and Louisiana the least civic. More important, however, is the impact of a state's civic culture on the performance of its government. According to Rice and Sumberg, a state's civic culture is "a powerful predictor of government performance."[58] Statistical analysis shows that the more civic the state, the more innovative and effective its government. Figure 4.3 displays the states' positions when civic culture and government performance are considered simultaneously. The closer a state is to the upper right corner, the better it is on both indicators. Conversely, states landing near the lower left corner score poorly on both factors. The lesson? Citizen participation matters, not only for the individual but also for the government.

| FIGURE 4.3 | **Civic Culture and Government Performance** |

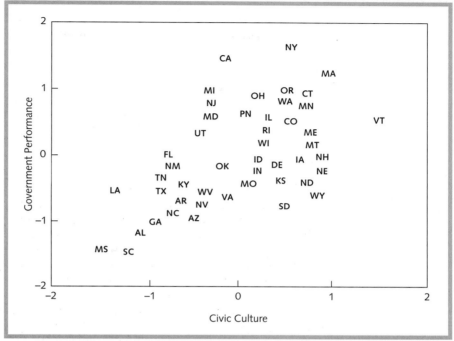

SOURCE: Tom W. Rice and Alexander F. Sumberg, "Civic Culture and Government Performance in the American States," *Publius: The Journal of Federalism* 27 (Winter 1997): 110. Reprinted by permission.

Chapter Recap

➤ Voter turnout rates vary dramatically from one state to another. The reasons have to do with the political culture of the state, the competitiveness of the political parties, and the way elections are administered.

➤ Republicans control more governorships than Democrats do and, as a result of the 2002 elections, control more legislative chambers, also.

➤ Almost half of the states have an initiative process; in those that do, it has become an important tool for policymaking.

➤ E-government is on the rise, with states and localities adopting more and more high-tech ways of interacting with citizens.

➤ Volunteerism is a way of bringing fresh ideas and energy into government and helps connect citizens to their community.

➤ State and local governments continue to make efforts to engage their citizens in meaningful participation. Doing so seems to make government work better.

Key Terms

participation *(p. 69)*
Voting Rights Act of 1965 *(p. 72)*
primary system *(p. 75)*
closed primary *(p. 76)*
open primary *(p. 76)*
blanket primary *(p. 76)*
runoff election *(p. 76)*
plurality *(p. 78)*
fusion *(p. 78)*
coattail effect *(p. 78)*

nonpartisan election *(p. 79)*
slating groups *(p. 80)*
popular referendum *(p.80)*
referendum *(p. 80)*
recall *(p. 80)*
open meeting laws *(p. 84)*
administrative procedure acts *(p. 85)*
advisory committee *(p. 85)*
volunteerism *(p. 87)*

Surfing the Net

The League of Women Voters is a preeminent organization that encourages informed and active participation of citizens in government. Its website is located at **www.lwv.org.** A good source for election information is the Federal Election Commission, at **www.fec.gov.** Although the primary focus is federal elections, the site contains some state-level information, as well as data on political action committees. The League of Women Voters sponsors the Democracy Network, a nonprofit, public policy research group located at **www.democracynet.org,** which provides citizens, public officials, and candidates a unique opportunity to debate issues of local and state interest. Candidates and elected officials can upload or update their positions in the database and citizens can access them. America's Promise: The Alliance for Youth at **www.americaspromise.org** encourages volunteers to create "communities of promise" in their hometowns. An interactive site that allows users to vote "yes" or "no" on current "hot button" issues is **www.vote.com.** For example, after the 2000 presidential election, the site e-polled public opinion on this question: "Does the Electoral College work fairly?" And for those interested in the initiative process, a wealth of information can be found at **www.iandrinstitute.org.**

5

POLITICAL PARTIES, INTEREST GROUPS, AND CAMPAIGNS

Political Parties
Political Parties in Theory and in Reality » Party Organization »
The Two-Party System » Is the Party Over?

Interest Groups
Types of Interest Groups » Interest Groups in the States »
Techniques Used by Interest Groups » Local-Level Interest
Groups

Political Campaigns
A New Era of Campaigns » Campaign Finance

On a cold day in 2000, the new governor of Mississippi—a Democrat—was chosen. But that cold day was not in November; it was in January. Moreover, it was not the voters who were doing the choosing, but the state legislature. According to the Mississippi constitution, to be elected governor, a candidate must win a majority of both the popular vote and the electoral vote. In the gubernatorial elections the preceding fall, the Democrat was slightly ahead in the popular vote (49.5 percent to 48.6 percent) but the two candidates had evenly split the electoral votes. Thus, as prescribed by the state constitution, the election was thrown into the Mississippi House of Representatives for resolution. In a straight party-line vote, the House selected Ronnie Musgrove, the Democratic candidate, over the Republican candidate.[1] Mississippi's rules for the electoral process may seem odd, but the larger point is this: Each state makes its own rules. As this chapter shows, state rules produce some interesting politics.

Political Parties

The two major parties offer slates of candidates to lead us. Candidates campaign hard for the glamorous jobs of governor, state legislator, mayor, and a variety of other state and local positions. In some states, even candidates for judicial positions compete in partisan races. But party involvement in our system of government does not end on election day—the institutions of government themselves have a partisan tone. Legislatures are organized along party lines; governors offer Republican or Democratic agendas for their states; county commissioners of different ideological stripes fight over the best way to provide services to local residents. Through the actions of their elected officials, political parties play a major role in the operation of government.

Lately, the condition of contemporary American political parties has been described with words such as *decline, decay,* and *demise.* A more precise description would use the word *transformation,* which reflects the change that parties are experiencing but stops short of an epitaph. Even the experts are unsure of what lies ahead for political parties. One book on the subject, *The Party's Just Begun,* lays out a blueprint for party renewal.[2] And although this chapter does not use similar words, such as *rejuvenation* and *revitalization,* we acknowledge that political parties continue to evolve.

Political Parties in Theory and in Reality

One ideal against which political party systems can be measured is called the **responsible party model,** which has several basic principles:

responsible party model

A theoretical ideal in which political parties are issue oriented, candidates toe the party line, and voters respond accordingly.

1. Parties should present clear and coherent programs to voters.
2. Voters should choose candidates according to the party programs.
3. The winning party should carry out its program once in office.
4. At the next election, voters should hold the governing party responsible for executing its program.[3]

According to this model, political parties carve out identifiable issue positions, base their campaign appeals on them, and endeavor to enact them upon taking office. Voters select candidates who represent their preferences and hold officeholders accountable for their performance.

Still, even a casual observer would recognize that U.S. political parties fall somewhat short of the responsible party mark. For example, U.S. political parties stand for different things in different places, so a single, coherent program is unworkable. Although Democratic politicians tend to be more liberal than their Republican counterparts, it would be difficult to find an abundance of liberals in a Democrat-controlled southern state legislature. Furthermore, voters display a remarkable penchant for **ticket splitting**—that is, voting for a Democrat for one office and a Republican for another in the same election. Many voters are fond of saying that they "vote for the person, not the party."

ticket splitting

Voting for candidates of different political parties in a general election.

Parties in the United States function as umbrella organizations that shelter loose coalitions of relatively like-minded individuals. A general image for each party is discernible: The Republicans typically have been considered the party of big business, the Democrats the party of workers. But even though many people identify with the party of their parents, they hold that identification more and more lightly. In what used to be called "the solid South," a label that indicated the region's historically overwhelming support for the Democratic party, one finds increasingly fewer "yellow dog Democrats"—people who would vote for the Democratic nominee "even if he was a yellow dog." At the same time, Republicans, once regarded as oddities in the region, have become respectable. Now the Republican party considers the South, where conservatives are aplenty, a good source of partisan support.

As noted, the responsible party model does not aptly describe politics and governance in the states. Therefore, does it matter which party controls the institutions of state government? One can reasonably answer "yes," given that the parties vary in their ideological composition. Americans have grown more ideologically conservative, and, at present, conservatives outnumber liberals in every state. However, states with proportionately higher numbers of liberals tend to have a more liberal direction to their public policies. The work of political scientists Robert Erikson, Gerald Wright, and John McIver emphasizes this point.[4] The variation across states is shown in Figure 5.1. Generally, the more conservative a state's populace, the lower a state's score on the policy liberalism index. As you move toward the liberal end of the ideological scale, a state's policy liberalism increases. New York and Massachusetts are very different from Mississippi and Oklahoma. Rhode Island, with a relatively liberal populace but public policies that are in line with more conservative states like Kansas, is a reminder that ideology and policies are not always in sync. And although ideology and partisanship are not completely interchangeable, the linkage is strong. States

---

FIGURE 5.1 **Ideology and State Policy Liberalism**

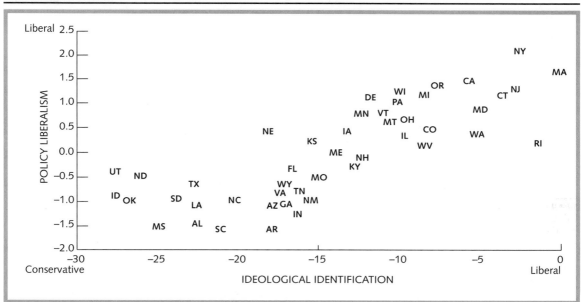

SOURCE: Robert S. Erikson, Gerald C. Wright, and John P. McIver, *Statehouse Democracy: Public Opinion and the American States.* Copyright © 1993. Reprinted with the permission of Cambridge University Press.

with proportionately more liberals are more likely to vote for Democrats; conservatives tend to favor Republicans. In the past, the South would stand as an exception to the rule; however, as noted above, these days conservative southerners are finding a home in the Republican party. For the Democrats, the increasing conservatism of the public has forced the party to move more toward the center of the ideological spectrum. The emergence of candidates who refer to themselves as "New Democrats" and speak the language of **pragmatism** is evidence of that movement.

pragmatism
A practical approach to problem solving, a search for "what works."

Party Organization

Political parties are decentralized organizations. There are fifty state Republican parties and fifty state Democratic parties. Each state also has local party organizations, most typically at the county level. Although they interact, each of these units is autonomous—a situation that is good for independence but not so helpful to party discipline. Specialized partisan groups, including the College Democrats, the Young Republicans, Democratic Women's Clubs, Black Republican Councils, and so on, have been accorded official recognition.[5] Party organizations are further decentralized into precinct-level clusters, which bear the ultimate responsibility for turning out the party's voters on election day. Figure 5.2 shows a typical state party organization.

State Parties   State governments vary in how closely and vigorously they regulate political parties. In states with few laws, parties have more discretion in their organization and functions.[6] Each state party has a charter or bylaws to govern its operation. The decisionmaking body is the state committee, sometimes called a central committee, which is headed by a chairperson and composed of members elected in party primaries or at state party conventions. State parties, officially at least, head their party's push to capture statewide elected offices. Although they may formulate platforms and launch party-centered fundraising appeals, their value to candidates is in the services they provide.[7] In many states, parties host "how to campaign effectively" seminars for party nominees, conduct research into the public's mood, and advertise on behalf of their candidates.

State party organizations vary widely in their organizational vitality and resources. Approximately one-quarter of them employ salaried chairpersons, and most have full-time executive directors as well as staffs numbering between six and thirteen people, with annual budgets in the $1.3 million range.[8] During election years the size of the staff swells, as does the party's budget. Republican organizations generally outstrip Democratic ones in these measures of organizational strength.

Local Parties   County party organizations are composed of committee members chosen at the precinct level. These workers are volunteers whose primary reward is the satisfaction of being involved in politics. But the work is rarely glamorous. Party workers are the people who conduct voter registration drives, drop off the lawn signs for residents' front yards, organize candidate forums, and stand at the polls and remind voters to "Vote Democratic" or "Vote Re-

| FIGURE 5.2 | **Typical State Party Organization** |

Most political party organizations look something like this. Party workers at the bottom of the chart are direct links to voters.

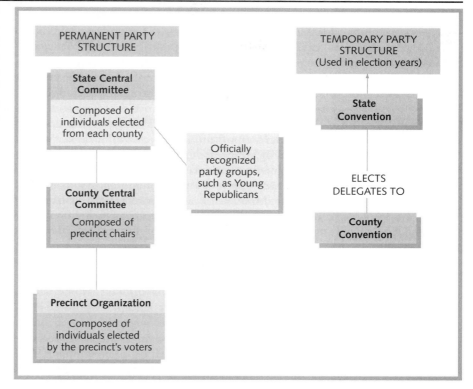

publican." Local party organizations kick into high gear come election time. On behalf of the party's candidates, they distribute campaign literature, contribute money, make calls to voters, and run newspaper advertisements. Because so many local elected offices are nonpartisan, as noted in Chapter 4, local party organizations focus primarily on state (and national) campaigns.

Local parties are less professionally organized than state parties. Although half of the local organizations maintain campaign headquarters during an election period, fewer than one-quarter operate year-round offices.[9] County chairpersons report devoting a lot of time to the party during election periods, but otherwise the post does not take much of their time. Most chairpersons lead organizations without any full-time staff, and vacancies in precinct offices are common.

Factions Political parties frequently develop *factions*—that is, identifiable subsets. These can be ideologically based, as exemplified by the struggle between moderates and liberals for control of state Democratic parties. They can be organized around particular political leaders—for instance, Giuliani (former mayor of New York City) Republicans versus Pataki (governor of New York) Republicans. Or they can reflect sectional divisions within a state; for example, south Florida Democrats battling with north Florida Democrats. When factions endure, they make it difficult for a party to come together in support of candidates and in support of policy. Persistent intraparty factions create opportunities for the opposing party.

A factional challenge to local Republican parties has come from evangelical Christian activists who want to move the party to a more conservative stance. In Minnesota, for instance, the state Republican party's tradition was one of moderately progressive social policies and fiscal restraint. The emergence of the Christian right with its conservative social agenda rocked the party.[10] By 1994, the Christian Coalition was sufficiently organized to dominate many local Republican party conventions. The case of Texas is illustrative. There, the religious right took over precinct meetings, gained control over many party committees, and was able to dictate platform positions. Thus in socially liberal Travis County, the GOP convention adopted an anti-abortion, anti-gay, pro-prayer in schools platform.[11] Minnesota and Texas reflect a near-national trend. The publication *Campaigns & Elections* reported that in eighteen states, the Christian right dominated the Republican party governing organization; in thirteen states its influence was considered substantial.[12]

Political parties continually face the problem of factions. The challenge for party leadership is to unite the factions into a winning force.

The Two-Party System

General elections in the United States are typically contests between candidates representing the two major political parties. Such has been the case for the past century and a half. The Democratic party has been in existence since the 1830s, when it emerged from the Jacksonian wing of the Jeffersonian party.[13] The Republican party, despite its label as the "Grand Old Party," is newer; it developed out of the sectional conflict over slavery of the 1850s.

Why Just Two?   There are numerous reasons for the institutionalization of two-party politics. Explanations that emphasize sectional dualism, such as East versus West or North versus South, have given way to those that focus on the structure of the electoral system. Parties compete in elections in which there can be only one winner. Most legislative races, for example, take place in single-member districts, in which only the candidate with the most votes wins; there is no reward for finishing second or third. Hence the development of radical or noncentrist parties is discouraged. In addition, laws regulating access to the ballot and receipt of public funds contribute to two-partyism by creating high start-up costs for third parties. Another very plausible explanation has to do with tradition. Americans are accustomed to a political system composed of two parties, and that is how we understand politics.

Interparty Competition   Most states exhibit meaningful two-party electoral competition. In other words, when you look at a general-election ballot, you will find both the Democrats and the Republicans offering credible candidates. Gone are the days when one party consistently dominated state politics without any opposition. Bastions of Republicanism such as New Hampshire and South Dakota have seen the Democratic party gain strength, while Democratically dominated states such as Georgia and Mississippi have experienced growth in the Republican party. The extension of interparty competition to states that lacked it in the past is a healthy development in American politics. Heated partisan competition turns a dull campaign into a lively contest. Citizen interest picks up and voter turnout increases. Citizens who are dissatisfied with the performance of the party in power have another choice. In the view of many, two parties are better than one.

Beyond electoral competition, an important consideration is which party controls the governor's office and the state legislature—the major policymaking institutions in the state. Even as more states develop competitive two-party politics, the pattern of institutional control varies.[14] In what is called **unified government,** one party controls both institutions, as the Democrats have done in Georgia and Hawaii and the Republicans have done in South Dakota. A condition known as **divided government** occurs when the governor's office and the legislature are controlled by different parties. In states like Ohio and Pennsylvania, partisan control of institutions has swung back and forth between the two parties.

Two-party competition is spreading at a time when states are becoming the battleground for the resolution of difficult policy issues. Undoubtedly, as governors set their agendas and legislatures outline their preferences, cries of "partisan politics" will be heard. But in a positive sense, such cries symbolize the maturation of state institutions. Partisan politics will likely encourage a wider search for policy alternatives and result in innovative solutions.

unified government
A situation in which both the governor's office and the legislature are controlled by the same party.

divided government
A situation in which one party controls the governor's office and the other party controls the legislature.

Third Parties   The assessment of former Alabama governor George Wallace that "there ain't a dime's worth of difference between Democrats and Republicans" raises questions about the need for alternative parties. Third parties (also called nonmajor or minor parties) are a persistent phenomenon in U.S. politics. Historically, third parties have achieved occasional success in certain states; examples include the Socialist party in New York in the early 1900s and the Progressive party of Wisconsin's Robert La Follette between the two world wars. Generally, however, third parties have not been particularly popular. There may be no substantial differences between the two major parties, but for the most part their positions reflect the public mood. Third parties suffer because the two established parties have vast reserves of money and resources at their disposal; new parties can rarely amass the finances or assemble the organization necessary to make significant inroads into the system. Further, third parties typically receive scant attention from the news media, and without it, credibility wanes.[15]

During the 1990s, third parties began to attract more adherents. One national survey reported that 53 percent of the electorate believed there should be a third major political party.[16] Many people indicated that their estrangement from the Democratic and Republican parties had reached the point that they would willingly affiliate with a third party that reflected their interests. Third-party options continue to expand as their electoral success increases. For example, the Libertarian party, which seeks to reduce the government's size, has been victorious in local races in thirty-seven states, with its greatest impact being in

California, New Hampshire, and Pennsylvania. And the Green party, which grew out of the environmental movement, has elected seventy-nine of its members to local offices in twenty-one states, including city council positions in cities such as Flagstaff, Arizona; Santa Monica, California; and Chapel Hill, North Carolina. The victory of the Reform party in the Minnesota gubernatorial race in 1998 provided further impetus for alternative parties. In 2000, the West Virginia governor's race included a candidate of the Mountain party, while in Vermont, a Progressive party candidate made a bid for the top job.

Is the Party Over?

This impertinent question is intended to spark debate. Have political parties, as we know them, outlived their usefulness? Should they be cast aside as new forms of political organization and communication emerge?

As some have argued, a more educated populace that can readily acquire political information is likely to be less reliant on party cues.[17] The members of today's generation are less loyal to political parties than their grandparents were and are not so likely to vote along party lines. But the trend toward **dealignment,** or weakening of individual partisan attachments, may have slowed, or even reversed. New research reports an increase in the proportion of people who say they "strongly identify" with a party.[18] And the number of pure Independents who reject all parties appears to have declined slightly. While that information may be encouraging to parties, other trends are not so reassuring. For example, parties no longer rule the roost when it comes to campaign finance. Challenges come from political action committees that pour huge amounts of money into campaigns and candidates, and from political operatives who use new technology creatively to build individual election teams.

dealignment
The weakening of an individual's attachment to political parties.

Political parties are not sitting idly by as their function in the political system is challenged. Research has shown that party organizations are making their operations more professional and have more money to spend and more staff to spend it.[19] The past several years have seen the development of party-centered advertising campaigns and a renewed commitment to get-out-the-vote drives.[20] In a few states with publicly funded campaigns, parties as well as candidates have been designated as recipients of funds. States formerly dominated by one party now find themselves with a resilient second party on their hands. All in all, it appears that parties are still viable parts of the political system.

Interest Groups

interest group
An organized body of individuals with shared goals and a desire to influence government.

Interest groups have become powerful players in our democratic system. Joining a group is a way for individuals to communicate their preferences—their interests—to government. Interest groups attempt to influence governmental decisions and actions by pressuring decisionmaking bodies to, for example, put more guidance counselors in public schools, restrict coastal development, keep a proposed new prison out of a neighborhood, or strengthen state licensing of family therapists. Success is defined in terms of getting the group's preferences enacted. In certain states, interest groups actually dominate the policy-making process.

In considering the role of groups in the political system, we must remember that people join groups for reasons other than politics. For instance, a teacher may be a member of a politically active state education association because the group offers a tangible benefit such as low-cost life insurance, but he may disagree with some of the political positions taken by the organization. In general, then, motivations for group membership are individually determined.[21]

Types of Interest Groups

Interest groups come in all types and sizes. If you were to visit the lobby of the state capitol when the legislature was in session, you might find the director of the state school boards association conversing with the chairperson of the education committee, or the lobbyist hired by the state hotel-motel association exchanging notes with the representative of the state's restaurateurs. If a legislator were to venture into the lobby, she would probably receive at least a friendly greeting from the lobbyists and at most a serious heart-to-heart talk about the merits of a bill. You would be witnessing efforts to influence public policy. Interest groups want state government to enact policies that are in their interest or, conversely, not to enact policies at odds with it.

The interests represented in the capitol lobby are as varied as the states themselves. One that is well represented and powerful is business. Whether a lobbyist represents a single large corporation or a consortium of businesses, when he or she talks, state legislators listen. From the perspective of business groups (and other economically oriented groups), legislative actions can cost or save their members money. Therefore, the chambers of commerce, industry groups, trade associations, financial institutions, and regulated utilities maintain a visible presence in the state capitol during the legislative session. Table 5.1 documents the influential nature of business interests at the state level. Of course, business interests are not monolithic; occasionally they even find themselves on opposite sides of a bill.

Other interests converge on the capitol. Representatives of labor, both of established AFL-CIO unions and of professional associations such as the state optometrists' group or sheriffs' association, frequent the hallways and committee meeting rooms. They, too, are there to see that the legislature makes the "right" decision on the bills before it. For example, if a legislature were considering a bill to change the licensing procedures for optometrists, you could expect to find the optometrists' interest group immersed in the debate. Another workers' group, schoolteachers, has banded together to form one of the most effective state-level groups. In fact, as Table 5.1 indicates, schoolteachers' organizations are ranked among the most influential interest groups in more states than any other group. In forty-one states, they are among the top groups.[22]

Many other interest groups are active in state government, and a large number of them are ideological in nature. In other words, their political activity is oriented toward some higher good, such as clean air or fairer tax systems or consumer protection. Members of these groups do not have a direct economic or professional

TABLE 5.1	The Twenty Most Influential Interests in the States

RANK		NUMBER OF STATES IN WHICH THE INTEREST WAS SEEN AS VERY EFFECTIVE
1	General business organizations (chambers of commerce, etc.)	40
2	Schoolteachers' organizations (predominantly the NEA)	41
3	Utility companies and associations (electric, gas, water, telephone, cable TV)	26
4	Lawyers (predominantly trial attorneys and state bar associations)	26
5	Health care organizations (mainly hospital associations)	17
6	Insurance: general and medical (companies and associations)	21
7	General local government organizations (municipal leagues, county organizations, etc.)	20
8	Manufacturers (companies and associations)	22
9	General farm organizations (mainly state farm bureaus)	17
10	Doctors/state medical associations	18
11	State and local government employees (other than teachers)	15
12	Traditional labor associations (predominantly the AFL-CIO)	14
13	Bankers' associations (includes savings and loan associations).	16
14	Contractors/builders/developers	11
15	Realtors' associations	11
16	K-12 education interests (other than teachers)	11
17	Gaming interests (race tracks/casinos/lotteries)	11
18	Individual banks and financial institutions	10
19	Environmentalists	7
20	Universities and colleges	6

SOURCE: Clive S. Thomas and Ronald J. Hrebenar, "Interest Groups in the Fifty States, *Comparative State Politics* 20 (August 1999), p. 7. Reprinted with permission from *Comparative State Politics,* University of Illinois at Springfield.

interest in the outcome of a legislative decision. Instead, their lobbyists argue that the public as a whole benefits from their involvement in the legislative process. Penn PIRG, for instance, describes itself as a nonprofit, nonpartisan watchdog group working on behalf of consumers, the environment, and good government in Pennsylvania. The group's motto, and that of other PIRGs (public interest research groups), is "Get active, speak out, make a difference."

Looking at a specific state reveals a mix of active, effective interest groups. For example, the list of effective interest groups in Rhode Island includes the standard set of economic interests such as business groups, labor unions, banks, and utilities. Other groups vying for legislative attention reflect diverse interests such as governmental reform groups, environmental groups, the media (especially the *Providence Journal-Bulletin* and radio talk shows), the city of Providence, senior citizens, and the liquor lobby.[23] In fact, a look across the states shows some fairly state-specific interests; some examples are the high-tech lobby in Oregon, the poultry federation in Arkansas, the stockgrowers' association in Montana, and the Ojibwa and Sioux tribes in Minnesota.

Interest Groups in the States

The actual interest-group environment is different from one state to another. There is variation not only in the composition of the involved groups but also in the degree of influence they exert. Research by political scientists Clive Thomas and Ronald Hrebenar, along with a team of researchers throughout the country, provides fresh insights into the interest-group scene. Table 5.2 classifies states according to the strength of interest groups vis-à-vis other political institutions in the policymaking process. Groups can dominate other political institutions such as political parties, complement them, or be subordinate to them.[24] As the listing in Table 5.2 shows, there are five states in which interest groups are dominant—that is, in which they wield an overwhelming and consistent influence on policymaking. At the other end of the spectrum, there are no states in which interest groups are completely subordinate. However, there is a cluster of four states in which interest groups are comparatively weak. Interest groups enjoy complementary, somewhat balanced, relationships with other political institutions in sixteen states. The pattern is less stable in the twenty-five states in the dominant/complementary category. In those states, there is likely to be more flux in the system as group power ebbs and flows.

For the most part, interest-group politics is defined by its state context.[25] First of all, interest groups and political parties have evolving, multidimensional relationships. Typically, in states where political parties are weak, interest groups are strong; where political parties are strong, interest groups tend to be weaker.[26] Strong parties provide leadership in the policymaking process, and interest groups function through them. In the absence of party leadership and organization, interest groups fill the void, becoming important recruiters of candidates and financiers of campaigns; accordingly, they exert tremendous influence in policymaking. Although the inverse relationship between parties and groups generally holds true, the politics in states like New York and Michigan offers an interesting

TABLE 5.2   Interest Group Impact

STATES IN WHICH THE OVERALL IMPACT OF INTEREST GROUPS IS			
Dominant (5)	Dominant/ Complementary (25)	Complementary (16)	Complementary/ Subordinate (4)
Alabama	Alaska	Colorado	Minnesota
Florida	Arizona	Delaware	Rhode Island
Nevada	Arkansas	Indiana	South Dakota
South Carolina	California	Hawaii	Vermont
West Virginia	Connecticut	Maine	
	Georgia	Massachusetts	
	Idaho	Michigan	
	Illinois	Missouri	
	Iowa	New Hampshire	
	Kansas	New Jersey	
	Kentucky	New York	
	Louisiana	North Carolina	
	Maryland	North Dakota	
	Mississippi	Pennsylvania	
	Montana	Utah	
	Nebraska	Wisconsin	
	New Mexico		
	Ohio		
	Oklahoma		
	Oregon		
	Tennessee		
	Texas		
	Virginia		
	Washington		
	Wyoming		

SOURCE: Clive S. Thomas and Ronald J. Hrebenar, "Interest Groups in the Fifty States, *Comparative State Politics* 20 (August 1999), p. 13. Reprinted with permission from *Comparative State Politics*, University of Illinois at Springfield.

variation. In these states, groups are active and can be influential, but they work with the established party system in a kind of symbiotic relationship.[27]

A second, related truth adds a developmental angle to interest-group politics. As states diversify economically, their politics are less likely to be dominated by a single interest.[28] Thus, we find that the interest-group environment is becoming more cluttered, resulting in *hyperpluralism,* or a multiplicity of groups. As states increasingly become the arena in which important social and economic policy decisions are made, more and more groups will go to statehouses, hoping to find a receptive audience.

Techniques Used by Interest Groups

Interest groups want to have a good public image. It helps a group when its preferences can be equated with what is "good for the state" (or the community). Organizations use slogans like "What's good for the timber industry is good for Oregon" or "Schoolteachers have the interests of New York City at heart." Some groups have taken on the label "public interest groups" to designate their main interest as that of the public at large. Groups, then, invest resources in creating a good image.

Being successful in the state capitol or at city hall involves more than a good public image, however. For example, interest groups have become effective at organizing networks that exert pressure on legislators. If a teacher pay-raise bill is in jeopardy in the senate, for instance, schoolteachers throughout the state may be asked by the education association to contact their senators to urge them to vote favorably on the legislation. To maximize their strength, groups with common interests often establish coalitions. For example, eighteen environmental groups in Arkansas formed an umbrella organization, the Environmental Congress of Arkansas, to get their message out. Sometimes related groups carve out their own niches to avoid direct competition for members and support.[29] For example, gay and lesbian groups, relatively new to state politics, focus on narrow issues such as ending prohibitions against same-sex marriages rather than on broad concerns.[30] This strategy allows more groups to flourish. Interest groups also hire representatives who can effectively promote their cause. To ensure that legislators will be receptive to their pressures, groups try to influence the outcome of elections by supporting candidates who reflect their interests.

A number of factors affect the relative power of an interest group. In their work, Thomas and Hrebenar have identified ten characteristics that give some groups more political clout than others:

- the degree of necessity of group services and resources to public officials;
- whether the group's lobbying focus is primarily defensive or offensive;
- the extent and strength of group opposition;
- potential for the group to enter into coalitions;
- group financial resources;

- size and geographical distribution of group membership;
- political cohesiveness of the membership;
- political, organizational, and managerial skills of group leaders;
- timing and the political climate; and
- lobbyist-policymaker relations.[31]

No single interest group is on the "high end" of all ten of these characteristics all of the time. However, returning to Table 5.1 for a moment, we find that the first ten groups listed, influential in two-thirds of the states, possess quite a few of these factors. When the timing is right, an indispensable group armed with ample resources, a cohesive membership, and skilled leaders can wield enormous influence in the state capitol. This is especially true when the group has taken a defensive posture—that is, when it wants to block proposed legislation. On the other hand, victory comes less easily to a group lacking these characteristics.

lobbying

The process by which groups and individuals attempt to influence policymakers.

Lobbying   **Lobbying** is the attempt to influence government decisionmakers. States have developed official definitions to determine who is a lobbyist and who is not. A common definition is "anyone receiving compensation to influence legislative action." A few states, such as Nevada, North Dakota, and Washington, require everyone who attempts to influence legislation to register as a lobbyist (even those who are not being paid), but most exclude public officials, members of the media, and people who speak only before committees or boards from this definition. Counting lobbyists is a tricky endeavor, but a recent survey put Arizona and New Hampshire at opposite ends of the "average number of lobbyists per legislator" spectrum.[32] On average, Arizona has twenty-eight lobbyists per legislator; New Hampshire's ratio is less than one lobbyist per legislator.

In most states, lobbyists are required to file reports indicating how and on whom they spent money. Concern that lobbyists would exert undue influence on the legislative process spurred states to enact new reporting requirements and to impose tougher penalties for violations. Maine and New Jersey, for instance, require lobbyists to report their sources of income, total and categorized expenditures, the names of the individual officials who received their monies or gifts, and the legislation they supported or opposed. Despite stringent disclosure laws, legislator-lobbyist scandals have caused many states to clamp down even harder. For example, in the wake of scandals in Kentucky, lobbyists and their employers are prohibited from giving *anything* of value (with the exception of meals) to legislators or their immediate family. Public employees in South Carolina and Wisconsin are prohibited from accepting a gift of value from lobbyists, even if it is no more than a cup of coffee. (Iowa's law is only slightly more relaxed: Officials may accept food and drink valued at $3 or less and consumed at one sitting.)[33]

As state government has expanded and taken on more functions, the number of interests represented in the state capital has exploded. A 1990 estimate put the number of registered lobbyists at 42,500—a jump of 20 percent in only four years.[34] This increase has a very simple, but important, cause: Interests that are affected by state government cannot afford to be without representation. An anecdote from Florida makes the point. Legislators supported a new urban development program that Florida cities had lobbied for but about which they could not agree on a funding source. After much debate, they found one: a sales tax on dry cleaning. Because the dry-cleaning industry did not have a lobbyist in Tallahassee, there was no one to speak out on its behalf. Indeed, since their views were not represented in the debate over funding sources, dry cleaners were an easy target.[35] (The dry-cleaning industry learned its lesson and hired a lobbyist a few days after the tax was enacted.)

To influence legislators in their decisionmaking, lobbyists need access, so they cultivate good relationships with lawmakers. In other words, they want connections; they want an "in." There are many ways of establishing connections, such as entertaining, gift giving, and contributing to campaigns. Lawmakers want to know how a proposed bill might affect the different interests throughout the state and in their legislative districts, and what it is expected to achieve. And lobbyists are only too happy to oblige. Social lobbying—wining and dining legislators—still goes on in many states, but it is being supplemented by the provision of information. A study of western states has revealed a new breed of lobbyists trained as attorneys and public relations specialists, skilled in media presentation and information packaging.[36] A study of the lobbying environment in three states—California, South Carolina, and Wisconsin—identified the kinds of techniques that lobbyists rely on. Table 5.3 lists the techniques that more than 80 percent of the 595 lobbyists surveyed said they used. Providing information is clearly a large part of a lobbyist's role, but a few of the techniques, such as having influential constituents contact a legislator's office, tend toward

TABLE 5.3	**The Most Popular Techniques Used by Lobbyists**
1.	Testifying at legislative hearings
2.	Contacting government officials directly to present point of view
3.	Helping to draft legislation
4.	Alerting state legislators to the effects of a bill on their districts
5.	Having influential constituents contact legislator's office
6.	Consulting with government officials to plan legislative strategy
7.	Attempting to shape implementation of policies
8.	Mounting grass-roots lobbying efforts
9.	Helping to draft regulations, rules, or guidelines
10.	Shaping government's agenda by raising new issues and calling attention to previously ignored problems
11.	Engaging in informal contacts with officials
12.	Inspiring letter-writing or telegram campaigns

SOURCE: Anthony Nownes and Patricia Freemann, "Interest Group Activity in the States," *Journal of Politics* 60 (February 1998), p. 92. Copyright © Southern Political Science Association. Reprinted by permission of Blackwell Publishers.

more of a "leaning on" approach. Notice, too, that lobbying is not confined to the legislative process. Lobbyists regularly attempt to shape the implementation of policies after they are enacted.

The influence of lobbyists specifically and of interest groups generally is a subject of much debate. The popular image is one of a mythical lobbyist whose very presence in a committee hearing room can spell the fate of a bill. In fact, his will is done because the interests he represents are widely considered vital to the state, he has assiduously laid the groundwork, and legislators respect the forces he can mobilize if necessary. Few lobbyists cast this long a shadow, however, and their interaction with legislators is seldom this mechanical. Much contemporary interest-group research suggests that patterns of influence are somewhat unpredictable and highly dependent on the state context.[37]

grassroots lobbying

Group mobilization of citizens to contact public officials on behalf of shared public policy views.

A not-so-new tactic that is enjoying a resurgence is **grassroots lobbying**— "the planned and orchestrated demonstration of public support through the mobilization of constituent action."[38] Since lobbying reforms have changed the political landscape, groups increasingly rely on their members to communicate with legislators (translation: bombard with mail, faxes, and telephone calls) on behalf of the group's issue. Grassroots lobbying is not just a technique for outsiders. A recent study found that citizen groups, unions, religious groups, charities, corporations, and trade and professional associations all use grassroots techniques.[39] This has given rise to the term *astroturfing,* or bogus grassroots lobbying.

political action committee (PAC)

An organization that raises and distributes campaign funds to candidates for elective office.

Political Action Committees   **Political action committees (PACs)** made extensive inroads into state politics in the 1980s. Narrowly focused subsets of interest groups, PACs are political organizations that collect funds and distribute them to candidates. PACs serve as the campaign-financing arm of corporations, labor unions, trade associations, and even political parties. They grew out of long-standing laws that made it illegal for corporations and labor unions to contribute directly to a candidate. Barred from direct contributions, these organizations set up "political action" subsidiaries to allow them legal entry into campaign finance. Probably the oddest PAC is "21st Century Vote," organized by a Chicago street gang called the Gangster Disciples.[40] In 1994, this PAC raised money on behalf of certain candidates in the Windy City and, with a membership of 30,000, even engaged in grassroots lobbying.

The impact of PACs on state politics is just beginning to become clear. Some Michigan legislators, for example, consider PACs a potentially dangerous influence on state politics because their money "buys a lot of access that others can't get."[41] And access can mean influence. Analysis of tobacco industry PACs suggests that their campaign contributions affect legislative behavior: "As legislators [in California, Colorado, Massachusetts, Pennsylvania, and Washington] received more tobacco industry campaign contributions . . . legislators were more likely to be pro–tobacco industry."[42]

States have responded to the proliferation of PACs by increasing their regulation. In New Jersey, for instance, PACs are required to register and to provide information regarding their controlling interests. In Kentucky, a candidate's total PAC contributions are limited to 35 percent of receipts or $5,000, whichever is larger.[43] One very likely possibility is that an independent interstate network of groups with money to spend could emerge as a real threat to political parties as recruiters of candidates and financiers of campaigns. The enactment of a law in Washington State that restricts contributions from out-of-state PACs is a harbinger of tighter regulation to come.

Local-Level Interest Groups

Interest groups function at the local level as well. Because so much of local government involves the delivery of services, local interest groups devote a great deal of their attention to administrative agencies and departments. Groups are involved in local elections and in community issues, to be sure, but their major focus is on the *actions* of government: policy implementation and service delivery.[44]

National surveys of local officials have indicated that although interest groups are influential in local decisionmaking, they do not dominate the process.[45] As is true at the state level, business groups are considered to be the most influential. Business-related interests, such as the local chamber of commerce or a downtown merchants' association, usually wield power in the community. An increasingly influential group at the local level is the neighborhood-based organization. Newer groups at the local level include women's organizations, ideological groups, and homosexual-rights activists. Thus far, however, these groups have not achieved the degree of influence accorded business and neighborhood groups.

Neighborhood organizations deserve a closer look. Some have arisen out of issues that directly affect neighborhood residents—a local school that is scheduled to close, a wave of violent crime, a proposed freeway route that will destroy homes and businesses. Others have been formed by government itself as a way of channeling citizen participation. For example, St. Paul, Minnesota, is divided into district councils; Portland, Oregon, uses district coalition boards to pull neighborhood representatives together. These arrangements not only empower citizens but also make local government more responsive to public preferences.[46]

direct action
A form of participation designed to draw attention to a cause.

Neighborhood groups, as well as others lacking a bankroll but possessing enthusiasm and dedication, may resort to tactics such as **direct action,** which includes protest marching at the county courthouse or standing in front of bulldozers clearing land for a new highway. Direct action is usually designed to attract attention to a cause; it tends to be a last resort, a tactic employed when other efforts at influencing government policy have failed. The nation witnessed a stunning example of extreme direct action when riots broke out in poor, predominantly black and Hispanic sections of Los Angeles in May 1992. Allegations of police brutality triggered violent upheaval, and the eventual uneasy calm that settled over the neighborhood brought with it increased government assistance.

Political Campaigns

Political parties and interest groups bump into each other all the time. This is especially true in political campaigns. Like so many things these days, political campaigns aren't what they used to be. State and local campaigns are no longer unsophisticated operations run from someone's dining room table. The new era of campaign technology and financing makes information accessible to almost everyone through television, the mailbox, and, most recently, the Internet. As a consequence, some argue, campaigns have taken on a different, sometimes negative tone.

A New Era of Campaigns

Campaigns of the past conjure up images of fiery oratory and county fairs. But campaigns orchestrated by rural courthouse gangs and urban ward bosses have given way today to stylized video campaigning, which depends on the mass media and political consultants.

Mass Media   The mass media, especially television, are intrinsic aspects of modern statewide campaigns. Even candidates for local offices are increasingly using the mass media to transmit their messages. Campaigners can either buy their time and newspaper space for advertising or get it free by arranging events that reporters are likely to cover. These events range from serious (a candidate's major policy statement) to gimmicky (a candidate climbing into the ring with a professional wrestler to demonstrate his "toughness"); either way, they are cleverly planned to capture media attention.

A candidate seeking free media attention needs to create visual events, be quotable, and relentlessly attack opponents or targeted problems. But as the magazine *Campaigns & Elections* advises, he or she must integrate gimmicks with a message that appeals to the electorate. In one of its issues, this magazine

Running for a third term as New York's governor, George Pataki campaigned vigorously in 2002. (© Chet Gordon / The Image Works)

contained articles aimed at candidates on "making a name for yourself," "nailing the opposition," and "effective targeting."[47] Televised debates offer another opportunity for free media time. In 2002, the Democratic candidates for governor in Texas debated twice during the primary election campaign. That was not particularly unusual; the distinction lay in that one of the debates was conducted in Spanish.[48]

Free media time is seldom sufficient. Candidates, particularly those running for higher-level state offices and for positions in large cities, rely on paid advertisements to reach the public. Paid media advertisements these days seem to be of two distinct varieties: generic and negative. Generic advertisements include

1. the *sainthood spot,* which glorifies the candidate and her accomplishments;
2. the *testimonial spot,* in which other people (celebrities, average citizens) attest to the candidate's abilities;
3. the *bumper-sticker policy spot,* which emphasizes the campaign's popular and noncontroversial themes (good schools, lower taxes, more jobs); and
4. the *feel-good spot,* which identifies and capitalizes on the spirit of a place and its people (for example, "Vermont's a special place" or "Nobody can do it better than Pennsylvania").[49]

Media advertising is important because it is frequently the only contact a potential voter has with a candidate. A candidate's personal characteristics and style—important considerations to an evaluating public—are easily transmitted via the airwaves. And, indeed, advances in communications technology offer new options to enterprising candidates. For instance, more candidates are now using cable television to cut media costs and to target audiences. One candidate for the Maryland House of Delegates distributed homemade videotapes to 7,000 targeted households in his district. Curious VCR-equipped voters could tune into the candidate whenever they wanted, pause the spiel, rewind the tape, and play it again.[50]

Negative Campaigning   The level of negativism in political campaigns, especially in advertising, has increased. Yet, nationwide, the public is registering its disapproval of mudslinging, take-no-prisoners campaigns. The strident tone projected in campaigns seems to have fueled cynicism about both government and politics, and may have the effect of reducing voter turnout. Tired of the unrelenting nastiness, states are exploring different ways of controlling negative campaigning.

Negative campaign advertising comes in three flavors: fair, false, and deceptive. A fair ad might emphasize some embarrassing aspect of an opponent's voting record or some long-forgotten indiscretion. A false ad, as the label implies, contains untrue statements. More problematic are deceptive advertisements. These misleading ads distort the truth about an opponent. The difficulty for states is to regulate negative campaign advertising without violating the free-speech guarantees of the U.S. Constitution. False advertising that is done with actual malice can be prohibited by a state, but deceptive ads, replete with accusation and innuendo, are more difficult to regulate.[51]

Twenty states have enacted laws prohibiting false campaign statements: Candidates who use false ads against their opponents can be fined. One of the problems with these laws is that the damage is done long before the remedy can be applied. Fining a candidate after the election is akin to latching the barn door after the horse has fled. Nine states have adopted a fair campaign practices code. These codes typically contain broad guidelines such as "Do not misrepresent the facts" or "Do not make appeals to prejudice based on race or sex." The limitation of the codes is that compliance is voluntary rather than mandatory.

In addition to government action, many newspapers have begun to report regularly on the content, presentation, and relative accuracy of campaign advertising. "Ad watches" or "truth boxes," as they are often called, occasionally have led to the retraction or redesign of ads. Despite the efforts of government and the media, however, negative campaign advertising persists because many candidates believe that if done cleverly, it can benefit their campaigns. After all, people may not like negative ads, but they certainly seem to remember them.

Political Consultants   Increasingly sophisticated campaigns have produced a new occupational specialty: political consulting. Individuals with expertise in polling, direct mail, fundraising, advertising, and campaign management hire themselves out to candidates. The occupation is undoubtedly here to stay, and several colleges and universities now offer degree programs in practical politics and campaign management.

Consultants form the core of the professional campaign management team assembled by candidates for state offices. They identify and target likely voters, both those who are already in the candidate's camp but need to be reminded to vote and those who can be persuaded. They use survey research and focus groups to find out what the public is thinking. They carefully craft messages to appeal to specific subsets of voters, such as the elderly, homeowners, and environmentalists. Advertising on cable television and through direct mail are two popular means of getting a candidate's message to targeted segments of the voting public.

Any number of factors can influence the result of an election, such as the presence of an incumbent in a race and the amount of funds a challenger has accumulated, but one significant factor is the ability to frame or define the issues during the campaign. Even in a quietly contested state legislative race, district residents are likely to receive mailings that state the candidate's issue positions, solicit funds, and perhaps comment unfavorably on the opposition. The candidate who has an effective political consultant to help set the campaign agenda and thereby put her opponent on the defensive is that much closer to victory.

Campaign Finance

To campaign for public office is to spend money—a lot of money. How do you define "a lot"? Return to the 2002 Democratic primary for governor of Texas mentioned earlier. The victorious candidate, Tony Sanchez, spent more than $20 million for the chance to face the Republican incumbent in the general election.[52] Much of the money came from Sanchez's own personal fortune. And big spending is not confined to gubernatorial contests. Expenditures in state legislative races topped the $1 billion mark for the first time in 2000.[53]

Just how important is money? One knowledgeable observer concluded: "In the direct primaries, where self-propelled candidates battle for recognition, money is crucial. Electronic advertising is the only way to gain visibility. Hence the outcome usually rewards the one with the largest war chest."[54] This does not bode well for an idealistic but underfunded potential candidate. Winning takes money, either the candidate's or someone else's. If the latter, it may come with a string or two attached. And as noted earlier, that is the real concern: To what extent do campaign contributions buy access and influence for the contributor?

Recent research has confirmed several long-standing truths about the costs of campaigning.[55] For instance, close elections cost more than elections in which one candidate is sure to win, since uncertainty regarding the outcome is a spur to spending. A candidate quickly learns that it is easier to get money from potential contributors when the polls show that she has a chance of winning. Also, elections that produce change—that is, in which an incumbent is unseated or the out-party gains the office—typically cost more. Taking on an existing officeholder is a risky strategy that drives up election costs. And an open race in which there is no incumbent represents an opportunity for the party out of office to capture the seat, thus triggering similar spending by the in-party in an effort to protect the seat. It is no wonder that campaign costs continue to rise.

Major candidates, especially incumbents, do not have to look too hard to find campaign money. As noted earlier, PACs loom larger and larger as heavy funders of state election campaigns. Data from legislative races in seventeen states show that PACs contribute heavily to incumbents.[56] In Utah, incumbent legislators rely on PACs for approximately 70 percent of their campaign funds; in Kansas, 66 percent. In Minnesota, however, PAC funding accounts for only 11 percent of an incumbent's funds.

State Efforts at Campaign Reform   Concern over escalating costs and the influence of wealthy special interests in campaigns has led reform groups such as Common Cause to call for improved state laws to provide comprehensive and timely disclosure of campaign finances; impose limitations on contributions by individuals and groups; create a combined public-private financing mechanism for primaries and general elections; and establish an independent commission to enforce tough sanctions on violators of campaign finance laws.

States have performed impressively on the first of these recommendations; in fact, all states have some sort of campaign-financing reporting procedure. In response to the fourth recommendation, twenty-six states have established independent commissions to oversee the conduct of campaigns, although they have found it somewhat difficult to enforce the law and punish violators. One study of state election commissions identified only four—in California, Connecticut, Florida, and New Jersey—as displaying "consistency and vigor" in their enforcement behavior.[57]

The other recommendations have proved more troublesome. States have grappled with the issue of costly campaigns but have made only modest progress in controlling costs. A 1976 decision by the U.S. Supreme Court in *Buckley* v. *Valeo* made these efforts more difficult: The Court ruled that governments cannot limit a person's right to spend money in order to spread his views on particular issues and candidates. In essence, then, a candidate has unlimited power to spend his own money on his own behalf, and other individuals may spend to their hearts' content to promote their own opinions on election-related issues. In 1996, in a lawsuit from Colorado, the Court decided that independent spending by political parties, so-called **soft money,** could not be limited, either. (The 2002 federal campaign finance reform law reacts to the Court's ruling by attempting to stem the flow of soft money.) What the Court let stand, however, were state limits on an individual's contributions to candidates and parties; it also ruled that if a candidate accepts public funds, he is then bound by whatever limitations the state may impose.

soft money
Unregulated funds contributed to national political parties.

Some states have established actual limits on the amount of money that organizations and individuals can contribute to a political race. In New York, for example, corporations are limited to a contribution maximum of $5,000 per calendar year, and individuals (other than official candidates) are restricted to $150,000. Florida allows corporations, labor unions, and PACs to contribute a maximum of $500 per candidate. The same limits apply to individuals, excluding the candidate's own contributions. Some states, such as Arizona, Connecticut, North Dakota, Pennsylvania, and Rhode Island, have gone even further by prohibiting contributions from corporations and labor unions.[58] But a totally different philosophy pervades the politics of a large number of states that continue to operate their election systems without any limitations on contributions. In Illinois, Missouri, and Utah, to name just a few, organizations and individuals can contribute as much as they wish.

States have also considered the other side of the campaign-financing equation: expenditures. Virtually all states require candidates and political committees to file reports documenting the expenditure of campaign funds. Although a few states continue to impose limits on a candidate's total expenditures, many have followed Hawaii's lead and set voluntary spending limits. Colorado, for example, has adopted a nonbinding $2 million spending cap for gubernatorial candidates. Michigan takes a different approach. There, gubernatorial candidates can raise up to $2 million, which is then matched with $1.1 million in public funding. Florida and Kentucky have similar systems in place for candidates receiving public funds. In just over half of the states, however, candidates campaign without any spending limits.

Public Funding as a Solution   Almost half the states have begun experimenting with public funding of campaigns. Individuals voluntarily contribute to a central fund, which is divided among candidates or political parties. The system is fairly easy to administer. In most of the public-funding states, citizens can use their state income tax form to earmark a portion (a dollar or two) of their tax liability for the fund. A checkoff system of this sort does not directly increase taxpayers' tax burden. In a few states, the public fund is amassed through a voluntary surcharge or an additional tax (usually $1, although California allows surcharges of $5, $10, and $25). Indiana has opted for an alternate approach: Revenues from the sale of personalized motor vehicle license plates support the fund.

In addition to checkoffs and surcharges, some of the public-funding states, including Minnesota and Ohio, offer taxpayers a tax credit (usually 50 percent of the contribution, up to a specific maximum) when they contribute to political campaigns. A more popular supplement to public funding is a state-tax deduction for campaign contributions, as used in Hawaii, Oklahoma, and North Carolina. A final though not widely explored approach is direct state appropriation of funds. Maryland, for instance, does not use checkoffs or surcharges but relies instead on a direct state appropriation to candidates for governor and lieutenant governor.[59]

Public campaign financing is supposed to rid the election process of some of its evils. Proponents argue that it will democratize the contribution process by freeing candidates from excessive reliance on special-interest money. Other possible advantages include expanding the pool of potential candidates, allowing candidates to compete on a more equal basis, and reducing the cost of campaigning.[60] A study of legislative races in Wisconsin indicated that as a proportion of total contributions, public dollars increased and PAC money declined.[61] By contributing to the fund, average citizens may feel that they have a greater stake in state elections. Citizen action, for example, led to Maine's approval in 1996 of an initiative that provides full public funding of campaigns for candidates who demonstrate grassroots support, agree to spending limits, and promise to forego private money. Voters in Arizona and Massachusetts approved similar "Clean Money Campaign Reform" measures in 1998.[62] In their efforts to regulate the role of money in campaigns, states can learn from a recent study of campaign finance reform. Public financing in combination with spending limits was found to be more effective in controlling spending than were contribution limits.[63]

Chapter Recap

➤ The past two decades have seen a growth in two-party competition. The number of Republican party identifiers has increased, as has Republican control of state institutions.

➤ Although many observers have predicted the decline of the two major parties, they have proved remarkably resilient. Third parties continue to enjoy only sporadic success.

➤ Interest groups exert a powerful force in state government, with business lobbyists and teachers' groups the most influential in the majority of states.

➤ The state interest-group system is changing: A more diverse set of interests lobbies at the state capital. Meanwhile, state governments have tightened their regulation of lobbyists.

➤ Campaigns for state and local offices still involve door-to-door canvassing, neighborhood "drop-ins," and public forums, but candidates increasingly use direct mail, electronic media, and political consultants.

➤ Running for public office can be an expensive proposition. To try to level the playing field and diminish the role of private money, most states limit contributions; many states provide public financing.

Key Terms

responsible party model (*p. 92*)
ticket splitting (*p. 92*)
pragmatism (*p. 94*)
unified government (*p. 97*)
divided government (*p. 97*)
dealignment (*p. 98*)

interest group (*p. 98*)
lobbying (*p. 104*)
grassroots lobbying (*p. 106*)
political action committee (PAC) (*p. 106*)
direct action (*p. 107*)
soft money (*p. 112*)

Surfing the Net

The major political parties have official websites: The Democrats' site is **www.democrats.org,** and the Republicans' site is **www.rnc.org.** These sites contain links to state-level party organizations. Some of the more interesting third-party websites are at the state level, such as the Green Party of California's **www.cagreens.org.** The organization known as Common Cause has a website devoted to state politics, especially campaign finance reform. That site is located at **www.commoncause.org/states/states.htm.** Another group devoted to cleaning up elections is Public Campaign, at **www.publicampaign.org.** For two different points of view, check out the websites for the American Civil Liberties Union, **www.aclu.org,** and the Christian Coalition, **www.cc.org.**

6

STATE LEGISLATURES

The Essence of Legislatures

Legislative Dynamics
The Senate and the House » Legislative Districts » Legislative Compensation » Legislative Leadership » Legislative Committees

Legislative Behavior
Legislative Norms » Legislative Cue-Taking

How a Bill Becomes Law (or Not)

Legislative Reform and Capacity
The Ideal Legislature » The Effects of Reform » Term Limits

Relationship with the Executive Branch
Dealing with the Governor » Overseeing the Bureaucracy

Legislatures and Capacity

These days, channel surfers may encounter unusual images as they check out one television channel after another. There, amid *Survivor* and *JAG,* is the state legislature. Nineteen states have made provisions to televise some or all of the legislative proceedings. Debate on the floor, testimony in committees, and reports of the staff are just some of the programming features. States vary as to whether the coverage is gavel-to-gavel (as in Minnesota) or limited to certain hours (as in Oregon); live (as in New Jersey) or tape-delayed (as in Nevada); produced by the legislature (as in California) or contracted out (as in Hawaii); available statewide (as in Kansas) or in limited markets (as in Ohio). Regardless of the variations, the legislature is making its way into citizens' living rooms. The rationale behind the programming is simple: to make the work of the legislature accessible to the public.[1] And the public just may be surprised by what it sees.

The Essence of Legislatures

The New Year dawns quietly in Boise, Idaho; Jefferson City, Missouri; and Harrisburg, Pennsylvania. But it does not remain quiet for long: State legislators are set to converge on their state capitol. Every January (or February or March in a few states; every other January in some others), state legislatures reconvene in session to do the public's business. More than seven thousand legislators hammer out solutions to intricate and often intransigent public problems.

Legislatures engage in three principal functions: *policymaking, representation,* and *oversight.* The first, policymaking, includes enacting laws and allocating funds. The start of the twenty-first century found legislators debating such issues as election reform, biotechnology, and urban sprawl. These deliberations resulted in the revision of old laws, the passage of new laws, and changes in spending. This is what policymaking is all about. Legislatures do not have sole control of the state policymaking function; governors, courts, and agencies also determine policy, through executive orders, judicial decisions, and administrative regulations, respectively. Nevertheless, legislatures are the dominant policymaking institutions in state government. Table 6.1 lists issues that attracted legislative attention in 2002. At the top of the agenda in most states was the budget crunch.

In their second function, legislators are expected to represent their constituents—the people who live in their district—in two ways. At least in theory, they are expected to speak for their constituents in the state capitol—to do "the will of the public" in designing policy solutions. This is not an easy task. On "quiet" issues, a legislator seldom has much of a clue as to what the public's will is. Moreover, on "noisy" issues, constituents' will is rarely unanimous. Individuals and organized groups with different perspectives may write to or visit their legislator to urge her to vote a certain way on a pending bill. In another representative function, legislators act as their constituents' facilitators in state government. For example, they may help a citizen deal with an unresponsive state agency. This kind of constituency service, or casework, as it is often called, can pay dividends at reelection time: Voters tend to look favorably on a legislator who has helped them out.[2]

The oversight function is one that legislatures took on in the 1980s. Concerned that the laws they passed and the funds they allocated frequently did not produce the intended effect, lawmakers began to pay more attention to the performance of the state bureaucracy. Legislatures have adopted a number of methods for checking up on agency implementation and spending. The oversight role takes legislatures into the administrative realm and, not surprisingly, is little welcomed by agencies, although legislatures see it as a logical extension of their policymaking role.

| TABLE 6.1 | Popular Legislative Issues in 2002 |

ISSUE	WHAT IT'S ALL ABOUT
The budget crunch	State revenues fell below expected levels; legislators had to determine which services and programs would be cut.
Antiterrorism	Security and public health concerns loomed large after the 9/11 attacks and the anthrax scare.
Welfare reform	With demand for welfare benefits rising amid falling revenues, legislators faced choosing which programs to curtail.
Medicaid costs	As costs of the health program continue to skyrocket, states looked for ways to contain increases in the cost of prescription drugs.
The power grid	Legislators debated issues surrounding deregulation of the industry.
Education and schools	A range of issues emerged, including funding, testing, accountability, teacher preparation, and school leadership.
Protection of privacy	New e-technologies raised questions about protecting consumer privacy.
Election reform	Legislators tackled topics such as voting machines, ballot design, recount standards, and voter registration lists.
Immigration issues	The ability of immigrants to get driver's licenses and identification cards came under scrutiny.
Genetics and biotech	Advances in cloning and genetic testing produced new debates over regulation.

SOURCE: Adapted from Melissa Conradi and Alan Greenblatt, "Ten Issues to Watch," *Governing* (January 2002): 24–25. Reprinted with permission, *Governing Magazine.* Copyright © 2002.

Legislative Dynamics

State legislative bodies are typically referred to as "the legislature," but their formal titles vary. In Colorado, the General Assembly meets every year; in Massachusetts, the General Court; and in Oregon, the Legislative Assembly. The legislatures of forty-four states meet annually; in six (Arkansas, Montana, Nevada, North Dakota, Oregon, and Texas), they meet every two years. (Kentucky had been among the biennial session group until 2000, when voters approved a switch to annual legislative sessions.) The length of the legislative session varies widely. For example, the Indiana General Assembly convened in Indianapolis on January 7, 2002, and adjourned nine weeks later. In states like Michigan and New Jersey, legislative sessions run nearly year-round.

The length of a state's legislative session can be a sensitive issue. In 1997, the Nevada legislature met for 169 days—the longest, most expensive session in its history.[3] Nevadans showed their displeasure the following year when they passed a measure limiting future legislative sessions to 120 days. Evidently in the public's view, it should not take more than four months—every two years—to conduct their state's business.

The Senate and the House

State legislatures have two houses or chambers, similar to those of the U.S. Congress. Forty-nine states are bicameral. (As noted in Chapter 3, the exception is Nebraska, which in 1934 established a unicameral legislature.) Bicameralism owes its existence to the postcolonial era, in which an "upper house" represented the interests of the propertied class, and a "lower house" represented everyone else. Even after this distinction was eliminated, states stuck with the bicameral structure, ostensibly because of its contribution to the concept of checks and balances. It is much tougher to pass "bad" bills when they have to survive the scrutiny of two legislative houses. Having a bicameral structure, then, reinforces the status quo. Unicameralism might improve the efficiency of the legislature, but efficiency has never been a primary goal of the consensus-building deliberative process.

In the forty-nine bicameral states, the upper house is called the senate; the lower house is usually the house of representatives. The average size of a state senate is 40 members; a house of representatives typically averages about 100 members. As with most aspects of state legislatures, chamber size varies substantially—from the Alaska senate with 20 members to the New Hampshire house with 400 representatives. Chamber size changes only rarely, but in 2001 Rhode Island began implementing a voter mandate that would reduce its 150-member legislature by one-fourth.

For senators, the term of office is usually four years; approximately one-quarter of the states use a two-year senate term. In many states, the election of senators is staggered. House members serve two-year terms, except in Alabama, Louisiana, Maryland, and Mississippi, where four-year terms prevail. As noted in Chapter 4, the 2002 elections shifted the partisan balance in state institutions. In state legislatures, the Republican party was the primary beneficiary of the public's changed mood. Voters put Republicans in control of both legislative chambers in twenty-one states. Democrats dominated both chambers in eighteen states. Ten states were split with one party in control of each chamber. This round of elections saw a relatively high degree of legislative turnover due to the combined impact of term limits and redistricting.

There are 7,424 state legislators in this country: 1,984 senators and 5,440 representatives. Overall, the proportion of Democrats and Republicans is similar at around 49 percent (with the remaining seats held by other parties); men outnumber women 78 to 22 percent. Legislatures are becoming more racially and ethnically diverse. African Americans occupy 7 percent of all legislative seats, Latinos 2 percent, Asian Americans 1 percent, and Native Americans .5 percent. Yet even these small proportions of women and racial-ethnic minorities represent a substantial increase relative to their virtual absence from most pre-1970s legislatures. In terms of occupations, attorneys remain the single largest occupational category (16 percent). Full-time lawmakers constitute the next largest category (15 percent), followed by business owners (10 percent), farmers (8 percent), and retirees (7 percent).[4]

Legislative Districts

Legislators are elected from geographically based districts. Each district has approximately the same number of inhabitants. In Nebraska, for instance, each member of the unicameral legislature represents 32,210 people, more or less. Dividing or apportioning a state into districts is an intensely political process. These decisions affect the balance of power in a state. In the 1960s, for example, the less populated panhandle area of Florida was overrepresented in the legislature at the expense of the heavily populated southern areas of the state. The balance of power lay with the northern rural regions. Therefore, despite Florida's rapid urbanization during that period, public policy continued to reflect the interests of a rurally based minority.

malapportionment
Skewed legislative districts that violate the "one person, one vote" ideal.

Malapportionment **Malapportionment,** or unequal representation, has characterized many legislative bodies. In the past, for example, some states allocated an equal number of senators to each county. (This system calls to mind the U.S. Senate, which has two senators per state.) Because counties vary in population size, some senators were representing ten or twenty times as many constituents as their colleagues were. New Jersey offered one of the most extreme cases. In 1962, one county contained 49,000 residents and another had 924,000; yet each county was allotted one senator, and each senator had one vote in the senate.[5] This kind of imbalance meant that a small group of people had the same institutional power as a group that was nineteen times larger. Such disproportionate power is inherently at odds with representative democracy, in which each person's vote carries the same weight.

Until the 1960s, the federal courts ignored the legislative malapportionment issue. It was not until 1962, in a Tennessee case in which the malapportionment was especially egregious (house district populations ranged from 2,340 to 42,298), that the courts stepped in. In that case, *Baker* v. *Carr,* the U.S. Supreme Court applied the Fourteenth Amendment guarantee of equal protection to state legislative apportionment.[6] With this decision as a wedge, the Court ruled that state legislatures should be apportioned on the basis of population. Two years later, in *Reynolds* v. *Sims* (1964), Chief Justice Earl Warren summed up the apportionment ideal by saying, "Legislators represent people, not trees or acres."[7] Accordingly, districts should reflect population equality: one person, one vote. In the aftermath of this decision, which overturned the apportionment practices of six states, a **reapportionment** fever swept the country, and district lines were redrawn in every state.

reapportionment
The redrawing of legislative district lines to conform as closely as possible to the "one person, one vote" ideal.

Reapportionment provided an immediate benefit to previously underrepresented urban areas, and increased urban representation led to a growing responsiveness in state legislatures to the problems and interests of cities and suburbs. Where reapportionment had a partisan effect, it generally benefited

Republicans in the South and Democrats in the North. Other impacts of reapportionment have included the election of younger, better-educated legislators and, especially in southern states, better representation of blacks.[8] In addition, state legislatures, in the opinion of those who served during the reapportionment period of 1967–1977, took a discernibly liberal turn.[9] All in all, reapportionment is widely credited with improving the representativeness of American state legislatures.

Reapportionment and Redistricting After the 2000 Census   State legislatures are reapportioned following the U.S. census, which is taken every ten years. Redistricting allows population fluctuations—growth in some areas, decline in others—to be reflected in redrawn district lines. Thirty-six legislatures redistrict themselves; twelve states attempt to depoliticize the process by using impartial commissions to develop their redistricting plans.[10] In two states, Alaska and Maryland, the governor plays a dominant role in redistricting.

District lines have traditionally been redrawn to maximize the strength of the party in power. The art of drawing district lines creatively was popularized in Massachusetts in 1812, when a political cartoonist for the *Boston Gazette* dubbed one of Governor Elbridge Gerry's district creations a **gerrymander** because the district, carefully configured to reflect partisan objectives, was shaped like a salamander. Gerrymandering has not disappeared. Political parties poured record sums of money into the 2000 state legislative elections, in large part because of looming reapportionment. The party controlling the legislature controls the districting process. When the Republicans gained control of the Kentucky senate, the Republican chair of the redistricting committee stated his philosophy this way: "Any party that's in control, charity begins at home."[11]

gerrymander
The process of creatively designing a legislative district to enhance the electoral fortunes of the party in power.

Mississippi lawmakers examine a series of maps outlining new legislative districts. (AP/Wide World Photos)

Redistricting has become a sophisticated operation in which statisticians and geographers use computer mapping to assist the legislature in designing an optimal districting scheme. Although "one person, one vote" is the official standard, some unofficial guidelines are also taken into consideration. Ideally, districts should be geographically compact and unbroken. Those who draw the lines pay close attention to traditional political boundaries such as counties and, as noted, to the fortunes of political parties and incumbents. As long as districts adhere fairly closely to the population-equality standard (if a **multimember district** contains three seats, it must have three times the population of a single-member district), federal courts tolerate the achievement of unofficial objectives. But redistricting does make for some oddly shaped districts resembling lobsters, spiders, and earmuffs.[12]

Increasingly, legislatures have to pay attention to the effects of their redistricting schemes on racial minority voting strength. In fact, amendments to the Voting Rights Act and subsequent court rulings instructed affected states to create some districts in which racial minorities would have majority status. After years of designing districts to minimize the political power of blacks, legislatures were forced by the courts to change their ways. States throughout the South spent the decade of the 1990s drawing and redrawing district lines to satisfy the courts. In Texas, a state covered under the Voting Rights Act, minority groups and Republicans challenged the reapportionment plan passed by the Democratic-controlled legislature. Eventually, a federal court substituted its own redistricting map in place of the plan designed by the Texas legislature. By carving out more black and Latino districts, the judicial plan boosted Republican fortunes as well. In other words, "packing" minorities into districts diluted the Democratic vote of nearby districts, thereby allowing more Republicans to win legislative seats.[13]

Redistricting after the 2000 census is proving to be somewhat different. States still have to achieve the one person, one vote standard, of course, but partisanship may play an even greater role in the wake of a U.S. Supreme Court decision. In *Easley* v. *Cromartie* (2001), the Court ruled that reliance on partisan considerations is an appropriate redistricting option. As one expert, political scientist Ronald Weber, put it, the strategy for line-drawers will be "to determine the best way to waste the vote of the partisans of the other party."[14] Armed with data on voter turnout and partisan preferences, many states have completed the redistricting process. Undoubtedly, many rounds of litigation await.

multimember district
A legislative district that contains more than one seat.

Legislative Compensation

Legislative compensation has increased handsomely in the past two decades, again with some notable exceptions. Before the modernization of legislatures, salary and per diem (money for daily expenses) levels were set in the state constitution and, hence, were impossible to adjust without a constitutional amendment. By the mid-1990s, only four states continued to have constitutional restrictions on legislative compensation.[15] The lifting of these limits put legislatures, as the policymaking branch of state government, in the curious position of setting their own compensation levels. Recognizing that this power is a double-edged sword (the legislators can vote themselves pay raises and the public can turn around and vote them out of office for doing so), almost half of the states have established compensation commissions or advisory groups to make recommendations on legislative remuneration.

As of 2001, annual salaries of legislators (excluding per diem) ranged from a low of $200 in New Hampshire to a high of $99,000 in California. Seventeen states paid their legislators more than $30,000 annually. Compare these figures with the more modest pay levels of legislators in Georgia ($16,200), Idaho ($15,646), and Nebraska ($12,000).[16] Generally, states paying generous compensation typically demand more of a legislator's time than do low-paying states. New Mexico legislators certainly cannot be accused of seeking elective office for the money. There, legislators receive no salary. What, then, is their financial reward for legislative service? One hundred twenty-four dollars per day for living expenses while in Santa Fe during the session.

Legislative pay is but a fraction of the cost of operating a legislature. Legislative staff salaries consume a large chunk of the expenditures, as do building maintenance and technological improvements. Unsurprisingly, large states such as California and New York spend the most on their legislatures. However, when legislative costs are calculated on a per capita basis, Alaska is at the top, followed by Hawaii and Rhode Island.[17]

Legislative Leadership

Legislatures need leaders, both formal and informal. Each chamber usually has four formal leadership positions. In the senate, a president and a president pro tempore (who presides in the absence of the president) are in charge of the chamber; in the house, the comparable leaders are the speaker and the speaker pro tempore. These legislative officials are chosen by the members, with voting following party lines. (In some states, the post of senate president is occupied by the lieutenant governor.) Both houses have two political party leadership positions: a majority leader and a minority leader.

The leaders are responsible for making the legislature run smoothly and seeing that it accomplishes its tasks. In a typical chamber, the presiding officer appoints committee members, names committee chairs, controls the activity on the floor, allocates office space and committee budgets, and, in some states, selects the majority leader and the holders of other majority-party posts.[18] The actual influence of the leadership varies from one chamber to another. One factor that affects leaders' power is whether the positions are rotated or retained. Leaders who have the option of retaining their position can build power bases, as did Ohio's Vern Riffe, speaker of the house of representatives from 1975 to 1994. In the case of rotation, however, one set of leaders is replaced with another on a regular basis, so the leaders are lame ducks when they assume the posts. On average, today's leaders are different from the caricatured wheeler-dealers of the past. Successful leaders are those who adapt as the membership changes and the institution evolves.[19]

A good illustration of adaptation was found in the Washington house of representatives in 1999. The chamber was evenly split between the two parties, so to avoid deadlock, a power-sharing arrangement was created. Lawmakers decided to use co-speakers and co-committee chairs. The speakership rotated daily between the Republican leader and the Democratic leader; the committee chairs did likewise.

As political parties become more competitive in the states, legislative behavior and decisions take on a partisan cast. There are Democratic and Republican sides of the chamber and Democratic and Republican positions on bills. The parties meet in caucuses to design their legislative strategies and generate camaraderie. In states where one political party continues to dominate, partisanship is less important. In one-party settings, the dominant party typically develops splits or factions at the expense of party unity. However, when the vastly outnumbered minority party begins to gain strength, the majority party usually becomes more cohesive. In the Texas house, historically a bastion of Democratic party strength, Republicans held about 48 percent of the seats by 2002. As Republican strength grew, the Democrats coalesced and organized a truly partisan Democratic caucus.[20] As a result, legislative voting patterns among Democrats show less factionalization.

In many states, legislative leaders have embraced a new function: fundraising. Leaders tap interest groups and lobbyists for money and divide it among their party's candidates for legislative seats. California has led the way with multimillion-dollar war chests. The amount of money raised is not as great in other states, of course, but it has become a significant source of campaign funding. Lobbyists find it difficult to say "no" to a request for funds from the leadership. The leaders then allocate the funds to the neediest candidates—those in close races. If those candidates are victorious, their loyalty to party leaders pays legislative dividends.

Legislative Committees

The workhorse of the legislature is the committee. Under normal circumstances, a committee's primary function is to consider bills—that is, to hear testimony, perhaps amend the bills, and ultimately approve or reject them. A committee's action on a bill precedes debate in the house or senate.

All legislative chambers are divided into committees, and most committees have created subcommittees. Committees can be of several types. A *standing committee* regularly considers legislation during the session. A *joint committee* is made up of members of both houses. Some joint committees are standing; others are temporary (sometimes called ad hoc, or select, committees) and are convened for a specific purpose, such as investigating a troubled agency or solving a particularly challenging public policy problem. A *conference committee* is a special type of joint committee that is assembled to iron out differences between house- and senate-passed versions of a bill. Most states use *interim committees* during the period when the legislature is not in session to get a head start on an

TABLE 6.2	Standing Committees of the Legislature

Both houses of state legislatures typically have standing committees dealing with these substantive issues:

Agriculture	Government operations
Banking/financial institutions	Health
Business and commerce	Insurance
Communications	Judiciary and criminal justice
Education	Local affairs
Elections	Public employees
Energy	Rules
Environment and natural resources	Social/human services
Ethics	Transportation

In addition, both houses have standing committees that address the raising and allocating of state funds. These committees may have different names in different chambers:

Appropriations
Finance and Taxation
Ways and Means

upcoming session. The number of committees varies, but most senates and houses have standing committees on the issues listed in Table 6.2. Most of these committees, in turn, have professional staffs assigned to them.

A substantive standing committee tends to be made up of legislators who are interested in that committee's subject matter.[21] Thus you would find farmers on the agriculture committee, teachers on the education committee, bankers on the banking committee, lawyers on the judiciary committee, and so on. These legislators bring knowledge and enthusiasm to their committees; however, they also bring a certain bias since they tend to function as advocates for their career interests.

The central concern of a standing committee is its floor success—getting the full chamber to accede to its recommendations on a bill. There are a number of plausible explanations for a committee's floor success.[22] For one thing, a committee with an ideological composition similar to that of the chamber is likely to be more successful than one whose members are at odds with the chamber. Also, committees full of legislatively experienced members generally have more floor success than committees composed of legislative novices. And committees that have a reputation for being tough have more floor success with their bills than committees that are easy and pass everything that comes before them.

Legislative Behavior

Legislatures have their own dynamics, their own way of doing things. Senate and house rule books spell out what can and cannot be done, in the same way that an organization's bylaws do. Legislatures, for the most part, function as self-regulating institutions. It is especially important, therefore, that participants know what is expected of them. To make certain that the chamber's rules are understood, most legislatures conduct orientation sessions for new members.

Legislative Norms

An understanding of the legislature involves not only knowledge of formal structures and written rules but also awareness of informal norms and unwritten policies. For example, nowhere in a state's legislative rules does it say that a freshman legislator is prohibited from playing a leadership role, but the unwritten rules of most legislatures place a premium on seniority. A primary rule of legislative bodies is that "you gotta go along to get along," a phrase that emphasizes teamwork and "paying your dues." Legislators who are on opposite sides of a bill to regulate horse racing might find themselves on the same side of a bill to lower the cost of prescription drugs. Yesterday's opponent is today's partner. For this reason, no one can afford to make bitter enemies in the legislature and expect to flourish.

Those who aspire to rise from rank-and-file legislator to committee chairperson and perhaps to party leader or presiding officer find consensus-building skills quite useful. These skills come in handy because many norms are intended to reduce the potential for conflict in what is inherently a setting full of conflict. For instance, a freshman legislator is expected to defer to a senior colleague. Although an energetic new legislator might chafe under such a restriction, one day he will have gained seniority and will take comfort in the rule. Moreover, legislators are expected to honor commitments made to one another, thus encouraging reciprocity: "If you support me on my favorite bill, I will be with you on yours." A legislator cannot be too unyielding. Compromises, sometimes principled but more often political, are the backbone of the legislative process. Very few bills are passed by both houses and sent to the governor in exactly the same form as when they were introduced.

It is worth noting that the internal organization of legislatures varies, as emphasized in a study of three legislatures—those in New York, Connecticut, and California.[23] New York has a stable organizational system in which seniority is the major criterion for advancement. Empire State legislators tend to be careerists who expect a long tenure in office. In Connecticut, where an unstable system prevails and few career incentives exist, members stay in the legislature a short time and then return to private life. California has an unstable system that is not seniority oriented; therefore, talented legislators can advance quickly. As a result, California legislators tend to be politically ambitious, and the structure allows them to act as entrepreneurs. The informal rules in these three legislatures are quite different, and the institutions tend to attract different types of legislators. Accordingly, the New York legislature is considered career oriented, Connecticut's legislature a dead end, and California's a springboard to higher office.[24]

Informal rules are designed to make the legislative process flow more smoothly. Legislators who cannot abide by the rules, those who refuse to "go along," find it difficult to get along. They are subjected to not-so-subtle behavior modification efforts, such as powerful social sanctions (ostracism and ridicule) and legislative punishment (the bottling up of their bill in committee or their assignment to an unpopular committee), that promote adherence to norms.

Legislative Cue-Taking

Much has been written about how legislators make public policy decisions, and a number of explanations are plausible. Legislators may adopt the policy positions espoused by their political party. They may follow the dictates of their conscience—that is, do what they think is right. They may yield to the pressures of organized interest groups. They may be persuaded by the arguments of other legislators, such as a committee chairperson who is knowledgeable about the policy area or a trusted colleague who is considered to be savvy; or they may succumb to the entreaties of the governor, who has made a particular piece of legislation the focus of her administration. Of course, legislators may also attempt to respond to the wishes of their constituents. On a significant issue—one that has received substantial media attention—they are likely to be subjected to tremendous cross-pressures.

Assuming that legislators are concerned about how a vote will be received back home, it seems logical that they would be particularly solicitous of public opinion. Some research on the subject, however, has shown that state legislators frequently hold opinions at odds with those of their constituents.[25] Moreover, they occasionally misperceive what the public is thinking; at such times it is difficult for them to act as mere **delegates** and simply fulfill the public's will. To improve the communications link, some legislators use questionnaires to poll constituents about their views; others hold town meetings at various spots in the district to assess the public's mood.

delegate
A legislator who functions as a conduit for constituency opinion.

It is quite probable that first-term legislators feel more vulnerable to the whims of the public than legislative veterans do. Hence the new legislator devotes more time to determining what the people want, whereas the experienced legislator "knows" what they want (or perhaps knows what they need) and thus functions as a **trustee**—someone who follows his own best judgment. Since the vast majority of legislators are returned to office election after election, it appears that there is some validity to this argument. Research on Oklahoma and Kansas legislators, for example, found that the members' personal values played a consistently important role in decision choices.[26]

trustee
A legislator who votes according to his or her conscience and best judgment.

In the final analysis, the determining factor in how legislators make decisions depends on the issue itself. On the one hand, "when legislators are deeply in-

politico
A legislator who functions as either a delegate or a trustee, depending on the circumstances.

volved with an issue, they appear to be more concerned with policy consequences" than with constituency preferences.[27] In this situation, the legislators are focused on a goal other than reelection. On the other hand, if the legislators are not particularly engaged in an issue that is important to their constituents, they will follow their constituents' preference. In that sense, they act as **politicos,** adjusting as the issues and cues change.

How a Bill Becomes Law (or Not)

A legislative bill starts as an idea and travels a long, complex path before it emerges as law. It is no wonder that of the 3,331 bills introduced in the Hawaii legislature in 2001, only 316 had become law by the end of the session.[29] A legislative session has a rhythm to it. Minor bills and symbolic issues tend to be resolved early, whereas major, potentially divisive issues take a much longer time to wend their way through the legislative labyrinth. The budget or appropriations bill is typically one of the last matters that the legislature debates during the session.

The lawmaking process has been described in many ways: a zoo, a circus, a marketplace. Perhaps the most apt description is "casino," because there are winners and losers, the outcome is never final, and there is always a new game ahead.[30] Figure 6.1 diagrams a typical lawmaking process, showing at just how many points a bill can be sidetracked.

The diagram of the legislative process shown in this figure cannot convey the dynamism and excitement of lawmaking. (Again, the casino analogy is appropriate.) Ideas for bills are everywhere: Constituents have them, as do interest groups and state agencies. Legislators may turn to their staffs or to other states for ideas. **Policy entrepreneurs,** people who are knowledgeable about certain issues and are willing to promote them, abound. Introducing a bill—"putting it in the hopper," in legislative parlance—is just the beginning.

policy entrepreneur
A person who brings new ideas to a policymaking body.

A bill does not make it through the legislative process without a lot of effort and even a little luck. A bill's chances of passage rise as more legislators sign on as cosponsors. If the cosponsors are legislative leaders, even better. Assignment of the bill to a favorable committee improves the likelihood that the bill will be scheduled for a hearing in a timely manner. (Many bills get bottled up in committee and never receive a hearing.) Strong support from key interest groups is a powerful advantage, as is the emergence of only weak opposition to the bill. Sometimes bill passage is a matter of fortuitous timing. If, for example, the bill provides funding for new prisons at a time when the state's crime rate is climbing, passage is likely to be easier.

Controversial issues such as abortion raise the stakes. The former speaker of the Wisconsin Assembly, Tom Loftus, described abortion politics in his state as "trench warfare" in which compromise was virtually impossible. Leadership on the issue came from legislators who felt strongly about the issue and who held safe seats. (In this instance, "safe" meant that taking a position was not likely to cost them too many votes or generate too many serious challengers when they

FIGURE 6.1 How a Bill Becomes Law

At each of the stages in the process, supporters and opponents of a bill clash. Most bills stall at some point and fail to make it to the end.

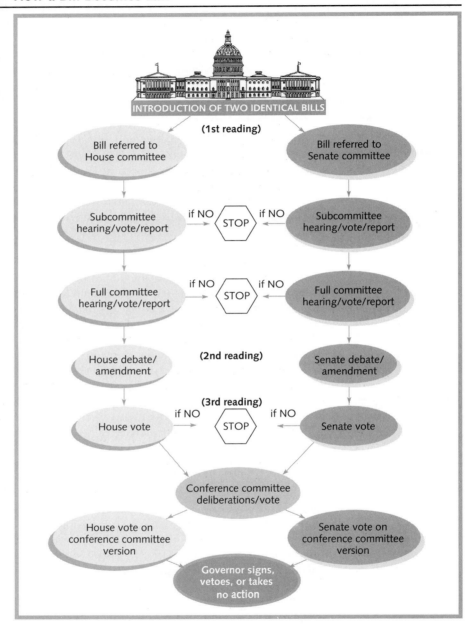

INTRODUCTION OF TWO IDENTICAL BILLS

(1st reading)

Bill referred to House committee — Bill referred to Senate committee

Subcommittee hearing/vote/report — if NO — STOP — if NO — Subcommittee hearing/vote/report

Full committee hearing/vote/report — if NO — STOP — if NO — Full committee hearing/vote/report

(2nd reading)

House debate/amendment — Senate debate/amendment

(3rd reading)

House vote — if NO — STOP — if NO — Senate vote

Conference committee deliberations/vote

House vote on conference committee version — Senate vote on conference committee version

Governor signs, vetoes, or takes no action

ran for reelection.) As anti-abortion bills were introduced, battle lines were drawn. According to the speaker:

> The pro-choice side, which included the Democratic leadership, tried to keep the bill bottled up in committee, and the pro-life side, through political pressure on the Republicans and conservative Democrats, tried to pull it out so the whole Assembly could vote on it on the floor of the chamber. If the pro-life people could get the bill to the floor for a vote, they would win. To accomplish this end, they needed to gain supporters from the pivotal middle group of legislators, usually moderates of both parties from marginal districts.[31]

The powerful anti-abortion group, Wisconsin Citizens Concerned for Life, pressured vulnerable legislators. These legislators were in a tough position because they knew that "regardless of how you voted, you were going to make a slew of single-issue voters mad."[32] Their strategy became one of parliamentary maneuvering and delay.

While bills are making their way (some quickly, some slowly, some not at all) through the legislative labyrinth, other events intervene. The Texas Bankers Association (TBA), the interest group representing bankers in the Lone Star State, pushed a home-equity-lending bill in the 1997 session. As the house was debating the bill, some banks around the state announced surcharges on ATM fees. The angry public reaction was heard by lawmakers; despite TBA's attempt to defuse the issue, very unfavorable amendments were attached to the home-equity bill.[33]

Even if a bill is successful in one chamber, potential hurdles await in the other chamber. Representatives and senators may see the same issue in very different terms. In Ohio in 1997, everyone agreed that the state's system for funding public education needed reform. (The Ohio Supreme Court had found the state's school-funding system unconstitutional and had given the legislature one year to devise a new system.) But initial efforts derailed when the house and senate could not agree on a plan. The senate approved a funding package that would have increased the sales tax, provided debt financing, and allowed local school boards to propose property tax increases.[34] The house, dominated by Republicans who had signed an antitax pledge the preceding year, approved a bill that did not include tax hikes. Each chamber rejected the other's plan. Hammering out a compromise agreeable to both chambers took a long time, even with the court's order as a spur to action.

Once conference or concurrence committees resolve differences and agreement is secured in both chambers, then the bill is enrolled (certified and signed) and sent to the governor. The governor may do one of three things: (1) sign the act (once passed, a bill is called an "act") into law, (2) veto it (in which case the legislature has a chance to have the last word by overriding the veto), or (3) take no action. If the governor does not take action and the session has ended, then in most states the act will become law without the governor's signature. Why not simply sign it if it is going to become law anyway? Sometimes it is a matter of political symbolism for the governor. In approximately one-third of the states, if the governor does not sign or veto the act and the legislature has adjourned, the act dies. (This outcome is referred to as a pocket veto, a topic discussed in somewhat more detail in the next chapter.)

During its 2001 session, the Hawaii legislature passed only 9 percent of the bills that were introduced. Is this a sign of success or failure? Connecticut's figures are lower than those of most states—20 to 25 percent is a common passage rate—but not necessarily a cause for alarm. Not all bills are good ones, and the inability to generate sufficient consensus among legislators may reflect that condition.

Colorado tried something new in a recent session: a process called "Getting to Yes."[35] A task force representing groups involved in education—teachers and their unions, administrators, school board members, business leaders, and legislators—met before the session to develop bills on evaluating and dismissing teachers. Participants agreed beforehand to focus on goals, not turf. Although the process was not conflict free, it did produce two bills that participants could agree on, thus increasing the likelihood of favorable legislative action.

Legislative Reform and Capacity

It was not easy to get state legislatures where they are today. Well into the 1960s, state legislatures functioned poorly. Malfunctioning legislatures resulted from three conditions: low pay for legislators; brief, biennial sessions; and insufficient staff resources.[36] During the 1970s, fundamental reforms occurred throughout the country as legislatures sought to increase their capacity and to become more professional. The modernization process never really ends, however.

The Ideal Legislature

In the late 1960s, the Citizens' Conference on State Legislatures (CCSL) studied legislative performance and identified five characteristics critical to legislative improvement.[37] Ideally, a legislature should be functional, accountable, informed, independent, and representative; the acronym is FAIIR.

The functional legislature has virtually unrestricted time to conduct its business. It is assisted by adequate staff and facilities, and has effective rules and procedures that facilitate the flow of legislation. The accountable legislature's operations are open and comprehensible to the public. The informed legislature manages its workload through an effective committee structure, legislative activities between sessions, and a professional staff; it also conducts regular budgetary review of executive branch activities. The independent legislature runs its own affairs separate from the executive branch. It exercises oversight of agencies, regulates lobbyists, manages conflicts of interest, and provides adequate compensation for its members. Finally, the representative legislature has a diverse membership that effectively represents the social, economic, ethnic, and other characteristics of the constituencies.

CCSL evaluated the fifty state legislatures and scored them according to the FAIIR criteria. The rankings offered a relatively scientific means of comparing one state legislature with another. Overall, the "best" state legislatures were found in California, New York, Illinois, Florida, and Wisconsin. The "worst," in the assessment of CCSL, were those in Alabama, Wyoming, Delaware, North Carolina, and Arkansas.

The CCSL report triggered extensive self-evaluation by legislatures around the country. Most states launched ambitious efforts to reform their legislatures. The results are readily apparent. In terms of the CCSL criteria, states have made tremendous strides in legislative institution building. The evidence of increased professionalism includes more staff support, higher legislative compensation, longer sessions, and better facilities. Many legislatures revamped their committee systems, altered their rules and procedures, and tightened their ethics regulations. The consequences of these actions are state legislatures that are far more FAIIR now than they were thirty years ago.

The Effects of Reform

Today's legislative institutions are different, but are they better? Initial research suggested that legislative professionalism had an independent, positive effect on social welfare policy.[38] In other words, policymaking in professional legislatures seemed to be more responsive to the needs of lower-income citizens. However, subsequent research arrived at a different conclusion: Professionalized legislatures did not seem to affect the direction of state public policy.[39] More recent studies have sought to clarify the relationship between the characteristics of a legislature and its public policy outputs. These studies have led to the recognition that legislative characteristics and a variety of other factors, such as a state's socioeconomic conditions and executive branch strength, affect policy decisions.[40]

The issue of legislative capacity continues to intrigue researchers. Recent analysis has confirmed the link between reformed institutions and legislative capacity. Legislatures that are closer to the FAIIR standards appear to have greater capacity than the remaining "less FAIIR" institutions do.[41] Furthermore, if the CCSL study were repeated today, it would show that the gap between the "best" legislature and the "worst" one has narrowed considerably.

But the legislative reform picture is not unequivocally rosy. Political scientist Alan Rosenthal, who has closely observed legislative reform, warns that "the legislature's recent success in enhancing its capacity and improving its performance may place it in greater jeopardy than before."[42] This prospect certainly was not an intended effect of the reform efforts. Rosenthal's argument is that a constellation of demands pulls legislators away from the legislative core. That is, the new breed of legislator gets caught up in the demands of reelection, constituent service, interest groups, and political careerism, and thus neglects institutional matters such as structure, procedure, staff, image, and community. The legislature as an institution suffers because it is not receiving the necessary care and attention from its members. Minnesota's highly reformed legislature performed poorly in the mid-1990s, mired in a period of bitter partisanship and personal scandal. Some observers blame reform.[43]

Consider the idea of a citizen-legislator, one for whom service in the legislature is a part-time endeavor. Since the onset of reform, the proportion of legislators who are lawyers, business owners, or insurance or real estate executives has dropped from almost one-half to slightly more than one-third.[44] This development has been accompanied by a rise in the number of full-time legislators. In states such as Michigan, Pennsylvania, and Wisconsin, roughly two-thirds of the lawmakers identify themselves as "legislators" having no other occupation. The critical issue is whether the decline of the citizen-legislator is a desirable aspect of modernization. Should a state legislature represent a broad spectrum of vocations, or should it be composed of career politicians? One perspective is this: "If I'm sick, I want professional help. I feel the same way about public affairs. I want legislators who are knowledgeable and professional."[45] Another view is represented by a Michigan legislator who believes that his careerist colleagues have lost touch with their constituents: "When you spend all your time in Lansing, you're more influenced by the lobbyists than by your constituents."[46] In effect, state legislatures are becoming more like the U.S. Congress. Legislators are staying in the legislature in record numbers. Modernization has made the institution more attractive to its members, so turnover rates are declining. But do we really want fifty mini-Congresses scattered across the land? Today's legislatures are more FAIIR than in the past, but reform has also brought greater professionalization of the legislative career, increased polarization of the legislative process, and more fragmentation of the legislative institution.[47] Figure 6.2 shows the pattern of citizen, professional, and "hybrid" state legislatures. The hybrid category reflects legislative changes that stop short of professionalization.

Change continues in state legislatures, but lately it has been cloaked in an anti-reform guise. Term limits are, of course, a major component in the effort to limit the legislature. And there are others. Voters in Louisiana registered their opposition to legislative reform by approving a constitutional amendment in 1993 that cut the length and limited the focus of even-year legislative sessions in that state. Now, in even-numbered years, the legislature is restricted to a thirty-day session that addresses only fiscal issues.[48] North Dakota, in the meantime, is trying to improve its legislature without sacrificing its part-time citizen-legislator tradition.

To some analysts, the reforms of the past two decades have produced a legislative monster. Richard Nathan, a veteran observer of the states, argues that the key to increased government productivity is the empowerment of the governor.[49] Therefore, the legislative Godzilla must be contained. Nathan advocates term limits, unicameral legislative bodies, rotation of committee memberships, and reduction of legislative staff and sessions as a means of reining in the legislature vis-à-vis the governor. If adopted, Nathan's recommendations would undo thirty-five years of legislative reform. And the governor's hand would be significantly strengthened. The legislative-gubernatorial nexus receives further analysis in a later section of this chapter.

Term Limits

In September 1990, Oklahoma voters took an action that has sent state legislatures reeling. Oklahomans overwhelmingly approved a ballot measure limiting the tenure of state legislators and statewide officers. As it turned out, limiting

FIGURE 6.2   **Legislatures: Three Flavors**

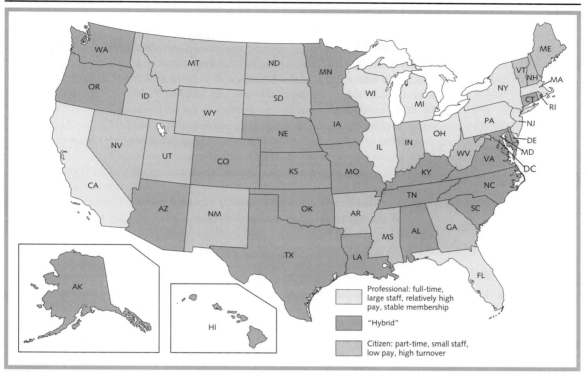

Professional: full-time, large staff, relatively high pay, stable membership

"Hybrid"

Citizen: part-time, small staff, low pay, high turnover

SOURCE: Used with permission from National Conference of State Legislatures; as appeared in Charles Mahtesian, "The Sick Legislature Syndrome," *Governing* 10 (February 1997): 20.

terms was not just a "Sooner" thing. Within two months, voters in California and Colorado had followed suit. With a close defeat in Washington State slowing it only slightly, the term-limits movement swept the country like a tidal wave. In Oregon, a group called LIMITS (Let Incumbents Mosey into the Sunset) grew out of a tax-limitation organization. In Wisconsin, a coalition known as "Badgers Back in Charge" took up the cause of term limitation. And political activists of many stripes—populists, conservatives, and libertarians—found a home in the term-limitation movements in Florida, Michigan, and Texas.[50] By 1996, twenty-one states had slapped limits on legislative terms. The term-limits laws eventually bore the intended fruit: More than 330 legislators in eleven states were barred from seeking reelection in 2002.

In most states, the measure limits service in each chamber separately. In Maine, for example, a legislator is limited to eight years in the house and eight years in the senate. It is quite possible, then, that an individual could serve a total of sixteen years in the legislature under this plan. In a few states, the restriction is on total legislative service. In Oklahoma, for instance, the limitation is twelve years, whether in the house, in the senate, or in a combination of the two.

Some term limits are for a lifetime (as in Arkansas and Nevada); others simply limit the number of consecutive terms (e.g., Ohio and South Dakota).

Limiting legislative terms has captured the fancy of a public angry with entrenched politicians. The measure offers voters a chance to strike back at an institution perceived as self-serving and out of touch. In California, for example, power brokers like Willie Brown—the speaker of the assembly and self-described "ayatollah" of the legislature—became symbols of legislative arrogance. (Term-limited in the state assembly, Brown was elected mayor of San Francisco in 1995.) Opponents of term limits have not been very successful in swaying public opinion. On a theoretical level, they argue that term limits rob voters of their right to choose their representatives. They contend that these measures unfairly disqualify a subset of the population—legislators—from seeking office. And, finally, they claim that term limits are unnecessary. Survey data show that, nationwide, three-quarters of the representatives and senators holding office in 1979 had left their respective chambers by 1989.[51]

Term limits appear to have several potential consequences. First, the domination of a chamber by powerful entrenched veteran legislators will end. Second, in any one session, the proportion of first-termers is likely to be substantial. These two consequences mean that the distribution of power within a legislature will fluctuate.[52] Term-limited legislators grouse that inexperienced newcomers are taking on leadership roles before they are "ready." Third, groups that have been underrepresented in the legislature, especially women and minorities, may have greater electoral opportunities because of the guarantee of open seats. (It should be noted, however, that preliminary research on that point is mixed.[53]) A fourth consequence is more ominous for the legislature: a shift in power to the governor and to lobbyists.[54] Term limits have changed the nature of the legislative process. Some have gone so far as to call it "a revolution in state legislatures."[55] The exodus of veteran legislators and the influx of inexperienced members have some observers shaking their heads in dismay. Data from term-limited Maine, Oregon, and California reflect procedural difficulties, a slower-working institution, and less deliberation in committees.[56] For affected legislatures, one solution has been to increase the amount of training new legislators receive. Another has been to increase the role of legislative staff. Replacing the lost institutional memory is a critical issue.

Popular though they may be, term limits may, in some instances, be unconstitutional. Courts in Massachusetts and Washington overturned term-limiting laws in those states in the late 1990s. In 2002, the Oregon Supreme Court ruled that the wording of the ballot measure imposing term limits violated the state constitution and, therefore, the law was voided. And in a surprising move, the Idaho legislature in 2002 repealed the term-limits law that was adopted via the initiative process in 1994. Idaho's governor had vetoed the repeal legislation but the legislature mustered sufficient votes to override the veto. Stung by the legislature's action, term-limits supporters immediately began circulating petitions to put the question on the ballot.[57] Table 6.3 compares the term-limits provisions of the states where the laws remain in force.

TABLE 6.3	Term Limits in the States					
STATE	**YEAR ADOPTED**	**SENATE**	**HOUSE**	**YEAR LAW TAKES EFFECT**	**REFERENDUM VOTE**	**BALLOT STATUS**
Arizona	1992	8	8	2000	74 to 26	Initiative
Arkansas	1992	8	6	2000/1998	60 to 40	Initiative
California	1990	8	6	1998/1996	52 to 48	Initiative
Colorado	1990	8	8	1998	71 to 29	Initiative
Florida	1992	8	8	2000	77 to 23	Initiative
Louisiana	1995	12	12	2007	76 to 24	Referendum
Maine	1993	8	8	1996	67 to 33	Indirect Initiative
Michigan	1992	8	6	2002/1998	59 to 41	Initiative
Missouri	1992	8	8	2002	74 to 26	Initiative
Montana	1992	8	8	2000	67 to 33	Initiative
Nebraska	2000	8	—	2008	56 to 44	Initiative
Nevada	1994	12	12	2006	70 to 30	Initiative
Ohio	1992	8	8	2000	66 to 34	Initiative
Oklahoma	1990	12	12	2002	67 to 33	Initiative
South Dakota	1992	8	8	2000	63 to 37	Initiative
Utah[a]	1994	12	12	2006	—	
Wyoming	1992	12	12	2004	77 to 23	Indirect Initiative

[a]The legislature adopted term limits in Utah, thus the question did not appear on the ballot.

SOURCE: State Legislative Term Limits (2001), http://www.termlimits.org and the Council of State Governments, *The Book of the States, 1998–1999* (1998); updated by the authors.

Relationship with the Executive Branch

In Chapter 7, you will read about strong governors leading American states boldly into the twenty-first century. In this chapter, you have read about strong legislatures charting a course for that same century. Do these institutions ever collide in their policymaking? Is there conflict between the legislature and the governor in a state? Of course there is. In the words of one observer, "Conflict is the chief manifestation of a new calculus of political and institutional power in state government today."[58]

Tension between the executive and legislative branches is inevitable, but it is not necessarily destructive. It is inevitable because both governors and legislators think that they know what is best for the state. It is not necessarily destructive because during the posturing, bargaining, and negotiating that produces a consensus, governors and legislators may actually arrive at the "best" solution.

Dealing with the Governor

The increased institutional strength of the legislature and its accompanying assertiveness have made for strained relations with a governor accustomed to being the political star. When a legislature is dominated by one party and the governor is of the other party, a condition referred to as divided government, the ingredients for conflict are assembled. This is a fairly new phenomenon in the Democratic-dominated southern states, which elected their first Republican governors since Reconstruction during the 1970s (in the Carolinas and Texas), 1980s (in Alabama and Louisiana), and 1990s (in Mississippi). In some states in the Rocky Mountain area, the reverse was the case. During the 1980s, popular Democratic governors and Republican-dominated legislatures governed Arizona, Colorado, Utah, and Wyoming. The product of divided government can be finger-pointing and blame shifting.

Having the governor's office and a legislature controlled by the same party does not necessarily make for easy relations, either. In fact, it may actually increase the strain between the two branches. Especially in states where the two parties are competitive, legislators are expected to support the policy initiatives of their party's governor. Yet the governor's proposals may not mesh with individual legislators' attitudes, ambitions, or agendas.

Executives have a media advantage over deliberative bodies such as a legislature. At the national level, we saw media use developed to a veritable art form during the Reagan years, when the media conveyed images of the president as leader and the Congress as a collection of self-interested politicians. A similar situation exists at the state level. The governor is the visible symbol of state government and, as a single individual, fits into a media world of thirty-second sound bites. The Colorado senate president offered an explanation from a distinctly legislative perspective: "We never win in Colorado in the public's eye. We, the legislature, are always the bad guys, and the governor is the white hat, and he has been very successful in making that appeal to the public through the news media."[59] In contrast, media images of the legislature often portray dealmaking, pork barrel politics, and general silliness. "Gotcha" journalism, the term for media efforts to catch public officials in seemingly questionable situations, certainly complicates legislative life.

Another weapon of the governor is the veto. In 1995, the New Mexico legislature found out just how powerful that can be when the Republican governor vetoed 200 bills. That's 200 out of the 424 bills that were passed: 47 percent. A political novice, the governor was thought by some legislators to be "ignorant of the political process."[60] Legislators quickly set about acquainting the governor with the veto override process. It should be noted that the veto-happy governor was reelected in 1998; he vetoed 150 legislative acts the following legislative session.

Sometimes governors who have previously served as legislators seem to have an easier time dealing with the lawmaking institution. For example, former Vermont governor Madeleine Kunin assumed the office after three terms in the legislature and one term as lieutenant governor, "knowing the needs of legislators, the workings of the legislative process, the sensitivities of that process."[61] Usually about two-thirds of the governors have had legislative experience, although the proportion has recently declined.

The legislature is not without its weapons. In recent years a popular battleground has been the state budget. As the New Mexico example showed, if the legislature can muster the votes, it can override a gubernatorial veto. Legislatures have also enacted other measures designed to enhance their control and to reduce the governor's flexibility in budgetary matters.[62] For example, some states now require the governor to get legislative approval of budget cutbacks in the event of a revenue shortfall. Others have limited the governor's power to initiate transfers of funds among executive branch agencies. These actions reflect the continuing evolution of legislative-executive relations.

Overseeing the Bureaucracy

Legislative involvement with the executive branch does not end with the governor. State legislatures are increasingly venturing into the world of state agencies and bureaucrats, with the attitude that "we've authorized the program, we've allocated funds for it, so let's see what's happening." Legislative oversight involves four activities: policy and program evaluation, legislative review of administrative rules and regulations, sunset legislation, and review and control of federal funds received by the state.[63]

Policy and Program Evaluation   Legislatures select auditors to keep an eye on state agencies and departments. In a few states, auditors are independently elected officials. Auditors are more than superaccountants; their job is to evaluate the performance of state programs as to their efficiency and effectiveness (a task sometimes known as the postaudit function). Specifically, they conduct periodic performance audits to measure goal achievement and other indicators of progress in satisfying legislative intent, a process that has been credited with both saving money and improving program performance.[64] In this respect, Virginia's Joint Legislative Audit and Review Commission (JLARC), regarded as a model for the rest of the country, was reinventing government before it became fashionable.[65] Throughout its thirty-year history, JLARC has conducted hundreds of evaluations of state programs. Its work has saved the state millions of dollars. The key to a useful auditing function is strong legislative support (even in the face of audits that turn up controversial findings) and, at the same time, a guarantee of a certain degree of independence from legislative interference.

Legislative Review of Administrative Rules   All state legislatures conduct reviews of administrative rules and regulations, but they vary in the way they do it. They may assign the review function to a special committee (such as a rule review committee) or to a specific legislative agency, or they may incorporate the review function in the budgetary process.

Legislative review is a mechanism through which administrative abuses of discretion can be corrected. Legislative bills frequently contain language to the effect that "the Department of Youth Services shall develop the necessary rules and regulations to implement the provisions of this act." Such language gives the agency wide latitude in establishing procedures and policies. The legislature wants to be certain that in the process, the agency does not overstep its bounds or violate legislative intent. If it is found to have done so, then the legislature can overturn the offending rules and regulations through modification, suspension, or veto, depending on the state.

This issue is a true gray area of legislative-executive relations, and court rulings at both the national and state levels have found the most powerful of these actions, the **legislative veto,** to be an unconstitutional violation of the separation of powers. For example, in 1997 the Missouri Supreme Court declared that the legislature's rule-review process was an unconstitutional intrusion into the executive branch's functions.[66] If legislative vetoes and similar actions are determined to be unconstitutional, more states will return to the traditional means of reviewing agency behavior—through the budgetary process. Increasingly, legislatures are requiring state agencies to furnish extensive data to justify their budget requests, and they can use their financial power to indicate their displeasure with agency rules and regulations.[67]

> **legislative veto**
> An action whereby the legislature overturns a state agency's rules or regulations.

> **sunset laws**
> Statutes that set automatic expiration dates for specified agencies and other organizations.

Sunset Legislation   Half the states have established **sunset laws** that set automatic expiration dates for specified agencies and other organizational structures in the executive branch. An agency can be saved from termination only through an overt renewal action in the legislature. Review occurs anywhere from every two years to every twelve years, depending on individual state statute, and is conducted by the standing committee that authorized the agency or by a committee established for sunset-review purposes (such as a government operations committee). The reviews evaluate the agency's performance and its progress toward achieving its goals.

During the 1970s, sunset legislation was widely hailed as an effective tool for asserting legislative dominion over the executive branch; but more than twenty years' experience with the technique has produced mixed results, and some states have repealed their sunset laws. Agency reviews tend to be time consuming and costly. And the process has become highly politicized in many states, involving not only agencies and legislators but lobbyists as well. One Texas representative commented that she "never saw so many alligator shoes and $600 suits as when some agency is up for sunset review."[68] On the positive side, sunset reviews are said to increase agency compliance with legislative intent. Statistics show that nationwide, only about 13 percent of the agencies reviewed are eventually terminated.[69] Termination is more a threat than an objective reality.

Review and Control of Federal Funds   Since the early 1980s, legislatures have played a more active role in directing the flow of federal funds once they have reached the state. Before this time, the sheer magnitude of federal funds and their potential to upset legislatively established priorities caused great consternation among legislators. The executive branch virtually controlled the disposition of these grant funds by designating the recipient agency and program. In some cases, federal money was used to fund programs that the state legislature did not support. Federal dollars were simply absorbed into the budget without debate and discussion, and legislators were cut out of the loop. By making disbursement of federal funds part of the formal appropriations process, however, legislators have redesigned the loop.

If legislatures are to do a decent job in forecasting state priorities, some control of federal funds is necessary. In the face of reduced federal aid to states, it is critical for legislators to understand the role that federal dollars have played in program operation. When funding for a specific program dries up, it is the legislature's responsibility to decide whether to replace it with state money.

How effectively are legislatures overseeing state bureaucracies? As with so many questions, the answer depends on who is asked. From the perspective of legislators, their controls increase administrative accountability. A survey of legislators in eight states found legislative oversight committees, the postaudit function, and sunset laws to be among the most effective bureaucratic controls available.[70] Another effective device, and one that legislatures use in special circumstances, is legislative investigation of an agency, administrator, or program. But from the perspective of the governor, many forms of legislative oversight are simply meddling and, as such, they undermine the separation of powers.[71]

Legislatures and Capacity

State legislatures are fascinating institutions. Although they share numerous traits, each maintains some uniqueness. Houses and senates have different traditions and styles, even in the same state. As Alan Rosenthal writes, "Legislatures are interwoven in the fabric of their states."[72]

The demands placed on state legislatures are unrelenting. Challenges abound. In these times, the ability of legislatures to function effectively depends on institutional capacity. The extensive modernization that virtually all legislatures underwent in the 1970s is evidence of institutional renewal. Structural reforms and a new breed of legislator have altered state legislatures and are sending them in the direction of increased capacity. How ironic, then, that with all their institutional success, reformed legislatures continue to struggle with their public image.[73]

One real concern is that some state legislatures are being marginalized through a citizen-empowering mechanism, the initiative, and an institution-weakening mechanism, term limits. It is no wonder, then, that in several states, legislators have mounted efforts to increase public knowledge of and respect for the legislative process.

Chapter Recap

➤ The three principal functions of legislatures are policymaking, representation, and oversight.

➤ Reapportionment is a battleground for state legislatures because drawing district lines is a partisan process.

➤ Legislatures operate with their own rules, both formal and informal. Violations of institutional norms result in punishment.

➤ The lawmaking process is a complex one with multiple opportunities for delay and obstruction. Most bills never make it through, and those that do seldom look like they did when they were introduced.

➤ Although legislatures perform more effectively than they used to, seventeen states have legislative term limits in place. Term limits create open seats, thereby increasing competition for legislative seats.

➤ Legislators vie with governors in the policymaking process. Governors have the power to veto, but legislators can override a gubernatorial veto. In addition, the legislature plays several oversight roles with regard to the bureaucracy.

➤ Legislative capacity has increased; at the same time, however, legislatures risk becoming marginalized in states with the initiative process and term limits.

Key Terms

malapportionment *(p. 119)*

reapportionment *(p. 119)*

gerrymander *(p. 120)*

multimember district *(p. 121)*

delegate *(p. 126)*

trustee *(p. 126)*

politico *(p. 127)*

policy entrepreneur *(p. 127)*

legislative veto *(p. 138)*

sunset laws *(p. 138)*

Surfing the Net

To find out what's up in state legislatures, the place to look is the National Conference of State Legislatures, located at **www.ncsl.org.** Most states have created websites that allow citizens to follow the progress of legislation during the session. See, for example, New Mexico's site, **legis.state.nm.us,** or South Dakota's, **http://legis.state.sd.us/index.cfm.** Another interesting website is Project Vote Smart, located at **www.vote-smart.org,** which tracks the performance of political leaders, including state legislators. To learn about model state laws, look at the site for the National Conference of Commissioners on Uniform State Laws, located at **www.nccusl.org.** For up-to-date coverage of the term-limits issue, see **www.termlimits.org.** The Center for Public Integrity is a watchdog organization that scrutinizes—and regularly criticizes—state legislatures. Its website is **http://www.50statesonline.org./dtaweb/home.asp.**

7

GOVERNORS

The Office of Governor
History of the Office » Today's Governors » Getting There:
Gubernatorial Campaigns

The Roles of the Governor: Duties and Responsibilities
Policymaker » Chief Legislator » Chief Administrator »
Ceremonial Leader » Intergovernmental Coordinator »
Economic Development Promoter » Party Leader

Formal Powers of the Governor
Tenure » Appointment Power » Veto Power » Budgetary Power »
Reorganization Power » Staffing Power » The Relevance of the
Formal Powers

Informal Powers
Tools of Persuasion and Leadership » Characteristics of a
Successful Governor

Removal from Office

Other Executive Branch Officials
Attorney General » Lieutenant Governor » Treasurer » Secretary
of State

The Vigor of U.S. Governors

Just a few years ago, the nation's governors were either routinely ignored by Congress or treated like any other of the many supplicants who appear regularly in Washington, D.C., appealing for congressional largess. Today, however, the governors speak with voices of authority on important national policy issues. Although they do not always agree on what they want, the governors have recently been influencing the Congress and president as never before in our history.

For example, the Republican governors played a leading role in nominating and electing Texas governor George W. Bush as president in November 2000. Increasingly, the governors have asserted themselves as a righteous third force. Speaking through the National Governors Association (NGA), they helped forge a path to the first balanced federal budget in a quarter-century. The governors played a major role in shaping federal welfare reform and education reform. And while Congress feuded along partisan lines over virtually all significant issues, the governors preached—and practiced—partisan peacemaking to reach common policy ground with their legislatures. As one respected Capitol commentator observed, "The senators and representatives talk about bills they are trying to pass or defeat, the governors about things they actually have done."[1]

Members of Congress have developed a new respect for the governors' ideas and for their practical knowledge of policies and problems and of how federal actions play out at the state and local levels. Indeed, it is no longer unusual for governors actually to sit at the table to help congressional committees draft laws that are of special consequence to the states.[2] And in the nation's time of need after September 11, 2001, President Bush sought out a sitting governor, Tom Ridge of Pennsylvania, to head up a new cabinet-level agency on domestic security.

The governors' enhanced visibility in the national domestic policy arena is a tribute to their policymaking capacity and responsiveness to common problems affecting the citizens of their respective states. It also reflects recognition of the policy leadership of the states in the U.S. federal system.

The Office of Governor

It has been said that the American governorship was "conceived in mistrust and born in a straitjacket." Indeed, because the excesses of some colonial governors appointed by the English Crown resulted in strong dislike and distrust of executive power by the early American settlers, the first state constitutions concentrated political power in the legislative branch.

History of the Office

Early governors were typically elected by the legislature rather than by the voters, were restricted to a single one-year term of office, and had little authority.[3] Two states, Pennsylvania and Georgia, even established a plural (multimember) executive. Slowly the governorships became stronger through longer terms, popular election, and use of the veto; but power did not come easily. The movement for popular democracy during the Jacksonian era led to the election of other executive branch officials, and reaction to the excesses of Jacksonian democracy resulted in numerous independent boards and commissions in the executive branch. Although governors did gain some power, they were not able to exercise independent authority over these executive boards and commissions.

In the early 1900s, along with their efforts to democratize national politics and clean up the corrupt city political machines, Progressive reformers launched a campaign to reform state government. Their principal target was the weak executive branch. Efforts to improve the state executive branch continued throughout the twentieth century. Today, in the beginning of the twenty-first century, we are in the latter stages of a long, highly comprehensive wave of reform that began around 1965 and has affected all the states. Its essential goal has been to increase the governors' powers to make them more commensurate with the office's increased duties and responsibilities. As a result, constitutional and statutory changes have fortified the office of the chief executive, reorganized the executive branch, and streamlined the structure and processes of the bureaucracy. The capacity of governors and the executive branch to apply state resources to the solution of emerging problems has thus been greatly enhanced.[4] And, as observed at the beginning of this chapter, the governors have become prominent players in national policymaking.

Today's Governors

Today, being governor is a high-pressure, physically demanding, emotionally draining job. As political scientist Larry Sabato states, "Governors must possess many skills to be successful. They are expected to be adroit administrators, dexterous executives, expert judges of people, combative yet sensitive and inspiring politicians, decorous chiefs of state, shrewd party tacticians, and polished public relations managers."[5] The job is also hard on the governor's private life. It consumes an enormous amount of waking hours at the expense of family activities, hobbies, and, in some cases, more significant money-making opportunities in law, consulting, or business.

Fortunately, governorships are attracting well-qualified chief executives. These "new breed" governors, first described by Sabato in *Goodbye to Goodtime Charlie: The American Governorship Transformed,*[6] are a far cry from the figureheads of the eighteenth and nineteenth centuries and the back-slapping, cigar-smoking wheeler-dealers of the first half of the twentieth century. Sabato's study of 357 governors holding office from 1950 to 1981 revealed "a thoroughly trained, well regarded, and capable new breed of state chief executive."[7] The pattern continues to hold true today, notwithstanding the occasional gubernatorial eccentric, such as Minnesota's former governor Jesse Ventura.

Today's governors are younger, better educated, and better prepared for the job than their predecessors were. The average age has declined by about five years since the 1940s. (The legal minimum age ranges from eighteen in California and four other states to thirty-one in Oklahoma; it is thirty in most states.) Formal education averages around 18 years,[8] and approximately two-thirds of the recent governors have held law degrees. Most of today's governors paid their political dues in state legislatures, gaining an understanding of important issues confronting the state, a working familiarity with influential figures in government and the private sector, and a practical knowledge of the legislative process and other inner secrets of state government (see Table 7.1). A majority have served previously as elected state executive branch officials. A handful have held a local elective office. Some have come straight from the private sector. The

TABLE 7.1		Background Data on Selected Governors			

NAME	STATE	PARTY	YEAR ELECTED	AGE FIRST ELECTED	PREVIOUS PUBLIC SERVICE
Gray Davis	CA	Democrat	2002	56	Governor (1998–2002); lieutenant governor; state controller; state legislature
John G. Rowland	CT	Republican	2002	37	Governor (1994–2002); U.S. congressman; state legislature
Ruth Ann Minner	DE	Democrat	2000	65	State legislature, lieutenant governor
John E. Bush	FL	Republican	2002	45	Governor (1998–2002); state secretary of commerce (1987–1988)
Sonny Perdue	GA	Republican	2002	55	State legislature
Dirk Kempthorne	ID	Republican	2002	51	Governor (1998–2002); U.S. senator; mayor
Frank O'Bannon	IN	Democrat	2000	66	Lieutenant governor; state legislature, governor (1996–2000)
Kathleen Sebelius	KS	Democrat	2002	54	State insurance commissioner
Jennifer Granholm	MI	Democrat	2002	43	State attorney general
Tim Pawlenty	MN	Republican	2002	42	State legislature
Bob Holden	MO	Democrat	2000	51	State legislature; state treasurer
Judy Martz	MT	Republican	2000	57	Lieutenant governor
Mike Easley	NC	Democrat	2000	50	Attorney general
Tim McGreevey	NJ	Democrat	2001	43	State legislature, mayor
George Pataki	NY	Republican	2002	49	Governor (1994–2002); mayor; state senator
Ed Rendell	PA	Democrat	2002	58	Mayor; state attorney general; state legislature
Mark Sanford	SC	Republican	2002	42	U.S. Congress
Phil Bredesen	TN	Democrat	2002	58	Mayor
Rick Perry	TX	Republican	2002	52	Governor (2000–2002); lieutenant governor; state commissioner of agriculture
Mike Leavitt	UT	Republican	2000	45	Governor (1992–2000)
Gary Locke	WA	Democrat	2000	46	State legislature, governor (1996–2000)
Bob Wise	WV	Democrat	2000	52	U.S. Congress, state legislature
Dave Freudenthal	WY	Democrat	2002	52	U.S. attorney general

attractiveness of the governorship is evident in the fact that several current chief executives left a congressional seat to take office. Why would someone desert the glamour of the nation's capital for the statehouse in Boise, Nashville, Harrisburg, or Hartford? For political power and the opportunity to make a difference in one's own state. More simply, being a state chief executive is just more fun. As John Ashcroft, a former two-term Missouri governor and U.S. senator currently serving as U.S. Attorney General, puts it, "Anyone who tells you that being senator is as much fun as being governor will lie to you about other things, too."[9]

Though still predominantly white males, today's governors are more representative of population characteristics than former chief executives were. Several Hispanics have served as governors in recent years, including Tony Anaya of New Mexico and Bob Martinez of Florida. In 1989, the first African American was elected governor—L. Douglas Wilder of Virginia. Gary Locke, the first Asian-American governor not from Hawaii, was elected governor of Washington in 1996. In earlier years, several women succeeded their husbands as governor, but since 1974 a growing number have won governorships on their own, including, in 2002, Jennifer Granholm (Michigan), Kathleen Sebelius (Kansas), Linda Lingle (Hawaii), and Janet Napolitano (Arizona).

A unique gubernatorial event occurred with the election of John E. (Jeb) Bush as Florida's governor in 1998. The younger Bush joined older brother George W. Bush (Texas, now president) as a state chief executive. (The Bush brothers are sons of former president George Bush.)

Getting There: Gubernatorial Campaigns

The lure of the governorship must be weighed against the financial costs. Campaigning for the office has become hugely expensive. Because candidates no longer rely on their political party to support them, they must continuously solicit great sums of money from donors to pay for the technology of campaigning—political consultants, opinion polls, air travel, advertisements in the media, telephone banks, direct mailings, websites, and interactive video links. Moreover, the growing attractiveness of the office has led to more competitive (and costlier) primary and general election races. To date, the most expensive governor's race was the 1998 election in California, in which Democrat Gray Davis defeated first two primary opponents and then Republican Dan Lungren in the general election; a total of $119.8 million was spent.[10] This official figure does not include in-kind donations such as free transportation, telephones, door-to-door canvassing, and other contributions from supporters. Generally, elections tend to cost more when they are close, held in a nonpresidential election year, involve a partisan shift (that is, when a Democrat succeeds a Republican, or vice versa), and are held in highly populated and geographically large states (for example, Florida, Texas, California, and New York).[11] On a cost-per-vote basis, races in states with a widely scattered population or hard-to-reach media markets, such as Alaska or Nevada, tend to be the most expensive. Cost per vote in recent gubernatorial elections ranged from $42.07 in Alaska to only $1.43 in

Vermont.[12] In the June 1998 California Democratic gubernatorial primary just mentioned, candidate Al Checchi spent $40 million of his own money—$59 per vote—only to lose to Lieutenant Governor Gray Davis, who spent only $5 per vote received.

Money has a profound influence on gubernatorial election results, but it isn't the only important factor.[13] As one veteran of political campaigns has reflected, "Everyone knows that half the money spent in a political campaign is wasted. The trouble is that nobody knows which half."[14] Other factors are also important in candidate success. The strongest influence is the strength of the candidate's political party in the state electorate,[15] as party identification usually translates into votes for a party's candidate. High-profile candidates stand a solid chance of being elected because they possess campaign skills, political experience, and other characteristics that help them raise the campaign funds needed to get their message and persona across to the electorate.[16] Of course, being independently wealthy doesn't hurt either.

Incumbency is a particularly important aspect of a candidate's profile. An incumbent governor running for reelection stands an excellent chance of victory; about three-quarters of incumbents have retained their seats since 1970. Incumbents enjoy a number of important advantages, including the opportunity while in office to cultivate both popularity with the voters and campaign donations from interest groups. However, reelection is no sure thing. Budget and tax woes can lead voters to toss chief executives out of office, particularly those who as candidates pledge not to raise taxes but then do so after election.[17]

The Roles of the Governor: Duties and Responsibilities

In performing the duties of the office, the governor wears the hats of top policymaker, chief legislator, chief administrator, ceremonial leader, intergovernmental coordinator, economic development promoter, and political party leader. Sometimes several of these hats must be balanced atop the governor's head at once. All things considered, these roles make the governorship one of the most difficult and challenging, yet potentially most rewarding, jobs in the world.

Policymaker

A governor is the leading formulator and initiator of public policy in his state, from his first pronouncements as a gubernatorial candidate until his final days in office. The governor's role as chief policymaker involves many other players, including actors in the legislature, bureaucracy, courts, interest groups, and voting public. However, few major policies that the governor does not initiate are enacted, and success or failure depends largely on how competently the governor designs and develops policy. The governor must also follow through to see that adopted policies are put into effect as originally intended.

Some issues are transitory in nature, appearing on the agenda of state government and disappearing after appropriate actions are taken. These issues are often created by external events, such as a federal court decision that mandates a reduction in prison overcrowding, a new national law requiring a state response, or an act of nature such as a tornado, flood, or forest fire. Examples include abortion rights, affordable health care, taxation of e-commerce, and preservation of open spaces.[18]

Most policy issues, however, do not emerge suddenly out of happenstance. Perennial concerns face the governor each year: education, corrections, social welfare, the environment, and economic development. Cyclical issues also appear, periodically increasing in intensity and then slowly fading away. Examples of the latter are consumer protection, ethics in government, reapportionment, and tax increases. Of course, national policy issues sometimes absorb the governor's time as well, such as preparing for and responding to acts of terrorism, providing health care insurance to the working poor and children, and dealing with proposals to drill for oil and gas in national parks.

Several factors have contributed to stronger policy leadership from the chief executives in recent years, including larger and more able staffs that are knowledgeable in important policy fields; a more integrated executive branch with department heads appointed by the governor; strengthened formal powers of the office, such as longer terms and the veto and budget powers; and the assistance of the National Governors Association, which offers ideas for policy and program development. Of no small importance is the high caliber of individuals who have won the office in recent years.

The top policy concern of the governors for the past two decades has been improving public education. The governors want to raise standards, increase teacher pay and quality, and boost student achievement. Specific policy approaches include smaller classes, tougher testing, an end to social promotions, and radical alternatives such as education vouchers and school privatization. Education improvement does not come cheap. The governors face the unenviable task of promoting new education programs in the context of serious fiscal problems and new outlays for homeland security and Medicaid.

Chief Legislator

This gubernatorial role is closely related to that of policymaker because legislative action is required for most of the chief executive's policies to be put into effect. In fact, the governor cannot directly introduce bills; party leaders and policy supporters in the house and senate must actually put the bills in the hopper. Dealing with legislators is a demanding role for a governor, consuming more time than any other role and representing for many the single most difficult aspect of the job.

Executive-Legislative Tensions   Developing a positive relationship with the legislature requires great expenditures of a governor's time, energy, and resources. Several factors hinder smooth relations between the chief executive and the legislature, including partisanship and personality clashes. Even the different natures of the two branches can cause conflict. Governors are elected by a statewide constituency and therefore tend to take a broad, comprehensive, long-range view of issues, whereas legislators, who represent relatively small geographical areas and groups of voters, are more likely to take a piecemeal approach to policymaking.[19]

According to one study, the amount of strife between the two branches is influenced by three factors: the size of the majority and minority parties, the personalities of the governor and legislative leaders, and the nearness of an election year.[20] Following the 2002 elections, there were twenty-eight Republican governors, and twenty-two Democratic governors. In a majority of the states, the governor has to deal with a one- or two-house majority from the opposing political party. When the opposition party is strong, the governor must seek bipartisan support to get favored legislation passed. Often a governor facing a large legislative majority from the opposing party has only the veto and the possibility of mobilizing public support as weapons against the legislature. Independent governors don't even have a minority party to count on. Former Maine Independent governor King observed that "I have no automatic friends in the legislature, but I have no automatic enemies. I have 186 skeptics."[21]

A governor who ignores or alienates members of the opposing political party can quickly find himself in the desert without a drink of water. Republican governor Gary Johnson of New Mexico took office proudly proclaiming his intention not to compromise his lofty principles with "a bunch of careerist Democratic officeholders who had brought the curse of bloated government upon the Land of Enchantment."[22] The comment led to overridden vetoes, an ineffective administration, and an exhausting shouting contest between Johnson and the legislature. Conversely, former Wisconsin governor Tommy Thompson's bipartisan, pragmatic approach to making government work was widely acclaimed and credited with major legislative triumphs in education and welfare policy reform. During budget time, when critical (and tough) spending decisions are at hand, serious conflicts typically erupt no matter how well the governor and legislators have gotten along.

The approach of statewide elections can also bring gubernatorial-legislative gridlock, as incumbents may be extremely cautious or overtly partisan in trying to please (or at least not to offend) the voters while discrediting their opponents. These three conflict-producing factors of partisanship, personalities, and proximity of an election are intensified during debates on the budget, when the principal policy and financial decisions are made.

Even in states where the governor's own party enjoys a large majority in both houses of the legislature, factions are certain to develop along ideological, rural-urban, geographical, or other divisions. Ironically, a very large legislative majority can create the greatest problems with factionalism, primarily because there is no sizable opposition to unite the majority party. A legislative majority of 60 to 70 percent helps a governor; after that, the majority party tends to degenerate into intraparty rivalries beyond the governor's control. As one governor lamented in the face of a 4-to-1 majority of his own party in the legislature, "You've got Democrats, you've got moderate Democrats, you've got suburban Democrats, you've got urban Democrats, you've got rural Democrats."[23]

Executive Influence on the Legislative Agenda   Despite the difficulties in dealing with the legislature, most governors do dominate the policy agenda, usually by working hand-in-hand with legislative leaders. The governor's influence begins with the State of the State address to the legislature and the general public, which kicks off each new legislative session, and in most states continues with the annual budget message. In 2002, the governors stressed fiscal problems and improvements in education.[24] During the session, the governor might publicly threaten to veto a proposed bill or appeal directly to a particular legislator's constituency.

Most of the drama, however, takes place behind the scenes. The governor might promise high-level executive branch jobs or judgeships (either for certain legislators or for their friends) to influence legislative votes. Or, she might offer some sort of **pork barrel** reward, such as funding a highway project in a legislator's district or approving an appropriation for the local Strawberry Festival. Private meetings or breakfasts in the governor's mansion flatter and enlist support from small groups or individual legislators. Successful governors are usually able to relate to representatives and senators on a personal level. Many are former members of the state legislature, so they know which strings to pull to win over key supporters.

In addition, all governors have legislative liaisons who are assigned to lobby for the administration's program. Members of the governor's staff testify at legislative hearings, consult with committees and individuals on proposed bills, and even write floor speeches for friends in the legislature. Some governors designate a floor leader to steer their priorities through the legislature. Most governors, however, are careful not to be perceived as unduly interfering in the internal affairs of the legislature. Too much meddling can bring a political backlash that undermines a governor's policy program. The role of chief legislator, then, requires a balancing act that ultimately determines the success or failure of the governor's agenda.

> **pork barrel**
> Favoritism, by a governor or other elected official, in distributing government monies or other resources to a particular program, jurisdiction, or individual.

Chief Administrator

As chief executive of the state, the governor is (in name, at least) in charge of the operations of numerous agencies, departments, boards, and commissions. In the view of many voters, the governor is directly responsible not only for pivotal matters such as the condition of the state's economy but also for mundane concerns such as the number and depth of potholes on state highways. Most governors are sensitive to their chief administrative responsibilities and spend a great amount of time and energy attending to them. Constitutional and statutory reforms, including the concentration of executive power in the office of the governor and the consolidation of numerous state agencies, have considerably strengthened the governor's capacity to manage the state. (See Chapter 8 for further discussion of public administration.) If governors are diligent in expeditiously appointing talented and responsive people to policymaking posts, they should feel no compulsion to micromanage the state's day-to-day affairs. Instead, they can focus their energies on leadership activities such as identifying goals, marshaling resources, and achieving results.[25]

In many respects, the governor's job is comparable to that of the chief executive officer of a large corporation. Governors must manage tens of thousands of workers, staggering sums of money, and complex organizational systems. They must establish priorities, manage crises, and balance contending interests. But there are important differences as well. For one, governors are paid proportionately far less for their responsibilities. In terms of expenditures and employees, most states are as big or bigger than *Fortune* 500 companies, whose chief executive officers typically earn tens of millions of dollars a year in salary and other forms of remuneration. Yet the 50 governors average only $104,500 annually, and Nebraska's makes but $65,000.[26] Moreover, governors confront several unique factors that constrain their ability to manage.

Restraints on Management   Reforms of the executive branch have allowed for more active and influential management, but significant restraints still exist. For example, the separation-of-powers principle dictates that the governor share his or her authority with the legislature and the courts, either or both of which may be politically or philosophically opposed to any given action. Changes in state agency programs, priorities, or organization typically require legislative approval, and the legality of such changes may be tested in the courts. The governor's ability to hire, fire, motivate, and punish is severely restricted by the courts, merit-system rules and regulations, collective bargaining contracts, independent boards and commissions with their own personnel systems, and other elected executive branch officials pursuing their own administrative and political agendas. Thus, most employees in the executive branch are outside the governor's formal sphere of authority and may challenge that authority almost at will. Career bureaucrats—who have established their own policy direction and momentum over many years, and who see governors come and go—usually march to their own tune. In sum, governors must manage through "third parties" in the three branches of government as well as in the private and nonprofit sectors. They have very little unilateral authority.

One of the most critical functions of the governor's role as chief administrator is crisis management. Immense problems may come crashing down on the chief executive as a result of natural or manmade disasters. Some governors are unfortunate enough to have a series of crises, none of their own making, befall the state during their administration. For instance, during Pete Wilson's eight years in office (1990–1998), California suffered the deadly 1992 Los Angeles riots, the worst drought in decades, followed by earthquakes, fires, and floods. Wilson could be forgiven for feeling like a biblical victim of holy wrath. When catastrophic events such as these occur, governors typically exercise their power to call out the National Guard for assistance.

Governors as Managers   Some governors minimize their managerial responsibilities, preferring to turn them over to trusted staff persons and agency heads. Others provide strong administrative and policy leadership in state government.

Consider the case of Utah Republican Mike Leavitt, a popular governor known for his management abilities. A former insurance executive, Leavitt used a collaborative decisionmaking style to attain remarkable gains in economic development and other areas. His state was named the nation's "best managed" by *Financial World* magazine.[27]

The constraints on the governor's managerial activities are not likely to lessen, nor are the potential political liabilities. The governors who courageously wade into the bureaucratic fray must invest a great deal of time and scarce political resources, yet they risk embarrassing defeats that can drag their administrations into debilitation and disrepute. Meanwhile, in the face of social and economic changes, the management of state government has become increasingly complex and the need for active managerial governors more critical than ever before.

Ceremonial Leader

Some governors thrive on ceremony and others detest it, but all spend a large portion of their time on it. Former governors remember ceremonial duties as the second most demanding of the gubernatorial roles, just behind working with the legislature.[28] Cutting the ribbon for a new highway, celebrating the arrival of a new industry, welcoming foreign businesspeople, receiving the queen of the Frog Jump Festival, announcing "Be a Good Neighbor Week," opening the state fair, and handing out high school or college diplomas are the kind of ceremonial duties that take a governor all over the state and often consume a larger portion of the workweek than any other role. (George A. Aiken, the late governor of Vermont, dreaded having to pin the ribbon on the winner of the Miss Vermont contest because he couldn't figure out how to put the pin in without getting under the bathing suit.)

Intergovernmental Coordinator

Governors serve as the major points of contact between their states and the president, Congress, and national agencies. For example, following the forays of Hurricanes Dennis and Floyd into the Tar Heel State in 1999, Governor Jim Hunt of North Carolina coordinated relief efforts with the Federal Emergency Management Agency, the Armed Forces, nonprofit organizations, and local governments. State-to-state relations to manage conflicts or settle disputes over cross-boundary water pollution and other environmental concerns are carried out through the governor's office. At the local level, governors are involved in allocating grants-in-aid, promoting cooperation and coordination in economic development activities, and a variety of other matters. Governors have also provided leadership in resolving disputes with Native American tribes over casino gambling and related issues.[29]

The role of intergovernmental coordinator is most visible at the national level, where governors are aided by the National Governors Association. In the 1960s, the NGA was transformed from a social club into a lobbying and research organization with a staff of more than one hundred and considerable clout. It now meets two times a year in full session to adopt policy positions and to discuss governors' problems and policy solutions. (C-SPAN covers national meetings of the governors.) The governors also meet in separate regional organizations. The NGA's staff analyzes important issues, distributes its analyses to the states, offers practical and technical assistance to governors, and holds a valuable seminar for new governors.

In addition, more than thirty-two states have established Washington offices to fight for their interests in Congress, the White House, and, perhaps most important, the many federal agencies that interact with states on a daily basis.[30] A governor's official inquiry can help speed up the progress of federal grant-in-aid funds or gain special consideration for a new federal facility. Washington offices are often assisted by major law and lobbying firms under contract to individual states.

The governor's role as intergovernmental coordinator is becoming more important with each passing year. It reflects the elevated position of the states in the scheme of American federalism and their increasing importance in national and international affairs. Acting together, the governors have exercised national policy leadership on critical issues such as taxation of Internet sales, public education, welfare and health care reform, economic development, and urban sprawl. Increasingly often, when the national government confronts a policy problem, it turns to the states for solutions.

Economic Development Promoter

As promoter of economic development, a governor works to recruit industry and tourists from out of state and to encourage economic growth from sources within the state (see Chapter 12). Governors attend trade fairs, visit headquarters of firms interested in locating in the state, telephone and email promising business contacts, and welcome business leaders. The role may take the governor and the state economic development team to Mexico, Korea, Germany, or other countries, as well as to other states. Governors also work hard to promote tourism and the arts. But mostly, development entails making the state's climate "good for business" by improving infrastructure, arranging tax and service deals, and engaging in other strategies designed to entice out-of-state firms into relocating and to encourage in-state businesses into expanding or at least staying put.

When a state enjoys success in economic development, the governor usually receives (or at least claims) a major portion of the credit. Sometimes the personal touch of a governor can mean the difference between an industrial plum and economic stagnation. Success stories include the cases of BMW's selection of South Carolina and Mercedes-Benz's and Honda's choice of Alabama as locations for new vehicle-assembly facilities. Some governors seek to define their state's economic future on a grand scale. Former Pennsylvania governor Ridge proclaimed that "One hundred years ago, Pennsylvania's coal fueled the Industrial Revolution. This time, our technology can provide the fire."[31] The economic development policies of Michigan governor Engler have helped turn "a listing industrial behemoth into a technically sophisticated . . . competitor."[32]

Party Leader

By claiming the top elected post in the state, the governor becomes the highest-ranking member of her political party. This role is not as powerful as it was several decades ago, when the governor controlled the state's party apparatus and legislative leadership, and had strong influence over party nominations for seats in the state legislature and executive branch offices. The widespread adoption of primaries, which have replaced party conventions, has put nominations largely in the hands of the voters. In addition, legislative leaders are a much more independent breed than before. Still, some governors get involved in legislative elections through campaign aid, endorsements, or other actions. If the governor's choice wins, he or she may feel a special debt to the governor and support him on important legislation.

The political party remains at least marginally useful to the governor for three principal reasons.[33] Legislators from the governor's own party are more likely to support the chief executive's programs. Communication lines to the president and national cabinet members are more likely to be open when the president and the governor are members of the same party. And, finally, the party remains the most convenient means through which to win nomination to the governor's office.

As a growing number of states have highly competitive political parties, governors find that they must work with the opposition if their legislative programs are to pass. For Independent governors a special challenge exists: how to govern without a party behind you to organize votes and otherwise push proposed laws through the convoluted legislative process. The recent record has been mixed.

Florida Governor Jeb Bush meets with President Ricardo Lagos of Chile at the presidential palace in Santiago to pursue economic development opportunities for his state. (© Reuters New Media Inc./ CORBIS)

Maine's Independent governor, Angus King, demonstrated a talent for working successfully with shifting legislative coalitions on a variety of issues. Reform party governor Jesse Ventura did not experience the same level of success with the Minnesota legislature.

Formal Powers of the Governor

formal powers
Powers of the governor derived from the state constitution or statute.

A variety of powers are attached to the governor's office. A governor's **formal powers** include the tenure of the office, the power of appointment, the power to veto legislation, the responsibility for preparing the budget, the authority to re-organize the executive branch, and the right to use professional staff in the governor's office. These powers give governors the *potential* to carry out the duties of office as they see fit. However, the formal powers vary considerably from state to state. Some governors' offices (Pennsylvania, New York) are considered strong and others (Alabama, Oklahoma) weak. Also, the fact that these powers are available does not mean that they are used effectively. Equally important are the

informal powers
Powers of the governor not derived from constitutional or statutory law.

informal powers that governors have at their disposal. These are potentially empowering features of the job or the person that are not expressly provided for in law. Many of the informal powers are associated with personal traits on which the chief executive relies to carry out the duties and responsibilities of the office. They are especially helpful in relations with the legislature.

Both sets of powers have increased over the past several decades. Indeed, governors are more influential than ever before because of their enhanced formal powers and the personal qualities they bring to the state capital. The most successful governors are those who employ their informal powers to maximize the formal powers. The term for this concept is *synergism,* a condition in which the total effect of two distinct sets of attributes working together is greater than the sum of their effects when acting independently. An influential governor, then, is one who can skillfully combine formal and informal powers to maximum effectiveness.

Tenure

There are two aspects of the governor's tenure power: the duration (number of years) of a term of office and the number of terms that an individual may serve as governor. Both have slowly but steadily expanded over the past two hundred years. From the onerous restriction of a single one-year term of office placed on ten of the first thirteen governors, the duration has evolved to today's standard of two or more four-year terms (only New Hampshire and Vermont restrict their governors to two-year terms). In addition, gubernatorial elections have become distinct from national elections now that thirty-nine states hold them in nonpresidential election years. This system encourages the voters to focus their attention on issues important to the state instead of allowing national politics to contaminate state election outcomes.

The importance of longer consecutive terms of office is readily apparent. A two-year governorship condemns the incumbent to a perpetual reelection campaign. As soon as the winner takes office, planning and fundraising must begin for the next election. For a new governor, the initial year in office is typically spent settling into the job. In addition, the first-term, first-year chief executive must live with the budget priorities adopted by his or her predecessor. A two-year governorship, therefore, does not encourage success in matters of legislation or policy. Nor does it enable the governor to have much effect on the bureaucracy, whose old hands are likely to treat the governor as a mere bird of passage, making him virtually a lame duck when his term begins.

In truth, two four-year terms are needed for a governor to design new programs properly, acquire the necessary legislative support to put them into place, and get a handle on the bureaucracy by appointing competent political supporters to top posts. A duration of eight years in office also enhances the governor's intergovernmental role, particularly by giving him sufficient time to win leadership positions in organizations such as the National Governors' Association. The record of an eight-year chief executive stands on its own, untainted by the successes or failures of the office's previous inhabitant.

The average time actually served by governors has grown steadily since 1955 as a result of fewer restrictions on tenure. The gubernatorial graybeard is Illinois governor Jim Thompson, who stepped down after serving his fourth consecutive term in 1990—a twentieth-century record. (North Carolina's Jim Hunt served two nonconsecutive four-year terms). Long periods in office strengthen the governor's position as policy leader, chief legislator, chief administrator, and intergovernmental coordinator, as shown by the policy legacy left in Illinois by Thompson and in North Carolina by Hunt.[34] Another sort of gubernatorial record was set by Cecil H. Underwood, who in 1956 became West Virginia's youngest governor at the age of thirty-four. He was reelected for a second term in 1996 as the state's *oldest* governor at seventy-four years of age, but lost in another bid for office in 2000.

There is still some resistance to unlimited tenure. More than one reelection creates fears of political machines and possible abuses of office. And, pragmatically speaking, a long period of "safe governorship" can result in stagnation and loss of vigor in the office. Even in states that do not restrict governors to two consecutive terms, the informal custom is to refrain from seeking a third term.

Appointment Power

Surveys of past governors indicate that they consider appointment power to be the most important weapon in their arsenal when it comes to managing the state bureaucracy. The ability to appoint one's own people to top positions in the executive branch also enhances the policy management role. When individuals who share the governor's basic philosophy and feel loyal to the chief executive and her programs direct the operations of state government, the governor's policies are more likely to be successful. Strong appointment authority can even help the governor's legislative role. The actual or implicit promise of important administrative and especially judicial positions can generate a surprising amount of support from ambitious lawmakers.

Unfortunately for today's governors, Jacksonian democracy lives on in the **plural executive.** Most states continue to provide for popular election of numerous officials in the executive branch, including insurance commissioners, public utility commissioners, and secretaries of agriculture. Proponents of popular election claim that these officials make political decisions and therefore should be directly responsible to the electorate. Opponents contend that governors and legislators can make these decisions more properly, based on the recommendations of appointed executive branch professionals who are not beholden to special interests.

plural executive
A system in which more than one member of the executive branch is popularly elected on a statewide ballot.

Perhaps appointment authority should depend on the office under consideration. Those offices that tend to cater to special interests, such as agriculture, insurance, and education, probably should be appointive. Less substantive offices such as secretary of state or treasurer probably should be appointive as well. However, it makes sense to *elect* an auditor and an attorney general because they require some independence in carrying out their responsibilities. (The auditor oversees the management and spending of state monies; the attorney general is concerned with the legality of executive and legislative branch activities.)

Many governors are weakened by their inability to appoint directly the heads of major state agencies, boards, and commissions. These high-ranking officials make policy decisions in the executive branch, but if they owe their jobs in whole or in part to legislative appointment, the governor's authority as chief executive is diminished significantly. Though nominally in charge of these executive branch agencies, the governor is severely constrained in her ability to manage. Such an arrangement would be unthinkable in a corporation.

The fragmented nature of power in the executive branch diminishes accountability and frustrates governors. Former Oregon governor Tom McCall once lamented that "we have run our state like a pick-up orchestra, where the members meet at a dance, shake hands with each other, and start to play."[35] When the assorted performers are not selected by the chief conductor, their performance may lack harmony, to say the least. And elected statewide offices provide convenient platforms for aspiring governors to criticize the incumbent.

Most reformers interested in "good government" agree on the need to consolidate power in the governor's office by reducing the number of statewide elected officials and increasing the power of appointment to policy-related posts in the executive branch. Most states have expanded the number of policymaking, or "unclassified," positions in the governor's staff and in top agency line and staff positions. But the number of elected branch officials has remained virtually the same since 1965. Table 7.2 shows the range and number of separately elected officials. The largest number are in North Dakota, where twelve statewide offices are filled through elections. At the bottom of the list are the reformer's ideal states, Maine, New Hampshire, and New Jersey, which elect only the governor. The average number of elected officials is about eight.

TABLE 7.2	Separately Elected State Officials

OFFICE	NUMBER OF STATES ELECTING
Governor	50
Lieutenant governor	42
Attorney general	43
Treasurer	40
Secretary of state	37
Education (superintendent)	14
Auditor	25
Secretary of agriculture	13
Controller	9
Public utilities commissioner	7
Insurance commissioner	11
Land commissioner	5
Labor commissioner	4
Mines commissioner	1
Adjutant general (National Guard)	1

SOURCE: Adapted with permission from *The Book of the States,* 2000–01 (Lexington, KY.: Council of State Governments, 2000), Table 2.10.

Why has it been so difficult to abolish multiple statewide offices? The primary answer is that incumbent education superintendents, agricultural commissioners, and others have strong supporters in the electorate. Special-interest groups, such as the insurance industry, benefit from having an elected official—the insurance commissioner—representing their concerns at the highest level of state government. Such groups can be counted on for fierce resistance to proposals to make the office appointive. Additional resistance may be credited to the fact that many citizens simply like having an opportunity to vote on a large number of executive branch officials.

Professional Jobs in State Government   The vast majority of jobs in the states are filled through objective civil service (merit-system) rules and processes. Governors are generally quite content to avoid meddling with civil service positions, and a few have actually sought to transfer many **patronage** appointments—those based on personal or party loyalty—to an independent, merit-based civil service.[36] (See Chapter 8.) Gubernatorial sacrifice of patronage power is comprehensible in view of the time and headaches associated with naming political supporters to jobs in the bureaucracy. There is always the possibility of embarrassment or scandal if the governor accidentally appoints a person with a criminal record, a clear conflict of interest, or a propensity for sexual harassment or

patronage
The informal power of a governor (or other officeholder) to make appointments on the basis of party membership and to dispense contracts or other favors to political supporters.

other inappropriate behavior; or someone who causes harm through simple incompetency. Moreover, those who are denied coveted appointments may become angry. One governor, just as he was about to name a new member of a state commission, is quoted as saying, "I now have twenty-three good friends who want on the Racing Commission. [Soon] I'll have twenty-two enemies and one ingrate."[37] A governor benefits from a stable, competent civil service that hires, pays, and promotes on the basis of knowledge, job-related skills, and abilities rather than party affiliation or friendship with a legislator or other politician.

The Power to Fire The power of the governor to hire is not necessarily accompanied by the power to fire. Except in cases of extreme misbehavior or corruption, it is very difficult to remove a subordinate from office, even if it is constitutionally permitted. For instance, if a governor attempts to dismiss the secretary of agriculture, he or she can anticipate an orchestrated roar of outrage from legislators, bureaucrats, and farm groups. The upshot is that the political costs of dismissing an appointee can be greater than the pain of simply living with the problem.

Several U.S. Supreme Court rulings have greatly restricted the governor's power to dismiss or remove from office the political appointees of previous governors. In the most recent case, *Rutan et al. v. Republican Party of Illinois* (1990), the Court found that failure to hire, retain, or promote an individual because of his or her political or party affiliation violates that person's First Amendment rights.[38]

A good appointment to a top agency post is the best way for a governor to influence the bureaucracy. By carefully choosing a competent and loyal agency head, the governor can more readily bring about significant changes in the programs and operations of that agency. Where appointment powers are circumscribed, the chief executive must muster his or her informal powers to influence activities of the state bureaucracy or rely on the seasoned judgment of professional civil servants.

Veto Power

The power to veto bills passed by the legislature is a means for influencing the bureaucracy: The governor can strike out an appropriation for a particular agency's programs if that agency has antagonized the governor. It also helps the governor as chief legislator; often the mere threat of a veto is enough to persuade a recalcitrant legislature to see the governor's point of view and compromise on the language of a bill. Vetoes are not easy to override. Most states require a majority of three-fifths or two-thirds of the legislature.

package veto
The governor's formal power to veto a bill in its entirety.

Types of Vetoes The veto can take several forms. The **package veto**, for instance, is the governor's rejection of a bill in its entirety. All governors hold package veto authority. North Carolina was the last to approve this gubernatorial power, in 1995. The package veto is the oldest form available to governors, having been adopted in the original constitutions of New York and Massachusetts.

<table>
<tr><td>

line-item veto

The governor's formal power to veto separate items in a bill instead of the entire piece of proposed legislation.

</td><td>

The **line-item veto** allows the governor to strike out one or more objectionable sections of a bill, permitting the remaining provisions to become law. It was first adopted by Georgia and Texas in 1868 and quickly spread to other states.[39] Only Nevada, Maine, and six other states forbid this gubernatorial power. Several states permit a hybrid form of line-item veto in which the governor may choose to reduce the dollar amount of a proposed item for purposes of holding down state expenditures or cutting back support for a particular program. In some states, the line-item veto is permitted only in appropriation bills.

</td></tr>
</table>

The **pocket veto,** which is available in fifteen states, allows the governor, after the legislature has enacted a bill and then adjourned, to reject it by refusing to sign it. In three states (Hawaii, Utah, Virginia), the legislature can reconvene to vote on a pocket veto. Otherwise, the bill dies. A governor might use the pocket veto to avoid giving the legislature a chance to override a formal veto or to abstain from going on record against a proposed piece of controversial legislation.

pocket veto

The governor's power to withhold approval or disapproval of a bill after the legislature has adjourned for the session, thus vetoing the measure.

A fourth type of veto is the **executive amendment,** formally provided for in fifteen states and informally used in several others. With this power a governor may veto a bill, recommend changes that would make the bill acceptable, and then send it back to the legislature for reconsideration. If the legislature concurs with the suggestions, the governor signs the bill into law.

executive amendment

A type of veto used by the governor to reject a bill and also to recommend changes that would cause the governor to reconsider the bill's approval.

Use of the Veto   The actual use of the veto varies by time, state, and issue. Some states, such as California and New York, often record high numbers of vetoes, whereas others, like Virginia, report few. On average, governors veto around 5 percent of the bills that reach their desks.[40] The variation among states reflects the tensions and conflicts that exist between the governor and the legislature. The largest number of vetoes typically occurs in states with divided party control of the executive and legislative branches.

Governors cast vetoes for many different reasons, including philosophical opposition to policies and budget items, or to make a powerful symbolic statement about an issue. Occasionally, the governor stands as the last line of defense against a flawed bill backed by the legislature because of powerful interest groups. It is not unknown for legislators to secretly ask the governor to veto a questionable bill they have just passed because the bill's contents are politically popular.[41]

Although the overall rate of veto utilization has remained steady, the proportion of successful legislative overrides has increased in the past two decades. This is an indication of the growing strength and assertiveness of state legislatures, the increase in conflict between the executive and legislative branches, and the prevalence of split-party government. Differences in party affiliation between the governor and the legislative majority probably provoke more vetoes than any other situation, especially when party ideology and platforms openly clash.

Conversely, when mutual respect and cooperation prevail between the two branches, the governor rarely needs to threaten or actually use the veto. Most governors interact with the legislature throughout the bill-adoption process. Before rejecting a bill, the governor will request comments from key legislators, affected state agencies, and concerned interest groups. He may ask the attorney general for a legal opinion. And before actually vetoing proposed legislation, the governor usually provides advance notification to legislative leaders, along with a final opportunity to make amendments.

The veto can be a powerful offensive weapon to obtain a legislator's support for a different bill dear to the governor's heart, particularly near the end of the legislative session. The governor may, for instance, hold one bill hostage to a veto until the legislature enacts another bill that he favors. Former Arizona governor Bruce Babbitt once threatened to veto a popular highway bill unless a teacher salary increase was passed—"No kids, no concrete." The legislature capitulated in the end.[42] In another instance, former Wisconsin governor Tommy G. Thompson's creative use of the line-item veto inspired a legislative revolt. Thompson applied the veto on some 1,300 occasions during a six-year period, even striking out certain words and letters to radically change the meaning of text.

Budgetary Power

The governor's budget effectively sets the legislative agenda at the beginning of each session. By framing the important policy issues and attaching price tags to them, the governor can determine the scope and direction of budgetary debates in the legislature and ensure that they reflect his overall philosophy on taxing and spending. All but a handful of governors now have the authority to appoint (and remove) the budget director and to formulate and submit the executive budget to the legislature. In Mississippi and Texas, budget authority is shared with the legislature or with other elected executive branch officials. And in these two states, two budgets are prepared each year: one by the governor and one by a legislative budget board.

Because full budgetary authority is normally housed in the office of the chief executive, the governor not only drives the budgetary process in the legislature but also enjoys a source of important leverage in the bureaucracy. The executive budget can be used to influence programs, spending, and other activities of state agencies. For example, uncooperative administrators may discover that their agency's slice of the budget pie is smaller than expected, whereas those who are attentive to the concerns of the governor may receive strong financial support. Rational, objective criteria usually determine departmental budget allocations, but a subtle threat from the governor's office does wonders to instill a cooperative agency attitude.[43]

During an economic downturn, governors find themselves in an extremely vulnerable political position. To balance the budget, a governor may cut spending, seek higher taxes, or both. None of these actions is likely to please many voters. It is particularly irksome when a newly elected governor inherits his predecessor's budget deficit, as Mark Warner did upon taking office in 2002, when Virginia faced a revenue shortfall of more than $1 billion.

The governor's budget requests are rarely, if ever, enacted exactly as put forward. Rather, they are usually argued and debated thoroughly in both houses of the legislature. A legislature dominated by the opposing political party is nearly certain to scorn or disparage the governor's budget. Ultimately, "the governor proposes, but the legislature disposes." In fact, no monies may be appropriated without formal action by the legislature. (The budget process is discussed further in Chapter 8.)

Reorganization Power

Reorganization power refers to the governor's ability to create and abolish state agencies, departments, and other offices and to reallocate administrative responsibilities among them. Reorganizations are usually aimed at the upper levels of the bureaucracy to streamline the executive branch and thereby make it work more efficiently and effectively. The basic premise is that the governor, as chief manager of the bureaucracy, needs the authority to alter administrative structures and processes to meet changing political, economic, and citizen demands. For instance, serious and recurring problems in coordinating the delivery of social services among several existing state agencies may call for a consolidated social services department with expanded powers. A governor with strong reorganization power can bring about such a department without approval of the legislature.

Traditionally, legislatures have been responsible for organization of state government; and in the absence of a constitutional amendment to the contrary or a statutory grant of reorganization power to the governor, they still are. But today, twenty-one states specifically authorize their chief executive to reorganize the bureaucracy through **executive order.** By this means, the governor can make needed administrative changes when she deems it necessary. All governors are permitted through constitution, statute, or custom to issue directives to the executive branch in times of emergency, such as during natural disasters or civil unrest.

executive order

A rule, regulation, or policy issued unilaterally by the governor to affect executive branch operations or activities.

Administrative reorganization today takes place under the assumption that streamlined government improves bureaucratic performance by cutting down on duplication, waste, and inefficiency. Achieving a more efficient and user-friendly government has been a top priority of governors. Recent "reinventing government" initiatives aim to make government more flexible and responsive by changing incentive systems for state employees, privatizing certain operations, reducing layers of bureaucracy, introducing e-government initiatives, and decentralizing human resource management agency activities. Governor Marc Racicot of Montana won legislative approval to abolish two departments and reorganize several others, saving the state an estimated $1.1 million. Ohio governor George Voinovich eliminated two departments and 3,200 state employees, saving $900 million.

Executive branch reorganization is widely practiced, but its actual benefits may be ephemeral. Reorganization typically achieves modest financial savings, if any at all.[44] Political scientist James K. Conant's analysis of reorganizations in twenty-two states indicates that such actions are not a cure for state fiscal ills. However, executive branch reorganization may help to provide a clearer focus on a particular problem or to contain administrative costs, and it may serve a variety of political purposes, such as rationalizing the pain of employee layoffs.[45]

The Politics of Reorganization   Reorganization is a politically charged process. Mere talk of it sounds alarms in the halls of the legislature, in the honeycombs of state office buildings, and in the offices of interest groups. Reorganization attempts usually spawn bitter controversy and conflict both inside and outside state government as assorted vested interests fight for favorite programs and organizational turf. Accordingly, reorganization proposals are frequently defeated or amended in the legislature, or even abandoned by discouraged chief executives. One study of proposed state reorganizations discovered that almost 70 percent resulted in rejection of the plan either in part or in entirety.[46] Even when enacted, reorganizations may generate extreme opposition from entrenched interests in the bureaucracy and, in the final analysis, be judged a failure. In the memorable words of former Kansas governor Robert F. Bennett:

> In the abstract, [reorganization] is, without a doubt, one of the finest and one of the most palatable theories ever espoused by a modern-day politician. But in practice it becomes the loss of a job for your brother or your sister, your uncle or your aunt. It becomes the closing of an office on which you have learned to depend. So there in many instances may be more agony than anything else in this reorganization process.[47]

Most governors who have fought the battle for reorganization would concur. Perhaps this helps explain the rarity of far-reaching executive branch restructuring in the past several years.

Staffing Power

The governor relies on staff to provide policy analyses and advice, serve as liaisons with the legislature, and assist in managing the bureaucracy. Professional staff members are a significant component of the governor's team, composing a corps of political loyalists who help the governor cope with the multiple roles of the office. From the handful of political cronies and secretaries of several decades ago, the staff of the governor's office has grown in number, quality, and diversity (with respect to gender and race).[48] The average number of professional and clerical staff members exceeds fifty today. And in the larger, more highly populated states, such as New York and California, staff members number well over one hundred. The principal staff positions of the governor's office may include those of chief of staff, legislative liaison, budget director, policy director, public relations director, legal counsel, press secretary, and intergovernmental coordinator.

A question of serious concern, especially in the states whose governors have large staffs, is whether too much power and influence are being placed in the hands of nonelected officials. Clearly, professional staff members have been highly influential in developing and promoting policies for the governor in some states, particularly in states where the governor lacks a coherent set of priorities and lets the staff have free rein. In other states the chief executive is very much in charge, relying on staff primarily for drafting bills and providing technical information.[49] Given their physical and intellectual proximity to the governor, staff members are in a highly advantageous position to influence their boss. In their role as the major funnel for policy information and advice, they can affect the governor's decisions by controlling the flow of information and individuals into his office.

The Relevance of the Formal Powers

In Table 7.3 the states are scored as to the strength of the governor's formal powers of office. As noted, governors have won stronger powers during the past three decades. But how helpful are the formal powers? Despite the major transformation of the governor's office, governors remain relatively weak because of the setting of state government. They must function in a highly complex and politically charged environment with formal authority that is quite circumscribed by the legislature, the courts, and constitutional and statutory law. Owing to the nature of our federal system, the national government effectively strips them of control over many policy and administrative concerns. Moreover, the business of state government is carried out in a fishbowl, open to regular scrutiny by the media, interest groups, talk-show hosts, and other interested parties. Notwithstanding the continued constraints on the exercise of their authority, however, today's governors as a group are more effective than their predecessors were in carrying out their varied responsibilities. Many of the "Goodtime Charlies" were quite powerful despite a lack of formal powers. But this reflects the weak and ineffective legislatures of years past as well as mastery of informal powers by some governors (see below). Today, the formal powers of the office are substantially strengthened, and highly qualified people are serving as chief executives.

In theory, governors with strong formal powers, such as the governors in New Jersey, Maryland, and West Virginia, should be more effective than their counterparts in Rhode Island and Vermont. In practice, that tends to be true— but not always. The potential for power and influence must not be confused with action. A governor with strong formal powers enjoys the capacity to serve

TABLE 7.3   **Institutional (Formal) Powers of the Offices of Governor**

	WEAK								MODERATE				STRONG			
2.7	2.8	2.9	3.0	3.1	3.2	3.3	3.4	3.5	3.6	3.7	3.8	3.9	4.0	4.1	4.2	4.3
RI	NH	SC	AL	MS	FL	NM	CA	AZ	CO	AK	MI	IA	HI	NJ	MD	WV
VT	OK		AR		OR	WA	DE	ID		KY	CT	MN	NY	IL		
			GA				ME	VA	TN	KS		ND	OH			
			IN				MO		WI	MA		SD	PA			
			LA						WY	MT		VT				
			NV							NE						
			NC													
			TX					US Average—3.5								

NOTE: The scale varies from 2.7 to 4.3. Six measures of power are assigned points for strength: tenure, appointment power, budget control, veto, whether governor and legislature belong to the same party, and number of other statewide elected officials.

SOURCE: Adapted from data collected by Thad L. Beyle, University of North Carolina at Chapel Hill.

effectively, but he may choose not to do so or, for various reasons, be unable to utilize the formal powers properly. Alternatively, a governor with weak formal powers can nonetheless be an effective, strong chief executive if she actively and skillfully applies the levers of power available in the constitution and in statutes.

Informal Powers

No doubt a governor with strong formal powers has an advantage over one without them. But at least equally important for a successful governorship is the exploitation of the informal powers of the office. These powers carry authority and influence that are not directly attached to the governorship through statute or constitution but, rather, are associated with the human being who happens to occupy the governor's mansion. Governors who can master these powers can be highly effective, even in the absence of strong formal powers.

The informal powers help transform the capacity for action into effective action. They react in synergy with the formal powers to create a successful governorship. An incumbent chief executive in the "strong governor" state of New Jersey will be hopelessly weak unless he also uses his personal assets in performing the multiple roles of the office. Alternatively, a chief executive in a "weak governor" state such as Oklahoma can be remarkably successful if he fully employs his informal powers [50] to become a "change master"—one who excels in persuading the state to adopt new ideas.[51] The informal powers are not as easy to specify as the formal powers are. However, they generally include such tools of persuasion and leadership as popular support, prestige of the office, special sessions, public relations and media skills, negotiating and bargaining skills, and pork barrel and patronage; and such personal characteristics as youth, ambition, experience, and energy.

Tools of Persuasion and Leadership

Popular support refers to public identification with and support for the governor and his or her program. It may be measured in terms of the margin of victory in the primary and general elections or in terms of the results of public opinion polls. Governors can parlay popular support into legislative acceptance of a policy mandate and otherwise channel the pressures of public opinion to their advantage. But popular support may erode when governors' actions alienate the voters. Jesse Ventura, for example, was elected Reform party governor of Minnesota in 1998. The 6'4" ex–Navy Seal, pro wrestler, radio personality, and actor captivated the voters with his unconventionality and straight talk. His approval ratings soared in 1999, as Minnesota's roaring economy permitted a $1.3 billion tax rebate. But following a *Playboy* interview in which he dismissed organized religion as a "sham" and made other controversial statements, Ventura's popular support plummeted. Without strong popularity to help push his policy ideas through a legislature containing no partisan allies, Ventura's clout diminished significantly, and he did not seek reelection in 2002.[52]

Prestige of the office helps the governor open doors all over the world that would be closed to an ordinary citizen. National officials, big-city mayors, corporate executives, foreign officials, and even the president of the United States recognize that the governor sits at the pinnacle of political power in the state, and they treat her accordingly. Within the state the governor typically makes use of the prestige of the office by inviting important individuals for an official audience, or perhaps to a special meal or celebration at the mansion.

The governor's informal power to call the legislature into *special session* can be employed to focus public and media attention on a particular part of the legislative program or on a pressing issue. In this way, the governor can delineate the topics that will be considered, thereby forcing the legislature's hand on divisive or controversial matters, such as environmental protection or a tax increase. In conjunction with popular support and with media and public relations skills, this informal power can work effectively to bend legislative will.

Other informal powers may be defined in terms of leadership skills. *Public relations and media skills* help the governor command the "big mike": the captive attention of the press, radio, and television. Any governor can call a press conference at a moment's notice and get a substantial turnout of the state's major media representatives, an advantage enjoyed by precious few legislators. Some chief executives appear regularly on television or radio to explain their policy positions and initiatives to the people. Others write a weekly newspaper column for the same purpose. Frequent public appearances, staged events, telephone calls, and correspondence can also help the governor develop and maintain popular support. Governors such as Mike Leavitt of Utah have used such techniques to attain statewide voter approval ratings of 85 percent and above.[53]

Indeed, the media can be a strong ally in carrying out the governor's programs and responsibilities. Effective governors know this instinctively and cultivate the press "like petunias."[54] But media relations are a two-way street. The media expect the governor to be honest, forthright, and available. If he instills respect and cooperation, observes political scientist Coleman B. Ransome, Jr., the governor's media relations can be "of incalculable value in his contest for the public eye and ear."[55] After all, most or all of what the public knows about the governor comes from the media.[56]

Negotiating and bargaining skills are leadership tools that help the governor to convince legislators, administrators, interest groups, and national and local officials to accept his point of view on whatever issue is at hand. These skills are of tremendous assistance in building voting blocs in the legislature, particularly in divided-power settings where hyperpluralism—such as exists in national politics—must be avoided. They also help persuade new businesses to locate in the state and effectively represent a state's interests before the national government. One governor who showed a special knack for finding common ground and brokering deals between warring parties was George W. Bush of Texas. As governor, Bush took great pride in his ability to bring contending elements of his legislature together. Weak in institutional power, Bush was willing to invest much time and energy negotiating the details of an agreement, eventually brokering a compromise through his powers of persuasion.[57]

Pork barrel and patronage are aspects of the seamier side of state politics. Although they are utilized much less frequently now than they were before the civil service reforms of the first half of the twentieth century, governors are still known to promise jobs, contracts, new roads, special policy consideration, electoral assistance, and other favors to influential citizens, legislators, and other politicians in return for their support. All governors have discretionary funds with which to help a special friend who has constituents in need. And although patronage appointments are severely limited in most jurisdictions, a personal telephone call from the governor can open the door to an employment opportunity in state government.

Characteristics of a Successful Governor

The *personal characteristics* that make for an effective governor are nearly impossible to measure. Research by political scientists indicates that age is the only statistically significant predictor of gubernatorial performance: Younger governors have been more successful than older ones.[58] However, as indicated earlier, leadership is generally agreed to be a very important quality of effective governors. Leadership traits are difficult to define, but former Utah governor Scott Matheson identified the best governors as "men and women who have the right combination of values for quality public service—the courage to stick to their convictions, even when in the minority, integrity by instinct, compassion by nature, leadership by perception, and the character to admit wrong and, when necessary, to accept defeat."[59]

A successful governor blends these qualities with the formal and informal powers of office in order to achieve her objectives. For example, following the political campaign to win the election, the governor must conduct a "never-ending campaign" to win the loyalty and support of her cabinet, state employees, the legislature, and the people, if she is to be effective.[60] Sixteen-hour workdays are not uncommon.

Successful governors, particularly those in "weak governor" states, know how to limit their policy agendas. Realizing that not all things are possible, they focus on a few critical issues at a time and marshal their formal and informal resources behind them. Eventually, the determined governor can wear down opponents. But more important, the successful governor exercises leadership by convincing the public that he is the person to pursue their vision and their interests. He prevails in the legislature by applying the pressure of public opinion and by building winning blocs of votes, and he leads the bureaucracy by personal example. Above all else, the successful governor must be persuasive.

In short, the formal powers of the office are important to any governor, but even strong formal powers do not guarantee success. As noted earlier, they must be combined with the informal powers to be effective. Whatever approach the governor chooses as chief executive, his or her individual skills are probably more important than formal powers.[61] Evidence of this conclusion is provided by Democratic governors in southern states who have won and held their state's top job and successfully pursued their policy agendas in the face of significant partisan opposition. Notable examples are Zell Miller of Georgia, Hunt of North Carolina, and Bush of Texas, who all combined the politics of pragmatism with outstanding interpersonal skills in exercising leadership. By contrast, those who lack appropriate individual skills, such as Jim Edgar of Illinois, are likely to bestow little policy legacy. Edgar's "wooden" speeches and below-average interpersonal skills left him unable to effectively communicate a policy vision during his second term.[62]

Removal from Office

Upon leaving office, the vast majority of governors simply continue their public service in another venue. Once out of office, many former governors continue to engage in public service. Sixteen now serve in the U.S. Senate, and, of course, several contemporary governors have run for president. Four (Carter, Reagan, Clinton, and Bush) have won in recent times, and others are interested in making a run for the White House. The experience of serving as a state's chief executive is widely believed to be excellent training for the top job in the nation. Former California governor Jerry Brown is the elected mayor of Oakland. After completing five gubernatorial terms and fifteen years in the insurance industry, former Iowa governor Robert Ray agreed to serve as acting mayor of Des Moines. Colorado's Roy Romer became superintendent of Los Angeles County schools.

Because state chief executives are held to higher standards today than ever before and are constantly under the microscope of the media and watchdog groups, illegal actions or conflicts of interest are likely to be found out and prosecuted. All states but one provide for the impeachment of the governor and other elected officials. (In Oregon, they are tried as regular criminal offenders.) Usually, impeachment proceedings are initiated in the state house of representatives, and the impeachment trial is held in the senate. A two-thirds vote is necessary for conviction and removal of the governor in most states. Of the more than 2,100 governors who have held office, only 17 have been impeached and 11 actually convicted and removed from office.

The most recent impeachment and conviction occurred in 1993 in Alabama. The case was that of Republican governor Guy Hunt, a Primitive Baptist (fundamentalist) preacher and farmer. Hunt's troubles began in 1991 when the state ethics commission ruled that Alabama's first Republican governor in 112 years had violated the ethics law by using the state's executive jet to fly to preaching engagements out of state and accepting "love offerings" from his flock. The elected Democratic attorney general of Alabama investigated and prosecuted Hunt on this and twelve other charges. Following indictment by a grand jury, the governor was convicted for illegally using his inaugural fund to channel $200,000 to personal use, including payment of his home mortgage and the purchase of cattle feed, a riding lawnmower, and a marble shower stall for his home.[63]

But Guy Hunt and the handful of other fallen governors are the gubernatorial black sheep—the oddities of contemporary state government who make interesting reading in the scandal sheets as political throwbacks to the Goodtime Charlies of yesteryear. They deflect proper attention from the vast majority of hard-working, capable, and honest chief executives who typify the American state governorship today.

Other Executive Branch Officials

The states elect more than 450 officials to their executive branches, not counting the 50 governors, ranging from attorneys general and treasurers to railroad commissioner (Texas). The four most important statewide offices are described here.

Attorney General

The attorney general (AG) is the state's chief legal counsel. The AG renders formal written opinions on legal issues (such as the constitutionality of a statute, administrative rule, or regulation) when requested to do so by the governor, agency heads, legislators, or other public officials. In most states, the attorney general's opinions have the force of law unless they are successfully challenged in the courtroom.

The attorney general represents the state in cases where the state government is a legal party and conducts litigation on behalf of the state in federal and state courts. The AG can initiate civil and criminal proceedings in most states. Increasingly, attorneys general have actively represented their states in legal actions contesting national government statutes and administrative activities in controversial fields such as hazardous and nuclear wastes and business regulation. Activist AGs such as New York's Eliot Spitzer have taken steps to protect consumers against mail fraud, Medicaid fraud, and misleading advertisements by rental-car firms, airlines, pharmaceutical companies, securities trading firms, and other businesses.[64]

Attorneys general received recent national attention by taking on the tobacco industry. AGs from forty states filed lawsuits against tobacco companies, seeking huge reimbursements for state funds spent to provide Medicaid-related health care for residents with smoking-related illnesses. Mississippi was the first to settle, in July 1997, for $3.6 billion; Florida was second at more than $11 billion later that year; and Texas was third with a record $15 billion settlement. The tobacco companies and the litigating states soon reached a national settlement for $206 billion and a pledge to drop billboard advertising of tobacco products along with sponsorship of sporting events, among other requirements.

Lieutenant Governor

This office was originally created by the states for two major reasons: to provide for orderly succession to a governor who is unable to fill out a term owing to death or other reasons, and to provide for an official to assume the responsibilities of the governor when the incumbent is temporarily incapacitated or out of the state. Eight states do not see the need for the office: Arizona, Maine, New

Hampshire, New Jersey, Oregon, Tennessee, West Virginia, and Wyoming. Others attach little importance to it, as indicated by a very low salary ($7,200 per year in Texas) or the absence of official responsibilities. The historical reputation of the lieutenant governor was that of a do-nothing; one former occupant of the office in Nevada characterized his major responsibility as "checking the obituaries to see if I should be in Carson City."[65]

Over the past twenty-five years, however, the lieutenant governorship in the majority of states has become a more visible, demanding, and responsible office. This trend is likely to continue as state governance grows increasingly complex and as additional states adopt the team election of governor and lieutenant governor. Many lieutenant governors hold important powers in the state senate, including serving as presiding officer and making bill assignments to committees. They are official members of the cabinet or of the governor's top advisory body in twenty-three states.[66] And virtually all lieutenant governors accept special assignments from the chief executive, some of which are quite visible and important. For example, Indiana's lieutenant governor acts as the state's commissioner of agriculture. In general, lieutenant governors' salaries, budget allocations, and staff have grown markedly during the past two decades.

A lingering problem is that nineteen states continue to elect the governor and lieutenant governor independently. This system can result in conflict and controversy when, for example, the chief executive is out of state and the two officeholders are political rivals or members of opposing political parties. On several recent occasions a lieutenant governor, assuming command, has proceeded to make judicial appointments, veto legislation, convene special sessions of the legislature, and take other actions at odds with the governor's wishes.

In order to avoid partisan bickering and politicking in the top two executive branch offices, twenty-four states now require team election. In addition to avoiding embarrassing factionalism, team election has the advantages of promoting party accountability in the executive branch, making continuity of policy more likely in the event of gubernatorial death or disability, and ensuring a measure of compatibility and trust between the two state leaders. But it doesn't entirely preclude problems. Lieutenant Governor Betsy McCaughey Ross shocked New York Republican governor George Pataki by changing her party stripes to Democrat in October 1997, a year before Pataki's first term expired. Needless to say, she was dropped from the Republican ticket in 1998.

Treasurer

The treasurer is the official custodian and manager of state funds. He or she collects revenues and makes disbursements of state monies. (The treasurer's signature is on the paycheck of all state employees and on citizens' state tax refunds.) Another important duty is the investment of state funds, including state employee pension monies. The failure to make profitable investments can cost the treasurer his job. West Virginia Treasurer A. James Manchin was impeached for losing $279 million in state funds through bad investments. Other treasurers have been criticized for leaving midterm for lucrative private-sector jobs (Connecticut, New Jersey), accepting gifts from financial firms (Massachusetts), or using their post to raise large sums of money from investment companies for their next election (nearly all states in which the treasurer is elected rather than appointed).

Secretary of State

In a majority of states the duties of this office are rather perfunctory. For the most part, they entail record-keeping and election responsibilities. Secretaries of state typically register corporations, securities, and trademarks, and also commission people to be notaries public. In their election-related responsibilities, they determine the ballot eligibility of political parties and candidates, receive and verify initiative and referendum petitions, supply election ballots to local officials, file the expense papers and other campaign reports of candidates, and conduct voter registration programs. The typical secretary of state also maintains state archives, files agency rules and regulations, publishes statutes and copies of the state constitution, and registers lobbyists.

The Vigor of U.S. Governors

The states have reformed their executive branches to enhance the capability of the governor as chief executive and to make the office more efficient, effective, accountable, and responsive. Indeed, the reforms discussed in this chapter not only have extended the formal powers and capacity of the office but also have improved the contemporary governor's performance in his many demanding roles.

In addition, today's governors are better educated, more experienced in state government, and more competent than their predecessors. They are better able to employ the informal powers of their office in meeting multiple and complex responsibilities. In a word, there is greater *vigor* in the governorships than ever before.

Chapter Recap

➤ The American governorship historically was institutionally weak, with very limited formal powers.

➤ Today's governors are better qualified, educated, and prepared for the office than governors of the past. However, winning the office is increasingly expensive.

➤ The roles of a governor include those of policymaker, chief legislator, chief administrator, ceremonial leader, intergovernmental coordinator, economic development promoter, and party leader.

➤ Formal powers of the office, which have strengthened over time, are tenure, appointment, veto, budgeting, reorganizing the executive branch, and staffing.

➤ To be successful, a governor must master the informal powers of the office and integrate them with the formal powers. Among the informal sources of power are tools of leadership and persuasion, such as public relations skills and negotiations and bargaining skills.

➤ Governors who violate the law may be removed from office through impeachment.

➤ Other key executive branch officials are the attorney general, lieutenant governor, treasurer, and secretary of state.

Key Terms

pork barrel (*p. 149*)
formal powers (*p. 154*)
informal powers (*p. 154*)
plural executive (*p. 156*)
patronage (*p. 157*)

package veto (*p. 158*)
line-item veto (*p. 159*)
pocket veto (*p. 159*)
executive amendment (*p. 159*)
executive order (*p. 161*)

Surfing the Net

The National Governors Association webpage is located at **www.nga.org.** It features, among other things, a subject index on a variety of state and local issues, including welfare reform. For western governors, see **www.westgov.org.** Information on sitting governors may be found on state homepages. Governors typically have personal webpages as well.

8

PUBLIC ADMINISTRATION: BUDGETING AND SERVICE DELIVERY

Public Employees in State and Local Governments: Who They Are, What They Do

Budgeting in State and Local Government
The Budget Cycle » The Actors in Budgeting » Pervasive Incrementalism » Types of Budgets

Personnel Policy in State and Local Government: From Patronage to Merit
The Merit System » State and Local Advances » Merit System Controversies

The Politics of Bureaucracy
Joining Administration and Politics » Professionals in State and Local Government »

Reinventing Government
Total Quality Management » Privatization » E-Government

The Quality of Public Administration

bureaucracy
The administrative branch of government, consisting of all executive offices and their workers.

Bureaucracy is a paradox. On the one hand, bureaucracy and public employees are sometimes portrayed as "the problem" with U.S. government at all levels. From the Internal Revenue Service, to the state department of motor vehicles, to the county tax assessor's office, bureaucracy is depicted as all-powerful and out of control, inefficient, wasteful, and drowning in red tape. Public employees (bureaucrats) are often seen as insensitive and uncaring, yet stay in their jobs forever.[1] Nearly everyone, from elected officials—presidents, governors, mayors, and legislators at all levels—to talk-show commentators and even product advertisers have stridently bashed the bureaucrats, blaming them for all imaginable sins of omission and commission (and all too often for their *own* personal shortcomings as well). The answer to the problem is no less than bureaucratic liposuction to "get the fat out."

On the other hand, bureaucracy can be beautiful.[2] Bureaucratic organization is indispensable to public administration. Legislative bodies and chief executives enact public policies through vague laws, depending on a variety of state and local agencies to deal with the specifics, such as operationally defining key components of the policies and putting the policies into effect. Some such "bureaucracies" make our lives more difficult, but others help the quality of our existence by enforcing the laws and punishing the criminals, putting out the fires, repairing and maintaining the roads, and helping the poor and disadvantaged among us. And who can forget that as corporate workers fled the burning twin towers, New York City police and firefighters rushed into the buildings to assist the injured survivors, only to perish themselves when the towers collapsed.

A theme of this chapter is that state agencies and local departments (the public administration) should not be treated as scapegoats for all the social, economic, and political maladies that befall society. The quality and capacity of public administration have improved markedly in the country's states, municipalities, and counties during the past twenty-five years in terms of the characteristics of employees and the efficiency, effectiveness, and professionalism with

New York City police take a break from searching for remains after the World Trade Center attack. (© Fabian Falcon/ Stock, Boston, LLC)

which they perform their duties. In fact, studies comparing public employees with cohort groups in the private sector find no important differences between them. Government workers are just as motivated, competent, and ethical as private-sector workers. Moreover, public employees tend to be more sensitive to other human beings, and more highly educated, than their counterparts in business and industry[3] (see Table 8.1). State and local employees are responding to citizens' demands by providing a wider range of services in greater quantities to more people than ever before; and publicly provided services are perceived to be just as good as the same services provided by private firms.[4]

Contrary to popular opinion, government work is not always a sunny day in the park. Public employees perform some of the most unpleasant and dangerous (but necessary) tasks imaginable, from taking abused or threatened children away from their parents to caring for the mentally ill and guarding prisoners who hurl feces at them. They act, often heroically, as our first—and continuing—response to disasters and terrorist events. It is only on those rare occasions when someone fouls up that a public outcry is raised; praise for consistency and excellence in public service delivery is seldom heard. In truth, dedicated public servants who work for the people should be saluted, not castigated, for jobs well done under difficult conditions. When government fails to perform effectively, blame occasionally may be laid at the feet of public employees. But more often than not, good government workers are the scapegoats for vague and poorly de-signed statutes and policies, failed political and corporate leadership, and other factors beyond the control of civil servants.

TABLE 8.1	Comparing Public- and Private-Sector Employees	

An extensive analysis of published studies on characteristics of public- and private-sector employees debunks certain stereotypes.

CHARACTERISTIC	ADVANTAGE
Motivation	Equal
Work habits	Equal
Competence	Equal
Education	Public employees have higher levels of educational achievement.
Values of public service and civic duty	Public employees
Compassion and self-sacrifice	Public employees
Ethics	Public employees
Helping other people	Public employees

SOURCE: Adapted from J. Norman Baldwin, "Public Versus Private Employees: Debunking Stereotypes," *Review of Public Personnel Administration* 11 (Fall 1990–Spring 1991): 1–27; James L. Perry, "Antecedents of Public Service Motivation," *Journal of Public Administration Research and Theory* 7(2) (1997): 181–97; and Gene A. Brewer, Sally Coleman Selden, and Rex L. Facer II, "Individual Conceptions of Public Service Motivation," *Public Administration Review* 60 (May/June, 2000): 254–264.

Public Employees in State and Local Government: Who They Are, What They Do

There are more than 16.7 million employees of states and localities. Their numbers have grown steadily since accurate counts were first compiled in 1929. Government work tends to be labor intensive, with the exception of national defense programs, which rely heavily on expensive technology. As a result of this fact and of inflation, personnel expenditures for states and localities have risen even faster than the number of workers. Total payroll costs for state and local governments exceed $475 billion.

Of course, the number of employees varies greatly among jurisdictions. Generally speaking, states and localities with large populations and high levels of per capita income provide more services and thus employ larger numbers of workers than do smaller, less affluent jurisdictions. Employment figures are further influenced by the distribution of functions and service responsibilities between states and their local jurisdictions. A state government may have hundreds of agencies, boards, and commissions. A municipality or county may have dozens of departments, boards, and commissions.

Such figures do not adequately account for the real people who work for states, cities, counties, towns, townships, and school districts. These include the police officer on patrol, the welfare worker finding a foster home for an abandoned child, the eleventh-grade English teacher, the state trooper, and even your professor of state and local government (if you are attending a public institution). Their tasks are as diverse as their titles: sanitation engineer, animal control officer, heavy-equipment operator, planner, physician, and so on. The diversity of state and local government work rivals that of the private sector, although there are important distinctions in the nature of the work (see Table 8.2). From the sewer-maintenance worker to the director of human services, all are public servants—often known as bureaucrats. Approximately one of every

TABLE 8.2	**Public Management and Private Management: What Are the Distinctions?**	
Public- and private-sector management differ in terms of constraints, clients, accountability, and purpose.	**PUBLIC MANAGEMENT**	**PRIVATE MANAGEMENT**
Constraints	Politics, public opinion, resources	Markets, resources
Clients	Citizens, legislatures, chief executives	Customers who purchase products or services
Accountability	To citizens and to elected and appointed officials	To customers, boards of directors, and shareholders
Purpose	To serve the public interest and the common good	To make profits and grow the organization

six working Americans is employed by government at some level. If bureaucrats are the enemy, we have met them and they are us.

Budgeting in State and Local Government

The budget is the very lifeblood of government bureaucracy. Without a budgetary appropriation, state and local organizations would cease to exist. The monies are allocated (usually on an annual basis) by legislative bodies, but the politics of the budgetary process involves all the familiar political and bureaucratic players: chief executives, interest groups, other government employees, the general public, and, of course, the recipients of legislative appropriations— the state highway department, the municipal police department, the county sanitation office, and so on. In a phrase, budget making is a highly charged political poker game with enormous stakes. To understand public administration, one must have a grasp of budgetary politics.

An often-quoted definition of politics is Harold Lasswell's famous line: "Politics is who gets what, when, where, and how."[5] The budget document provides hard dollars-and-cents data in answer to this question. It is a political manifesto—the most important one you will find in state and local government. The budget is a policy statement of what government intends to do (or not do), detailing the amount of the taxpayers' resources that will be dedicated to each program and activity. The outcomes of the budgetary process represent the results of a zero-sum game—for every winner there is a loser—because public resources are limited. An extra million dollars for corrections can mean that much less for higher education.

The Budget Cycle

The process of governmental budgeting is best understood as a cycle with overlapping stages, five of which can be identified: preparation, formulation, adoption, execution, and audit (see Figure 8.1). Several stages are simultaneously taking place at any given time. For example, while the 2003 budget is being executed and revenues and expenditures are being monitored to guard against an operating deficit, the governor and the legislature are developing the 2004 budget. Meanwhile, the 2002 budget is being audited to ensure that monies were properly spent and otherwise accounted for.

Budgets are normally based on a *fiscal* (financial) *year* rather than on the calendar year. Fiscal years for all but three states run from July 1 through June 30 (the exceptions are Alabama, Michigan, and Texas). Twenty-one states, including Oregon, Indiana, and Kentucky, have biennial (two-year) budget cycles. Most local governments' fiscal years also extend from July 1 to June 30.

The initial phase of the budget cycle involves demands for slices of the budget pie and estimates of available revenues for the next fiscal year. State and local agency heads join the chorus of interest groups and program beneficiaries seeking additional funding (with no concern for "profits," agencies have little

FIGURE 8.1	**The Budget Process**

The budget process has built-in "checks and balances," since all spending is approved or audited by more than one agency or branch.

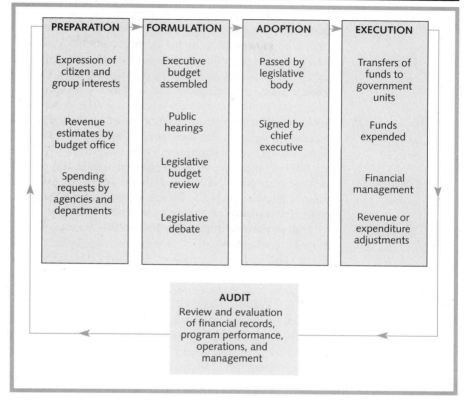

incentive to ask for less funding instead of more). Large state agencies are typically represented by their own lobbyists, or "public information specialists." State and local administrators develop estimates of revenues based on past tax receipts and expected economic conditions, communicating them to their respective state agencies or municipal departments, which then develop their individual spending requests for the fiscal year. Such spending requests may be constrained by legislative and executive "guidance," such as agency or program dollar ceilings and program priorities.[6]

Formulation, or initial development, of the budget document is the responsibility of the chief executive in most states and localities. Exceptions include states in which the balance of power rests with the legislature (such as Arkansas, Mississippi, and South Carolina) and local governments in which budgeting is dominated by a council or commission. The executive budget of the governor or mayor is presented to the appropriate legislative body for debate, review, and modification. The lengthy review process that follows allows agencies, departments, interest groups, and citizens to express their points of view. Finally, the legislative body enacts the amended budget.

The state legislature or city council must ensure that the final document balances revenues with expenditures. Balanced-budget requirements are contained in the constitutions or statutes of forty-eight states and operate through precedent in Vermont and Indiana. These requirements usually apply to local governments as well and, in many localities, are found in municipal ordinances. Balanced-budget requirements force state and local governments to weigh projected expenditures against expected revenues, but they may be circumvented to some extent.[7] One popular device is the "off-budget," in which costs and revenues for public enterprises such as government corporations or for special projects are exempt from central review and are not included in budget documents and figures. Another tactic is to borrow money from employee pension funds or next year's revenues to cover the current year's deficit. Before the budget bill becomes law, the chief executive must sign it. Last-minute executive-legislative interactions may be needed to stave off executive vetoes or to override them. Once the chief executive's signature is on the document, the budget goes into effect as law, and the execution phase begins.

Budget making during the 2002–2003 fiscal year well illustrates the difficulty of making ends meet when revenues are declining and expenditure demands are rising. The terrorist assaults of September 11 hit state and local budgets hard. The national economy had already slipped into recession. The aftershocks of the attacks rattled the economy further, particularly in California, Florida, New York City, Washington, D.C., and other jurisdictions highly reliant on travel and tourism revenues. California alone forecast a $12.4 billion shortfall for 2002. Shortly thereafter, projected economic growth rates plummeted across the country, even as new spending on security measures and personnel at key facilities shot up rapidly. Most states had to raise taxes, reduce expenditures, cut services, or use some combination thereof to balance the budgets—unpopular choices all. During the initial response to the economic reversal, governors imposed a variety of money-saving measures, including hiring and travel freezes, layoffs, furloughs, and across-the-board spending reductions. Rainy day funds were tapped as well (see Chapter 12). Local governments implemented similar strategies, including spending reductions, tax or fee hikes, short-term borrowing, and delayed or canceled capital expenditures.

During budget execution, monies from the state or local "general fund" are periodically allocated to agencies and departments to meet payrolls, purchase goods and materials, help average citizens solve problems ranging from a rabid raccoon in the yard to a raging forest fire, and generally to try to achieve program goals. Accounting procedures and reporting systems continually track revenues and outlays within the agencies. If revenues have been overestimated, the chief executive or legislative body must make adjustments to keep the budget in the black. In a crisis, the governor may call the legislature into special session, or the mayor may request a tax increase from the city council.

The final portion of the budget cycle involves several types of audits, or financial reviews—each with a different objective. Fiscal audits seek to verify that expenditure records are accurate and that financial transactions have been made in accordance with the law. Performance audits examine agency or department activities in relation to goals and objectives. Operational and management audits review how specific programs are carried out and assess administrators' performance. Either the executive or the legislative branch may employ the auditors. Some jurisdictions retain professional auditors from the private sector to ensure complete objectivity.

The Actors in Budgeting

There are four main actors in the budget process: interest groups, agencies, the chief executive, and the legislative body. Interest groups organize testimony at budget hearings and pressure the other three actors to pursue favored policies and programs. The role of the agency or department is to defend the base—the amount of the last fiscal year's appropriation—and to advocate spending for new or expanded programs. Agency and department heads are professionals who believe in the value of their organization and its programs, but they often find themselves playing Byzantine games to get the appropriations they want, as set forth in Table 8.3.

The late political scientist Aaron Wildavsky described the basic quandary of agency and departmental representatives as follows:

> Life would be simple if they could just estimate the costs of their ever-expanding needs and submit the total as their request. But if they ask for amounts much larger than the appropriating bodies believe is reasonable, their credibility will suffer a drastic decline. . . . So the first decision rule for agencies is: do not come in too high. Yet the agencies must also not come in too low, for the assumption is that if the agency advocates do not ask for funds they do not need them.[8]

What agency heads usually do is carefully evaluate the fiscal-political environment. They take into consideration the previous year's events, the composition of the legislature, the economic climate, policy statements by the chief executive, the strengths of clientele groups, and other factors. Then they put forward a figure somewhat larger than they expect to get.[9]

The chief executive has a very different role in the budget process. In addition to tailoring the budget to his program priorities as closely as possible, he acts as an economizer. Individual departmental requests must be reconciled, which means that they must be cut, since the sum total of requests usually greatly exceeds estimated revenues. Of course, an experienced governor or mayor recognizes the games played by administrators; he knows that budget requests are likely to be inflated in anticipation of cuts. In fact, various studies on state and local budgeting indicate that the single most influential participant is the chief executive.[10] Not surprisingly, astute administrators devote time and other resources to cultivating the chief executive's support for their agency's or department's activities.

The role of the legislative body in the initial stage of the budget cycle is essentially to respond to and modify the initiatives of the chief executive. The governor, mayor, or city manager proposes, and the legislature or council reacts. Later in the budget cycle, the legislative body performs another important function through its review of agency and department spending and its response to constituents' complaints.

TABLE 8.3	**The Games Spenders Play**
The following are tactics used by state and local officials to maximize their share of the budget during negotiations and hearings with governors, local chief executives, and the legislative body.	
MASSAGE THE CONSTITUENCY	Locate, cultivate, and utilize clientele groups to further the organization's objectives. Encourage them to offer committee testimony and contact legislative members on your behalf.
ALWAYS ASK FOR MORE	If your agency or department doesn't claim its share of new revenues, someone else will. The more you seek, the more you will receive.
SPEND ALL APPROPRIATED FUNDS BEFORE THE FISCAL YEAR EXPIRES	An end-of-year surplus indicates that the elected officials were too generous with you this year; they will cut your appropriation next time.
CONCEAL NEW PROGRAMS BEHIND EXISTING ONES	Incrementalism means that existing program commitments are likely to receive cursory review, even if an expansion in the margin is substantial. An announced new program will undergo comprehensive examination. Related to this game is *camel's nose under the tent,* in which low program start-up costs are followed by ballooning expenses down the road.
"HERE'S A KNIFE; CUT OUT MY HEART WHILE YOU'RE AT IT"	When told that you must cut your budget, place the most popular programs on the chopping block. Rely on your constituency to organize vigorous opposition. Alternatively, state that all your activities are critically important, so the elected officials will have to decide what to cut (and answer for it to voters).
A ROSE BY ANY OTHER NAME	Conceal unpopular or controversial programs within other program activities. And give them appealing names (for instance, call a sex education class "Teaching the Values of Family").
"LET'S STUDY IT FIRST" (AND MAYBE YOU WON'T BE REELECTED)	When told to cut or eliminate a program, argue that the consequences would be devastating and should be carefully studied before action is taken.
SMOKE AND MIRRORS	Support your requests for budget increases with voluminous data and testimony. The data need not be especially persuasive or even factual, just overwhelming. Management writer James H. Boren calls this "bloatating" and "trashifying."
A PIG IN A POKE	Place an unneeded item in your budget request, so you can gracefully give it up while protecting more important items.
END RUN	If the chief executive initiates a budget cut, run quickly to friends in the legislature.
EVERY VEIN IS AN ARTERY	Claim that any program cut would so completely undermine effectiveness that the entire program would have to be abandoned.

Pervasive Incrementalism

In a perfect world, budgeting would be a purely rational enterprise. Objectives would be identified, stated clearly, and prioritized; alternative means for accomplishing them would be considered; revenue and expenditure decisions would be coordinated within the context of a balanced budget.

That is how budgeting *should* be done. However, state and local officials have to allocate huge sums of money each year (more than $1 trillion) in a budgetary environment where objectives are unclear or controversial and often conflict with one another. It is nearly impossible to prioritize the hundreds or thousands of policy items on the agenda. Financial resources, time, and the capacity of the human brain are severely stretched.

In order to cope with such complexity and minimize political conflict over scarce resources, decisionmakers "muddle through."[11] They simplify budget decisionmaking by adopting decision rules. For example, instead of searching for the optimal means for addressing a public policy problem, they search only until they find a feasible solution. As a result, they sacrifice comprehensive analysis and rationality for **incrementalism** in which small adjustments (usually an increase) are made to the nature and funding base of existing programs. Thus the policy commitments and spending levels of ongoing programs are usually accepted as a given—they become the base for next year's funding. Decisions are made on a very small proportion of the total budget: the increments from one fiscal year to the next. If the budget has to be cut, it is done decrementally; small percentage adjustments are subtracted from the base. In this way, political conflict over values and objectives is held to a minimum.

The hallmarks of incremental budgeting are consistency and continuity: The future becomes an extension of the present, which is itself a continuation of the past. Long-range commitments are made, then honored indefinitely. This is not to say that state and local budget making is a simple affair. On the contrary: It is as tangled and intricate as the webs of a thousand spiders on amphetamines.

incrementalism
A decisionmaking approach in the budgetary process in which the previous year's expenditures are used as a base for the current year's budget figures.

Types of Budgets

A budget document can be laid out in various ways, depending on the purposes one has in mind: control, management, or planning. Historically, *control,* or fiscal accountability, has been the primary purpose of budgeting, incrementalism the dominant process, and the line-item budget the standard document.

line-item budget
A budget that lists detailed expenditure items such as personal computers and paper, with no attention to spending goals or objectives.

Control Through Line-Item Budgets   The **line-item budget** facilitates control by specifying the amount of funds each agency or department receives and monitoring how those funds are spent. Each dollar can be accounted for with the line-item budget—which lists every object of expenditure, from police uniforms to toilet paper—on a single line in the budget document. Line-item budgets show where the money goes, but they do not tell us how effectively the money is spent.

Budgeting for Management and Planning   Increasingly, government decisionmakers are focusing on obtaining *results*. Budget formats that stress *management* and *planning* are intended to help budget makers move beyond the narrow constraints of line items and incrementalism toward more rational and flexible decisionmaking techniques that help attain program results. Chief executives and agency officials seek to ensure that organizational units properly carry out priorities set forth in the budget—the management aspect of budgeting. Formal program and policy evaluations are a necessary step in ensuring proper performance and public accountability. The planning part involves orienting the budget process toward the future by anticipating needs and contingencies. A budget format that emphasizes planning is one that specifies objectives and lays out a financial plan for attaining them.

Several techniques permit budgeting for management and planning, but the most important today is performance budgeting. In **performance budgeting,** now required in forty-seven states, the major emphasis is on activities, or programs. The idea is to focus attention on how efficiently and effectively work is being done rather than on what things are being acquired. Whereas line-item budgets are input oriented, performance budgets are output and outcome oriented. Governments decide what they want to accomplish and measure these accomplishments versus expenditures. For example, the performance of a fire department can be evaluated by response times to emergency calls and by how quickly a fire is contained once firefighters arrive at the scene. By focusing on program objectives and work performance, performance budgets can assist managers, elected officials, and citizens in improving the quality of government operations.

performance budgeting
Budgeting that is organized to account for the outcomes of government programs.

Capital Budgets   The budget formats described above apply to operating budgets whose funds are depleted within a year. Capital outlays are made over a longer period of time and are composed of "big ticket" purchases such as hospitals, university buildings, libraries, new highways, and major computer systems. They represent one-time, nonrecurring expenditures that call for special funding procedures, or a **capital budget.** Because such items cannot be paid for within a single fiscal year, governments borrow the required funds, just as most individuals do when buying a house or an expensive automobile. The debt, with interest, is paid back in accordance with a predetermined schedule.

capital budget
A budget that plans large expenditures for long-term investments, such as buildings and highways.

Capital projects are funded through the sale of general obligation or revenue bonds. *Bonds* are certificates of debt sold by a government to a purchaser, who eventually recovers the initial price of the bond plus interest. *General obligation bonds* are paid off with a jurisdiction's regular revenues (from taxes and other sources). In this instance, the "full faith and credit" of the government is pledged as security. *Revenue bonds* are usually paid off with user fees collected from use of the new facility (for example, a parking garage, auditorium, or toll road). Payments for both types of bonds are scheduled over a period of time that usually ranges from five to twenty years. The costs of operating a new facility, such as a school or recreation area, are met through the regular operating budget and/or user fees.

Personnel Policy in State and Local Government: From Patronage to Merit

Whether the tasks of state and local government are popular (fighting crime, educating children) or unpopular (imposing and collecting taxes and fees), serious (saving a helpless infant from an abusive parent) or mundane (maintaining the grass on municipal sports fields), they are nearly always performed by public employees. The 5 million state workers and 11.7 million city, county, and town employees are the critical links between public policy decisions and how those policies are implemented. Agencies and departments must be organized to solve problems and deliver services effectively and efficiently. Personnel rules and procedures must determine how public employees are recruited, hired, paid, and fired.

In the nation's first decades, public employees came mainly from the educated and wealthy upper class and, in theory, were hired on the basis of fitness for office. During the presidency of Andrew Jackson (1829–1837), who wanted to open up national government jobs to all segments of white, male society, the *patronage* system was adopted to fill many positions. Hiring often depended on party affiliation and other political alliances rather than on job-related qualifications.

Patronage became entrenched in many states and cities where jobs were awarded almost entirely on grounds of partisan politics, personal friendships, family ties, or financial contributions. This system made appointees accountable to the governor, mayor, or whoever appointed them, but it did nothing to ensure honesty and competence. By the beginning of the Civil War, "spoils" permeated U.S. governments at all levels. The quality of public service plummeted.

The Merit System

merit system
The organization of government personnel providing for hiring and promotion on the basis of knowledge, skills, and abilities rather than patronage or other influences.

The concept of the **merit system** is usually associated with the national campaign for passage of the Pendleton Act of 1883. Two key factors led to its realization. First, Anglo-Saxon Protestants were losing political power to urban political machines dominated by "new" Americans of Catholic faith and Irish, Italian, and Polish descent. Second, scandals rocked the administration of an allegedly alcoholic president, Ulysses S. Grant, and spawned a public backlash that peaked with the assassination of President James Garfield in 1881 by an insane attorney seeking a political appointment. The Pendleton Act set up an independent, bipartisan *civil service* commission to make objective, merit-based selections for national job openings.

neutral competence
The concept that public employees should perform their duties competently and without regard for political considerations.

The *merit principle* was to determine all personnel-related decisions. Those individuals best qualified would receive a job or a promotion based on their knowledge, skill, and abilities. Far from perfect, the merit system was thoroughly overhauled by the Civil Service Reform Act of 1978. As a result of the Pendleton Act and similar laws adopted by the states, the negative effects of patronage and spoils politics in national selection practices were largely eliminated. **Neutral competence** became the primary criterion for obtaining a job, as public servants were expected to perform their work competently and in a politically neutral manner.

New York was the first state to enact a merit system. It did so in 1883, the year of the Pendleton Act, and Massachusetts followed in 1884. The first municipal merit system was established in Albany, New York, in 1884; a year later, Cook County, Illinois, became the first county with a merit system. Ironically, both Albany and Cook County (Chicago) were later consumed by machine politics and spoils-ridden urban governance.

By 1949, twenty-three states and numerous local governments had enacted merit-based civil service systems. Congressional passage of the 1939 amendments to the Social Security Act of 1935 gave additional impetus to such systems. This legislation obligated the states to set up merit systems for employees in social service and employment security agencies and departments that were at least partly funded by national grants-in-aid under the Social Security Act. All states are thus now required to establish a merit system for a sizable segment (around 20 percent) of their work force; most of them (thirty-four) have in fact developed comprehensive systems that encompass virtually all state employees. Common elements of these modern personnel systems include recruitment, selection, and promotion in accordance with knowledge, skills, and ability; regular performance appraisals; and equal employment opportunity.

Some merit systems work better than others. In a handful of states and localities, they are mere formalities—lifeless skeletons around which a shadowy world of patronage, spoils, favoritism, and incompetence flourishes.[12] Such conditions came to public attention when terrorists boarded and hijacked two commercial aircraft at Boston's Logan Airport on September 11, 2001. For years, gubernatorial patronage appointees with little or no experience in security or law enforcement had run Logan's security operations.[13] Rigid personnel rules, a lack of training programs, and inadequate salaries and retirement plans continue to plague some jurisdictions. Political control over merit-system employees is limited everywhere because most cannot be fired without great difficulty. Georgia and Florida are exceptions: In these states, new employees are hired on contracts and not granted tenure in the job.

State and Local Advances

On balance, however, state and local personnel systems have been greatly improved, and the process continues.[14] Nonnational governments are experimenting with recruitment and testing innovations, pay-for-performance plans and other incentive systems, participative management innovations, new performance-appraisal methods, electronic training programs, the decentralization of personnel functions, and many other concepts.[15] Virtually every state is reforming its civil service in some way. General public dissatisfaction with government at all levels, combined with increasing needs for government to become more sophisticated and responsive to its clients, means that efforts to "reinvent" personnel administration are certain to grow.

These reforms are designed to make the executive branch leaner and more responsive to the chief executive, to improve service capacity, to elevate efficiency and effectiveness in providing services, and to enhance flexibility for chief executives, agency heads, city managers, and other officials. Reformers remain dedicated to the principle of protecting the civil service from unnecessary and gratuitous interference by politicians with patronage considerations in mind. But they also want to increase the capacity of government executives to manage programs and people in their organizations and to achieve desired results.

Merit-System Controversies

As we shall see, state and local governments have taken the lead in addressing controversial questions that involve merit-system principles and practices, including affirmative action, sexual harassment, and labor unions.

Affirmative Action   This controversial policy is grounded in a related concept—namely, **representative bureaucracy.** The concept of representative bureaucracy suggests that the structure of government employment should reflect major sexual, racial, socioeconomic, religious, geographic, and related components in society. The assumptions behind this idea are (1) that a work force representative of the values, points of view, and interests of the people it governs will be responsive to their special problems and concerns, and (2) that a representative bureaucracy provides strong symbolic evidence of a government "of the people, by the people, and for the people." These assumptions have been widely debated. For example, empirical research indicates that the specific agency a person works for and the profession she belongs to are better predictors of public policy preferences than racial, sexual, and other personal characteristics.[16] However, the symbolic aspects of representative bureaucracy are important. A government that demonstrates the possibility of social and occupational mobility for all sorts of people gains legitimacy in the eyes of its citizens and expands the diversity of views taken into account in bureaucratic decisions.

> **representative bureaucracy**
> The concept that all major groups in society should participate proportionately in government work.

A controversial question is how to *achieve* a representative work force, particularly at the upper levels of government organizations, without sacrificing the merit principle. *Equal employment opportunity (EEO)*—the policy of prohibiting employment practices that discriminate for reasons of race, sex, religion, age, physical disability, or other factors not related to the job—is embodied in the Fourteenth Amendment to the U.S. Constitution, in various federal civil rights and equal opportunity acts, and in several U.S. Supreme Court decisions interpreting these acts. This policy has been the law for well over a hundred years; yet progress was very slow until the past twenty-five years or so, when **affirmative action** policies were adopted throughout government.

> **affirmative action**
> Special efforts to recruit, hire, and promote members of disadvantaged groups in order to eliminate the effects of past discrimination.

Affirmative action recognizes that equal opportunity has not been sufficient. Governments must take special steps to hire and retain those categories of workers legally defined as "protected classes," who have suffered discrimination in the past. These measures are required under certain conditions specified by the U.S. Equal Employment Opportunity Commission (EEOC), the regulatory body created to enforce EEO, and, in some instances, by the courts.[17] They include goals, timetables, and other preferential selection and promotion devices intended to make the work forces of public and private organizations more representative of the racial, sexual, and other characteristics of the available labor pool.

Under affirmative action, the absence of overt discrimination in employment is not sufficient; organizations must implement preferential hiring and promotion schemes to redress existing imbalances. The legitimacy of affirmative action policies imposed on employers by the EEOC has been put in question by a series of U.S. Supreme Court decisions during the past two decades[18] and by state legislative actions and referendums.

Obviously, affirmative action is highly controversial. Establishing specific numerical goals and timetables for hiring and promoting minorities does not necessarily correspond with selection or promotion of the "best person for the job." In other words, affirmative action appears to conflict with the merit principle. Furthermore, it has alienated a large proportion of white males, who feel that they have become victims of "reverse discrimination."

Legal clashes among the federal courts, the Congress, and the states and localities continue but have not produced a coherent interpretation of affirmative action's legal standing. Two recent events show the complexity of issues surrounding affirmative action policy. The first arose from a 1992 lawsuit against the University of Texas Law School filed by four white applicants (three men and a woman), who alleged that they had not been admitted despite having LSAT scores higher than those of black and Hispanic applicants who were accepted. The first federal judge to hear this case, in *Hopwood* v. *Texas*,[19] ruled against the white applicants. But on appeal, the Fifth Circuit Court judges agreed that the university had violated the students' constitutional rights. According to the court, the use of race as a selection criterion "is no more rational . . . than would be choices based upon the physical size or blood type of applicants." The Fifth Circuit Court's decision applied to universities in Texas, Louisiana, and Mississippi.

Texas attorney general Dan Morales appealed to the U.S. Supreme Court, which refused to hear the case, thereby keeping the circuit court's ruling in effect. Yet, to Texas's astonishment, the U.S. Department of Education warned the state, in an official letter, that Texas could lose all federal financial aid if it ended its affirmative action programs as ordered by the courts! After a furious reaction by Texas's powerful congressional delegation, the Department of Education backed down. The effects of federal court intrusion into Lone Star affirmative action were soon registered at the University of Texas Law School, where black and Hispanic admission fell precipitously.

National confusion and uncertainty about affirmative action are further illustrated by the 1996 passage in California of Proposition 209, which amended the state constitution by prohibiting race and gender consideration in contracting decisions and in hiring for state and local jobs. The initiative was approved by nearly 55 percent of the voters. Soon, however, a federal judge blocked enforcement on the grounds that "Prop 209" was discriminatory and therefore unconstitutional. About six months later, judges for the Ninth Circuit Court of Appeals reinstated the standing of Proposition 209, an action that was upheld by the U.S. Supreme Court.

Proposition 209 prohibits the state of California from granting "preferential treatment . . . on the basis of race, sex, color, ethnicity, or national origin." Supporters say this is both fair and constitutional. Opponents, including the American Civil Liberties Union, charge that the new law perpetuates discrimination by banning racial, gender, and ethnic preferences while ignoring other preferences such as those for veterans seeking jobs or state contracts. The debate in California presaged similar conflicts elsewhere. In 1998, Washington voters approved an anti-discrimination initiative, and in 2000, Governor Jeb Bush of Florida eliminated racial preferences in his state through an executive order.

Despite such confusion and political invective, substantial progress toward representative bureaucracy has been made, especially in recruiting and hiring protected-class individuals for entry-level positions. Granted, minorities and women continue to bump against a "glass ceiling" as they try to penetrate the upper levels of state and local agencies.[20] But gradual progress is being seen even with respect to this final barrier to representative bureaucracy, as indicated both by descriptive data (for instance, the number of female city managers rose from seven in 1971 to around one hundred in 1986 and to 435 in 1997, and the percentage of Hispanic professionals in state and local government doubled between 1974 and 1990) and by scholarly research on improvements in and attitudes toward minority employment. Female and minority employment at all levels of state and local government exceeds that in the private sector.[21]

Sexual Harassment   Sexual harassment has long been a problem in public and private employment, but it has only recently gained widespread recognition. Sexual harassment can consist of any of a variety of incidents: obscene or sexually oriented jokes that a listener finds personally insulting, unwanted touching or other physical contact of a sexual nature, implicit or overt sexual propositions, or (in one of its worst forms) extortion of a subordinate by a supervisor who demands sexual favors in return for a promotion or a raise. A "hostile working environment" that discriminates on the basis of gender also constitutes sexual harassment.[22] Examples in this category include repeated leering, sexual joking or teasing, and lewd calendars or photographs at the workplace. Isolated incidents of sexual teasing or innuendo do not constitute sexual harassment.[23]

Sexual harassment is undoubtedly common in the workplace: Surveys of women reveal that at least half of the respondents report being a victim. Approximately 14 percent of men have experienced sexual harassment. Such behavior subverts the merit principle when personnel decisions such as hiring or promotion are influenced by illegal or discriminatory considerations of a sexual nature, or when an employee cannot perform his or her assigned duties because of sexual harassment. Unfortunately for the recipient of unwanted sexual attention, there are seldom any witnesses. The matter becomes one person's word against another's. And when one of the parties is the supervisor of the second party, a formal complaint may be decided in favor of the boss.

Sexual harassment is illegal according to the federal courts. Considered sex discrimination under Title VII of the 1964 Civil Rights Act and a form of punishable employee misconduct under civil service rules, it is increasingly being prosecuted in the courts.

Much of the official activity aimed at stopping sexual harassment has been concentrated in the states, with local governments rapidly following suit. Michigan was the first to adopt a sexual harassment policy, in 1979; since then, nearly every other state has adopted a statewide sexual harassment policy through legislation or executive order. States offer employee-training programs that help workers and supervisors identify acts of sexual harassment, establish procedures for effectively addressing it, and enforce prompt, appropriate disciplinary action against offenders.[24]

The consequences of sexual harassment go well beyond the personal discomfort or injury suffered by victims. The problem also results in significant financial costs to organizations whose employees lose productive work time. Such misconduct is unacceptable today in a national work force that is almost 50 percent female. An emerging issue of significant proportions is the legal responsibility of teachers and school administrators to prevent flagrant sexual harassment of one student by another in the schools.

Unions   Nearly always controversial in government, *public-employee unions* present a potentially serious threat to the merit principle. They usually insist on seniority as the primary criterion in personnel decisions, often seek to effect changes in merit-system rules and procedures, and regularly challenge management authority. Moreover, unions aggressively seek higher pay and benefits, threatening to drive up the costs of government and, in some instances, prompting tax increases.

Until the 1960s, unionization was largely a private-sector phenomenon boosted by national legislation in the early 1930s. This legislation protected the rights of workers in industry to organize and engage in **collective bargaining** with their employers over wages, benefits, and working conditions. Workers then organized in record numbers. By the late 1950s, however, private-sector union growth began to decline for a number of reasons, including corporate opposition, the shift in the U.S. economy from manufacturing to services, and the globalization of labor markets.

Unionization in state and local government developed and flourished in the 1960s and 1970s, more than tripling during the 1960s alone. Why the sudden growth? In retrospect, several reasons are apparent.

First, the rise of unionism in government was spurred by the realization by state and local employees that they were underpaid and otherwise maltreated in comparison to their private-sector counterparts, who had progressed so well with unionization and collective bargaining. Second, the bureaucratic and impersonal nature of work in large government organizations encouraged unionization to preserve the dignity of the workers. A third reason for the rise of state and local unionism was the employees' lack of confidence in many civil service systems. Not only were pay and benefits inadequate, but grievance processes were controlled by management, employees had little or no say in setting personnel policies, and "merit" selection, promotion, and pay were often fraught with management favoritism. Fourth, public employees got caught up in the 1960s' fervor of social change. They saw other groups in American society winning concessions from government authorities and decided to join in.

Perhaps most important, the growth of unions in government was promoted by a significant change in the legal environment of labor relations. The rights of state and local employees to join unions and bargain collectively with manage-

collective bargaining
A formal arrangement in which representatives of labor and management negotiate wages, benefits, and working conditions.

ment were guaranteed by several U.S. Supreme Court rulings, state legislation, local ordinances, and various informal arrangements that became operative during the 1960s and 1970s. Wisconsin was the first state to permit collective bargaining for state workers, in 1959. Today, forty-two states specifically allow at least one category of state or local government employees to engage in collective bargaining.

The extent of unionization and collective bargaining is greatest in the states of the industrial Midwest and Northeast—the same areas so fertile for the growth of private-sector unions. A handful of traditionalistic states, including Arizona, Mississippi, Utah, Virginia, and the Carolinas, continues to resist the incursion of state and local unions (see Figure 8.2). Public employees in these jurisdictions have the legal and constitutional right to join a union, but their government authorities do not have a corresponding duty to bargain with them over wages, benefits, or conditions of work.

Approximately 38 percent of all state and local government workers belong to unions, compared with less than 10 percent of workers in private industry. The highest proportions of union workers are found in education, highways, public welfare, police protection, fire protection, and sanitation.[25]

The surge in the fortunes of state and local unions was partially arrested by the taxpayer revolt of the late 1970s and by President Reagan's successful effort

FIGURE 8.2 **Collective Bargaining Rights in the States**

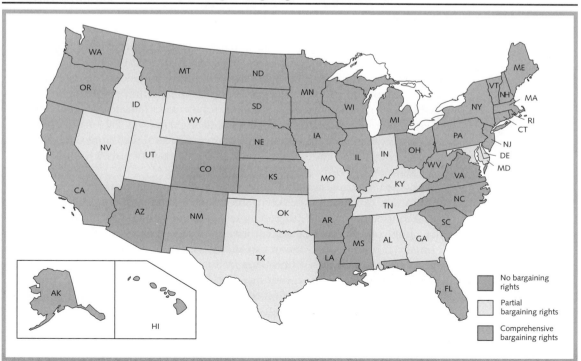

to "bust" a federal air traffic controllers' union. Also, a severe recession in the early 1980s slowed the growth of government employment and halted the rapid gains in salary levels that had accompanied the growth of unions and collective bargaining. Further resistance to unions developed in the 1990s and early 2000s as governments downsized and privatized, seeking greater efficiencies. Taxpayer resistance helped stiffen the backbones of public officials, who had been criticized in some jurisdictions for giving the unions too much.

As a result of these factors, unionism in state and local government has leveled off in some jurisdictions. Substantial gains in membership and bargaining rights are not likely in the near future; indeed, there are tentative signs of reversals in some states. Nonetheless, unions remain an important and highly visible component of many state and local government personnel systems.

What is the impact of collective bargaining in state and local government? Market forces, such as profit levels and the supply and demand for labor, largely determine the outcomes of bargaining between a union and a firm in the private sector. In government, however, political factors are much more important. The technical process of negotiating over wages and other issues in government is very similar to that in business. But the setting makes government labor relations much more complex, mostly because the negotiating process culminates in the political allocation of *public* resources.

Four factors make government labor relations highly political.[26] First, public officials are under greater pressure than private employers to settle labor disputes. Public services are highly visible and often monopolistic in nature; for example, there are no other convenient suppliers of police and fire protection. Accordingly, elected officials who confront a controversial labor dispute in an "essential service" may fear that it will derail their opportunity for reelection.

Second, public-employee unions have considerable political clout. Their members can influence election outcomes, particularly at the local level. A recalcitrant mayor or city council member who opposes a hefty wage increase may suffer defeat at the polls in the next election if the municipal union members vote as a bloc. Unions may actively engage in politics by raising money, writing letters to the editor about candidates, knocking on doors to get out the vote, formally endorsing candidates, or using any of the other electoral techniques employed by interest groups. The larger unions have professional lobbyists to represent them at the state capitol or in city hall.

A third politicizing factor in government labor relations is the symbiotic relationship that can develop between unions and elected officials. In exchange for special consideration at the bargaining table and perhaps elsewhere, the unions can offer public officials two valued commodities: labor peace and electoral support.

Finally, a hard-pressed union can use the strike or a related job action (such as a slowdown or a picket line) as a political weapon. In the private sector, a strike is not likely to have widespread public repercussions unless it involves goods or services that the nation relies on for its economic well-being (such as air transportation, coal mining, or, as a 1997 United Parcel Service strike demonstrated, communications). In government, however, a strike can directly involve the health and safety of all the citizens of a jurisdiction. For instance, a general strike involving police officers, firefighters, and sanitation workers has the potential to turn a city into filthy, life-threatening anarchy. The simultaneous strike by 4,300 bus and train drivers and 42,000 other Los Angeles County employees in 2000 is a case in point. Nearly half a million commuters had to make other arrangements to get to work, and thousands more encountered delays at health clinics and other facilities.

Strikes and other job actions by public employees are illegal in most jurisdictions, although twelve states permit work stoppages by "nonessential" workers under strictly regulated conditions. However, teachers, health care workers, firefighters, and others sometimes walk off the job anyway. The nightmare of a defenseless populace terrorized by acts of violence during a police strike, or of the stench of garbage piling up on city streets for weeks during the hot months of July and August, has convinced many an elected official to seek prompt settlement of government-labor impasses.

Given these politicizing factors, one might expect unions in government to be extravagantly successful at the bargaining table. In fact, this is not the case at all. Public-employee unions have raised wages and salaries an average of 4 to 8 percent, depending on the service, place, and time period under consideration (for example, teachers earn around 5 percent more, and firefighters around 8 percent more, if represented by a union). These figures are much lower than those representing the union-associated wage impacts that have been identified in the private sector. Greater success has come in the form of better benefits, such as generous pensions and health care insurance. It should be noted that union-driven wage and benefit hikes in the private sector are absorbed through profits, layoffs, productivity gains, or higher product prices. In government, by contrast, the choices are to raise taxes or fees, cut services, increase productivity, or contract out to a private firm.

Certain personnel impacts have also been associated with collective bargaining in government. Clearly, unions have gained a stronger voice in management decisionmaking. All personnel-related issues are potentially negotiable, from employee selection and promotion procedures to retention in the event of a reduction in force. As a result of collective bargaining, many government employers have altered civil service rules, regulations, and procedures. In heavily unionized jurisdictions, two personnel systems coexist uncomfortably—the traditional civil service system and the collective bargaining system.[27] Certainly the rights of public employees have been strengthened by unions.

Generally speaking, governments and collective bargaining have reached an uneasy accommodation. The principle of merit in making personnel decisions is still largely in place; and it is usually supported strongly by the unions, so long as seniority is fully respected as an employment decision rule. In an increasing number of jurisdictions, unions are cooperating with management to increase productivity in government services through participative decisionmaking techniques, labor-management partnerships, and worker empowerment programs.

The Politics of Bureaucracy

In an ideal democracy, political officials popularly elected by the people would make all decisions regarding public policy. They would delegate to public administrators in the executive branch the duty of carrying out these decisions through the agencies of state and local government. In the real world of bureaucratic politics, however, the line dividing politics and administration is transparent. Politicians frequently interfere in administrative matters, as when a legislator calls an agency head to task for not treating a constituent favorably. Administrators play politics at the state capitol and in city hall by participating in and influencing policy formulation decisions.

Joining Administration and Politics

Bureaucrats are intimately involved in making public policy, from the design of legislation to its implementation. Government workers are often the seedbed for policy ideas that grow to become law, in large part because they are more familiar with agency, departmental, and clientele problems and prospects than anyone else in government. It is not unusual, for instance, for law enforcement policy to originate with police administrators or higher-education policy to be the brainchild of university officials.

bureaucratic discretion
The ability of public employees to make decisions interpreting law and administrative regulations.

Once a bill does become law, state and local employees must interpret the language of the legislation in order to put it into effect. Because most legislation is written in very general terms, civil servants must apply a great deal of **bureaucratic discretion** in planning and delivering services, making rules for service delivery, adjudicating cases and complaints, and otherwise managing the affairs of government. All states have legal systems for hearing and acting on disputes over agency rules and regulations; one example is the application of regulations for local drinking-water cleanliness. These administrative procedures permit individuals and firms to challenge agency rules and regulations before an administrative law judge, who issues an order settling the dispute. In a very real sense, the ultimate success or failure of a public policy depends on the administrators who are responsible for its implementation. Experienced legislators and chief executives understand this, and they bring relevant administrators into the legislative process at a very early stage. The knowledge and expertise of these administrators are invaluable in developing an appropriate policy approach to a specific problem, and their cooperation is essential if a policy enacted into law is to be carried out as the lawmakers intend.

clientele group
A group that benefits from a specific government program, such as contractors and construction firms in state highway department spending programs.

Thus bureaucratic power derives from knowledge, expertise, information, and discretionary authority. It also comes from external sources of support for agency activities—that is, from the chief executive, legislators, and interest groups. Those who receive the benefits of government programs—the clientele, "stakeholders," or "customers"—are also frequently organized into pressure groups. All government programs benefit some interest—agricultural policy for the farm community, public assistance policy for the poor—and these **clientele groups** often are capable of exerting considerable influence in support of policies that benefit them.

Their support is critical for securing the resources necessary to develop and operate a successful government program. They serve as significant political assets to state agencies and municipal and county departments that are seeking new programs or additional funding from legislative and executive bodies, and they can become fearsome political in-fighters when their program interests are threatened.[28] Often, clientele and other concerned interest groups align with relevant government agencies and legislative committees to dominate policymaking and implementation in a particular policy field. These "iron triangles" or "subgovernments" may be found in fields ranging from health care policy to public education.

The problem of politics and administration, then, has two dimensions. First, elected officials have the duty of holding administrators responsible for their decisions and accountable to the public interest, as defined by the constitution and by statute. Second, political oversight and intrusion into administrative activities should be minimized so that administrative decisions and actions are grounded in objective rules and procedures—not in the politics of favoritism. For example, legislators have the duty of ensuring that decisions by a state department of environmental protection guard the public from harmful effects of pollution while treating polluting companies fairly. Nevertheless, state representatives should not instruct agency employees to go easy on a favored business constituent. Most government agencies discharge their tasks competently and professionally, and therefore require little direct oversight. Occasionally, however, a "rogue" agency or department head may strike out in the wrong direction.

An example of the proper balance of politics and administration is the lobbying of public administrators by legislative officials. Such lobbying occurs when legislators and council members perform casework for members of their constituency. Although on occasion the legislator-lobbyist seeks favorable treatment that borders on illegality, the bulk of legislative casework comprises responses to citizens' inquiries or complaints, or requests for clarification of administrative regulations. Such legislative casework is useful in that it promotes both feedback on the delivery of services and helpful exchanges of information with elected officials. If inquiries determine bias in the means by which services are being delivered, corrective political actions can be taken.[29]

In sum, state and local politics are intricately joined with administration. Public policy is made and implemented through the interaction of elected officials, interest groups, and public administrators. Nonetheless, the vast majority of administrative decisions are based on the neutral competence and professionalism of public employees. Generally, administrators identify and balance a variety of often conflicting interests in carrying out their responsibilities.

Professionals in State and Local Government

The growth of professionalism in government is a controversial phenomenon that has generated much discussion among scholars.[30] Virtually every profession in the United States is represented in state and local government, including law, medicine, teaching, certified public accounting, social work, librarianship, and city planning. In addition, there is the emerging profession of public administration itself, which embraces administrative generalists such as city managers and department heads. The proportion of professionals in state and local government employment has risen steadily, and an increasing number of government workers hold graduate degrees or professional licenses.

Critics bemoan professionalism in government. Each profession, they say, has its own narrow view of the world, grounded in its education process and specialized knowledge. Some fear that a professionalized bureaucracy pursues only its own limited notion of what is in the public interest (and in the interest of the profession), rather than balancing the interests of the citizenry, clientele groups, and elected officials.

Actually, a strong case can be made that professionalism encourages administrators to respond neutrally, objectively, and competently to competing interests in government.[31] Certainly professional norms, standards, and codes of ethics provide public administrators with a means for deciphering and responding to diverse public interests. They also promote accountability for work activities and encourage a sense of personal duty.[32]

Excellent examples of the value of professionalism can be found in case studies of urban service delivery in Houston, Chicago, San Antonio, Oakland, Detroit, and other cities. Such studies reveal that bureaucratic decision rules, usually based on professional standards, serve as the basis for allocating services in police and fire protection, recreation, street repair, and other areas. This finding is important, because it indicates that urban services are generally provided without discrimination on the basis of wealth or color.[33] When, for example, the municipal transportation department must decide which streets to repave, a formula is applied that takes into account such factors as date of the last repaving, intensity of public usage, and the condition of the road.

This is not to say that such decisions are never made on the basis of political favoritism. Sometimes political pressures influence bureaucratic discretion. On the whole, however, state and local services are provided in an unbiased fashion through the application of professional norms and standards.

Reinventing Government

State and local government employment has burgeoned since the 1960s at a rate much faster than that of population growth. In Texas, the number of state workers jumped from 112,000 in 1970 to 223,000 in 1990 and 1,140,226 in 1998; in New Jersey during the same twenty-eight-year period, the increase was from 58,000 to 431,350 workers. The total state and local government payroll exceeds about $400 billion per year. Explanations for this huge expansion in the size and costs of government are numerous, taking into account federal mandates, public-employee unionization, partisan politics, and the power of incremental budgeting.

Are the quantity and quality of services better than ever? Not according to most citizens, as we pointed out at the beginning of this chapter. Still, taxpayer ire and criticism of government at all levels seems to have peaked in 2001, when the heroic actions of public employees and military personnel in response to terrorist events helped citizens once again understand the value of public service. Calls for making government more efficient and effective have also played a role.

Many new strategies are being tried in an effort to improve the performance, productivity, and responsiveness of state and local governments.

The most far-reaching approach is called reinventing government, based on a widely read book with the same name written by David Osborne and Ted Gaebler.[34] According to these authors, governments today are preoccupied with rules and regulations and hierarchy; their bureaucracies are bloated, inefficient, and altogether poorly suited for meeting the demands being made on them. The solution is for governments to tap the powers of entrepreneurialism and market competition to design and provide efficient and effective services to state and local "customers." In short, governments should "steer, not row," by stressing a facilitative or cooperative approach to getting services to citizens rather than delivering all services directly. Among the alternative service-delivery systems described by the authors are public-private partnerships, volunteerism, voucher plans, and technical assistance. Once transformed, the governments would be enterprising, mission driven, outcome oriented, focused on their customers' needs, and prepared to "do more with less."

Osborne and Gaebler's book was met with great enthusiasm by many people in government. President Clinton and Vice President Gore commissioned the National Performance Review to make recommendations on reinventing the federal government. However, critics soon appeared like ants at a picnic. First one or two came forward; then a horde of academics and practitioners emerged to question and even ridicule the assumptions and examples associated with reinventing government. Among the forbidding obstacles to such profound change in government activities and behavior are rule-bound civil service systems, which tend to discourage risk taking; the inevitable inertia that plagues public organizations having no "bottom line" and few market-driven incentives; the difficulties of innovating in organizations created essentially to regulate; the need for politicians to buy into and support the movement, which implies greater autonomy and discretion for administrative agencies, but more risks and more mistakes as well; and the certain opposition by powerful vested interests, such as public-employee unions, that feel threatened by change.

Undeterred by the carping critics and maligning malcontents, many state and local governments have adopted a reinventing attitude in tackling various problems. They have placed their bets on (1) total quality management, (2) the privatization of government services, and (3) e-government.

Total Quality Management

Total quality management (TQM) is in use in several states. Designed by the late management guru W. Edwards Deming, TQM stresses worker participation in decisionmaking, continuous improvement in work processes, and treatment of organizational clients as customers whose satisfaction is the major goal. Quality improvement and excellence are the principal values. Applied successfully in some state and local settings, TQM is credited with reducing costs and improving service quality.[35] Critics, however, have pronounced it an overblown fad, inappropriate for the public sector. It is expensive and time consuming to put into place, they insist, and elected officials derive few benefits from supporting it. Perhaps for these reasons, TQM's popularity had faded by 2002.

Privatization

Privatization, which shifts government functions to private or nonprofit organizations through such service arrangements as vouchers, franchises, and contracting out, is a widely heralded reform that garners much support today, especially among conservatives, Republicans, and others who want to see a "businesslike" approach to government. Virtually any government service is a candidate for contracting out ("outsourcing"), from jails to janitorial work, and from teaching to trash collection. (In theory, most government facilities could even be sold to private interests and operated as businesses. Airports and bridges are obvious examples.) The purported benefits of privatization include cost savings, higher-quality services, and more efficient service delivery, making it an increasingly popular strategy for reducing service costs. To date, privatization has been most frequently used to outsource vehicle towing, solid waste collection, building security, street repair, ambulance services, printing, and social welfare services.[36]

In choosing the privatization route to reinventing government, Massachusetts has contracted out mental health care, prison health care, various highway maintenance functions, and operations of interstate highway rest stops, among many other functions.[37] New York has contracted out the processing of state personal income tax returns. Riverside, California, has privatized operations of its public libraries, while Chicago outsources window washing, sewer cleaning, and compost processing. Privately built and operated toll roads and bridges operate in a growing number of states.

Still, privatization isn't as easy as it sounds, and it doesn't guarantee savings.[38] It usually elicits virulent opposition from public-employee unions, who fear the loss of jobs or reductions in pay and benefits. Unless governments carefully monitor the quality and effectiveness of privatized services, performance may decline and costs may actually rise. Insufficient oversight on the part of some jurisdictions has resulted in cost overruns, shoddy services, and fraud or corruption by the contractors. Service disruptions have occurred when a firm's workers have walked off the job. Indeed, successful outsourcing requires not only careful government planning, design, and analysis of what the jurisdiction and its citizens need and want to have done but also a recognition that government accountability cannot be negotiated. The state, county, or city must remember that ultimately it will be held accountable for successful, reliable delivery of a service. If anything goes wrong, government officials will be blamed and held responsible—not the private provider. Successful contract monitoring requires inspections, performance reports, and assiduous investigations of citizen complaints.[39]

To keep contractors honest, some governments use multiple, competing firms or nonprofit organizations to deliver the same service to different state agencies or localities. Phoenix, for instance, devised a garbage-collection plan that permitted the city public works department to compete against private collectors for long-term contracts in five service districts. The city workers were consistently noncompetitive in their bids. But after garbage-truck drivers re-designed routes and work schedules and adopted one-person collection vehicles, the public works department eventually won back all five district contracts. In this case, government, prodded by "managed competition" or "competitive contracting," was able to do more with less and achieve greater operating efficiencies than private firms could.[40] Arizona state employees compete head-to-head with a national firm in administering public assistance programs. Led by pioneers Phoenix and Indianapolis, other jurisdictions are developing public-private partnerships. Such collaboration between governments, nonprofit organizations, and private firms saved Indianapolis some $100 million in four years through negotiated arrangements in wastewater treatment, recycling, sewer billing, street sweeping, and many other services.[41]

Is privatization worthwhile? Local officials believe that outsourcing improves service delivery in most cases, and research suggests that privatization saves cities about 16 to 20 percent for most service categories. Studies of the alleged benefits of privatization have been criticized on methodological and statistical grounds.[42] It is not a cure-all for the problems besetting states and local governments, but privatization does represent one potentially useful alternative for reinventing government.

E-Government

Finally, e-government is reinventing, or reengineering, the way a variety of government activities are conducted and making the face of government more friendly. Some improvements are rather mundane and commonsensical. For instance, in many states, renewal of auto licenses and registrations can now be accomplished at home or work, by telephone or online, and paid for with a credit card. Seattle, Miami, Little Rock (Arkansas), Scottsdale (Arizona), and other cities have established "Little City Halls" in major neighborhoods to make local government more convenient for residents. Other improvements are more futuristic. Arizonians can vote in primary elections on the Web and view live proceedings of the state senate and house of representatives. New York City and Washington State have mounted computer-synchronized attacks on crime that electronically track incidents and suspects, spot emerging crime patterns, and coordinate some crime-fighting activities with other state and local jurisdictions. Pennsylvania saved $2 million in one year through online state income tax filing.[43] Management of personnel systems has been vastly improved in Wisconsin through online job bulletins, walk-in testing services, and rapid hiring of employees for hard-to-fill positions.[44]

Unmistakably, we are well on the road to electronic government. "Virtual offices" operating through the Internet are establishing new, convenient, twenty-four-hour-a-day connections among citizens, businesses, nonprofit organizations, and their governments. From a home or office personal computer or a conveniently located PC in the neighborhood library, citizens can obtain everything from English-language lessons online in Boston to legal aid from "Victor, the cyber-lawyer" in Arizona. Massive filing systems for documents and other hard copy are no longer needed. Instead, paperless offices use imaging technology to scan, store, and access important records of marriages, births, deaths, business licenses, and a host of other documents.

Meanwhile, telecommuting permits county employees throughout Los Angeles and in an increasing number of other state and local jurisdictions to work at home several days a week, saving workers commuting time, enhancing productivity, and cutting down on air pollution. Welfare case-processing activities are being reengineered in many jurisdictions. In Minnesota, New Jersey, and Wisconsin, for instance, welfare recipients use "smart cards" to draw monthly benefits, thereby reducing paperwork, program administration costs, and the number of stolen checks. To further cut down on fraud, Connecticut, Texas, and other states use finger-imaging systems to establish the identification of welfare recipients.

Is the move toward reinventing government merely a fad (as many critics said of TQM)?[45] Definitely not. Responsive states and localities have been reinventing their operations and services ever since they were created, and will continue to do so for as long as they exist. In the short run, some governments will be reinvented, or at least changed in fundamental ways, while others continue to do things the old way. Change is politically risky, and inertia is a powerful force. Ultimately, it is the responsibility of citizens and the elected officials who represent them to bring about change and reforms.

Meanwhile, at least three hurdles are slowing the diffusion of e-government: the enormous investments required to finance the computer hardware and software; unresolved questions of liability, privacy, and security; and the fact that about half of U.S. citizens do not have ready access to personal computers. Nevertheless, the potential of e-government to make government more accessible, understood, and efficient is enormous.

The Quality of Public Administration

Despite the quantity of criticism hurled at government agencies, departments, and workers by the popular media, elected officials, and others, the quality of public administration in state and local government has improved markedly. Of course, there is considerable variance among jurisdictions; that quality is generally of a higher level in those that are affluent, highly educated, industrialized, and urban.

The results of a two-year study of state government administrative performance are found in Table 8.4. Known as the Government Performance Project, and conducted by *Governing* magazine and the Maxwell School of Citizenship and Public Affairs at Syracuse University, this study examined state performance in five key administrative areas: financial management, capital management, human resources, managing for results, and information technology.

Administrative quality is a critical factor in support of the revitalization and responsiveness of states and localities. State and local governments, particularly through partnerships with private and nonprofit organizations, have the capacity to accomplish more and on a grander scale than ever before; and the movement to reinvent government is continuing this trend. The basics of providing

TABLE 8.4	State Administrative Report Card					
STATE	FINANCIAL MANAGEMENT	CAPITAL MANAGEMENT	HUMAN RESOURCES	MANAGING FOR RESULTS	INFORMATION TECHNOLOGY	AVERAGE GRADE
Alabama	D+	D–	C–	F	D	D
Alaska	C	C+	C–	C–	C–	C
Arizona	B–	D+	C+	B–	D+	C
Arkansas	B–	C	C+	D	D	C–
California	C–	C–	C–	C–	C+	C–
Colorado	C	C	B	C	C	C+
Connecticut	C–	C+	C–	D+	D+	C-
Delaware	A–	B	B	B	B	B
Florida	B	C	C+	B	C–	C+
Georgia	C+	C	B–	C+	C	C+
Hawaii	C–	B–	C–	C–	F	C–
Idaho	B–	B–	C	C–	D+	C
Illinois	B+	B–	B	C	D+	B–
Indiana	B	C	C+	C	C	C+
Iowa	A–	B–	B+	B+	C+	B
Kansas	B–	B	B+	C	C+	B–
Kentucky	B+	A–	B	B	C+	B
Louisiana	B–	B	C+	B	C–	B–
Maine	B–	C–	C+	C	C	C
Maryland	A–	A–	B	B–	C	B
Massachusetts	B	B+	C+	C	C	B–
Michigan	A–	B+	B+	B	B+	B+
Minnesota	A–	A–	C+	B	B	B
Mississippi	B	B	C+	C	C–	C+
Missouri	A–	A	B	A–	B+	A–
Montana	B	B+	B–	C	B–	B–
Nebraska	B+	A–	B–	B–	C+	B
Nevada	B	B+	D	C	C	C+
New Hampshire	B–	C	B	D+	C	C+
New Jersey	B–	B+	C–	B–	B–	B–
New Mexico	C–	D	B–	D+	C	C–
New York	D+	C–	C	D+	C	C–
North Carolina	B	B+	B+	B–	C	B
North Dakota	B	B+	B–	D	B–	B–
Ohio	B+	B	B	C+	B	B

TABLE 8.4   **State Administrative Report Card (cont.)**

STATE	FINANCIAL MANAGEMENT	CAPITAL MANAGEMENT	HUMAN RESOURCES	MANAGING FOR RESULTS	INFORMATION TECHNOLOGY	AVERAGE GRADE
Oklahoma	B–	C	C–	D+	C–	C
Oregon	B	B–	C+	B+	C+	B–
Pennsylvania	A–	B	B	B–	B	B
Rhode Island	B–	C+	F	C	D	C–
South Carolina	B+	B–	A–	B–	B	B
South Dakota	B+	B	C+	D	B	B–
Tennessee	B	B–	C+	C	B+	B–
Texas	B	C	B	B+	B	B
Utah	A	A	B+	B+	B+	A–
Vermont	B	B	B–	B–	C	B–
Virginia	A	A	B	A–	A–	A–
Washington	A–	A	B+	B+	A	A–
West Virginia	B	C+	C+	C	C	C+
Wisconsin	C+	A–	B+	C	B	B
Wyoming	C+	C+	B–	C	D+	C
US Average	B	B–	B–	C+	C+	

NOTE: These grades are the results of a study called the Government Performance Project. The column headings are defined as follows. (1) *Financial Management:* managing a state's financial resources, including cash management, cost accounting, and rainy day fund. (2) *Capital Management:* managing large-scale projects, upkeep on buildings. (3) *Human Resources:* managing personnel policies, procedures, and pay systems. (4) *Management for Results:* strategic planning, performance measurement. (5) *Information Technology:* data management, information planning, procurement, and training; use of information technology to transmit information to citizens and stakeholders.

SOURCE: Adapted from Katherine Barrett and Richard Greene, "Grading the States," *Governing* (February 1999): 17–90; and from data collected by the Maxwell School of Citizenship and Public Affairs at Syracuse University.

services, from disposing of dead animals to delivering healthy human babies, will continue to depend on government employees with high standards of performance and professionalism.

Chapter Recap

➤ The quality and capacity of public administration have greatly improved in the great majority of the states and local governments.

➤ State and local government employment has grown rapidly during the past three decades.

➤ State and local operating budgets must be balanced each year.

➤ Interest groups, agencies, the chief executive, and the legislative body are the four principal actors in the budgetary process.

➤ Budgets tend to expand (or contract) incrementally.

➤ The trend in accounting for revenues and expenditures is toward performance-based budgeting.

➤ Most state and local jobs are situated in a merit system and filled based on knowledge, skills, and experience.

➤ Affirmative action has led to gains in advancement of minorities and women in state and local employment, but it is very controversial.

➤ States are addressing the problem of sexual harassment in public agencies.

➤ Unions and collective bargaining present a special challenge to many state and local governments.

➤ Bureaucratic discretion makes public employees important decisionmakers.

➤ There has been growth in professionalism in state and local government.

➤ The movement to reinvent government through privatization, e-government, and other steps is a major development.

Key Terms

bureaucracy (*p. 172*)
incrementalism (*p. 181*)
line-item budget (*p. 181*)
performance budgeting (*p. 182*)
capital budget (*p. 182*)
merit system (*p. 183*)

neutral competence (*p. 183*)
representative bureaucracy (*p. 185*)
affirmative action (*p. 185*)
collective bargaining (*p. 188*)
bureaucratic discretion (*p. 192*)
clientele group (*p. 192*)

Surfing the Net

Most major municipalities and all states have webpages. Many provide links to jobs, reinventing-government initiatives, service-provision information, and other data. An innovative, award-winning website is Indianapolis's at **www.indygov.org**. An interesting site on technology and government is located at **www.govtech.net**. An informative public-employee union website is that of the American Federation of State, County and Municipal Employees, at **www.afscme.org**. For publications and information on public-private partnerships, see **www.ncppp.org**. For a step-by-step illustration of a state budget process, see **http://www.state.ny.us/dob/citizen/process/process.html**. An interesting e-government site is **www.servicearizona.ihost.com**. To view streaming video of public meetings in Indiana, see **www.stream.hoosier.net/cats**. Finally, information on the Government Performance Project can be found at **www.maxwell.syr.edu/gpp** and at **www.governing.com**.

THE JUDICIARY

The Structure of State Court Systems
The Two Tiers of Courts » Structural Reforms

How Judges Are Selected
Legislative Election » Partisan Popular Election » Nonpartisan Popular Election » Merit Plan » Gubernatorial Appointment » Which Selection Plan Is Best? » Removal of Judges

Judicial Decisionmaking
In and Out of the Trial Court » Inside the Appellate Court » Influence of the Legal System » Personal Values, Attitudes, and Characteristics of Judges

New Judicial Federalism
Judicial Activism in the States » Current Trends in State Courts

State Court Reform
Financial Improvements » Dealing with Growing Caseloads » Compensating the Judges » State Courts Enter the 2000s

Crime and Criminal Justice

In the case of *Barnes* v. *Glen Theatre Inc.* (1991), a prudish U.S. Supreme Court ruled that nude dancing, being dangerous to "order and morality," is not protected as free expression under the First Amendment of the U.S. Constitution. This case, which arose in Indiana, was tried in the federal courts under national constitutional law.

Yet in Boston, a city once known for banning all manner of objects and activities deemed to be immoral, totally naked women grind, bump, and pirouette at tacky cabarets, fully confident that their activities are legal. In Massachusetts, the voluntary display of a naked body has been protected under the *state* constitution as a form of expression since the state supreme court ruled it so in 1984.[1] As the U.S. Supreme Court has become increasingly conservative, from the Chief Justiceship of Earl Warren (1953–1969) to today's Rehnquist Court, state courts have become more popular with individuals and groups advocating liberal causes such as civil rights, free speech, and freedom of expression. All sorts of conflicts and problems find their way to state and local courts, from the profound (abortion rights) to the profane (nude dancing). And courts at this level are very busy; New York State's cases alone outnumber those filed in all federal courts by a factor of 9 to 1. The state courts are fully engaged in a variety of legal activities. Many are innovative in their decisionmaking and administration; in addition, they are more accessible to the people and responsive to their concerns than are the federal courts.

Sometimes, state supreme courts act as policymakers. As the third branch of government, the judiciary is, after all, the final authority on the meaning of the language of laws and constitutions, as well as the ultimate arbiter of disputes between the executive and legislative branches. It also makes public policy through rulings on questions of political, social, and economic significance, and may serve as the last chance for minority interests to defend themselves from the decisions of the majority. As noted in Chapter 3, state courts have become more active policymakers in recent years and have increasingly based important decisions on state constitutions rather than on the national constitution. And as with the other branches of state government, their structures and processes have been greatly reformed and modernized. In our lifetimes, nearly all of us will experience the judicial branch as direct participants. At times, the courts are more accessible to us than are the other branches of government. Disputes that cannot be resolved through ordinary legislative, executive, and political processes frequently wind up before a judge, as litigation.

The work of the fifty state court systems is divided into three major areas: civil, criminal, and administrative. In **civil cases,** one individual or corporation sues another over an alleged wrong. Occasionally, a governmental body is party to a civil action. Typical civil actions are property disputes and suits for damages arising from automobile or other accidents. **Criminal cases** involve the breaking of a law by an individual or a corporation. The state is usually the plaintiff; the accused is the defendant. Murder, assault, embezzlement, and disorderly conduct are common examples. **Administrative cases** concern court actions such as probating wills, revoking driver's licenses, or determining custody of a child. Some administrative cases involve administrative law judges and quasi-judicial (less formal) proceedings.

State courts adjudicate (take actions to administer justice) by interpreting state statutes, the state and federal constitutions, and common law. In developing and deciphering the **common law,** courts are concerned with the legal rules and expectations that have developed historically in a state through the citizens' custom, culture, and habits, and that have been given standing through the courts. The most important applications of common law today concern enforcing contracts (contract law), owning and selling property (property law), and establishing liability for death or injuries to people as well as damage to property (tort law).

civil case
A case that concerns a dispute involving individuals or organizations.

criminal case
A case brought by the state against persons accused of a crime or other offense.

administrative case
A case in which a government agency applies rules to settle a legal dispute.

common law
Unwritten law based on tradition, custom, or court decisions.

The Structure of State Court Systems

State courts have evolved in response to changes in their environment. In colonial days, they developed distinctly, influenced by local customs and beliefs. Owing to a shortage of trained lawyers and an abiding distrust of English law, the first judges were laymen who served on a part-time basis. It did not take long for the courts to become overwhelmed with cases: Case overloads were reported as long ago as 1685.[2] More than three centuries later, case backlogs still plague our state judiciaries.

As the population and the economy grew, so did the amount of litigation. Courts expanded in number and in degree of specialization. However, their development was not carefully planned. Rather, new courts were added to existing structures. The results were predictably complex and confusing, with overlapping, independent jurisdictions and responsibilities. For instance, Chicago offered an astounding array of jurisdictions, estimated at one time to number 556.[3] State court systems were beset as well by a host of other serious problems, including administrative inefficiency, congestion, and excessive delays. In short, the American system of justice left much to be desired.

The organization of the state courts is important because it affects the quality and quantity of judicial decisions and the access of individuals and groups to the legal system. It also influences how legal decisions are made. An efficiently organized system, properly staffed and administered, can do a better job of deciding a larger number of cases than a poorly organized system can. Court structure is of great interest to those who make their living in the halls of justice—namely, lawyers and judges. It can also be an issue of concern to citizens who find themselves in court.

The Two Tiers of Courts

general jurisdiction
The power of a court to both hear a case first and review cases decided by lower courts

original jurisdiction
The power of a court to hear a case first.

appellate jurisdiction
The power of a court to review cases previously decided by a lower court.

Most states today have a two-tiered court structure: trial courts and appellate courts. Each tier, or level, has a different *jurisdiction,* or range of authority. Trial courts, which comprise the lower tier, may be of (1) limited jurisdiction or (2) **general jurisdiction.** Limited, or "special," jurisdiction trial courts have **original jurisdiction** over specialized cases, such as those involving juveniles, traffic offenses, and small claims. Original jurisdiction gives courts the power to hear certain types of cases first, in contrast to **appellate jurisdiction,** which gives the courts power to review cases on appeal after they have been tried elsewhere. Most states have three to five courts of limited jurisdiction, with names that reflect the type of specialized case: traffic court, police court, probate court, municipal court, and so on. Criminal cases here are usually restricted by law to misdemeanor violations of municipal or county ordinances that are punishable by a small fine, a short jail term, or both. Additional courts of limited jurisdiction have been created to deal with special types of cases or circumstances. For example, all states now have drug courts with the dual aims of processing drug-related offenses more efficiently and reducing the recidivism rates of drug offenders on probation or parole. And water courts have been established in Colorado and Montana to hear disputes over water rights.

Present in almost all states are *small-claims courts,* which offer a relatively simple and inexpensive way to settle minor civil disputes without either party having to incur the financial and temporal burdens of lawyers and legal procedures. Small claims courts are usually divisions of county, city, or district trial courts. In the cases they hear, the plaintiff (the person bringing the suit) asks for monetary recompense from the defendant (the individual or firm being sued) for some harm or damage. Claims are limited to varying amounts, usually around $1,000.

The proceedings are informal. Each party presents to a judge the relevant facts and arguments to support his or her case. The party with the preponderance of evidence on his or her side wins. Most disputes involve tenant-landlord conflicts, property damage, or the purchase of goods (for example, shoddy merchandise or the failure of a customer to pay a bill).

major trial court
Court of general jurisdiction that handles major criminal and civil cases

The second type of trial court is the **major trial court,** which exercises general authority over civil and criminal cases. Most cases are filed initially under a major trial court's original jurisdiction. However, trial courts also hear cases on appeal from courts of limited jurisdiction. Major trial courts are often organized along county or district lines. Their names—circuit courts, superior courts, district courts, courts of common pleas—vary widely.

supreme court
The highest state court, beyond which there is no appeal except in cases involving federal law.

The upper tier consists of appellate courts: **supreme courts** (sometimes called courts of last resort) and, in most states, **intermediate appellate courts.** Oklahoma and Texas have two supreme courts, one for criminal cases and the other for civil disputes. Thirty-nine states have intermediate appellate courts (Alabama, Oklahoma, Oregon, Texas, Pennsylvania, and Tennessee have two, typically one each for criminal and civil cases). Most intermediate appellate courts are known as courts of appeals. Their work generally involves cases on appeal from lower courts. Thus, these courts exercise appellate jurisdiction. By contrast, state supreme courts have original jurisdiction in certain types of cases, such as those dealing with constitutional issues, as well as appellate jurisdiction.

intermediate appellate court
A state appellate court that relieves the case burden on the supreme court by hearing certain types of appeals.

Intermediate appellate courts constitute the most notable change in the structure of the state court system during the past thirty years. They are intended to increase the capability of supreme courts by reducing their caseload burden, speeding up the appellate process, and improving the quality of judicial decisionmaking. The bulk of the evidence points to moderate success in achieving each of these objectives.[4] Case backlogs and delays have been reduced, and supreme court justices are better able to spend an appropriate amount of time on significant cases. Counteracting this positive trend, however, is the growing number of mandatory appeals, such as those for death penalty cases, that now make up more than 60 percent of the caseload.[5]

If a state supreme court so chooses, it can have the final word on any state or local case except one involving a national constitutional question, such as First Amendment rights. Some cases can be filed in either federal or state court. For example, a person who assaults and abducts a victim and then transports him across a state line can be charged in state court with assault and in federal court with kidnapping. Some acts violate nearly identical federal and state laws; possession or sale of certain illegal drugs is a common example. Other cases fall entirely under federal court jurisdiction, such as those involving treason, mail theft, or currency-law violations.

Thus, there exists in the United States a *dual system* of courts that is sometimes referred to as *judicial federalism*. Generally, state courts adjudicate, or decide, matters of state law, whereas federal courts deal with national law. The systems are separate and distinct. Although state courts cannot overturn federal law, they can base certain rulings on the federal constitution. Recently, state courts have decided cases governed by both state and federal law in areas such as hate crimes, the right to die, and gay rights. It is very unusual for a case decided by a state supreme court to be heard by the U.S. Supreme Court or any other federal court. An important exception to the custom occurred in the aftermath of the 2000 presidential election, when the U.S. Supreme Court overturned a Florida Supreme Court decision that had ordered a recount of ballots in three counties. The intervention of the nation's highest court effectively awarded the presidency to George W. Bush.

Structural Reforms

The court reform movement that swept across the states in the 1960s and 1970s sought, among other things, to convert the state courts into more rational, efficient, and simplified structures. A driving goal was to increase the capacity and responsiveness of state and local judicial systems. One important legacy of that movement is the *unified court system*.[6]

Although the two tiers of state courts appear to represent a hierarchy, in fact they do not. Courts in most states operate with a great deal of autonomy. They have their own budgets, hire their own staff, and use their own procedures. Moreover, the decisions of major and specialized trial courts usually stand unchallenged. Only around 5 percent of lower-court cases are appealed, mostly because great expense and years of waiting are certain to be involved.

Unified court systems consolidate the various trial courts with overlapping jurisdictions into a single administrative unit and clearly specify each court's purpose and jurisdiction. The aim of this arrangement, which includes centralized management and rule making, is to make the work of the courts more efficient, saving time and money and avoiding confusion. Instead of a system whereby each judge runs her own fiefdom, such responsibilities as rule making, record-keeping, budgeting, and personnel management are standardized and centralized, usually under the authority of the state supreme court.

Centralization relieves judges from the mundane tasks of day-to-day court management so that they can concentrate on adjudication. Additional efficiencies are gained from *offices of court administration*, which exist in all states. Court administration in an increasing number of states involves actively managing, monitoring, and planning the courts' resources and operations.

Computer technology is permitting tremendous improvements in how the courts manage criminal cases. In Los Angeles County, which has the largest local government justice system in the country, a Consolidated Criminal History

Reporting System, called "Cheers," consolidates the databases of fifty law enforcement agencies, twenty-one prosecutor's offices, twenty-four municipal courts, and sixty-two other authorities. Now, judges and other law enforcement authorities have instant access to case histories of defendants, as well as to computerized fingerprint-matching technology.[7] Responsiveness to the public is also growing. An increasing number of state courts are using the World Wide Web to disseminate court documents, judicial rulings, and general information such as instructions for jury duty, maps showing directions to the courthouse, and answers to commonly asked questions about the courts. Some display photographs and biographies of judges, many permit interested citizens to ask questions via e-mail, and others even broadcast cases live over the Internet.[8] (See "Surfing the Net" at the end of the chapter.)

Despite consolidation and centralization, court structures and processes continue to vary widely among the states, as shown in Figure 9.1. Generally, the most modern systems are found in the western states, including Alaska and Hawaii, while some of the most antiquated are situated in southern states, among them Arkansas and Georgia.

| FIGURE 9.1 | **Simplicity and Complexity in State Court Systems** |

State court systems can vary from the simple to the very complex, as illustrated by Alaska and Georgia.

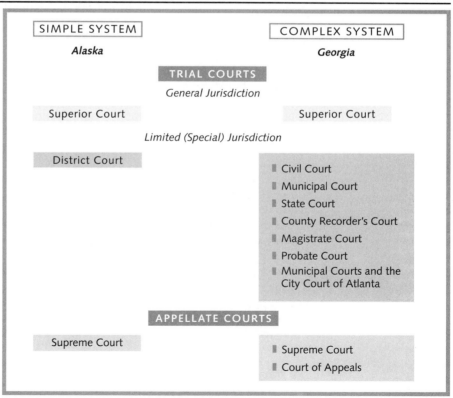

SIMPLE SYSTEM — *Alaska*

COMPLEX SYSTEM — *Georgia*

TRIAL COURTS
General Jurisdiction

Superior Court   Superior Court

Limited (Special) Jurisdiction

District Court

- Civil Court
- Municipal Court
- State Court
- County Recorder's Court
- Magistrate Court
- Probate Court
- Municipal Courts and the City Court of Atlanta

APPELLATE COURTS

Supreme Court

- Supreme Court
- Court of Appeals

SOURCE: State Court Organization, 1998. Washington D.C.: U.S. Bureau of Justice Statistics.

How Judges Are Selected

In large part, the quality of a state court system depends on the selection of competent, well-trained judges. According to the American Bar Association (ABA), the leading professional organization for lawyers, judges should be chosen on the basis of solid professional and personal qualifications, regardless of their political views and party identification. Judges should have "superior self-discipline, moral courage, and sound judgment."[9] They should be good listeners, broadly educated, and professionally qualified as lawyers. An appellate or general trial court judge should also have relevant experience in a lower court or as a courtroom attorney.

For a great many years, however, controversy has swirled over the selection of state judges. Should they be elected by popular vote? Should they be appointed by the governor? by the legislature? Many critics insist that judicial selection be free from politics and interest-group influences. Others claim that judges should regularly be held accountable to a majority of the people or to elected officials for their decisions.

The conflict between judicial independence and accountability is manifest in the five types of selection systems used in the states: legislative election, partisan popular election, nonpartisan popular election, the merit plan, and gubernatorial appointment. Most states use a single selection system for all appellate and major trial court judges. The others take separate approaches to selecting judges, depending on the tier. Figure 9.2 shows the popularity of these selection techniques for appellate and major trial courts. Some states have rather elaborate systems. Oklahoma, for example, utilizes a merit plan for the supreme court and court of criminal appeals, nonpartisan elections for its other appellate courts and district courts, and city council appointment of municipal judges.

Legislative Election

In South Carolina and Virginia, the legislature elects judges by majority vote from among announced candidates. Not surprisingly, the vast majority of judges selected under this plan are former legislators (in South Carolina, the proportion has been close to 100 percent). In these two states, a judgeship is viewed as a highly valued reward for public service and a prestigious cap to a legislative career.

Few people other than legislators approve of legislative election. Indeed, the method is open to criticism. The public has no role in either choosing judges or reelecting them, so democratic accountability is minimal. The judges may be independent, but since the major criterion for selection is service as a legislator, they often lack other qualifications. Legislative service has little connection to the demands of a judgeship.

Partisan Popular Election

This plan enjoyed popularity during the Jacksonian era as a means of ensuring a judiciary answerable to the voters. In theory, partisan election maximizes the

| **FIGURE 9.2** | **Appellate and Major Trial Court Selection Plans** |

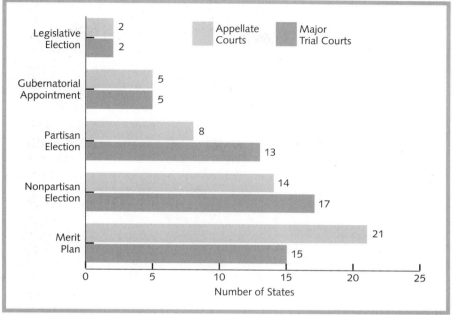

NOTE: Kansas and Missouri select some major trial court judges through a merit plan and others through partisan elections.

SOURCE: Adapted from State Court Organization, 1998. Washington, D.C.: U.S. Bureau of Justice Statistics, 1999, Tables 4 and 5.

value of judicial accountability to the people. Judges, identified by party label, must run for office on the same ticket as candidates for other state offices. And, like other candidates, they must raise and spend money for their election campaigns and publicly deal with political issues. The American Bar Association Code of Judicial Conduct forbids judicial campaigning on legal issues, but this prohibition was essentially struck down by a 2002 U.S. Supreme Court ruling that threw out a ban on issue discussions by judicial candidates in Minnesota as a violation of Free Speech.[10] As in other electoral contests, negative campaigning is on the rise in judicial elections. Even more serious is the problem that occurs when judges elected on a partisan ballot are accused of pandering to special interests during election campaigns and of favoring them in court decisions. In Texas, for instance, supreme court justices deciding a $10.5 billion judgment against Texaco in favor of Pennzoil were criticized for accepting huge campaign contributions from both parties. Nonpartisan elected judges have been open to similar charges, especially since political action committees (PACs) have boosted their contributions to candidates for state court judgeships.[11]

Wisconsin Chief Justice Shirley Abrahamson acknowledges a crowd of supporters following her reelection to the State Supreme Court in the costliest race in that state's court history. (AP/Wide World Photos)

Nonpartisan Popular Election

This selection technique won favor during the first half of the twentieth century, when reformers sought to eliminate party identification in the election of judges and certain other officials in state and local government. Political parties are prohibited from openly taking sides in nonpartisan judicial elections. In fact, they sometimes play a covert role in such contests. Approximately 95 percent of all judges have a political party preference;[12] most list it in the official biographies that are available to interested voters during campaigns.

One problem with nonpartisan elections is that they tend to reduce voter participation since party identification is an important voting cue for many citizens. However, voter turnout is very low in most judicial elections anyway, whether partisan or nonpartisan. This is a major criticism of both methods of electing judges: The winners are not truly accountable to the people, contrary to the principal advantage commonly associated with elections. Low rates of voter interest and participation frequently combine with low-key, unexciting, and issueless campaigns to keep many incumbent judges on the bench as long as they run for reelection. In addition, popular elections are criticized for the growing amount of money necessary to win a state judgeship. In some cases, the implication is that judges have sacrificed their independence and professionalism for crass electoral politics, complete with attack advertising and million-dollar war chests.

Following the trend set in executive and legislative contests, judicial campaign spending has skyrocketed. The largest campaign contributors are usually trial lawyers and other groups with a stake in judges' decisions, such as labor unions, business interests, and various professions, such as insurance or medicine.[13]

It looks as though judges running for election are forfeiting their independence in certain legal disputes while offering accountability only to the highest bidders instead of to the general public. If indeed this is the case, neither independence nor accountability is achieved. According to the president of the Ohio State Bar Association, "The people with money to spend who are affected by court decisions have reached the conclusion that it's a lot cheaper to buy a judge than a governor or an entire legislature, and he can probably do a lot more for you."[14]

If, as some people argue, it is unethical for a judge to rule on a case in which he or she has accepted money from one or more of the interested parties, then it would be difficult to bring together enough judges to hear cases in some states. Increasingly, the general sentiment is that judges should be both qualified and dignified, and that elections do not further either objective. Three states—Montana, North Carolina, and Wisconsin—have public financing for judges' campaigns to help contain spiraling costs. (Candidates for two Ohio supreme court seats spent an estimated $9 million in 2000.) Some states are also imposing spending restrictions and penalties for false campaign advertising.[15]

Merit Plan

Dissatisfaction with the other methods for selecting judges has led to the popularity of the so-called *merit plan*. Incorporating elements of gubernatorial appointment and elective systems, the merit plan attempts to provide a mechanism for appointing qualified candidates to the bench while permitting the public to evaluate a judge's performance through the ballot box.

First recommended by the ABA in 1937 and strongly supported today by virtually the entire legal community, the merit plan has been adopted by nearly all of the states that have changed their selection systems since 1940. Missouri became the initial adopter in that year. Since then another twenty-two states have adopted the merit plan, and others are considering merit selection.

The Missouri Plan   Commonly referred to as the Missouri Plan, the basic merit plan involves three steps:

1. A judicial nominating commission meets and recommends three (or more) names of prospective judges to the governor. Members of this bipartisan commission usually include a sitting judge (often the chief justice), representatives chosen by the state bar association, and laypersons appointed by the governor. The nominating commission solicits names of candidates, investigates them, chooses those it believes to be the three (or more) best-qualified individuals, and then forwards their names and files to the governor.
2. The governor appoints the preferred candidate to the vacant judgeship.
3. A retention election is held, usually after one or two years, in which the newly appointed judge's name is placed before the voters on a nonpartisan ticket. The voters decide whether or not the judge should be retained in office. If he

or she is rejected by a majority vote, the judicial nominating commission begins its work anew. Subsequent retention elections may be held every eight or twelve years, depending on the merit plan's provision.

Various hybrids of the basic plan are also in use. For example, the California Plan for choosing appellate judges begins when the governor identifies a candidate for a vacancy on the bench and sends that person's name to the Commission on Judicial Appointments. The commission, composed of two judges and the attorney general, hears testimony regarding the nominee and votes to confirm or reject. The new judge is then accepted or rejected in a retention election in the next regularly scheduled gubernatorial contest. Thus, although the governor appoints, the new judge is subject to confirmation by both the Commission on Judicial Appointments and the voters. In New Mexico's multistage merit plan, a judge is nominated by a commission and appointed by the governor. During the next general election the judge must run in a partisan election. If she wins, she must run unopposed in a nonpartisan retention election on the next general-election ballot.

The object of the merit plan is to permit the governor some appointive discretion while removing politics from the selection of judges. If it works as intended, election or direct gubernatorial appointment is replaced with a careful appraisal of candidates' professional qualifications by an objective commission. The process is intended to ensure both the basic independence of judges and their accountability to the people.

The Politics of Merit Selection   The merit plan looks great on paper, but in practice it has not fulfilled its promise. First, it certainly has not dislodged politics from judicial selection. A judgeship is too important a political office in any state ever to be immune from politics. It is a prized job and an important point of judicial access for numerous individuals, firms, and interest groups, especially the powerful state bar association.

Studies of judicial nominating commissions show that politics—partisan and otherwise—is rampant in the review and nomination of candidates.[16] For better or worse, the legal profession often dominates the process. Counting the judge who presides over the nominating commission, lawyers make up a commission majority in most of the states. Bar association lobbying is often the prime reason that merit plans are adopted in the first place. However, the legal profession is not monolithic in its politics, often dividing into two camps: plaintiff's attorneys and defendant's attorneys.

Furthermore, the influence of the governor can be exceptionally strong. The laypersons he appoints to the nominating commission may hold the judge in awe, but they are there to represent the governor's point of view and sometimes to promote specific candidates or the agenda of the governor's political party.[17] In six states, the majority of commission members are laypersons. The member who is a judge may also respect the governor's preferences, particularly if he owes his appointment to that chief executive.

A second criticism of the merit plan is that the procedure intended to ensure judicial accountability to the people—the retention election—rarely generates voter interest and seldom results in the departure of an incumbent judge from office.[18] Turnout in retention elections is normally very low and, on average, favors the incumbent by more than 70 percent.[19] Few incumbent judges have been voted out in retention elections—only a handful in sixty years. In most cases, then, merit selection essentially means a lifetime appointment.[20]

However, voter backlashes have occurred against judges whose decisions are distinctly out of step with public opinion. In 1986, California Chief Justice Rose Bird and two associate justices were swept from the state supreme court by large margins in retention elections, as voters reacted negatively to a series of supreme court rulings that significantly expanded the rights of the accused and of convicted felons. Bird had voted to overturn all sixty-one capital punishment cases brought to the court during a period when polls showed 80 percent support for the death penalty in California.[21] Ten years later, in 1996, Tennessee Supreme Court Justice Penny White was rejected in a retention election for failing to support the death penalty for the perpetrator of a particularly heinous crime.[22]

The final charge leveled against the merit plan is that despite reformers' claims to the contrary, it does not result in the appointment of better-qualified judges or of more women and minorities. When background, education, experience, and decisionmaking are taken into account, judges selected through the merit plan are comparable to those selected through other plans.[23] A large majority are white males. Most leave private practice for the bench in their forties and stay there until retirement. Approximately 20 percent come from a family in which the father or grandfather held political office (often a judgeship).[24] And a substantial majority were born, raised, and educated in the state in which they serve.

Gubernatorial Appointment

All gubernatorial appointment states are former colonies, reflecting the early popularity of the plan. As a method per se, gubernatorial appointment rates fairly high on independence, since the judge is appointed without an election; but it is weak on accountability because the judge is beholden to only one person for his or her job.

Although only five states formally recognize it, gubernatorial appointment is in fact the most common method for selecting a majority of appellate and major trial court judges in the United States. Judges in states with popular elections or merit plans often resign or retire from office just before the end of their term.[25] Under most state legal systems, the governor has the power to make interim appointments to vacant seats until the next scheduled election or the commencement of merit-plan selection processes. The governor's temporary appointee then enjoys the tremendous advantage of running as an incumbent for the next full term. Gubernatorial appointment is also used to replace a judge who dies before the expiration of the term.

What criteria does a governor apply in making appointments to the bench? Political considerations usually come first. The governor can use the appointment to reward a faithful legislator, to shore up support in certain regions of the state, to satisfy the demands of party leaders and the state legal establishment, or to appeal to women's or minority groups.[26]

Which Selection Plan Is Best?

The ongoing debate over which is best among the five formal selection systems is unlikely to be decided convincingly. Legislative election and gubernatorial appointment probably maximize the value of judicial independence, but may be the least desirable; judges selected under these systems tend to come from a rather specific political occupation (the legislature), and the general public has little opportunity to hold them accountable. Judicial accountability is maximized when judges and judicial candidates must face voters, but few incumbents are defeated in elections—only about 8 percent in state supreme courts since 1980. However, significant policy issues involving the courts can rouse voters to the polls in certain instances, meaning that elected judges who want to stay on the bench must pay attention to public opinion. None of the three remaining systems produces "better" judges, although gubernatorial appointment is more likely to benefit women than the other selection systems are.[27] And minorities have not done well under any selection plan. Hispanics and blacks fill fewer than 5 percent of state court seats. Gubernatorial appointment and legislative election apparently increase the selection opportunities for African-American judges, but significant gains probably await the development of a larger pool of Hispanic and black attorneys.

Politics, of course, is what raises all judges into office, regardless of the selection method. According to research by political scientists, the path a judge takes to the bench matters. Those chosen through elective systems tend to view the judiciary in more political—as opposed to juridical—terms than do those who reach the bench through gubernatorial or merit appointment systems. Elected judges also tend to be more activist in their decisionmaking, and they are more likely to dissent from other judges in their opinions than are appointed judges.[28] In other words, judges who attain their jobs through electoral politics tend to behave like elected officials in the executive and legislative branches of state government by emphasizing political—rather than legal—factors in their decisionmaking.[29]

Removal of Judges

Like anyone else, judges can and do break the law, go mad, suffer senility, or become physically incapable of carrying out their responsibilities. If a judge displays serious deficiencies, he or she must be removed from the bench. Forty-five states provide for impeachment, wherein charges are filed in the state house of representatives and a trial is conducted in the senate. Other traditional means for removing justices include the legislative address and popular recall. In the legislative address, both houses of the legislature by two-thirds vote must ask the governor to dismiss a judge. Popular recall requires a specified number of registered voters to petition for a special election to recall the judge before the term has expired. These traditional mechanisms are slow, cumbersome, uncertain, and hence seldom used.

In recent years, states have begun utilizing more practical methods for removing judges. Problems related to senility and old age are avoided in at least thirty-seven states by a mandatory retirement age (generally seventy years) or by the forfeiture of pensions for judges serving beyond the retirement age. Such measures have the added benefit of opening up the courtrooms to new, and younger, judges, even in situations where advancing age does not impair performance.[30] Most states have established special entities to address behavioral problems. *Courts of the judiciary,* whose members are all judges, and *judicial discipline and removal commissions,* composed of judges, lawyers, and laypersons, are authorized to investigate complaints about judges' qualifications, conduct, or fitness. These entities may reject allegations if they are unfounded, privately warn a judge if the charges are not serious, or hold formal hearings. Hearings may result in dismissal of the charges, recommendation for early retirement, or, in some states, outright suspension or removal.[31]

The discipline, suspension, or removal of state court judges is uncommon, but it becomes necessary in all states at one time or another. Judges have been found guilty of drunkenness and drug abuse; sexual misconduct with witnesses and defendants; soliciting and accepting bribes; buying and selling verdicts; and just about every other kind of misconduct imaginable. Sometimes judicial ethics seems to be in seriously short supply. In Rhode Island, a state not celebrated as a paragon of political virtue, two consecutive supreme court chief justices vacated the bench when faced with impeachment. Chief Justice Joseph A. Bevilacqua resigned in 1986 following allegations and testimony that he associated with criminals and had adulterous relations with two women in a Mafia-linked motel, among other things. And in 1994, Chief Justice Thomas F. Fay pleaded guilty to using court money to pay for personal expenses, assigning $45,000 in court work to a legal partner, and ordering his secretary to destroy financial records. He also wrote letters on official supreme court stationery to fix friends' and relatives' speeding tickets.[32]

Judicial Decisionmaking

What factors influence the rulings of state court judges? Why are some judges widely recognized as "liberal" and others as "tough on crime"? Why does a prosecutor prefer to file a case before one judge rather than another? Isn't justice supposed to be blind, like its symbol of the woman holding the scales?

Judges, alas, are mortal beings just like the rest of us. The legal formalities and argot of the courtroom tend to mask the fact that judges' decisions are no less discretionary and subjective than the decisions of a governor, legislator, or agency head. Before we examine the factors that affect judicial decisionmaking, however, we must distinguish between the legal settings of appellate courts and trial courts.

In and Out of the Trial Court

Approximately 95 percent of all civil and criminal cases are actually resolved outside of the courtroom. In many civil cases, the defendant never appears in court to defend himself, thereby implicitly admitting his guilt, and so loses the case by default. Other civil cases are settled in a pretrial conference between the defendant and the plaintiff (where, for instance, payments on an overdue debt might be rescheduled).

plea bargaining
Negotiation between a prosecutor and a criminal defendant's counsel that results in the defendant's pleading guilty to a lesser charge or pleading guilty in exchange for a reduced sentence.

The process of settling criminal cases out of court at the discretion of the prosecutor and the judge is called **plea bargaining.** Although some defendants plead guilty as originally charged, acknowledging guilt for a lesser charge is more typical in criminal proceedings. With the possible exceptions of the victim and the general citizenry, everyone potentially benefits from plea bargaining, a fact that accounts for its extensive use. The accused gets off with lighter punishment than she would face if the case went to trial and she lost. The defense attorney frees up time to take on additional legal work. The prosecuting attorney increases his conviction rate, which looks good if he has political ambitions. The judge helps cut back the number of cases awaiting trial. Even police officers benefit by not having to spend time testifying (and waiting to testify) and by raising the department's clearance rate (the number of cases solved and disposed of).

Out-of-court settlements through plea bargaining are negotiated in a very informal atmosphere in the judge's chamber, or between attorneys in the halls of the court building, or over drinks in a neighboring tavern. This is a disturbingly casual way to dispense justice. The process is secretive and far removed from any notion of due process. The prosecuting (district) attorney enjoys enormous discretion in making deals. Often her propensity to settle depends on the length of her court docket or her relationship with the accused's attorney, rather than on the merits of the case. All too often, an innocent person pleads guilty to a lesser offense for fear of being wrongly convicted of a more serious offense, or because he cannot post bail and doesn't want to spend any unnecessary time behind bars. Equally disturbing—particularly to a victim—is the fact that plea bargaining can soon put a guilty person back on the streets, perhaps to search for another victim.

Nonetheless, plea bargaining is widely practiced. It is almost inevitable when the prosecutor's case hinges on weak evidence, police errors, a questionable witness, or the possibility of catching a bigger fish. Negotiation of a guilty plea for a lesser offense can occur at any stage of the criminal justice process.

bench trial
A trial by a single judge, without a jury.

trial by jury
A trial in which a jury decides the facts and makes a finding of guilty or not guilty.

If the accused is unable to reach a compromise with the prosecuting attorney, he faces either a **bench trial** by a single judge or a **trial by jury.** Both involve a courtroom hearing with all the legal formalities. In some jurisdictions and for certain types of cases, the defendant has a choice. In other situations, state legal procedures specify which trial format will be utilized. For murder cases, a jury is always mandatory.

In a bench trial, the judge alone hears all arguments and makes rulings on questions of law. Jury trials depend on a panel of citizens who share decision-making power. Although at least one study has found that juries and judges come to identical decisions in more than 75 percent of criminal cases,[33] the uncertainty introduced by twelve laypersons is usually great enough to convince a defendant to choose a bench trial. Fewer than 1 percent of all cases are resolved by jury trial.

Attorneys seek to limit the unpredictable nature of juries by extensively questioning individuals in the jury pool. Each side in the dispute has the right to strike the names of a certain number of potential jurors without giving a specific reason. Others are eliminated for cause, such as personal knowledge of the case or its principals. In high-stakes cases, the jury selection process involves public opinion surveys, individual background investigations of potential jurors, and other costly techniques.

Inside the Appellate Court

Appellate courts are substantially different from trial courts. No plaintiffs, defendants, or witnesses are present. The appeal consists of a review of court records and arguments directed by the attorneys, who frequently are not the same lawyers who originally represented the parties. There is no bargaining and no opportunity for predecision settlement. Appellate court rulings are issued by a panel of at least three judges. Unlike decisions in most trial courts, appellate court decisions are written and published. The majority vote prevails. Judges voting in the minority have the right to make a formal, written dissent that justifies their opinion.

State supreme courts vary dramatically in ideology. A recent study indicates that the supreme courts in Hawaii, Rhode Island, and Maryland are much more liberal than those in Arizona, Mississippi, New Hampshire, Iowa, and Kansas.[34] There is marked variation in the dissent rates of state appellate courts. Some courts maintain a public aura of consensus on even the most controversial matters by almost always publishing unanimous opinions. Other courts are racked by public disputes over legal questions. Personal, professional, partisan, political, and other disagreements can escalate into open hostility over casework.[35] Supreme courts in states such as California, New York, and Michigan have a history of contentiousness, whereas others, like those in Rhode Island and Maryland, are paragons of harmony. Dissent rates appear to be positively related to state socioeconomic and political complexity, such as urbanization and partisan competition. More dissent occurs in courts with a large number of justices[36] and in states with intermediate appellate courts. According to one analysis of quarreling on the Missouri Supreme Court, the more time the justices have at their disposal, the more likely they are to find reasons to disagree.[37]

Influence of the Legal System

In addition to the facts of the case itself, judicial decisionmaking is influenced by factors associated with the legal system, including institutional arrangements, accepted legal procedures, caseload pressures, and the ease with which certain interested parties gain access to the legal process.

Institutional Arrangements The level, or tier, of court is a structural characteristic that influences decisionmaking. Trial court judges enforce legal norms and routinely *apply* the law as it has been written and interpreted over the years.

The trial court permits direct interpersonal contacts among the judge, the jury, and the parties (usually individuals and small businesses). Divorce cases, personal injury cases, and minor criminal cases predominate in trial courts.

Appellate courts are more apt to interpret the law and create public policy. Cases typically involve governments and large corporations. State constitutional issues, state-local conflicts, and challenges to government regulation of business are the kinds of issues likely to be found in appellate courts. From time to time a particular case in a high court has an enormous impact on public policy, as judges depart from established precedent or offer new interpretations of the law. Rulings on capital punishment, abortion, affirmative action, and the financing of public education offer good examples, as does court settlement of executive-legislative disputes.

Another important institutional arrangement is the selection procedures for judges. For instance, judicial decisions may be influenced by partisan electoral competition. Especially when a judge facing reelection votes on an issue highly salient to voters, public opinion can affect the judge's ruling.[38] Death penalty cases provide a good example of this point. In a study of judicial decisionmaking in Texas, North Carolina, Louisiana, and Kentucky, political scientist Melinda Gann Hall found that judges seeking reelection tend to uphold death sentences. In these traditionally conservative states, a decision in support of the death penalty helps to avoid unwanted preelection criticism from political opponents and angry voters.[39]

Judges may also be sensitive to other governmental actors. Legislatures and governors determine salaries, court funding, and in some of the states, judicial appointments, so judges do not take actions that offend them without careful consideration.[40]

precedent
The legal principle that previous court decisions should be applied to future decisions.

Legal Procedures and Precedent   On the basis of **precedent,** the principles and procedures of law applied in one situation are applied in any similar situation. In addition, lower courts are supposed to follow the precedents established by higher courts. Although an individual decision may seem unimportant in itself, when taken in the context of other, similar cases it helps judicial policy evolve. Through this practice, the doctrine of equal treatment before the law is pursued. When lower-court judges refuse to follow precedent or are ignorant of it, their decisions can be overturned on appeal. Of course, there may be several conflicting precedents related to a case; in such instances, a judge is permitted to choose among them in justifying his ruling. In this regard, precedent can be a misleading explanation for judicial decisionmaking.

Where do judges look to find existing precedent? Within a state, supreme court decisions set the norms. Supreme courts themselves, however, must scan the legal landscape beyond state boundaries. In the past, decisions of the U.S. Supreme Court heavily influenced those of the state supreme courts. Increasingly, however, state supreme courts are practicing "doctrinal diversity" and looking to one another for precedent.[41] State appellate judges borrow from the experiences of other states.[42] They especially tend to rely on the more professional, prestigious supreme courts, such as those of Massachusetts and New York. State courts also tend to "network" with courts in the same region of the country, where cultural and other environmental factors are similar.[43]

Caseload Pressures   Caseload affects the decisions of judges. The number of cases varies in accordance with crime rates, socioeconomic characteristics of the jurisdictions, state laws, the number of judges, and many other variables. It stands to reason that the quality of judicial decisionmaking is inversely related to caseload. Judges burdened by too much litigation are hard-pressed to devote an adequate amount of time and attention to each case before them.

Access to the System   The final legal-system characteristic affecting judicial decisions is the access of individuals, organizations, and groups to the court system. Wealthy people and businesses are better able to pay for resources (attorneys, legal research, alternative dispute settlement, etc.) and therefore enter the legal system with a great advantage over poorer litigants. Special-interest groups also enjoy certain advantages in affecting judicial decisions. They often have specialized knowledge in areas of litigation, such as environmental or business regulation. Lobbying by interest groups is much less prominent in the judicial branch than in the legislative and executive branches, but groups can affect outcomes by providing financial aid to litigants in important cases and by filing amicus curiae (friend of the court) briefs supporting one side or the other in a dispute.

The states have implemented several reforms to increase access to the judicial system for those who are disadvantaged. For example, court interpreter training is now available in Arizona, Florida, and other states with large Hispanic populations. Physical and communication barriers are being removed so that persons with disabilities can fully participate in all aspects of the legal system. Racial, ethnic, and gender biases are being addressed. Night courts remain open past closing hours for people who have difficulty getting off their day jobs to appear in court. And daycare is being provided for children of plaintiffs, defendants, witnesses, and jurors. Gradually, the state courts are responding to changes in the nature of society.[44]

Personal Values, Attitudes, and Characteristics of Judges

Simply put, judges do not think and act alike. Each is a product of his or her individual background and experiences, which in turn influence decisions made in the courtroom. Studies of state court justices have found that decisions are related to the judges' party identification, political ideology, prior careers, religion, color, age, and sex. In other words, personal characteristics predispose a judge to decide cases in certain ways.

For example, Democratic judges tend to favor the claimant in civil rights cases, the government in tax disputes, the employee in worker's compensation cases, the government in business regulation cases, the defendant in criminal contests, the union in disagreements with management, and the tenant in landlord-tenant cases. Republicans tend to support the opposite side on all these issues.[45] Female judges are more supportive of women on feminist issues, more likely to favor the accused in death penalty and obscenity cases, and, in general, are more liberal than their male colleagues.[46] And, finally, the judge's race appears to have little effect on the sentences handed down to black and white defendants, although according to one study, Anglo judges tend to be tougher on Hispanic defendants than Hispanic judges are.[47] Obviously, these distinctions do not hold in all situations, but the point is that "justice" is a complex concept subject to individual interpretation and discretion.

The personal characteristics and preferences of judges may be similar enough to paint the entire court with an ideological hue. A Pennsylvania study found that black judges are more likely to send criminal defendants to prison than are white judges, but that legal training and socialization are much more important factors in how judges determine sentences.[48]

New Judicial Federalism

During the 1950s and 1960s, the U.S. Supreme Court was far and away the leading judicial actor in the land. Under the Chief Justiceship of Earl Warren (1953–1969) and his liberal majority, the Court handed down a long series of rulings that overturned racial segregation, mandated legislative reapportionment, extended voting rights, and expanded the rights of accused criminals. Significant reversals of state court decisions were commonplace.

Beginning with Chief Justice Warren Burger (1969–1986) and a growing faction of conservative justices, however, the Supreme Court changed directions in the 1970s and 1980s.[49] Since 1988, a conservative majority has been in control. The Court has been less intrusive in state and local affairs and has, through its caution, flashed a green light to state courts inclined to activism. The result is **new judicial federalism,** in which state courts look first to state constitutional and statutory law in rendering legal judgments on important state and local issues once addressed mostly by the federal courts.

new judicial federalism

A trend in which state constitutional and statutory law are consulted and applied over federal law.

judicial activism

Judges' making of public policy through decisions that overturn existing law or effectively make new laws.

Judicial Activism in the States

Judicial activism is a term with value-laden and ideological dimensions.[50] When associated with politically liberal Court decisions, it is decried by conservatives. However, some conservative judges are also tagged as activists. Whether liberal or conservative, all tend to show strong ideological tendencies.[51]

An objective definition of judicial activism, then, points to court-generated change in public policy that is perceived as illegitimate by opponents who favor the status quo.[52] Judicial activism is in the eye of the beholder; it holds a pejorative association for some people and a positive one for others, depending on the issue at hand.

Regardless of one's feelings on the matter, state supreme courts have clearly become *more* activist by expanding into new policy areas. They are more likely to be involved in the policymaking process by making decisions that affect policy in the executive branch, and they even appear to preempt the lawmaking responsibility of the legislature when they invalidate a statute based on constitutional grounds. Examples of this new judicial federalism include the following:

- California, Connecticut, and Massachusetts courts have expanded women's right to abortion on demand and the right to state financial aid for abortions. (Virginia, on the other hand, requires parental consent before an abortion for a woman under legal age.)
- Although the U.S. Supreme Court has upheld state sodomy prohibitions, courts in New York, Pennsylvania, and other states have struck down sodomy laws as violations of the right to privacy, as spelled out in state constitutions. And courts in New York, Wisconsin, Mississippi, Minnesota, and elsewhere have rejected a Burger Court ruling that permits prosecutors to introduce evidence obtained through a defective search warrant.
- Oregon's supreme court rejected a U.S. Supreme Court decision that provided guidelines for declaring certain printed and visual materials to be obscene. The Oregon court noted that its state constitution had been authored "by rugged and robust individuals dedicated to founding a free society unfettered by the governmental imposition of some people's views of morality on the free expression of others." The court went on to declare, "In this state, any person can write, print, read, say, show or sell anything to a consenting adult even though that expression may be generally or universally considered 'obscene.'"[53]

How can the state courts override the decisions of the highest court in the land? The answer is that they are grounding their rulings in their own constitutions instead of in the national Constitution.[54] In several decisions, the U.S. Supreme Court has upheld the right of the states to expand on the minimum rights and liberties guaranteed under the national document. Of course, when there is an irreconcilable conflict between state and federal law, the latter prevails.

Current Trends in State Courts

The new wave of state court activism is not carrying all the ships of state with it. Many state supreme courts remain caught in the doldrums, consistently endorsing—rather than repudiating—U.S. Supreme Court decisions. Some of them are so quiet, as one wag suggested, "that you can hear their arteries harden." But even traditionally inactive courts, such as those in Wisconsin, North Carolina, and Mississippi, have been stirred into independent actions recently, and the trend is continuing.[55] The U.S. Supreme Court is likely to have a conservative majority for many years to come, permitting the state courts to explore the legal landscape further. Meanwhile, state court activism seems to be contagious, as courts utilize their own information and case networks instead of those of the Supreme Court.

Of course, with rare exceptions, judges cannot seize issues as governors and legislators can; they must wait for litigants to bring them to the courthouse. And although judges can issue rulings, they must depend on the executive and legislative branches to comply with and enforce those rulings. Nonetheless, many state supreme courts are becoming more active in the policymaking process. The reluctance of the federal courts to address important and controversial issues comprehensively has resulted in more cases for state supreme courts to decide.

State court activism does have some negative points. First, some courts may overstep their authority and try to go too far in policymaking, intruding into the proper domain of executive and legislative actors. Judges have little expertise in the substance of public policy or in the policymaking process. They have no specialized staff to perform in-depth policy research on particular policy issues, and they cannot realistically depend on lawyers to do policy research for them. After all, lawyers are trained and practiced in legal reasoning, not social science or political science.[56] Second, state courts are increasingly issuing policy decisions that have significant budgetary implications. Court rulings on school finance, prison overcrowding, and treatment of the mentally ill have severely affected state budgets. Such court actions rarely take into account their related financial effects. A third problem is that in the context of state constitutional rights, geography is destiny. A state-by-state approach may not be appropriate for such policies as civil rights, clean air, or safe food, which should be equal for all citizens.

State Court Reform

We have already discussed several important judicial reforms: intermediate appellate courts; court unification and consolidation; merit selection plans for judges; more practical means for disciplining and removing judges; and administrative and organizational improvements, including those of a financial nature. This last category remains important.

Financial Improvements

The exorbitant costs of some trials can bankrupt local jurisdictions if state financial assistance is not forthcoming. For example, one child molestation case in Los Angeles County lasted two and a half years and carried a tab of $15 million. (Neither of the two defendants was convicted.) The price tag for a murder trial and subsequent appeals can also be counted in the millions. Given such contingencies, more than half of the states have assumed full financial responsibility for the operation of state and local courts.

Another financial reform, centralized budgeting, has been adopted by more than half of the states. Also referred to as *unified court budgeting,* this reform entails a consolidated budget for all state and local courts, prepared by the chief administrative officer of the state court system, that details all personnel, supplies, equipment, and other expenditures.[57] It is intended to enhance financial management and help maintain judicial independence from the executive and legislative branches, which lose their authority to alter the judiciary's budget. A unified court system, centralized management and financing, and unified budgeting are all similar in that they share the objective of bringing a state's entire court system under a single authoritative administrative structure.

Dealing with Growing Caseloads

Recently, court reformers have recognized the need to deal more effectively with case backlogs. State courts confront more than 100 million new cases each year. And some judges participate in more than 300 opinions annually. Delays of two years or more have not been uncommon for appellate court hearings, and the unprecedented pressure is growing.

Excessive caseloads are caused by numerous factors, including the greater propensity of losing parties to appeal lower-court decisions, the tremendous growth in litigation, huge increases in drug-related and drunk-driving cases, and poor caseload management procedures. Exacerbating the problem is the sheer number of lawyers in the United States, which accounts for nearly two-thirds of all the lawyers in the world.

The paramount concern is that long delays thwart the progress of justice. The quality of evidence deteriorates as witnesses disappear or forget what they saw, and victims suffer from delays that prevent them from collecting damages for injuries incurred during a crime or an accident. Even accused (and perhaps innocent) perpetrators can be harmed by the experience of being held in prison for long periods while awaiting trial.

Reducing excessive caseloads is not a simple matter. Common sense dictates establishing intermediate appellate courts and adding new judgeships. But much like a new highway draws more traffic, intermediate appellate courts tend to attract more appeals by their very existence.[58] And although additional judges can speed up the trial process in lower courts, they may also add to appellate backlogs. Expanding the number of judges in an appellate court is also problematic; hearings may actually take longer because of more input or factional divisions among judges.

The stubborn persistence of case backlogs has led to some interesting and promising new approaches.

1. *Alternative dispute resolution.* Almost all states today use mediation, arbitration, or other techniques to help settle litigation prior to or in between formal courtroom proceedings. Third-party mediation by retired judges or attorneys and voluntary binding arbitration are promising approaches. In some states, including California and Washington, civil litigants in search of timely settlement have hired private judges to decide their disputes.[59]

2. *Fines against lawyers and litigants.* New laws or court rules provide for monetary fines to be levied by judges against lawyers and litigants guilty of delaying tactics, frivolous litigation, or standards violations that require cases to be heard within a specified time period.

3. *Case management systems.* Managerial judges can take charge of their dockets and impose an aggressive case management system.[60] Although individual systems vary widely, a typical approach is multitracking, or differentiated case

management. It distinguishes between simple and complex cases, as well as between frivolous and potentially significant cases, and treats them differently. Complex and significant cases are waved on down the traditional appellate track. Simple and frivolous cases take a shorter track, usually under the direction of staff attorneys. Experiments with multitracking have been successful in reducing case delays in Arizona, Maine, New Hampshire, and several other states. Another case management innovation designed to speed up the wheels of justice involves so-called *boutique courts*, in which environmental law disputes, drug cases, or others with special characteristics are heard by judges in specialized courts.

4. *New technology.* Technological innovations are also improving the quality and quantity of court operations. Electronic databases (for example, LEXIS and WESTLAW) are used to store case information and legal research and to transmit information from law offices to courts. Automation helps track child support payments, court administrative systems, and traffic tickets. Videotaping of witnesses' testimony is becoming commonplace. Arraignment procedures, during which suspects are formally charged, are also videotaped to save time or to prevent potential problems from a disruptive defendant. "Video courtrooms," in which trials are filmed by TV cameras, create a more accurate trial record and cost much less than a written transcript by a court stenographer. And audiovisual and Internet technology permits hearings, motions, pleas, sentencing, and other proceedings to be conducted long distance between jail and courthouse, thereby both saving money and enhancing security.

5. *Performance standards.* The National Center for State Courts has developed performance standards for state trial courts to aid self-assessment and improvement.[61] A growing number of states are not only adopting quantitative indicators of the speed with which cases are processed but also trying to measure broader concerns such as access to justice; fairness and integrity; public trust and confidence; and the quality of judges' decisionmaking.

Compensating the Judges

At first glance, judicial salaries seem high enough. In 2001, state supreme court judges earned an average of approximately $117,000.[62] (The variation is great: California justices make $162,409; their counterparts in Montana are paid only $89,381.) Trial court judges were paid 10 to 20 percent less. However, these amounts are substantially below what an experienced, respected attorney can expect to make. A successful lawyer who gives up private practice for the bench must be willing to take a considerable cut in income. Unlike legislators, state judges are permitted very little outside income. Therefore, it is reasonable to ask whether the best legal minds will be attracted to judgeships, given that judicial compensation is relatively low.[63] This is a dilemma at all levels and in all branches of public service, from the municipal finance officer to the highway patrol officer, since most state and local government compensation lags behind pay for comparable jobs in the private sector. If we expect our judges, law enforcement officers, and other public employees to be honest, productive, and highly qualified, they must be compensated adequately. Recent salary increases for state judges seem to reflect this principle.

State Courts Enter the 2000s

Like the other two branches of government, the state judiciary has been touched significantly by reform. Court systems have been modernized and simplified, intermediate appellate courts have been added, processes have been streamlined, and case delays have been reduced. Moreover, disciplinary and removal commissions now make it easier to deal with problem judges. As a result, courts are striving for greater independence from political pressures and favoritism and more accountability for their actions. Justice may at times still appear to be an ephemeral ideal, and an expensive one at that; but it is more likely to be approximated in state judicial decisions today than ever before.

Although the changes in state court systems have not gone far enough in some instances, one can't help but be amazed that so much has happened in so short a period of time to such a conservative, slow-moving institution of government. The courts, like the rest of society, are no longer immune to the technological age. New innovations and approaches will follow the recommendations of commissions in states now studying the needs of state judicial systems in the new century.

Court modernization and reform have been accompanied by increased judicial activism. The newly assertive state courts have far surpassed the federal courts in public policy activism. They sometimes blatantly disagree with federal precedents and insist on decisions grounded in state constitutional law rather than in the national constitution. In short, the state courts are actively responding to public concern with crime and the administration of justice.

Crime and Criminal Justice

The judiciary is the critical institutional link to the policy problem of crime. Governors exercise criminal justice policy leadership, legislatures determine what constitutes violations of the law and establish sentencing rules, and law enforcement personnel enforce the law—but it is the courts that decide questions of guilt or innocence and impose punishments.

Sometimes the criminal justice system misfires, with dreadful consequences the result. People may be convicted for crimes they did not commit. For instance, four men who dwelled in an Illinois penitentiary for sixteen years on double-murder charges were released in 1998 after a Northwestern University journalism class proved their innocence. At least seventy-three individuals have been freed from death row during the past twenty years after their murder convictions were cast into serious doubt or revoked because of new evidence.[64] Wrongful convictions can result from lack of solid evidence of a crime, dishonest police claims of a confession, incompetent legal representation, and many other factors. But the critical element in avoiding such problems is the court.

There is much controversy today regarding what should be done with properly convicted criminals. The debates over correctional policy range from the desirability of capital punishment to what, if anything, to do about "victimless" crimes such as prostitution and drug use. To an important degree, the role of the courts in applying the law and in sentencing is significantly restricted by sentencing mandates. Judges once exercised great discretion in deciding the number of years for which an offender should be sentenced to prison. But the current trend is toward *determinate sentencing,* in which offenders are given mandatory terms that they must serve without possibility of parole. Half the states have enacted "three strikes and you're out" laws, which mandate tough sentences—perhaps even life without parole—for habitual felons who are convicted of a third serious crime. The goal is to reduce sentencing disparity among judges, but this approach comes at the expense of flexibility. Isn't it more appropriate to make the punishment fit the crime? Longer sentences, combined with a greater propensity toward locking up people convicted of nonviolent crimes, have also led to tremendous growth in the nation's prison population.

The United States imprisons a higher proportion of its citizens than any other nation except Russia. One of every 150 Americans is behind bars. Louisiana, Texas, and Oklahoma hold more of their citizens in "stir" than other states. Minnesota, Maine, and North Dakota are the states least likely to lock up their citizens. Overall, inmate rolls have doubled since 1987, reaching a total of nearly 2 million. Approximately one-half of these prisoners are considered nonviolent offenders, convicted of such crimes as consuming or dealing drugs, passing bad checks, and burglary.

Prison overcrowding has produced a serious policy dilemma for the states, which have been busily experimenting with methods to ease the problem. Three basic strategies are being employed: back-door strategies, front-door strategies, and capacity enhancement. *Back-door strategies* are designed to extract inmates from correctional institutions before they serve their full sentences. Early release, probation, and parole remain options in many states. A relatively new measure is electronic house detention, whereby a released inmate wears a transmitter (usually on the ankle) that emits a steady signal to a receiver in his or her home. Failure to detect a signal causes the receiver to dial a central computer that brings the matter to the attention of law enforcement officials. This technique is much less expensive than incarceration, and it enables offenders not only to work to pay their own share of the program's costs but also to repay their victims financially. (The central computer is programmed to "know" when the inmates are permitted to be away from home.)

Front-door strategies are intended to keep offenders out of prison in the first place by directing them into alternative programs. Creative sentencing grants judges flexibility in designing punishments that fit the crime, yet permit the offenders to remain in society. An increasingly popular alternative sentence is community service, which ranges from cleaning up parks or streets to working in a hospital. Some sentences are creative indeed. A judge in Wake County, North Carolina, has been known to seize valuable items of clothing and personal stereos from larceny offenders. A municipal judge in Colorado requires young offenders to listen to musical artists they don't like, such as Wayne Newton or Barney the Dinosaur. And in California, judges have the option of offering child molesters surgical or chemical castration. Other front-door approaches include intensive probation supervision, which combines house arrest with intrusive surveillance for nonviolent criminals, and boot camps, in which young, first-time offenders are given the option of either doing jail time or spending several months in "shock incarceration." The latter involves rigorous Marine boot camp–style training intended to promote self-discipline.

Capacity enhancement usually entails construction and operation of new prison facilities—a seriously expensive undertaking that has hamstrung many a state budget. Texas has built so many new prisons that it currently rents cells to states with surplus prisoners. Other states have chosen the privatization route to capacity enhancement. Prisons run by firms such as Correctional Corporation of America can now be found in thirty-nine states. Savings appear to be marginal, and troubling legal questions have arisen concerning violations of inmate rights, the training and aptitude of guards, the quality of food and lodging, and related issues.

Crime and corrections present major challenges to state and local governments. How they meet these challenges will go a long way toward determining their future role in American federalism. More innovation and experimentation are certain to occur.

Chapter Recap

➤ State courts are organized into two tiers: appellate courts and trial courts.

➤ The five methods for selecting judges are legislative election, partisan election, nonpartisan election, the merit plan, and gubernatorial appointment. Each selection plan has certain advantages and disadvantages—there is no "one best way."

➤ Many factors influence judicial decisionmaking, including institutional arrangements; legal procedures; case precedent; caseload pressures; access to the legal system; and personal values, attitudes, and characteristics of judges.

➤ Judicial federalism is related to increased capability and judicial activism in many state courts.

➤ Efforts to reform state courts are in full swing, including financial improvements, better caseload management, and improved compensation for judges.

Key Terms

civil case (*p. 203*)
criminal case (*p. 203*)
administrative case (*p. 203*)
common law (*p. 203*)
general jurisdiction (*p. 204*)
original jurisdiction (*p. 204*)
appellate jurisdiction (*p. 204*)
major trial court (*p. 205*)

supreme court (*p. 205*)
intermediate appellate court (*p. 205*)
plea bargaining (*p. 216*)
bench trial (*p. 216*)
trial by jury (*p. 216*)
precedent (*p. 218*)
new judicial federalism (*p. 220*)
judicial activism (*p. 220*)

Surfing the Net

The National Center for State Courts maintains a list of courts and their Internet addresses at **www.ncsconline.org.** Interesting sites include the following: California at **www.courtinfo.ca.gov,** Florida at **www.flcourts.org,** and Alaska at **www.state.ak.us/courts/.** The American Bar Association's website provides an analysis of current, controversial cases and other legal information. It's located at **www.abanet.org.** The Law Forum Legal Resources site, located at **www.lawforum.net,** has links to all online state and local courts. For a peek at live cases underway in the courtroom and other interesting features, see the website of Florida's Ninth Judicial Circuit at **www.ninja9.org/courtadmin/ mis/courtroom_23.htm.**

10

STATE-LOCAL RELATIONS

The Distribution of Authority
The Amount and Type of Authority » A State-Local Tug of War »
State Mandates » An Uneasy Relationship » What Local
Governments Want from the States

State-Local Organizations

Metropolitics: A New Challenge for State Government
Smart Growth versus Urban Sprawl » Regional Governance

States and Their Rural Communities

The Interaction of States and Localities

Alarmed by the rate at which cell phone–chatting drivers were getting into automobile accidents, the county commissioners of Miami–Dade County, Florida, took action. In 2002, the county adopted an ordinance that banned the use of hand-held cell phones while operating a motor vehicle in the county. But the county's action was overridden by the state of Florida. In their 2002 legislative session, lawmakers passed a bill—later signed into law by Governor Jeb Bush— decreeing that only the state could regulate how cell phones are used by drivers.[1] In effect, local governments in Florida lost the power to make their own rules regarding cell phone use. This example underscores a larger point: A state can supersede the local governments within its boundaries.

The relationship between states and their communities is often strained. On the one hand, state government gives local governments life; that is, local governments exist only with state approval. On the other hand, state governments historically have not treated their local governments very well. It appears, however, that states have realized that mistreating their governmental offspring is counterproductive, and many have launched a sometimes-uncoordinated process of assistance and empowerment of local government.

Capturing this evolution is the statement of the National Conference of State Legislatures (NCSL) Task Force on State-Local Relations: "Legislators should place a higher priority on state-local issues than has been done in the past. The time has come to change their attitude toward local governments—to stop considering them as just another special interest group and to start treating them as partners in our federal system."[2] Stronger, more competent local governments are an asset to state government.

The Distribution of Authority

In essence, local governments are creatures of their states. Federal and state courts have consistently upheld the dependency of localities on the state since Iowa judge John F. Dillon first laid down **Dillon's rule** in 1868. Dillon's rule established that local governments may exercise only those powers explicitly granted to them by the state, those clearly implied by these explicit powers, and those absolutely essential to the declared objectives and purposes of the local government. Any doubt regarding the legality of a specific local government power is resolved in favor of the state.[3]

Thus, in the words of the U.S. Advisory Commission on Intergovernmental Relations (ACIR), "State legislatures are the trustees of the basic rules of local governance in America. The laws and constitutions of each state are the basic legal instruments of local governance."[4] The ACIR statement denotes the essence of the distribution of authority between a state and its localities. In short, it is up to the state to determine the amount and type of authority a local government may possess. As specified by Dillon's rule, localities depend on the state to imbue them with enough powers to operate effectively.

> **Dillon's rule**
> A rule that limits the powers of local government to those expressly granted by the state, those closely linked to expressed powers, and those essential to the locality's purposes.

The Amount and Type of Authority

There is wide variation in how much and what kind of authority states give their local governments. Some states grant their localities wide-ranging powers to restructure themselves, to impose new taxes, and to take on additional functions. Others, much more conservative with their power, force local governments to turn to the legislature for approval to act. Empowerment also depends on the type of local government. General-purpose governments such as counties, cities, and towns typically have wider latitude than special-purpose entities like school districts. (The concept of general-purpose governments is discussed in Chapter 11.) Even among general-purpose governments, there are different degrees of authority; counties tend to be more circumscribed than cities in their ability to modify their form of government and expand their service offerings.[5]

In general, states' regulatory reach is great. For example, states may regulate local finances (by, among other things, establishing debt limits and requiring balanced budgets), personnel (setting qualifications for certain positions, prescribing employee pension plans), government structure (establishing forms of government, outlawing particular electoral systems), processes (requiring public hearings and open meetings, mandating financial disclosure), functions (ordering the provision of public safety functions, proscribing the pursuit of enterprise activities), and service standards (adopting solid waste guidelines, setting acceptable water-quality levels). The preceding list makes the point: The state capitol casts a long shadow.

Building codes offer an interesting illustration of the variability in state-local authority. Researcher Peter May examined all fifty states to determine the amount of discretion allowed local governments to adopt and enforce building codes.[6] He found several different patterns. Twelve states (Kentucky and Michigan among them) played an aggressive role, imposing mandatory building codes on their local governments and overseeing local compliance. Thirteen states (including Indiana and Wyoming) had mandatory local codes but stopped short of state review or oversight. The rest of the states gave their local governments more leeway. In eight states (Iowa and Nebraska among them), local governments themselves decided whether to enforce the state building code. And in seventeen states (including Delaware and Oklahoma), there were no comprehensive building codes; thus local governments were free to design and enact their own. The building code example underscores an important point: States vary in their treatment of local government.

second-order devolution

A shift in power from state government to local government.

Devolution, the shift in power from the national government to state capitals, has also occurred between states and their local governments. In the state-local case, it is called **second-order devolution.** The more recently a state has adopted its constitution, the more likely the document is to contain provisions that strengthen local governments.[7] Many state constitutions set forth a provision for **home rule.** Although home rule falls short of actual local self-government, it is an important step in the direction of greater local decision-making.[8]

home rule

The legal ability of a local government to run its own affairs, subject to state oversight.

A State-Local Tug of War

Local governments want their states to provide them with adequate funding and ample discretion. Local officials are supremely confident of their abilities to govern, given sufficient state support. These same local officials express concern that neither their policymaking power nor their financial authority has kept pace with the increased administrative responsibilities placed on them by state government.[9] The recognition and correction of such conditions are the states' responsibility.

To learn more about the changes in state-local relations, the ACIR conducted a major survey. The research examined and compared state laws, as of 1978 and 1990, in six categories: form of government, annexation and consolidation, local elections, administrative operations and procedures, financial management, and personnel management.[10] Two hundred and one specific items were included in the ACIR survey. The findings were instructive. On average, states have 86 local government laws on the books. Ohio has the most, 113, followed by Florida and Montana with 112 each. States with the fewest local government laws tend to be located in the Northeast: Rhode Island and Vermont have 47; Connecticut has 51. During the period from 1978 to 1990, states increased their regulation of local government by passing an average of 16 new

| TABLE 10.1 | Regional Comparisons and Changes in State Laws Governing Administrative Operations and Procedures of Localities | | | | | |

| | REGION | | | | | |
	South	West	North Central	Northeast	TOTAL	CHANGE SINCE 1978
N=	16	13	12	9	50	
1. State law requires that all local government meetings at which official action is taken be open to the public.	15	13	12	8	48	+7
2. State law requires that local government records be open to public inspection at reasonable hours.	16	10	11	8	45	+15
3. State law mandates a procedure for adoption of municipal ordinances and/or resolutions.	11	11	8	3	33	+4
4. State law mandates a procedure for adoption of county ordinances and/or resolutions.	9	7	4	2	22	+8
5. State law authorizes initiative and referendum on local ordinances and/or resolutions.	3	11	9	3	26	+11
6. Local elected officials are subject to a state-imposed Code of Ethics.	8	7	3	3	21	+4
7. Sovereign immunity for local government torts has been waived by the state.	12	9	10	5	36	+4

SOURCE: U.S. Advisory Committee on Intergovernmental Relations, *State Laws Governing Local Government Structure and Administration* (Washington, D.C.: ACIR, 1993), p. 61.

statutes or constitutional amendments. With the stroke of the same pen, they decreased their involvement somewhat by repealing an average of 8 laws dealing with local government. Table 10.1 presents a selection of the laws that states have enacted with regard to the administrative operations and procedures of local governments. It is important to remember that, in the absence of a state law on a particular subject, a local government may have adopted its own law, or **ordinance.**

ordinance

Enacted by the governing body, it is the local government equivalent of a law.

To a certain extent, the evaluation of state-local relations depends on who is doing the assessment. State officials are apprehensive of awarding local governments carte blanche authority. Local officials, though they angle for more authority, also want more money. The tug of war will continue.

State Mandates

Although local governments generally want increased autonomy, state governments have shared their policymaking sphere with reluctance. Rather than letting these "subgovernments" devise their own solutions to problems, states frequently prefer to impose a solution. For instance, when solid waste management became a concern in Florida, the state legislature's reaction was to require counties to establish recycling programs. Not only were counties required to initiate programs, they were ordered to achieve a recycling rate of 30 percent.[11] This kind of requirement or order is an example of a *mandate*. Unfunded mandates are a persistent source of friction between state and local levels of government.

From the perspective of state government, mandates are necessary to ensure that vital activities are performed and desirable goals are achieved. State mandates promote uniformity of policy from one jurisdiction to another (for instance, regarding the length of the public school year or the operating hours of precinct polling places). In addition, they promote coordination, especially among adjacent jurisdictions that provide services jointly (as with a regional hospital or a metropolitan transportation system).

Local governments see the issue quite differently. They have three basic complaints:

1. State mandates, especially those that order a new service or impose a service quality standard, can be quite expensive for local governments.
2. State mandates displace local priorities in favor of state priorities.
3. State mandates limit the management flexibility of local governments.[12]

mandate-reimbursement requirements
Measures that take the sting out of state mandates.

Taken together, these problems make for unhappy local officials. Recognizing the problem, many states have adopted **mandate-reimbursement requirements.** These measures require states to either reimburse local governments for the costs of state mandates or give local governments adequate revenue-raising capacity to deal with them. For example, New Jersey voters in 1995 approved limiting the state legislature's ability to impose mandates on localities without providing adequate funding. Seven states do not permit mandates to become binding until formally approved by the local governments. Mandate-reimbursement requirements tend to make state officials unhappy. They argue that mandates are frequently necessary to prod reluctant local governments into assuming their rightful responsibilities. As for paying for mandates, state governments protest that they cannot afford to do so. In Arizona and Illinois in 1996, efforts to restrict state mandates fell short despite vigorous lobbying by local officials.[13] Still, mandate relief is an issue whose time has come.[14] Governor Pataki of New York put it well when he said, "Mandates are fiscal time bombs."[15]

It is no wonder that the NCSL's Task Force on State-Local Relations has urged states to consider relaxing or eliminating mandates and assuming the cost of compliance[16] Mandates dealing with local personnel policies, environmental standards, service levels, and tax-base exemptions are due reconsideration. As a result, several states have taken a long, hard look at their policies on mandates, with an eye on reforming them.

An Uneasy Relationship

A conflicted relationship exists between states and local governments when it comes to money. Cities, counties, and other local governments will always live within the constitutional constraints of their states. Localities enjoy their own sources of revenue—property taxes, user fees, and business license fees—but depend on the states for much of their income. They suffer the frustration of having to cope with rising expenditure demands from their residents while their authority to raise new monies is highly circumscribed by state law. No wonder localities turned to the national government in the 1960s and 1970s to seek direct financial aid that "bypassed" the states.

The historical insensitivity of states to the economic problems of their cities and counties began slowly changing in the 1970s, largely because reapportionment brought urban interests greater standing in state legislatures. In the 1980s, the states had to assume an even more attentive posture. National aid to localities declined substantially during the eight years of the Reagan administration. Today, only about 16 percent of all federal grant-in-aid dollars goes directly to cities and counties. The states funnel twelve times more money to local governments than the national government does.[17]

The single largest source of local revenues is the state. More than one-third of all state expenditures (more than $279 billion) goes to local governments. But like federal grants-in-aid, state grants come with lots of strings attached. Most state dollars (three out of every four) are earmarked for public education and social welfare; state aid accounts for more than 50 percent of total local education expenditures and 80 percent of public welfare spending. Other state assistance is earmarked for roads, hospitals, and public health. The result is that local governments have very little spending discretion.

Naturally, there is much diversity in the levels of encumbered (earmarked) and unencumbered state assistance to local jurisdictions, much of which is related to the distribution of functions between a state and its localities. Highly centralized states such as Hawaii, South Carolina, and West Virginia fund and administer at the state level many programs that are funded and administered locally in decentralized states such as Maryland, New York, and Wisconsin. In states where taxation and expenditure limitations have hampered the ability of local jurisdictions to raise and spend revenues, the trend has been toward fiscal centralization. Greater centralization has also resulted from state efforts to reduce service disparities between wealthy and poor jurisdictions, and to lessen the dependence of local governments on the property tax.

There is much diversity in state aid to local governments, varying from $1,601 per capita in Alaska to $123 in Hawaii; the average is $1,032. This surprisingly large variation has been explored in empirical research by political scientists. It appears that the most important predictors of state aid to localities are centralization of functions (centralized states allocate less for local governments), state wealth (rich states provide more money than poor states), fiscal need (fiscally stressed localities need greater state aid), and legislative professionalism (professional legislatures are willing to spend more on education, social welfare, and other local programs).[18]

What Local Governments Want from the States

What local governments want from their states and what they actually get may be a cosmos apart. Today, states and their local jurisdictions conduct nearly constant dialogue over financial matters. Increasingly, the states are willing to recognize and want to respond to local financial problems—subject, of course, to their own fiscal circumstances and their judgment as to what is best for all state residents.

In a nutshell, what localities want most is *more money*. But they also want more power to raise it and more control over how it is spent. The tax revolt, terminations and reductions in federal grants-in-aid, and pressing infrastructure needs have left local jurisdictions in a financial bind. State governments must provide help, and in general they have done so. State aid for all local governments has grown every year since 1981, substantially outstripping inflation over that period.

Most increases in state aid are devoted to education, corrections, health care, and social services. Recently, however, states have been more willing to share revenues that cities or counties may spend as they desire. Many states distribute a portion of their tax revenues based on local fiscal need, thus tending to equalize or level economic disparities between local jurisdictions. But by the same token, when a state's finances are stretched thin, aid to localities slows.[19]

The specific means for sharing revenues takes many forms. More than half the states make special payments to local governments that host state buildings or other facilities, which are exempt from property taxes but cause a drain on local services. Such payments are of particular concern to capital cities, in which large plots of prime downtown property are occupied by state office buildings.

In addition, local governments want the *legal capacity to raise additional revenues themselves*, especially through local option sales and income taxes (although a slice of gasoline, tobacco, and other tax benefits is greatly appreciated). The key is local option, whereby jurisdictions decide for themselves which, if any, taxes they will exact. More than two-thirds of the states have authorized an optional sales or income tax for various local governments, and some permit localities to adopt optional earmarked taxes. For example, Florida empowers its counties to place an accommodations tax on local hotel and motel rooms; the resulting revenues are dedicated to tourism development projects. Local option taxes are attractive because they provide local jurisdictions with the flexibility to take action as they see fit in response to local needs. What protects citizens against "taxaholic" local legislative bodies in the aftermath of the taxpayer revolt is the state requirement that local tax hikes must be approved by the voters in a referendum.

As noted in the State Mandates section of this chapter, *localities also want limitations on and reimbursements for state mandates.* Local governments believe that they should not have to obey *and* pay; rather, states should reimburse them for expenses incurred in carrying out mandates.

State-Local Organizations

Legal, administrative, and financial ties link state and local governments. Additional interaction occurs when state governments establish organizations such as local government study commissions and advisory panels of local officials. Among the most prevalent structures are task forces, advisory commissions on intergovernmental relations, and departments of community affairs.

Task forces tend to be focused organizations set up by the governor or the state legislature in response to a perceived local-level problem. If a state wants to investigate the ramifications of changing its annexation statutes, the legislature might create a Task Force on Annexation and Boundary Changes (or something similar), probably composed of state and local officials, community leaders, and experts on the subject of annexation. The task force would proceed as follows: First, it would collect information on how other states handle the annexation question; next, it would conduct a series of public hearings to get input from individuals and groups interested in the issue; and, finally, it would compile a report that included recommendations suitable for legislative action. Its work completed, the task force would then disband, although individual members might turn up as advocates when the task force's recommendations receive legislative attention. Task forces are quick organizational responses to local problems that have become too pressing for state government to ignore. A task force is a low-cost, concentrated reaction that gives the appearance of action and, in some instances, actually influences legislative deliberations.

In an ongoing, comprehensive effort at state-local cooperation, many states have created state-level *advisory commissions on intergovernmental relations*, modeled after the commission, now defunct, created by the U.S. Congress in 1959. State-level ACIRs are designed to promote more harmonious, workable relations between the state and its governmental subdivisions. They are intended to offer a neutral forum for discussion of long-range state-local issues— a venue where local officials can be listened to and engaged in focused dialogue; conduct research on local developments and new state policies; promote experimentation in intergovernmental processes, both state-local and interlocal; and develop suggested solutions to state-local problems.[20] And to prevent their recommendations from gathering dust on some forgotten shelf, many state-level ACIRs have added marketing and public relations to their list of activities. Generally, state-level ACIRs return real benefits to local government. Whether in their narrowest form, as arenas for discussion of local issues, or in their broadest, as policy developers and initiators, ACIRs are useful to state and local governments. But their greatest impact will occur if they are given the authority and resources to do something more than simply discuss issues. Virginia's ACIR, for instance, has four primary duties:

- Providing a forum for the discussion of intergovernmental concerns;
- Conducting research and issuing reports on intergovernmental topics;
- Resolving specific issues and problems as they arise; and
- Promoting needed policies.[21]

Another way that states can generate closer formal ties with their local governments is through specialized administrative agencies. All fifty states have created *departments of community affairs* (DCAs) that are involved in local activities. They have different labels (Kentucky calls its DCA the Department for Local Government; Ohio's is known as the Department of Economic and Community Development), but their function is similar: to offer a range of programs and services to local governments.[22] DCAs are involved in housing, urban revitalization, antipoverty programs, and economic development; they also offer local governments such services as planning, management, and financial assistance. DCAs vary on several dimensions: their niche in state government, the sizes of their budget and staff, and whether they include an advisory board of local officials. Each of these dimensions contributes to the clout wielded by any DCA. For example, a DCA that has cabinet-level status (as thirty-five of them do) is likely to be more influential than one located within another state agency (as in nine states) or within the governor's office (as in six states). DCAs with bigger budgets and staffs tend to have more influence. The existence of an advisory board is problematic, however. Half of the DCAs have advisory boards, but few of them are active or effective in an array of local policy areas.[23]

Compared to state-level ACIRs, DCAs function much more as service deliverers and much less as policy initiators. Therefore, these two types of organizations tend to complement rather than compete with one another. Both, however, function as advocates for local government at the state level.

Metropolitics: A New Challenge for State Government

State governments often find their dealings with local governments to be confounded by the side effects of urbanization. Regardless of which state we examine, its urban areas show the effects of three waves of suburbanization. An early wave occurred during the 1920s, when automobiles facilitated the development of outlying residential areas. Although the dispersion slowed during the Great Depression and World War II, its resurgence in the 1950s triggered a second wave, during which retail stores followed the population exodus. The "malling of America" has led to the third wave of suburbanization: the development of office space beyond the central city.[24] This is happening with a vengeance in New York City and Atlanta, in Cheyenne and Nogales. It is this third wave that has caught the attention of state governments.

As a result of the transformation of American metropolitan areas, central cities have lost their prominence as the social, economic, and political focal points of these areas.[25] People have moved to surrounding suburbs and beyond; businesses and firms have sprung up in the hinterlands; communities have formed their own service and taxing districts. The outward flow of people and activities has fundamentally altered metropolitan areas, which are now composed of "a series of relatively self-contained and self-sufficient decentralized regional units."[26] Not simply residential, these new "boom towns" include business, retail, and entertainment activities. Wal-Mart, the ubiquitous discount retailer, may be the symbol of twenty-first-century urbanization. *Washington Post* reporter Joel Garreau spent several years exploring the new developments on the urban fringes, places that he calls **edge cities.**[27] With their office towers, shopping malls, and jogging paths, edge cities are the new frontier for an urbanized United States. Figure 10.1 shows the edge cities that have developed—and continue to develop—around Phoenix.

edge cities
New urban centers that spring up beyond a city's downtown area. Some edge cities have official governments, others do not.

| FIGURE 10.1 | **Living on the Edge in Phoenix** |

In the fast-growing Phoenix area, new work-play-sleep communities are springing up beyond downtown.

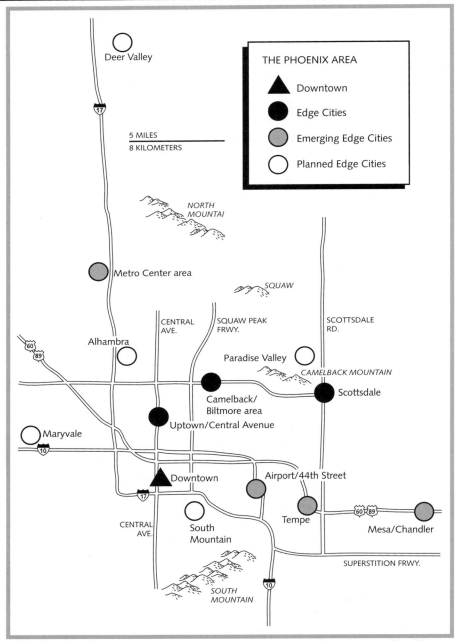

SOURCE: From *Edge City* by Joel Garreau, © 1991 by Joel Garreau. Used by permission of Doubleday, a division of Random House, Inc.

The de-emphasis of the central city suggests the need for changes in outmoded state government policy toward metropolitan jurisdictions. A serious concern is that rapid, unplanned growth is producing sprawl. A logical question is, What is state government doing while all of this is occurring? The answer: more than it used to, as the next section of the chapter explains.

Smart Growth versus Urban Sprawl

urban sprawl
Development characterized by low population density, rapid land consumption, and dependence on the automobile.

Urban Sprawl   One of the hottest issues of the early twenty-first century is **urban sprawl.** Urban sprawl is a term that carries negative connotations, but it refers to development beyond the central city that is characterized by low densities, rapid land consumption, and dependence on the automobile. It is often called "leapfrog" development because it jumps over established settlements. Sprawl is resource intensive and costly. It is also the subject of much political debate. Figure 10.2 plots population growth in the Denver area against land-area growth. The difference is noteworthy. The population grew by 15 percent from 1990–1996; the urbanized land area increased by 65 percent during that same period.[28]

Las Vegas may offer the best contemporary example of a fast-growing city. According to the city's statistics, "two hundred new residents arrive in Las Vegas every day; a house is built every fifteen minutes."[29] According to an official in the county's public works department, "Traffic is probably 100 times worse

FIGURE 10.2   **Growth in the Denver Area**

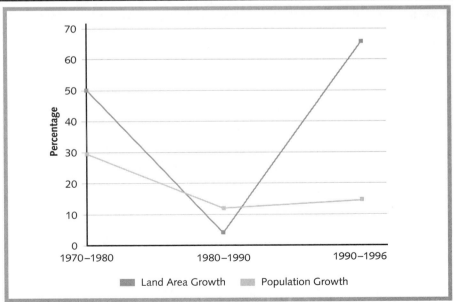

SOURCE: Retrieved from www.sierraclub.org/sprawl/report 98/denver.html. *The Dark Side of the American Dream: The Costs and Consequences of Suburban Sprawl.* Copyright © 1998 Sierra Club.

impact fee
A fee, levied by a government on developers, that is intended to shift some of the societal costs of growth to the developer.

than it was 10 years ago."[30] Maintaining an adequate water supply is a persistent problem in this desert city. Local government is pressed to provide schools, parks, and roads. Bottom line: Growth has outstripped the infrastructure needed to support it. The mayor of Las Vegas has proposed a $2,000 per house **impact fee** to mitigate the effects of growth, but the city lacks the authority to levy the fee. The Nevada legislature will have to approve the proposal before it can take effect. Other places do not have the furious pace of development that Las Vegas has, but they face serious challenges related to growth nonetheless. Table 10.2 lists the concerns of five cities in different parts of the United States.

smart growth
Government efforts to limit urban sprawl by managing growth.

Smart Growth The majority of land-use decisions occur at the local level. Many states have begun to provide localities with more tools to manage growth as subdivisions and strip malls spring up where forests and farms used to be. It costs a lot of money for government to provide infrastructure—streets, water and sewer lines, schools—to these new developments. At the same time, many inner cities are plagued by empty storefronts, vacant lots, and abandoned factories. There, the infrastructure is already in place. The **smart growth** movement is an effort by governments to reduce the amount of sprawl and minimize its impact. Maryland was one of the first states to take action to limit sprawl. Calling sprawl "a disease eating away at the heart of America," Governor Parris Glendening signed the Smart Growth Areas Act into law in 1997.[31] Simply put, the state rewards local governments that target new growth to areas that already have infrastructure, and it denies state funding for infrastructure projects that

TABLE 10.2	Growth-Related Challenges Facing Five Metropolitan Areas
METROPOLITAN AREA	**GROWTH-RELATED CHALLENGES**
Albuquerque, NM	Providing enough water to support growth
	Conducting land-use planning in an area surrounded on three sides by federal and tribal land
Atlanta, GA	Addressing an average daily commute that is among the highest in the nation
	Improving air quality in an area where ozone pollution exceeds the Clean Air Act standard
Burlington, VT	Maintaining the area's rural character
	Maintaining traditional downtown centers and villages
Columbus, OH	Preserving farmland
	Providing the water-sewer infrastructure needed to support growth
Fresno, CA	Preserving prime agricultural land in the metropolitan area—which includes the highest-producing agricultural county in the nation
	Maintaining an adequate water supply

SOURCE: U.S. General Accounting Office, _Local Growth Issues—Federal Opportunities and Challenges_ (Washington, D.C.: U.S. GAO, September 2000), p. 88.

Rapid consumption of land by sprawling development, as pictured here, has sparked the "smart growth" movement.
(© A. Ramey/Stock, Boston, LLC)

encourage sprawl. By enacting this legislation, the state of Maryland has established itself as a major influence in local governments' land-use decisions.

As the Maryland example demonstrates, one of the key aspects of these new state approaches is a stronger link between land use and infrastructure planning. A Sierra Club report in 1999 rated Oregon, Maryland, Vermont, and Maine among the most effective states in doing so.[32] Tennessee and Wisconsin are two states that are fairly new to the ranks of smart growth states.[33] Tennessee adopted legislation in 1998 that requires local governments to establish growth boundaries. In 1999, Wisconsin promulgated uniform comprehensive planning requirements that protect farmland and open space. Not everyone, however, thinks that sprawl is so bad. In fact, to some, sprawl is simply the consequence of the unfettered workings of a free-market system.[34] Given a choice, they contend, Americans prefer a spread-out, car-centered lifestyle. There is some truth to that argument.

Regional Governance

regional government
An areawide structure for local governance, designed to replace multiple jurisdictions.

Regional governments provide structural recognition of the interdependence of proximate communities. Under a regional government, local jurisdictions give up some of their power and authority to a larger government in exchange for areawide solutions to local problems. State legislatures are important players in this process because, aside from the state constitution, they create the rules of the game. Their actions either facilitate or hinder local government reorganization into regional units.

City-County Consolidation   In the United States, the closest thing to regional government is **city-county consolidation,** whereby area jurisdictions are absorbed into a single countywide government. Structure and function are unified. In a pure consolidation, there is one police department, one fire department, one water and sewer system serving the entire county. The functions of local government—public safety, public works, health and human services, community and economic development, and recreation and arts programs—are provided by a single jurisdiction. There are thirty-two city-county consolidated governments. Some of these consolidated governments—San Francisco's, Philadelphia's, and New Orleans's, for example—reflect political decisions of the nineteenth century. Among the most prominent mergers of the past forty years are those of Indianapolis–Marion County, Indiana; Jacksonville–Duval County, Florida; and Nashville–Davidson County, Tennessee. Table 10.3 lists the consolidations that have occurred since 1991.

city-county consolidation
The merger of city and county governments into a single jurisdiction.

Regional government seems so rational, yet it has proven to be quite elusive. Voters typically defeat proposals to consolidate city and county government. During the 1990s, voters rejected the mergers of Des Moines and Polk County, Iowa; Spokane and Spokane County, Washington; and Knoxville and Knox County, Tennessee.

To reformers, this lack of success is perplexing. The logic is straightforward: If small local governments in a metropolitan area merge to form a larger local government, two positive outcomes will occur. First, stubborn public policy problems can be tackled from an areawide perspective. For example, the pollution generated by city A but affecting city B can be handled as a regional problem rather than as a conflict between the two cities. Second, combining forces

TABLE 10.3   **Recent City-County Consolidations**

JURISDICTION	YEAR
Athens–Clarke County, GA	1991
Augusta–Richmond County, GA	1996
Lafayette–Lafayette Parish, LA	1996
Kansas City–Wyandotte County, KS	1997
Louisville–Jefferson County, KY	2000

produces *economies of scale* in service delivery. Instead of a situation in which each jurisdiction constructs and operates jails, for example, one large regional facility can be maintained, providing jail service at a lower cost to each participating jurisdiction.

But there is another side to the regional government coin. Research compared the taxing and spending policies of a consolidated jurisdiction with a comparable but unconsolidated area in the same state.[35] In Florida, both taxes and expenditures increased in consolidated Jacksonville–Duval County relative to those of unconsolidated Tampa–Hillsborough County. A study of preconsolidation city and county budgets in Kansas City and Wyandotte County predicted only modest cost savings at best as a result of consolidation.[36] Another criticism of regional government is that it can be inaccessible and destructive of the hard-won political gains of minorities. Compared to a city or town government, regional government is farther away, both literally and figuratively. Residents of small towns fear the loss of identity as their community gets swept into "big government." The effect on minority political strength, though not as obvious, is no less troublesome. Because the proportionate number of minorities may be lessened when jurisdictions are combined, their voting strength can be diluted. Minorities will likely find it more difficult to elect one of their own to the regional governing board. Considerations like these have made regional government a hard sell in most jurisdictions.

Metropolitan Government   The former mayor of Albuquerque, David Rusk, after thinking long and hard about the relationship between a central city and its suburbs, jumped into the regionalism debate with this statement: "The real city is the total metropolitan area—city and suburb."[37] He uses the concept of "elastic" (and "inelastic") to signify the ability of a city to expand its city boundaries (or not). In a sense, a city's elasticity is its destiny. Elastic cities have been able to capture suburban growth; by adjusting their boundaries through annexation, they can keep pace with urban sprawl. Conversely, many inelastic cities trapped in existing boundaries have suffered population loss and tax-base erosion, resulting in higher levels of racial and class segregation.

The solution offered is a familiar one: metropolitan government. But to be effective, the metropolitan government must include the central city and at least 60 percent of the area's population. How to do this? It depends on the characteristics of the metropolitan area. In single-county metropolitan areas, empowerment of the urban county would effectively create metropolitan government, as would city-county consolidation. And in multicounty metropolitan areas, a single regional government could be created out of existing cities and counties. Obviously, the restructuring of local governments in these ways would engender substantial opposition; as Rusk acknowledges, however, there are few alternatives in areas with low elasticity.

Overcoming traditional antiregionalism sentiment will not be easy, but regional approaches may be necessary for effective competition in an increasingly global economy. And there is some evidence that thinking regionally is gaining favor. For example, recent federal legislation, the Intermodal Surface Transportation Efficiency Act (ISTEA), has revitalized metropolitan planning organizations by requiring them to develop transportation plans for their regions. With the federal government putting more emphasis on regions, it is likely that states and localities will do the same. Consider these comments by the mayors of two very different cities. The mayor of Missoula, Montana (population 43,000), remarked: "It is not possible for Missoula to understand itself, or its future, except in a regional context. The city draws its strength from the region."[38] And the mayor of Detroit, referring to his city and nearby suburbs, said, "It's not Detroit versus Livonia or Auburn Hills or Grosse Pointe. . . . It's the Detroit region versus the Cleveland region."[39] The motivation for regionalism is simple: By joining together and pooling resources, jurisdictions within metropolitan areas are better prepared to meet the challenges confronting them.

It's Up to the States   In many areas of the country, studies have found growing public enthusiasm for regionalism in its various forms. Researchers Larry Gerston and Peter Haas, in studying the San Jose area, have concluded that public concern about serious urban problems has generated new support for regional government. As they note, "With government boundaries and modern political problems increasingly not confluent, leaders and citizens alike must devise new schemes to overcome old jurisdictional lines."[40] One place that has done so is Portland, Oregon, where the city has joined with its suburbs and outlying jurisdictions to develop a regionwide vision for the future. The 2040 Plan, as it is called, aims at accommodating orderly growth while maintaining a desirable quality of life in the region. The planning process involved extensive public participation, including citizen surveys and public forums. In addition, the plan's backers launched media campaigns and loaned videos to acquaint residents with the proposal. The 2040 Plan is enforced by an elected, regionwide council that works to secure the compliance of local governments.[41]

It would be erroneous, however, to assume that everyone everywhere is embracing regionalism. For instance, in southern California, surveys of the public report persistent negative attitudes toward regionalism.[42] In the final analysis, it is up to state government to provide a sufficiently supportive environment in which regionalism can take root. The example of the Minneapolis–St. Paul area of Minnesota is particularly relevant. Since the 1970s, jurisdictions in the Twin Cities area have contributed 40 percent of their new commercial and industrial tax base to a regional pool. The money in this pool is redistributed to communities throughout the region on the basis of financial need, thereby reducing fiscal disparities across jurisdictions. Thus, for instance, a new industry locating in one city becomes a benefit to neighboring cities as well. With regional tax-base sharing as a start, Minnesota went even further in 1994 when the state legislature placed all regional sewer, transit, and land-use planning in the hands of a regional organization—the Metropolitan Council of the Twin Cities.[43] This significantly empowered council makes crucial decisions about growth and development in the Twin Cities area from a regional perspective. Only a few states, however, have endorsed regionalism with the enthusiasm of Minnesota.

States and Their Rural Communities

When the local Dairy Queen closes its doors, a small town in rural America knows that it is in trouble. The Dairy Queen, like the coffee shop on Main Street, serves as a gathering place for community residents. Its demise symbolizes the tough times that a lot of rural communities face. In fact, some analysts argue that the major distinctions in regional economics are no longer between Sunbelt and Frostbelt, or East Coast and West Coast, but between metropolitan America and the countryside.[44] Even as America's economy flourished in the 1990s, several old rural towns in the Great Plains states became veritable ghost towns. Isolated rural areas located miles from an interstate highway, without a coastline or a major city nearby, and lacking an economic engine are particularly at risk.

The decline of rural America has provoked a question: What can state governments do to encourage the right kind of growth in rural areas? Short of pumping enormous amounts of money into the local economy, they can encourage the expansion of local intergovernmental cooperation, whereby small rural governments join together to increase their administrative capacity to deliver services and achieve economies of scale. Two state actions facilitate such cooperation. One is the reforming of state tax codes so that jurisdictions can share locally generated tax revenues. Rather than competing with one another for a new manufacturing plant or a shopping mall, local governments can cooperate to bring the new facility to the area; regardless of where this facility is located, all jurisdictions can receive a portion of the tax revenue. A second useful state action is the promotion of statewide land-use planning. As one observer has noted, "Currently too many rural local governments engage in wasteful inter-community competition, mutually antagonistic zoning, and contradictory development plans."[45]

In 1990, a new federal initiative offered states a means of redesigning their rural development efforts. Concerned that existing rural programs were fragmented and only partially successful, the national government selected eight states for a pilot study.[46] In those states, newly established Rural Development Councils brought together—for the first time—federal, state, and local officials involved in rural development. And rather than mandating the structure of the councils and their agendas, the federal government assumed a hands-off posture and simply provided the necessary start-up funds. In the ensuing years, each council designed its own initiative aimed at specific conditions and problems confronting the state. Mississippi, for example, worked on a tourism and recreation project, South Dakota developed an online resource database, and Washington undertook the issues of affordable housing and job retraining. During the decade many successful projects were completed. The promise of these state-based interorganizational networks is substantial; thinking optimistically, the federal government has extended the initiative to another thirty states.

The Interaction of States and Localities

Constitutionally, state governments are supreme in their dealings with local governments. New York State empowers its cities; nevertheless, New York City—8 million strong and larger than most states—is affected by laws enacted by the state legislature. Yet there is evidence that the state-local relationship is shifting.[47] Leaders in state government are increasingly aware that clinging vines—local governments with limited legal and fiscal authority—do not function well. During the 1990s, states strengthened their local governments so that they could flourish. Strong local governments make for resurgent state governments. Increased capacity and proactivity will be the result. The words of New York governor George Pataki are apropos: "As a former mayor, I know firsthand the importance of freeing our cities, towns, and counties from the heavy hand of state government."[48]

It might be a surprise to find Montana leading the way in the restructuring of state-local relations, but that state is indeed at the forefront. The Governor's Task Force to Renew Montana Government made several recommendations that would substantially alter the state-local connection. In general, the recommendations would diminish the influence of the state in what are considered purely local issues. As the chair of a task force committee noted, "The sheer size of the law regulating local governments is overwhelming. It's the size of *War and Peace* and the Task Force believes it should be reduced to the size of *A River Runs Through It*."[49] Adoption of the recommendations would give local governments substantial powers of self-determination. For example, one recommendation would permit local voters to authorize local taxes. Under existing Montana law, state legislative approval is required before a locality can impose a sales or income tax. In the view of the task force, local voters should decide community tax questions.

Yet one should not be surprised at Montana's willingness to rethink state-local relations. The state constitution contains a provision that gives Montanans the right to review and possibly change the structure and organization of local government. In the spring of 1994, citizens in thirty-three counties and seventy-nine cities voted to begin local "self-examinations." Nonpartisan local government study commissions were elected in the fall and had two years to develop and debate ballot proposals to redesign their governments. Although only relatively modest changes were made—for example, Missoula dropped its partisan elections in favor of nonpartisan ones—the self-examinations were useful. Other states have embraced the Montana approach and have begun their own rethinking of the state-local relationship.

Chapter Recap

> ➤ States vary in the amount and type of authority they give their local governments. During the past two decades, the trend has been toward increased state assistance and empowerment of localities.

➤ Local governments want more money from the state, more power to generate revenues, and more control over how the revenues are spent.

➤ Three types of state-local organizations are common: task forces, advisory commissions on intergovernmental relations, and departments of community affairs.

➤ Urban sprawl has become a major issue in state-local relations. States have begun to adopt "smart growth" laws that are designed to help localities manage growth.

➤ Regionalism continues to be advocated as a solution to many local problems. More jurisdictions are creating regional organizations to link their local governments.

➤ With many rural communities in decline, states are seeking ways of revitalizing them.

➤ The interaction of states and localities is becoming more positive.

Key Terms

Dillon's rule (*p. 230*)

second-order devolution (*p. 231*)

home rule (*p. 231*)

ordinance (*p. 232*)

mandate-reimbursement
   requirements (*p. 233*)

edge cities (*p. 237*)

urban sprawl (*p. 239*)

impact fee (*p. 240*)

smart growth (*p. 240*)

regional government (*p. 242*)

city-county consolidation (*p. 242*)

Surfing the Net

The website of the Association of Bay Area Governments has won awards for its information and design. That site is located at **www.abag.ca.gov.** Two state-level ACIRs with helpful websites are Virginia's and Indiana's, at **www.acir.state. va.us** and **iacir.spea.iupui.edu,** respectively. The Urban Institute's research on economic and social policy in urban areas can be accessed via its website at **www. urban.org.** For an antisprawl argument, see the Sierra Club's website, **www. sierraclub.org/sprawl/.** If your interest is more rural, the website of the National Rural Development Partnership will be useful. Located at **www.rurdev. usda.gov/nrdp,** it has links to state-level rural councils. A particularly interesting rural council is the one in Texas, accessible at **www.trdc. org.**

11

LOCAL GOVERNMENT: STRUCTURE AND LEADERSHIP

Five Types of Local Governments
   Counties » Municipalities » Towns and Townships » Special
   Districts » School Districts

Leadership in Local Government
   Mayors and Managers » City Councils

The Issue of Governance

In 1999, America's second largest city, Los Angeles, did something that it had not done for three-quarters of a century: It rewrote its charter. The charter, which sets out the city's structure and functions, had been amended four hundred times in its history and had grown to an unwieldy and complicated seven hundred pages. The mayor had little real authority over the nearly five-hundred-square-mile city, sharing power with the city council, boards of commissioners, and professional general managers. In essence, the city's structure was a blueprint for failure. Over time, citizens of Los Angeles grew increasingly weary of dealing with an unresponsive city government. When the charter reform question was put on the ballot, voters approved it by a 60 percent to 40 percent margin.[1] But no sooner had this new era in Los Angeles government begun when another challenge emerged: the potential secession of a portion of the city located in the San Fernando Valley.

American local governments were not planned according to some grand design. Rather, they grew in response to a combination of citizen demand, interest-group pressure, and state government acquiescence. As a consequence, no rational system of local governments exists. What does exist is a collection of autonomous, frequently overlapping jurisdictional units. The number of local governments varies from state to state. Consider the case of Kansas and its 3,950 local jurisdictions. The state contains 105 counties, 627 cities, 1,370 townships,

1,524 special districts, and 324 school districts.[2] Nevada, on the other hand, has a grand total of 205 local governments.

What do citizens want from local governments? The answer: to be governed well. They want governmental structures that work and leaders who are effective. And they want jurisdictions with adequate capacity to resolve the tough public problems of our times. But as this chapter demonstrates, "governed well" is hard to achieve. Even with improved capacity, local governments confront a series of challenges that make proactivity difficult. As the Los Angeles example shows, just as soon as they solve one problem, another crops up.

Five Types of Local Governments

general-purpose local government
A local government that performs a wide range of functions.

single-purpose local government
A local government, such as a school district, that performs a specific function.

Local government is the level of government that fights crime, extinguishes fires, paves streets, collects trash, maintains parks, provides water, and educates children. Some local governments provide all of these services; others, only some. (Native American reservations are not a type of local government, even though they perform many local government functions.) A useful way of thinking about them is to distinguish between general-purpose and single-purpose local governments. **General-purpose local governments** are those that perform a wide range of governmental functions. These include three types of local governments: counties, municipalities, and towns and townships. **Single-purpose local governments,** as the label implies, have a specific purpose and perform one function. School districts and special districts are single-purpose governments. In the United States, the number of local governments exceeds 87,000. Table 11.1 classifies those governments.

Regardless of the purpose of a local government, we must remember its relationship to state government. Local citizens may instill a community with its flavor and its character, but state government makes local government official. *Dillon's rule* and *home rule,* both mentioned in Chapter 10, are at work here.

Being so close to the people offers special challenges to local governments. Citizens are well aware when trash has not been collected or when libraries do

TABLE 11.1   **Number and Types of Local Governments**

TYPE OF LOCAL GOVERNMENT	1977	NUMBER IN 1987	1997
County	3,042	3,042	3,043
Municipality	18,862	19,200	19,372
Town/township	16,822	16,691	16,629
Special district	25,962	29,532	34,683
School district	15,174	14,721	13,726
TOTAL	79,862	83,186	87,453

SOURCE: U.S. Bureau of the Census, 1977, 1987, and 1997 *Census of Governments, Volume I: Government Organization* (Washington, D.C.: U.S. Government Printing Office, 1977, 1987, and 1999).

not carry current bestsellers. Moreover, they can contact local officials and attend public hearings—and they do. A recent survey asked a national sample of Americans about their interaction with government. More than 40 percent said that they had contacted an elected official or attended a community meeting.[3] The interactive nature of local government makes the questions of capacity and responsiveness all the more critical.

Counties

State governments have carved up their territory into 3,043 discrete, general-purpose subunits called counties (except in Louisiana, where counties are called parishes, and in Alaska, where they are called boroughs). Counties exist everywhere, with only a few exceptions. The exceptions include Connecticut and Rhode Island, where there are no functional county governments; Washington, D.C., which is a special case in itself; municipalities in Virginia that are independent jurisdictions and are not part of the counties that surround them; and cities like Baltimore and St. Louis, which, as the result of past political decisions, are not part of a county. Also, there are jurisdictions—Philadelphia and San Francisco, for example—that are considered cities but are actually consolidated city-county government structures.

Counties vary dramatically in terms of size. At one extreme is Los Angeles County, California, which, with its more than 9 million residents, is larger than many states. Loving County, Texas, at the other extreme, has fewer than 100 people spread over its 673-square-mile territory.

Why We Have County Government   Counties were created by states to function as their administrative appendages. In other words, counties were expected to manage activities of statewide concern at the local level. Historically, their basic set of functions included property tax assessment and collection, law enforcement, elections, record-keeping (land transactions, births, and deaths), and road maintenance.[4]

The twin pressures of modernization and population growth placed additional demands on county governments. As a result, their service offerings expanded and now include health care and hospitals, pollution control, mass transit, industrial development, social services, and consumer protection.[5] Counties are increasingly regarded less as simple functionaries of state government than as important policymaking units of local government. By 2000, thirty-eight states had adopted home rule provisions for at least some of their counties, thereby granting them greater decisionmaking authority and flexibility.[6]

Even with their gradual empowerment, counties, like other local governments, continue to chafe at the traditionally tight reins of state government control. In a recent survey, county officials blamed "state requirements without state funding" for many of the problems plaguing their government.[7] Also ranking high on their list of complaints were "state limits on authority." The issue of empowerment is unlikely to fade away soon.

How County Governments Are Organized   The typical structure of county government is based on an elected governing body, usually called a board of commissioners or supervisors, that is the central policymaking apparatus in the county. The board enacts county ordinances, approves the county budget, and appoints other officials (such as the directors of the county public works department and the county parks department). One of the board members acts as presiding officer. This form of government is the most popular; about three-quarters of U.S. counties use it. A typical county commission has three or five members and meets in regular session twice a month.

The board is not omnipotent, however; a number of other county officials are elected as well, thereby forming a plural executive structure. In most places, these officials include the sheriff, the county prosecutor (or district attorney), the county clerk (or clerk of the court), the county treasurer (or auditor), the county tax assessor, and the coroner. These officials can become powerful political figures in their own right by controlling their own bureaucratic units. Figure 11.1 sketches the typical organizational pattern.

There are two primary criticisms of this type of organization. First, it has no elected central executive official, like the mayor of a city or the governor of a

| **FIGURE 11.1** | **Traditional Organization of County Government** |

The most common form of county government lacks a central executive.

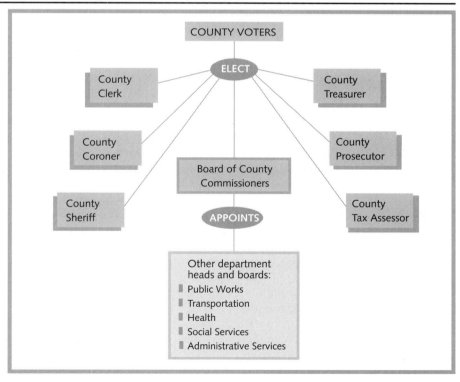

state. County government is run by a board. Second, there is no single professional administrator to manage county government, the way a city manager does in a municipality. Elected officials are responsible for administering major county functions.

These criticisms have led to two alternative county structures. In one, called the county council–elected executive plan, the voters elect an executive officer in addition to the governing board. The result is a clearer separation between legislative and executive powers—in effect, a two-branch system of government. The board still has the power to set policy, adopt the budget, and audit the financial performance of the county. The executive's role is to prepare the budget, administer county operations (in other words, implement the policies of the board), and appoint department heads. Just under four hundred counties have adopted this arrangement. In the other alternative structure, the council-administrator plan, the county board hires a professional administrator to run the government. The advantage of this form of government is that it brings to the county a highly skilled manager with a professional commitment to efficient, effective government. Approximately eight hundred counties have variations of the council-administrator structure.

Determining the most effective structural arrangements for county government is an ongoing issue. Defections from the long-standing commission form of county government and experimentation with alternatives continue, especially in the most populous counties.

The Performance of County Government   The last word on counties has not been written. Granted, counties are now more prominent than they were in the old days, when they were considered the shadowy backwaters of local governments. As urban populations spill beyond the suburbs into the unincorporated territory of counties, the pressure on local governments grows.[8] A county and the cities located within it may find themselves at odds on myriad issues. The county-state relationship is rocky, primarily because of spiraling costs of state-imposed mandates for programs such as indigent services and long-term health care. In addition, counties are expected to tackle tough dilemmas of affordable housing and land-use planning at the same time that they are expanding their services to include such matters as disaster preparedness and consumer protection.

Concerned that county governments were overwhelmed, the speaker of the California assembly introduced legislation in 1991 to create a tier of regional governments in his state.[9] Under the proposal, California would have been divided into seven regions that would be governed by thirteen-member elected boards. These regional "supergovernments" would assume many of the development and infrastructure functions currently assigned to county governments. Although the bill did not pass, the issue has not disappeared. In Massachusetts, where cities and towns provide most local services, the state legislature has abolished several counties, contending that they are superfluous in the Bay State.[10] Although these threats to counties are isolated, county governments must continue to modernize and focus on the big picture or run the risk of being bypassed.

Municipalities

Municipalities are cities; the words are interchangeable in that each refers to a specific, populated area, typically operating under a charter from state government. Cities differ from counties in terms of how they were created and what they do. Historically, they have been the primary units of local government in most societies—the grand enclaves of human civilization.

Creating Cities   A city is a legal recognition of settlement patterns in an area. In the most common procedure, residents of an area in a county petition the state for a charter of **incorporation.** The area slated for incorporation must meet certain criteria, such as population or density minimums. In most cases, a referendum is required. The referendum enables citizens to vote on whether they wish to become an incorporated municipality. If the incorporation measure is successful, then a **charter** is granted by the state, and the newly created city has the legal authority to elect officials, levy taxes, and provide services to its residents. Not all cities have charters, however. Most California cities, for example, operate under general state law rather than a charter. New cities are created every year. For instance, from 1990 to 1996, 145 places incorporated around the country (and 33 cities disincorporated, or ceased to exist as official locales).[11]

Like counties, cities are general-purpose units of local government. But unlike counties, they typically have greater decisionmaking authority and discretion. Almost all states have enacted home rule provisions for cities, although in some states, only those cities that have attained a certain population size can exercise this option. (One of the few states without home rule for cities, New Hampshire, sought to provide it through a constitutional amendment in 2000. The measure was defeated by voters.) In addition, cities generally offer a wider array of services to their citizenry than most counties do. Public safety, public works, parks, and recreation are standard features, supplemented in some cities by publicly maintained cemeteries, city-owned and -operated housing, city-run docks, city-sponsored festivals, and city-constructed convention centers. It is city government that picks up garbage and trash, sweeps streets, inspects restaurants, maintains traffic signals, and plants trees.

City Governmental Structure   City governments operate with one of three structures: a mayor-council form, a council-manager form, or a city commission form. In each structure, an elected governing body, typically called a city council, has policymaking authority. What differentiates the three structures is the manner in which the executive branch is organized.

1. *Mayor-council form.* In the mayor-council form of government, executive functions such as the appointment of department heads are performed by elected officials. This form of government can be subdivided into two types, depending on the formal powers held by the mayor. In a **strong-mayor–council** structure, the mayor is the source of executive leadership. As noted

incorporation
The creation of a municipality through the granting of a charter from the state.

charter
A document that sets out a city's structure, authority, and functions.

strong mayor
An elected chief executive who possesses extensive powers in the city government structure.

weak mayor
An elected chief executive who shares power with other officials in the city government structure.

later in the chapter, strong mayors run city hall like governors run the statehouse. They are responsible for daily administrative activities, the hiring and firing of top-level city officials, and budget preparation. They have a potential veto over council actions. The **weak-mayor**–council structure limits the mayor's role to that of executive figurehead. The council (of which the mayor may be a member) is the source of executive (and legislative) power. The council appoints city officials and develops the budget. The mayor has no veto power. He performs ceremonial tasks such as speaking for the city, chairing council meetings, and attending ribbon-cutting festivities. A structurally weak mayor can emerge as a powerful political figure in the city, but only if he possesses informal sources of power. Figure 11.2 highlights the structural differences between the strong- and weak-mayor–council forms of city government.

FIGURE 11.2   **Mayor-Council Form of Government**

The primary difference between these two structures concerns the power and authority possessed by the mayor. Strong mayors are more ideally situated to exert influence and control.

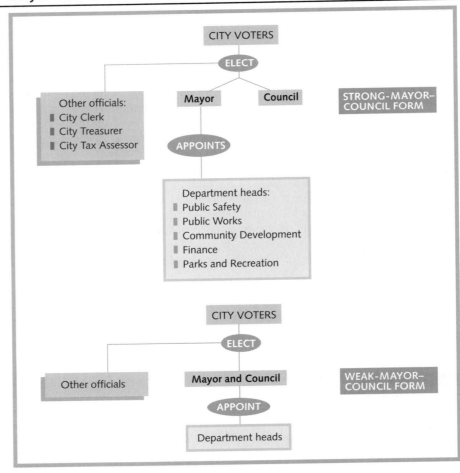

More than half of the cities in the United States use a mayor-council structure. Mayor-council systems are popular both in large cities (populations greater than 250,000) and in small cities (populations less than 10,000). In large cities, the clash of conflicting interests requires the leadership of an empowered politician, a strong mayor. In small communities, however, the mayor-council structure is a low-cost, part-time operation. Some large cities, in which the administrative burdens of the mayor's job are especially heavy, have established the position of general manager or chief administrative officer.

2. *Council-manager form.* The council-manager form of government emphasizes the separation of politics (the policymaking activities of the governing body) from administration (the execution of the policies enacted by the governing body). Theoretically, the city council makes policy, and administrators execute policy. Under this structure, the council hires a professional administrator to manage city government. Figure 11.3 sketches this structure.

The administrator (usually called a city manager) appoints and removes department heads, oversees service delivery, develops personnel policies, and prepares budget proposals for the council. These responsibilities alone make the manager an important figure in city government. Add to them the power to make policy recommendations to the city council, and the position becomes very powerful. When offering policy recommendations to the council, the manager is walking a thin line between politics and administration.[12] Managers who, with the acquiescence of their council, carve out an activist role for themselves may be able to dominate policymaking in city government.[13]

The council-manager form of city government predominates in cities of 10,000 to 25,000 people, especially in homogeneous suburban communities

---

FIGURE 11.3 **Council-Manager Form of Government**

The council-manager form places administrative responsibility in the hands of a skilled professional. The intent is to make the operation of city government less political.

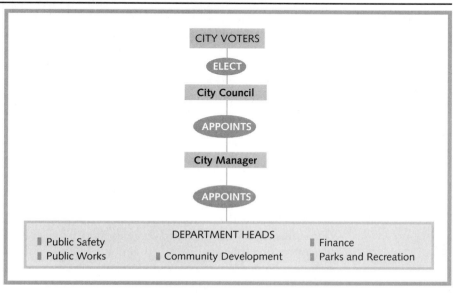

FIGURE 11.4   **City Commission Form of Government**

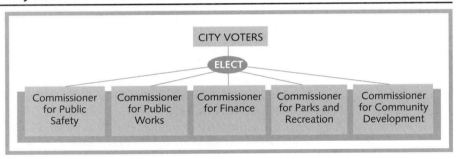

Executive leadership is fragmented under a commission form of government. Individually, each commissioner heads a department; together they run city hall.

and in the newer cities of the Sunbelt region. Even some large cities, such as Dallas, Phoenix, San Diego, and Cincinnati, use the council-manager structure.

3. *City commission form.* Under the city commission form of government, illustrated in Figure 11.4, legislative and executive functions are merged. Commissioners make policy as members of the city's governing body; they also head the major departments of city government. They are both policymakers and policy executors. One of the commissioners is designated as mayor simply to preside over commission meetings.

The commission form of government got its start in Galveston, Texas, and quickly spread to other Texas cities. By 1920, more than 160 other municipalities (including Des Moines, Pittsburgh, Buffalo, Nashville, and Charlotte) had adopted the structure. Its appeal was its ostensible reduction of politics in city government. But almost as fast as the commission form of government appeared on the scene, disillusion set in. One problem stemmed from the predictable tendency of commissioners to act as advocates for their own departments. Each commissioner wanted a larger share of the city's budget allocated to his department. Another problem had to do with politicians acting as administrators: Elected officials do not always turn out to be good managers. The result was that public enthusiasm for the commission form declined. One study showed that of the almost two hundred cities reporting a commission structure in 1970, more than 42 percent had replaced it with another form by 1980.[14] By the 1990s, only a few cities were operating with a commission structure. Notable among them was Portland, Oregon, with its modified commission form of government.

Which Form of City Government Is Best?   Experts disagree about many things, and one of them is which city government structure is best. Most would probably agree that structures lacking a strong executive officer are generally less preferable than others. By that token, the weak-mayor–council and the commission forms are less favorable. The strong-mayor–council form of government is extolled for fixing accountability firmly in the mayor's office, and the council-manager system is credited with professionalizing city government by bringing in skilled administrators to run things. Yet strong-mayor structures are criticized for overconcentrating power in one office; council-manager forms are taken to task for their depoliticization of city government. Bottom line: It is up to community residents to decide which form of government they want. For some cities, a hybrid form that combines features may be the answer. For instance, in 1998, voters in Oakland, California, approved a measure scrapping their council-manager form of government in favor of a modified strong-mayor structure that retained the position of city manager. However, two years later, Hartford, Connecticut, voters turned down a charter revision that would have strengthened the mayor. The best advice may be for a city to use whichever form of government works, while remaining receptive to structural improvements.

Towns and Townships

The word *town* evokes an image of a small community in which everyone knows everyone else, government is informal, and local leaders gather at the coffee shop to make important decisions. These connotations are both accurate and inaccurate. Towns generally are smaller, in terms of population, than cities or counties. And the extent of their governmental powers depends on state government. But even where they are relatively weak, town government is increasingly becoming more formalized.

How Do We Know a Town When We See One? Towns and townships are general-purpose units of local government, distinct from county and city governments. Only twenty states, primarily in the Northeast and Midwest, have official towns or townships. In some states these small jurisdictions have relatively broad powers; in others they have a more circumscribed role.

New England towns, for example, offer the kinds of services commonly associated with cities and counties in other states. Many New England towns continue their tradition of direct democracy through a town-meeting form of government. At a yearly town meeting, residents make decisions on policy matters confronting the community. They elect town officials, pass local ordinances, levy taxes, and adopt a budget. In other words, the people who attend the town meeting function as a legislative body. Although the mechanism of the town meeting exemplifies democracy in action, it often falls short of the ideal. One concern is the relatively low rate of citizen participation in meetings. Often, fewer than 10 percent of a town's voters actually attend the meeting. Larger towns in Connecticut and Massachusetts rely on representatives elected by residents to vote at the meetings.

New England towns, along with those in New Jersey, Pennsylvania, and to some degree Michigan, New York, and Wisconsin, enjoy fairly broad powers. In large measure, they act like other general-purpose units of government. In the remainder of the township states (Illinois, Indiana, Kansas, Minnesota, Missouri, Nebraska, North Dakota, Ohio, and South Dakota), the nature of township government is more rural. Rural townships tend to stretch across thirty-six square miles of land (conforming to the surveys done by the national government before the areas were settled), and their service offerings are often limited to roads and law enforcement. A part-time elected board of supervisors or trustees commonly rules the roost in townships. In addition, some of the jobs in government may be staffed by volunteers rather than salaried workers. However, the closer these rural townships are to large urban areas, the more likely they are to offer an expanded set of services to residents.

Townships and the Future   The demise of the township type of government has long been expected. As rural areas become more populated, they will eventually meet the population minimums necessary to become municipalities. In 2000, for instance, residents of a Minnesota township decided to incorporate as a municipality to ward off annexation by a neighboring city.[15] Other towns face a different problem. Many are experiencing a substantial population exodus and, in the process, losing their reason for existence. These towns may die a natural death, with other types of government (perhaps counties or special districts) providing services to the remaining residents. The question is whether towns and townships are needed in twenty-first-century America.

Townships have not sat idly by as commentators speculated on their dim future. Many small towns have embarked upon ambitious economic development strategies: industrial recruitment, tourism promotion, and amenity enhancement.[16] They formed an interest group, the National Association of Towns and Townships (NATaT), to lobby on their behalf in Washington, D.C. NATaT spawned a spinoff organization, the National Center for Small Communities, to provide training and technical assistance to towns.

Despite dire predictions, towns and townships have proved to be remarkably resilient. According to the U.S. Census Bureau, there were 16,629 of them in 1998, down only 62 from the 1987 figure. Indeed, some see towns and their grassroots governments as the last hope for democracy in the twenty-first century. A political scientist and a state senator in Vermont teamed up to advocate redesigning their state government around a system of reinvigorated towns and regional governments they called shires.[17]

Special Districts

Special districts are supposed to do what other local governments cannot or will not do. They are created to meet service needs in a particular area. Special districts can be formed in three different ways. First, states can create them through special enabling legislation. Second, a general-purpose local government may adopt a resolution establishing a special district. Third, citizens may initiate districts by petition, which is often followed by a referendum on the question. Some districts have the power to levy taxes; others rely on user fees, grants, and private revenue bonds for funding. Taxing districts typically have elected governing boards; nontaxing districts—called **public authorities**—ordinarily operate with appointed boards.[18] There are approximately 35,000 special districts around the country, and that number is increasing. From 1992 to 1997, more than 3,000 new special districts were created; only around 250 were terminated.

public authority
A type of special district funded by nontax revenue and governed by an appointed board.

Not all special districts are organized alike. Ninety-two percent of them provide a single function, but the functions vary. Natural resource management, fire protection, housing and community development, and water and sewer service are the most common. The budget and staff size of special districts range from minuscule to mammoth. Some of the more prominent include the Port Authority of New York and New Jersey, the Chicago Transit Authority, and the Los Angeles County Sanitation District.

Are Special Districts Needed? Special districts overlay existing general-purpose local governments, and some question their necessity. The ACIR puts the question bluntly: "If general-purpose local governments are set up to perform a broad spectrum of functions and if they collectively cover practically every square foot of territory in a state, why [are] special districts needed at all?"[19] The answer has traditionally focused on the deficiencies of general-purpose local governments.[20] Three general categories of "deficiencies" are worth examining: technical conditions, financial constraints, and political explanations.

First are the technical conditions of a general-purpose local government. In some states, cities cannot extend their service districts beyond their boundaries. Moreover, the problem to be addressed may not fit neatly within a single jurisdiction. A river that runs through several counties may periodically overflow its banks in heavy spring rains—a problem affecting small portions of many jurisdictions. A flood control district covering only the affected areas of these jurisdictions may be a logical solution. Furthermore, there are problems of scale. A general-purpose local government simply may not be able to provide electric service to its residents as efficiently as a special utility district that covers a multitude of counties. Finally, there may be prohibitions against joint jurisdictional ventures. For example, some states do not allow their counties to offer services jointly with other counties. Management of a two-county library requires that a special two-county library district be established.

A second set of deficiencies has to do with financial constraints. Local general-purpose governments commonly operate under debt and tax limitations. Demands for additional services that exceed a jurisdiction's revenue-raising ceiling or lead to the assumption of excessive debt cannot be accommodated. By using special districts, existing jurisdictions can circumvent the debt and tax ceilings. Special districts are better suited than general-purpose governments for service-charge or user-fee financing, whereby the cost of the service can be directly apportioned to the consumer, as with water or sewer charges.

Technical and financial deficiencies of general-purpose local governments help to explain the creation of special districts, but political explanations shed even more light. Restrictive annexation laws and county governments with limited authority are political facts of life that encourage the use of special districts. For residents of an urban fringe area, a public service district (which may provide more than one service) may be the only option. Some special districts owe their existence to a federal mandate. For example, national government policy has spurred the creation of soil conservation and flood control districts throughout the country.

Once created, a special district may become a political power in its own right. In places where general-purpose governmental units are fully equipped legally, financially, and technically to provide a service, they may encounter resistance from special-district interests fighting to preserve the district.

Uneasiness About Special Districts   The arguments in favor of special districts revolve around their potential for efficient service provision and the likelihood that they will be responsive to constituents whose demands are not otherwise being met.[21] But for the most part, scholarly observers look at special districts with a jaundiced eye. The most frequently heard complaint is that special districts lack accountability. The public is often unaware of their existence, so they function free of much scrutiny. And, as research by Nancy Burns reminds us, the establishment of special districts is a costly political act.[22] Well-placed groups such as businesses, developers, and home owners' associations are among the beneficiaries of special-district creation. A new study of one hundred airport and seaport districts found that those with an elected governing board were no more likely to be responsive to public preferences than were those with appointed boards.[23]

One thing is certain: The proliferation of special districts complicates the development of comprehensive solutions to public problems. The metropolitan areas of two large Texas cities, Houston and Dallas, contain 779 active special districts.[24] The presence of such an array of districts makes it difficult for general-purpose governments to set priorities. It is not uncommon for cities and counties to be locked in governmental combat with the special districts in their area. Further, special districts may actually drive up the costs of service delivery. A recent study of three hundred metropolitan areas found that compared with general-purpose governments, services provided by special districts have a higher per-capita cost.[25]

Cognizant of these concerns, state governments are looking more closely at special districts and the role they play in service delivery. Colorado, Arizona, and Florida have taken actions that give their general-purpose local governments more input into the state's decision to create special districts.[26]

School Districts

School districts are a type of single-purpose local government. They are a distinct kind of special district and, as such, are considered one of the five types of local government. The trend in school districts follows the theory that fewer is better. Before World War II, more than 100,000 school districts covered the countryside. Many of these were rural, one-school operations. In many small towns, community identity was linked to the local schoolhouse. Despite serving as a source of pride, small districts were so expensive to maintain that consolidations occurred throughout the nation, and by 1998 the number of districts was less than 14,000. Nebraska exemplifies the trend. In 1952, there were 6,392 school districts in the state; by 1997, there were 681.

School Politics   The school board is the formal source of power and authority in the district. It is typically composed of five to seven members, usually elected in nonpartisan, at-large elections. Their job is to make policy for the school district. One of the most important policy decisions involves the district budget—how the money will be spent.

School districts are governed by these boards and managed by trained, full-time educational administrators. Like city governments, school districts invested heavily in the reform model of governance, and the average district has become more professional in operation in the past forty years. An appointed chief administrator (a superintendent) heads the school district staff, the size of which is dependent on the size of the district.

Revamping public education has been a hot topic for the past decade.[27] Concern over mismanagement of funds and low student achievement has led some states to shift control of schools away from the school district itself and place it in the hands of city government. Cleveland and Detroit are two of the most prominent examples; and in 2002, the new mayor of New York City, Michael Bloomberg, suggested a similar action for the Big Apple's schools.[28] At the same time, other school districts have sought to decentralize, shifting power to the school level. This school-based management approach has meant greater involvement of the private sector in some schools; in others it has enhanced the role of parents.

Parental influence in school district policy is most clearly emerging in the matter of **school choice.** School districts around the country have begun to adopt measures that allow parents to decide whether their child will attend the neighborhood school or one elsewhere in the district, perhaps a charter school. In effect, schools are competing for students. Schools are anxious to attract students because district and state funds are allocated on a per-pupil basis. To increase their appeal, some schools specialize in a particular academic area, such as arts or sciences; others emphasize certain teaching styles. Advocates of parental choice claim that this approach offers poor families some of the options that wealthy families have always had with private schools. They argue that competition among schools will generate creativity and responsiveness among teachers and principals. At the same time, some groups are agitating for a return to neighborhood schools. In Boston in 1999, an advocacy group called Boston's Children First sued the school system, demanding neighborhood schools.[29]

school choice
Market-based approach to education improvement that permits parents to choose which school their child will attend. Examples include charter schools and voucher programs.

School District Concerns   There are always controversies in education. The burning issues in school districts range from corporal punishment to the dropout rate, but one recurring central issue is finances. Although the relationship is a bit more complex than "you get what you pay for," there is widespread agreement that children in well-funded school districts are better off educationally than those in poorly funded ones.

A history of serious disparities in school funding, caused by great differences in the available property taxes that provide most of the revenue for local school districts, has led to the increasing financial involvement of state government. State governments use an **equalization formula** to distribute funds to school districts in an effort to reduce financial disparities. Under this formula, poorer school districts receive a proportionately larger share of state funds than wealthier districts do. Although these programs have increased the amount of funding

equalization formula
A means of distributing funds (primarily to school districts) to reduce financial disparities among districts.

for education, they have not eliminated the interdistrict variation. Wealthier districts simply use the state guarantee as a foundation on which to heap their own resources. Poorer school districts continue to operate with less revenue. By 1990, this situation had prompted state courts in Montana, Texas, New Jersey, and Kentucky to declare their public-school finance systems unconstitutional. In those states, the legislatures struggled to design new, more equitable financial arrangements. Texas, for example, responded with a controversial property-tax-sharing system that was defeated by voters in a referendum. Michigan went even further by lowering property taxes for schools and substituting sales taxes and other revenues. In South Carolina, voters approved a state lottery in 2000 in large measure because the proceeds were earmarked for education. In fact, the official name of the game is the "South Carolina Education Lottery." The issue of money for schools is one that stays at the top of legislative agendas, year in and year out.

Leadership in Local Government

Leadership goes hand in hand with governance. Regardless of the jurisdiction, leadership can make the difference between an effectively functioning government and one that lurches from one crisis to another. The terms that conjure up images of leadership in local government circles these days include *initiative, persistence, entrepreneurship, innovation,* and *vision.* These words share a common element: They denote activity and engagement. Leaders are people who "make a difference."[30]

elite theory
A theory of government asserting that a small group possesses power and rules society.

Real questions about who is running the show in local government do arise. At the risk of being accused of naiveté, we might suggest that "the people" run government, local and otherwise. Unfortunately, there is much evidence to persuade us otherwise. But we should not become too cynical, either. Citizen preferences do have an impact on public policy decisions. Can we assume, therefore, that those who occupy important positions in government, such as the mayor and the city council, are in fact in charge? Are they the leaders of the community?

pluralist theory
A theory of government asserting that multiple open, competing groups possess power and rule society.

In sorting through the issue of "who's running the show," we find that several different theories have been advanced. In general, they revolve around the concentration of power and the influence of different groups. For instance, **elite theory** argues that a small group of leaders called an elite possesses power and rules society;[31] **pluralist theory,** conversely, posits that power is dispersed among competing groups, whose clash produces societal rule.[32] Another approach, **regime analysis,** contends that certain individuals and groups possess systemic power and enjoy a strategic advantage in influencing government decisions.[33] It is important to remember that not all communities are organized alike; furthermore, even within a single community, power arrangements shift as time passes and conditions change. A case in point is Athens, Georgia, where the rock group R.E.M. has become a power broker in the city's politics.[34]

regime analysis
An approach asserting that certain individuals and groups possess systemic power and enjoy a strategic advantage in influencing government decisions.

Mayors and Managers

Mayors tend to be the most prominent figures in city government, primarily because their position automatically makes them the center of attention.

Differences Between Strong and Weak Mayors   As discussed earlier in the chapter, strong mayors are different from weak mayors. It is important to note that these labels refer to the *position*, not to the person who occupies it. Similarly, a structure creates opportunities for leadership, not the certainty of it. True leaders are those who can take what is structurally a weak-mayor position and transform it into a strong mayorship.

A strong-mayor structure establishes the mayor as the sole chief executive who exercises substantive policy responsibilities. Directly elected by the voters rather than selected by the council, a strong-mayor serves a four-year (not a two-year) term of office and has no limitations on reelection. She also has a central role in budget formulation, extensive appointment and removal powers, and veto power over council-enacted ordinances.[35] The more of these powers a mayor has, the stronger her position is and the easier it is for her to become a leader.

A weak-mayor structure does not provide these elements. Its design is such that the mayor shares policy responsibilities with the council and perhaps a manager, and serves a limited amount of time in office. (In an especially weak-mayor system, the job is passed around among the council members, each of whom takes a turn at being mayor.) A weak-mayor structure often implies strong council involvement in budgetary and personnel matters.

Mayoral leadership was the subject of a recent point-counterpoint.[36] One side argued that large, diverse communities grappling with complex problems are better served by a structure that fixes leadership and accountability in the mayor's office. In response, the other side contended that a too-powerful mayor could run amok, building political machines based on the exchange of benefits. Structural differences can indeed have consequences. It is important to remember, however, that individuals who work within structures are the essential factor. As David Morgan and Sheilah Watson note, "Even in council-manager communities—where mayors have the fewest formal powers—by negotiating, networking, and facilitating the efforts of others, mayors clearly rise above the nominal figurehead role."[37] In the words of one politician: "The bottom line is good people committed to good governance."[38]

Black Mayors, Women Mayors   By 2002, there were black mayors in more than 350 cities across the country. (Approximately 70 of them are women.) A list of black mayors in large American cities is presented in Table 11.2. Called by some scholars a "new generation," these mayors consider themselves problem solvers, not crusaders; political pragmatists, not ideologues.[39]

Increased success by African Americans in mayoral elections has led some observers to talk of deracialization, that is, the de-emphasis of race as a campaign issue in an effort to attract white voter support.[40] Instead of making racial ap-

TABLE 11.2   Big-City Black Mayors, 2002

CITY	BLACKS AS PERCENTAGE OF CITY POPULATION	MAYOR
Arlington, TX	8.4	Elzie Odom
Atlanta, GA	66.6	Shirley Franklin
Birmingham, AL	55.6	Bernard Kincaid
Columbus, OH	22.6	Michael Coleman
Denver, CO	12.8	Wellington Webb
Detroit, MI	63.1	Kwame Kilpatrick
Houston, TX	26.9	Lee Brown
Memphis, TN	54.8	Willie Herenton
Newark, NJ	58.2	Sharpe James
New Orleans, LA	55.3	Marc Morial
Philadelphia, PA	39.9	John Street
Rochester, NY	31.5	William Johnson
St. Louis, MO	47.5	Clarence Harmon
San Francisco, CA	10.9	Willie Brown
Washington, D.C.	70.3	Anthony Williams

SOURCE: From National Conference of Black Mayors, Atlanta, Ga., 2000 and retrieved from www.blackmayors.org/members/demographics.html. Copyright © 2000 National Conference of Black Mayors. Updated by the authors.

peals, candidates offer a race-neutral platform that stresses their personal qualifications and political experience.[41] Wellington Webb could not have been elected mayor of Denver without the support of large numbers of white voters. The same is true for several of the mayors listed in the table.

More women, too, are running for and winning local elective offices. The data from cities with populations of 30,000 or more are instructive. In 1973, fewer than 2 percent of the cities in that population range had female mayors. A quarter-century later, the number of women mayors had increased to 202, or 21 percent, in cities of 30,000 or more. Recent studies of female mayoral candidates have dispelled several electoral myths. For example, women do not appear to experience greater difficulty in raising money or gaining newspaper endorsements than do men.[42] Women mayors, however, do tend to be political novices. Few female mayors in Florida, for instance, had held elective office before their mayoral election; if they had, it tended to be a city council seat. Other research indicates that mayors, regardless of gender, see their political environments similarly. That makes sense: Successful local politicians know their communities.

Sharon Sayles Belton, the female, African-American former mayor of Minneapolis, offers an instructive story. In her first campaign for mayor in 1993, she crafted a platform that appealed broadly to the electorate, regardless of sex or race. She cruised to victory with no discernible gender gap, receiving 91 percent of the black vote and 67 percent of the white vote. However, rising crime rates and declining student test scores led to a degree of dissatisfaction with the incumbent mayor. In her bid for reelection in 1997, she faced a former city councilwoman—a white female Republican—who had become a radio talk-show host. A tough campaign ensued, one with "unmistakable racial overtones," according to some analysts, but Mayor Sayles Belton prevailed with 55 percent of the vote.[43] By 2001, when she ran for a third term, the bloom was off the rose. Minneapolis voters were in the mood for change. Mayor Sayles Belton received only 35 percent of the vote, losing to political novice R. T. Rybak. In the same election, seven newcomers, including two members of the Green party, won seats on the city council.[44]

City Managers   City managers (as well as county administrators and appointed school superintendents) exemplify the movement toward reformed local government. Local government reform was a Progressive Era movement that sought to depose the corrupt and inefficient partisan political machines that controlled many American cities. To the reformers, local government had become too political; what was needed, they believed, was a government designed along the lines of a business corporation. To achieve their goals, reformers advocated such fundamental structural changes in local government as the abolition of partisan local elections, the use of at-large electoral systems, and the installation of a professionally trained city manager. Altering the structure of local government has had profound consequences for local government leadership. City managers— the professional, neutral experts whose job it is to run the day-to-day affairs of the city—have become key leaders.

In the original conception, managers were to implement but not formulate policy. Administration and politics were to be kept separate. The managers' responsibility would be to administer the policies enacted by the elected officials— the city councils—by whom they were hired (and fired). But it is impossible to keep administration and politics completely separate. City managers are influenced not only by their training and by the councils that employ them but also by their own political ideologies.[45] When it comes to making choices, they balance professional norms, the politics of the issue, and their own predispositions. Hence city managers typically end up being far more influential on the local government scene than their neutral persona might suggest.

As time has passed and more governments have adopted the council-manager system, the issue of whether the city manager should be a policy leader or a functionary of the city council has become paramount.[46] Should a city's policy initiation and formulation process involve a well-trained, highly competent administrator? The International City/County Management Association, the city managers' professional association (and lobbyist), says yes: The role of the manager is to help the governing body function more effectively.[47] The manager-in-training is taught that "the manager now is also expected to be a full partner in the political side of the policymaking process."[48] Ways in which the manager can assume a larger role in policymaking include proposing community goals and service levels; structuring the budget preparation, review, and adoption process so that it is linked to goals and service levels; and orienting new council members to organizational processes and norms. Another indisputable role for the manager is as an information source for the busy, part-time city council.

One new trend is the hiring of professional managers in *non*council-manager cities. That is, some cities with mayor-council or commission forms of government are employing "managing directors" or "chief administrative officers." These individuals have the educational credentials and professional experiences of city managers, and their role in a strong-mayor city would be limited to administrative matters.

City Councils

Local legislatures include city councils, county commissions, town boards of aldermen or selectmen, special-district boards, and school boards. They are representative, deliberative, policymaking bodies. In this section we focus on city councils, because that is where most of the research has taken place; but many of the points made are applicable to the other local legislative bodies as well. And although the ensuing discussion focuses on patterns across councils, it is important to remember that there may be significant variations from one city to another. For example, in some communities, council members receive high salaries, are assisted by clerical and research staff, and have no limits on the number of terms they can serve.[49] In other words, the council enjoys more resources in these places.

Being a city council member involves a lot of listening to constituents. (© Bob Daemmrich/Stock, Boston, LLC)

City Council Members: Old and New   A former member of the city council of Concord, California, defines "the good old days" on local governing boards with this comment: "When I first came on the city council, it was like a good-old-boys' club."[50] The standard view was that the city council was a part-time, low-paying haven for public-spirited white men who did not consider themselves politicians. Most councils used at-large electoral mechanisms, so individual council members had no specific territorially based constituency. Council members considered themselves volunteers.[51] Research on city councils in the San Francisco Bay–area cities in the 1960s found that these volunteer members were fairly unresponsive to public pressures and tended to vote their own preferences.

These days, circumstances have changed. City councils are less white, less male, and less passive than they were in the past. Some of this change is due to modifications in the electoral mechanism. Many cities have abandoned citywide, at-large elections for the council and switched to district (or ward) elections. In **at-large elections,** a city voter can vote for as many candidates as there are seats to be filled. In **district (ward) elections,** a city voter can vote only in the council race in her district. From the perspective of candidates, the at-large system means that a citywide campaign must be mounted. With districts, the candidate's campaign is limited to a specific area of the city. Figure 11.5 displays the district map for the Board of Supervisors of San Francisco, a city that recently made the change to districts. (San Francisco is a consolidated city-county jurisdiction; thus, its legislative body is called a board of supervisors.) Other cities have chosen to retain some at-large seats while dividing the city into electoral districts. Houston, a strong-mayor city, is an example: Of the fourteen members of the Houston city council, five are elected at large and nine are elected from districts. (Table 11.3 shows the wide variation both in council size and in number of members elected at large and from districts.) Changes in election mechanisms signaled a change in council composition. There are more African Americans, Hispanics, and women on city councils than ever before, and they are taking their governance roles seriously.

Much research has been done on the impact of structural considerations—for example, the at-large election format, the size of the council, and the use of nonpartisan elections—on minority council representation.[52] Other factors such as the size of the minority group, its geographical concentration, and its political cohesiveness affect electoral success. In general, a higher proportion of African-American council members can be found in central cities that use a mayor-council structure and in southern cities with large black populations. Councils with higher-than-average Hispanic representation tend to be found in the West, particularly the Southwest, in larger central cities using council-manager structures. Thus far, Asian representation has been clustered primarily in the Pacific Coast area in larger council-manager central cities. And Native American representation is highest in very small communities using commission structures in the southwestern and Pacific Coast regions of the country. The increase in nonwhites on councils has policy consequences. Data from 351 city council members indicate that nonwhites are pursuing a more liberal policy agenda than whites.[53]

---

at-large elections
Citywide (or countywide) contests to determine the members of a city council (or county commission).

district (ward) elections
Elections in which the voters in one district or ward of a jurisdiction (city, county, school district) vote for a candidate to represent that district.

FIGURE 11.5   **San Francisco's Districts**

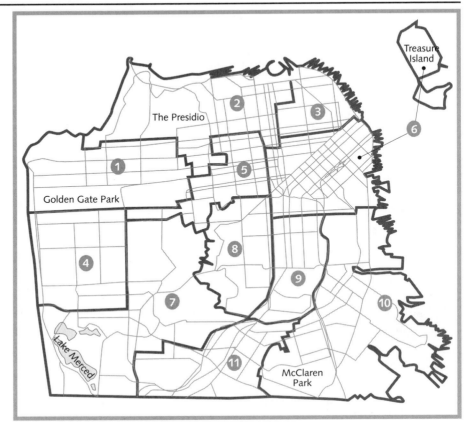

SOURCE: www.ci.sf.ca.us/bdsupvrs/dmap.htm.

Local governing boards in cities and counties are becoming more diverse in another way: The number of openly gay and lesbian elected officials is on the rise. A 1999 estimate for local governing boards of all types placed the number at 120.[54]

Councils in Action: Increasing Conflict   In earlier times, when members of the council came from the same socioeconomic stratum (in some communities, all members of the at-large council came from the same neighborhood) and when they shared a common political philosophy, governing was a lot easier. Members of the council could come together before the meeting (usually at breakfast) and discuss the items on the agenda. That way they could arrive at an informal resolution of any particularly troubling items and thereby transform the actual council meeting into a "rubber-stamp" exercise. No wonder that the majority of council votes were often unanimous; members were merely ratifying what they had already settled on.

| TABLE 11.3 | City Councils of the Twenty Largest U.S. Cities |

CITY	2000 POPULATION	COUNCIL SIZE	NUMBER ELECTED AT-LARGE	NUMBER ELECTED FROM DISTRICTS
New York, NY	8,008,278	51	0	51
Los Angeles, CA	3,694,820	15	0	15
Chicago, IL	2,896,016	50	0	50
Houston, TX	1,953,631	14	5	9
Philadelphia, PA	1,517,550	17	7	10
Phoenix, AZ	1,321,045	8	0	8
San Diego, CA	1,223,400	8	0	8
Dallas, TX	1,188,580	14	0	14
San Antonio, TX	1,144,646	10	0	10
Detroit, MI	951,270	9	9	0
San Jose, CA	894,943	10	0	10
Indianapolis, IN	791,926	29	4	25
San Francisco, CA	776,733	11	0	11
Jacksonville, FL	735,617	19	5	14
Columbus, OH	711,470	7	0	7
Austin, TX	656,562	7	7	0
Baltimore, MD	651,154	19	1	18
Memphis, TN	650,100	13	0	13
Milwaukee, WI	596,974	17	0	17
El Paso, TX	563,622	8	0	8

SOURCE: Census 2000 Population Data, U.S. Bureau of the Census (May 2001).

Council members elected by districts report more factionalism and less unanimity than do their counterparts elected at large. Data from surveys of council members in 218 cities in forty-two states shed more light on this question.[55] Conflict on councils revolves around three types of rivalries: development interests versus others, business versus neighborhoods, and tax cutters versus opponents. The growing tendency of cities to move away from complete reliance on at-large electoral mechanisms suggests that council discord will be on the rise in the future. Fifty-five percent of the city council members responding to a recent national survey reported that such conflict was a serious source of frustration to them.[56] Ten years earlier, only 33 percent voiced a similar concern.

The Chicago city council offers intriguing cases of intracouncil friction. A deliberative body as large as the Chicago council (totaling fifty members, called "aldermen"), and operating with a strong-mayor structure, has several potential patterns of conflict.[57] In a low-conflict council dominated by a large voting bloc loyal to the mayor, the council rubber-stamps the mayor's agenda. Greater conflict occurs in fragmented councils in which many small, loosely structured voting blocs contend for power. The instability of the coalitions requires that they be reassembled each time the council votes. Tremendous uncertainty results. A different pattern of conflict exists in council wars, in which two large factions—one pro-mayor, the other anti-mayor—battle. When Harold Washington served as Chicago's mayor during the 1980s, he could count on a large bloc of African American, Latino, and white "reform" aldermen for support. However, he could also expect a large bloc of primarily white ethnic "machine" aldermen to oppose every piece of legislation he proposed. Stalemate was the consequence. The lesson of Chicago is this: The amount and type of conflict in a council affect its ability to make policy.

The Issue of Governance

Let us return to the governance issue that was raised early in this chapter and has been alluded to throughout it: How do we know when a community is well governed? We have seen communities restructure their governments with the intent of improving governance. Voters defeat incumbents and elect new council members in a similar effort. And conflict over local government spending priorities ensues.

There is no set of universally accepted criteria for evaluating the quality of governance. But efforts toward this end have been made. The National Municipal League, a group that got its start during the reform movement, annually bestows its "All-America City" designation on a few select communities that display "civic energy."[58] Perhaps the key to governance is energy.

Another attempt to isolate characteristics that are plausibly related to governance has settled on seven elements.[59] According to this study, well-governed communities exhibit the following:

1. tranquillity among public officials—an absence of squabbles and bloodletting;
2. continuity in office of top-level managerial officials—a stable corps of administrative personnel;
3. use of analytical budgeting and planning processes—reliance on comprehensive, multiyear methods;
4. participative management—less commitment to hierarchical models and more employee-oriented management;
5. innovativeness—receptivity to new ideas;
6. active public-private partnerships—a minimization of the traditional barrier between government and the private sector; and
7. citizen input into government decisions—the use of formal mechanisms to increase public involvement in government.

The items on the list provide a seedbed for capacity and responsiveness. In other words, local governments that listen and experiment are local governments that lead. The governance question goes back to Plato and Aristotle, and we are unlikely to resolve it here. But these seven elements do offer some guidance for continued rumination about government structure and leadership.

Chapter Recap

➤ There are five types of local governments: counties, municipalities, towns and townships, special districts, and school districts. There are more than 87,000 local governments in the United States.

➤ Counties were created by states to serve as their local administrative arms, while cities operate with a charter of incorporation.

➤ Special districts are both the most prevalent and the least understood of the five types of local government.

➤ The public wants well-governed communities. Local governments redesign their structures in hopes of improving governance.

➤ Mayors tend to be the central figures in city politics and government, even if they operate in formally weak-mayor structures.

➤ City managers, as top-level appointed officials, have become policy leaders.

➤ City councils have changed from the good-old-boy clubs of the past. They are more active, they are more diverse, and there is more conflict on the council.

Key Terms

general-purpose local government *(p. 249)*	school choice *(p. 261)*
single-purpose local government *(p. 249)*	equalization formula *(p. 261)*
incorporation *(p. 253)*	elite theory *(p. 262)*
charter *(p. 253)*	pluralist theory *(p. 262)*
strong mayor *(p. 253)*	regime analysis *(p. 262)*
weak mayor *(p. 254)*	at-large elections *(p. 267)*
public authority *(p. 258)*	district (ward) elections *(p. 267)*

Surfing the Net

There are national associations for most of the types of government, and they have websites. These include the National Association of Counties at **www.naco.org,** the National League of Cities at **www.nlc.org,** and the National Association of Towns and Townships at **www.natat.org/natat.** For school districts, the relevant website is that of the National School Boards Association, **www.nsba.org.** Interesting websites for individual counties include Miami–Dade County's homepage at **www.miamidade.gov** and Los Angeles County's at **www.co.la.ca.us.** For cities, check out the Big Apple at **www.ci. nyc.ny.us.** (An alternative way to get to the site is to use **home.nyc.gov.** Mayors of cities with populations of 30,000 or more may join a national organization, the U.S. Conference of Mayors. Its website is located at **www.usmayors.org.** Within an individual state, mayors frequently belong to a statewide organization such as the one in New Jersey at **www.njmayornet.com.** Specialized constituency groups often have their own organizations and websites, such as the National Conference of Black Mayors at **www.blackmayors.org.** Finally, those interested in learning more about professional city management should examine the International City/County Management Association's website at **www.icma.org.**

TAXING AND SPENDING

The Principles of Finance
Interdependence » Diversity

Revenues
Criteria for Evaluating Taxes » Major State and Local Taxes »
User Fees » Severance Tax » Gambling: Lotteries and Casinos

The Political Economy of Taxation
Spending » Tax Revolt » Fiscal Stress » Limited Discretion

Borrowing and Debt
Estimating Revenues » Rainy Day Funds » Other Financial
Management Practices

Where All the Money Goes: State and Local Spending
Economic Development » Education Policy » Social Welfare and
Health Care Policy

State and Local Finance in the 2000s

Things looked terrific for Tennessee in 1999, the last year of a
decade-long economic boom. The Volunteer State enjoyed triple-A credit ratings and a big budget surplus. Two years later, a mob of angry tax protesters,
stirred up by talk-radio zealots, descended on the Capitol building in Nashville,
screaming at legislators and hurling rocks. Tennessee's credit ratings were down-
graded. Public schools were forced to delay opening the new school year because of a cash shortage. State colleges hiked tuition by 15 percent. A national
recession had caused a significant drop in state revenues, even as expenditure demands continued rising. Making Tennessee particularly susceptible to an economic downturn was its heavy dependence on a 6 percent sales tax for nearly 60
percent of the state's total revenues.

When the state's economy was based primarily on manufacturing and agriculture, the sales tax was a highly productive cash cow. But with an increasing

untaxed, service-based economy and growing (untaxed) Internet and catalog sales, revenues nose-dived and the projected deficit accelerated rapidly. The legislature was within a couple of votes of enacting a state income tax when the tax protesters frightened it into using the state's $560 million share of the national tobacco settlement instead.[1] In July 2002, the sales tax was hiked to 7 percent.

This chapter deals with state and local finance: the politics and policies of taxing and spending. It is a topic of continuing, visceral interest in state and local jurisdictions, and an activity characterized by much change and experimentation. From taxpayer revolts to rainy day funds, the fiscal landscape has profoundly changed during the past twenty-five years. More change is certain as state and local governments strive to meet taxpayer service demands economically and creatively.

The Principles of Finance

A major purpose of government is to provide services to citizens. But this costs money: Equipment must be purchased and employees must be paid. Governments raise needed funds through taxes, fees, and borrowing. In a democracy, the voters decide what range and quality of services they desire and register those opinions through elected representatives. Sometimes, when elected officials don't listen, voters revolt and take matters directly into their own hands.

Two basic principles describe state and local financial systems as they have evolved: *interdependence* and *diversity*. State and local fiscal systems are closely interlinked and heavily influenced by national financial activities. Intergovernmental sharing of revenues is a pronounced feature of our interdependent federal fiscal system. Yet our state financial structures and processes are also highly diverse. Though affected by national activities, their own economic health, and competitive pressures from one another, the states enjoy substantial autonomy in designing individual revenue systems in response to citizens' policy preferences.

Interdependence

own-source revenue
Monies derived by a government from its own taxable resources.

intergovernmental transfers
The movement of money or other resources from one level of government to another.

U.S. governments raise huge amounts of money. In 2000, the national government took in more than $1.9 trillion, and the states and localities more than $1.7 trillion. Most of this money is **own-source revenue,** garnered from taxes, charges, and fees applied to people, services, and products within the jurisdiction of each level of government. Nonnational governments also benefit from **intergovernmental transfers.** The national government contributes almost one-quarter of all state and local expenditures. For their part, states pass on more than $220 billion to their cities, counties, and special-purpose governments.[2] Some of the states are economic powerhouses. In 2001, California's $1.33 trillion total economy displaced France's as the fifth largest in the world.

From 1902 (the first year such data were published) to the late 1970s, state and local governments gradually grew more and more dependent on federal revenue transfers. In 1980, 27.5 percent of total state revenues came from Washington, D.C., in the form of grants-in-aid and other sources; the corresponding percentage of intergovernmental (that is, national and state) contributions to local government was 44.1 percent.[3] During the 1980s, the importance of intergovernmental sources declined for both states and localities, primarily because of national aid reductions and the termination of the general revenue sharing program. A turnaround occurred in 1990, and today federal aid accounts for about 24 percent of state and local spending.

Actually, the impact of federal cutbacks is significantly understated. More than 62 percent of all federal aid to nonnational governments is passed through to *individual* recipients (for example, people receiving Medicaid or Medicare), rather than retained by state and local governments for general purposes. As a result, fewer retained federal grant dollars are available for the traditional functions of state and local governments, such as education, transportation, and public health.

Local governments rely heavily on the states, and to a lesser degree on the national government, for financial authority and assistance. Only the states can authorize localities to levy taxes and fees, incur debt, and spend money. State constitutions and laws place many conditions on local government taxing and spending. As federal aid declined in importance, states increased their monetary support of local governments through state grants-in-aid and revenue sharing; they also assumed financial responsibility for activities previously paid for by localities—in particular, school and social welfare costs. The emergence of the states as senior financial partners in state-local finance has been challenged in some states (especially those without state income taxes) by the need for large local tax increases to fund school improvements or local services.

Although federal grants to local governments have dropped (in constant dollars) since 1978, state-local finances continue to be linked very closely to activities of the national government. When national monetary and fiscal policies lead the nation into a recession, as happened in 2001, it is state and local governments that suffer most. And when the federal government changes the tax code, it can wreak havoc on those thirty-five states that base their own income tax on that of the federal government. For instance, Congress's repeal of the estate tax in 2001 is projected to cost the states upwards of $5.5 billion over the next ten years—$1 billion for California alone![4]

Diversity

The second basic principle of state and local finance systems is diversity of revenue sources. Each level of government depends on one type of revenue device more than others. For the national government it is the income tax; for the states, the sales tax; and for local governments, the property tax. But diversity triumphs among the states. Differences in tax capacity (wealth), tax effort, and tax choices are obvious even to the casual observer. Most states tax personal income and merchandise sales, but a handful do not. A large number of states operate lotteries and pari-mutuel betting facilities.

Some states, such as Alaska and Hawaii, tax with a heavy hand. Others, including New Hampshire, South Dakota, and Texas, are relative tax havens. Most fall somewhere in the middle. If the basic objective of taxing is to pluck the maximum number of feathers from the goose with the minimum amount of hissing, the wealthy states hold a great advantage, since they can reap high tax revenues with much less effort than poor states, which must tax at high rates just to pull in enough money to pay for the basics. Per-capita state and local tax revenues vary from $3,987 in New York to $1,878 in Tennessee. The U.S. average is $2,597.[5] There is a fairly close relationship between state wealth (as measured by personal income) and tax burden. Table 12.1 shows how the states compare in state and local tax revenues, controlling for personal income. Tax levels can reflect such factors as citizen attitudes, population characteristics and trends, business climate, and the quality as well as quantity of government services. And taxing is only one means of plucking the public goose. State and local governments increasingly rely on fees and charges for services rendered. Examples include entrance fees for parks and recreation facilities; sewer and garbage fees; and severance taxes on oil, natural gas, and minerals.

tax capacity
The taxable resources of a government jurisdiction.

tax effort
The extent to which a jurisdiction exploits its taxable resources.

There is an important difference between **tax capacity,** the potential ability to raise revenues from taxes, and **tax effort,** the degree to which a state exploits its fiscal potential. High tax capacity is associated with high levels of urbanization, per-capita income, economic development, and natural resources. But simply because a state has high revenue-raising capacity does not necessarily mean that it will maximize its tax-collecting possibilities. Indeed, many states with high revenue potential, such as Alaska and Wyoming, actually tax at relatively low rates, indicating low tax effort.[6] Tax effort depends largely on the scope and level of services desired by the people.

Revenues

Although the state and local finance systems have their own strengths, weaknesses, and peculiarities, certain trends can be found in all of them. The property tax is increasingly unpopular. It is no longer a significant source of revenue in most states; its contribution to total own-source local revenues, though, is still strong. User fees and other miscellaneous charges are gradually increasing. States continue to depend heavily on the sales tax, but alternatives are being used more widely. In fact, tax diversification is an important trend in all state and local tax systems (see Figure 12.1).

Criteria for Evaluating Taxes

Numerous criteria can be used to evaluate taxes. Moreover, what one person or interest group likes about a tax may be what another dislikes. Nevertheless, political scientists and economists agree that among the most important criteria are equity, yield, elasticity, ease of administration, political accountability, and acceptability.

TABLE 12.1	**State and Local Taxes as a Percentage of Personal Income, 2002, in Descending Order**		

	STATE/LOCAL TAXES AS % OF INCOME		STATE/LOCAL TAXES AS % OF INCOME
Maine	13.6	Kansas	10.2
New York	12.9	Delaware	10.1
Wisconsin	11.9	North Carolina	10.0
Vermont	11.7	Illinois	9.9
Connecticut	11.6	Montana	9.9
Hawaii	11.6	Oklahoma	9.9
Rhode Island	11.4	California	9.8
Minnesota	11.3	Missouri	9.8
New Mexico	11.1	Florida	9.7
Arkansas	10.9	Maryland	9.7
Nebraska	10.9	Georgia	9.6
Mississippi	10.8	Nevada	9.6
Ohio	10.8	Arizona	9.5
Utah	10.7	Massachusetts	9.5
Kentucky	10.6	Virginia	9.5
Michigan	10.6	Oregon	9.4
North Dakota	10.5	South Carolina	9.3
West Virginia	10.5	Wyoming	9.2
Idaho	10.4	Alabama	9.1
New Jersey	10.4	Texas	9.0
Washington	10.4	South Dakota	8.9
Louisiana	10.3	Colorado	8.4
Pennsylvania	10.3	Tennessee	8.3
Indiana	10.2	New Hampshire	7.6
Iowa	10.2	Alaska	6.3
		U.S. average	10.2%

SOURCE: Data from Tax Foundation, *Tax Bites.* www.taxfoundation.org., March 14, 2002. Reprinted by permission of the Tax Foundation.

Equity If citizens or firms are expected to pay a tax, they should view it as fair. In the context of taxation, equity usually refers to the distribution of the tax burden in accordance with ability to pay: High income means greater ability to pay and, therefore, a larger tax burden. Equity has other dimensions as well, such as the relative tax burden on individuals versus firms and the impact of various types of taxes on income, age, and social class.

| FIGURE 12.1 | **Distribution of Total State Tax Revenue by Source, 2002** |

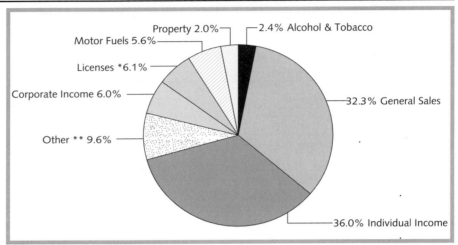

*Includes motor vehicle, hunting/fishing, alcoholic beverage, public utility, and occupation and business license fees.

**Includes insurance, death and gift, and severance taxes, and non-license taxes on public utilities.

SOURCE: Council of State Governments, *The Book of the States,* vol. 34 (Lexington, Ky: Council of State Governments, 2002): 299.

regressive tax
A tax in which the rate falls as the base or taxable income rises.

Taxes may be regressive, progressive, or proportional. A **regressive tax** places a greater burden on low-income citizens than on high-income citizens. Thus the ability-to-pay principle is violated, with the result that upper-income groups contribute a smaller portion of their incomes than lower-income groups do. Most state and local levies, including property and sales taxes, are regressive. For example, both low-income and high-income people would pay, say, a 5 percent sales tax. The latter will likely make more purchases and contribute more total dollars in sales tax, but at a lower percentage of their total income than the low-income individuals.

progressive tax
A tax in which the rate rises as the base or taxable income rises.

A **progressive tax** increases as a percentage of a person's income as that income rises. The more you make, the greater proportion of your income is extracted by the progressive tax. Thus, those better able to pay carry a heavier tax burden than the poor. The national income tax is the best example of a progressive tax. The more you earn, the higher your *income tax bracket.*

proportional (flat) tax
A tax in which people pay an identical rate regardless of income or economic transaction.

A **proportional tax,** sometimes called a **flat tax,** burdens everyone equally, at least in theory. For instance, a tax on income of, say, 10 percent that is applied across the board is a proportional tax. Whether you earn $100,000 or $10,000, you pay a flat 10 percent of the total in taxes. Of course, it can be argued that a low-income person is more burdened by a proportional tax than a high-income person (as in the case of the sales tax).

benefit principle
The principle that taxes should be levied on those who benefit directly from a government service.

In place of ability to pay, some people advocate the **benefit principle.** Under this principle, those who reap more benefits from government services should shoulder more of the tax burden than people who do not avail themselves of service opportunities to the same degree. As a hypothetical example, it might be argued that parents whose children attend public schools should pay higher taxes for education than should senior citizens, childless couples, or single people without children. The benefit principle is the theoretical underpinning for user fees, which charge a taxpayer directly for services received.

Yield Taxes can also be evaluated on the basis of efficiency, or how much money they contribute to government coffers compared to the effort expended to collect them. The administrative and other costs of applying a tax must be taken into consideration when determining yield. Taxes that return substantial sums of money at minimal costs are preferred to taxes that require large outlays for moderate revenues. Income and sales taxes have high yields because of the low administration costs. Property taxes have lower yields because they are more expensive to assess and collect. Yield depends on base and rate. The broader the tax base, the higher the yield. For example, a sales tax applied to all purchases yields much more than a sales tax on cigarette purchases.

Elasticity This criterion is related to yield. Tax yields should be automatically responsive to changes in economic conditions, and revenue devices should expand or contract their yields as government expenditure needs change. Specifically, as per capita income grows within the state and its localities, revenues should keep pace without increases in the tax rate. Tax reductions should accompany economic recession and declines in per capita income, so that citizens' tax burdens are not increased during hard times. The national income tax is considered to be elastic, because revenues increase as individuals earn more money and move into higher tax brackets, and decline as income falls. Property taxes and user fees generally do not move in tandem with economic conditions and are therefore considered to be inelastic.

Ease of Administration Taxes should be simple to understand and compute. They should also be easy to apply in a nonarbitrary fashion and difficult to evade. Income taxes are fairly easy to collect because most are deducted directly from employee paychecks and remitted to the state by employers. Local property taxes are difficult to administer, because of the time and expense involved in regularly appraising property values and the inherent subjectivity of placing a dollar value on buildings and land. The sales tax is easy to administer at the time and place of sale, and nearly impossible to evade. (Exceptions to this rule involve out-of-state catalog and Internet sales and consumers who cross state borders to avoid high sales taxes on merchandise, cigarettes, gasoline, and alcohol.)

Political Accountability Tax increases should not be hidden. Instead, state and local legislative bodies should have to approve them deliberately—and publicly. Citizens should know how much they owe and when it must be paid. For example, some state income taxes are silently hiked as wages rise in response to cost-of-living increases. After inflation is accounted for, taxpayers make the same income as they did before, but they are driven into a higher income bracket for tax purposes. This phenomenon, known as bracket creep, can be eliminated by **indexing** income tax brackets to changes in the cost of living.

---

indexing

A system in which tax brackets are automatically adjusted to account for inflation.

Acceptability   The type and mix of taxes imposed should be congruent with citizen preferences. No tax commands wild enthusiasm, but some are less disagreeable than others. Tax acceptability varies from place to place depending on numerous factors, including equity implications and the perceived pain of paying. Large, one-time payments, such as the annual property tax, inflict greater pain than small, frequently paid sales taxes. And a tax on someone else is always preferable. As Senator Russell Long of Louisiana put it many years ago, "Don't tax me, don't tax thee; tax that man behind the tree."

Major State and Local Taxes

The principal types of taxes are those on property, sales, and income. Various other miscellaneous taxes also provide much-needed revenue for state and local governments.

Property Tax   In 1942, taxes on personal and corporate property accounted for 53 percent of all state and local tax revenues. Today they represent only 30 percent of tax revenues, and only 21 percent of all forms of revenue. Many states hardly utilize the property tax at all today—it accounts for less than 3 percent of their total revenues—but local governments continue to depend on it for three-quarters of all their own-source revenues. Other revenue sources have augmented the property tax, with the result that its proportionate contribution has diminished. As always, there is considerable state-by-state variation. New Hampshire, which has no sales or income taxes, depends on property taxes for 67 percent of its total state and local tax revenues. The state least committed to this particular tax is New Mexico, which derives only 12.2 percent of state and local tax revenues from property taxes.[7]

The best thing about the property tax is that it is certain; owners of property must pay it or the government may seize and sell their land, buildings, or other taxable possessions. However, it has lost acceptability in recent years because it tends to be regressive, lacks political accountability, is hard to administer, and sometimes must be paid in a large lump sum. At first thought, it seems that property taxes cannot be truly regressive, because only those people who own property pay taxes on it directly; however, renters pay property taxes indirectly through their monthly checks to the landlord. When property tax assessments climb, so do rental charges. Property taxes can also violate the ability-to-pay principle when housing values spiral upward, as they have recently in Utah, Colorado, Oregon, and Arizona. Retirees and other homeowners on fixed incomes discover with alarm that their annual property tax bills are rising sharply as housing prices escalate.

Just this sort of situation helped precipitate California's Proposition 13, which was credited with kicking off a taxpayer revolt across the United States. In the Los Angeles and San Francisco Bay areas during the 1970s, property taxes doubled and then tripled in only a few years. Some senior citizens were forced to sell their homes in order to pay their property tax. Proposition 13 reduced property tax bills by approximately $7 billion in the first year; in addition, it imposed strict limitations on the ability of local governments to raise property and other taxes in the future. California dropped from being the eighth-highest property tax state to the twenty-eighth. This illustrates the problem of political accountability: When property values rise to lofty heights, taxpayers' bills keep pace, even though elected officials do not explicitly vote to hike property taxes.

Property taxes are difficult to administer; they also are somewhat arbitrary. The process of levying an annual fee on "real property" (land and buildings) begins with a government assessor's making a formal appraisal of the market value of the land and the buildings on it. Then property values are "equalized" so that similarly valued real estate is taxed at the same level. Time is set aside to make corrections and to review appeals on appraisals that the owner believes to be too high. Next, an assessment ratio is applied to the property. For instance, houses might be assessed for tax purposes at 80 percent of market value. A rate is placed on the assessed value to calculate the annual tax amount. (Assessed at $100,000, taxed at a ratio of .80 and a rate of $3 per $100 [30 mils], a house would produce a tax due of $2,400.) This last step may seem fairly straightforward, but ultimately the appraised market value depends on the findings of the assessor, who may or may not be properly trained for the job or be fully aware of conditions in the local housing market (computer-assisted appraisals remove some of the guesswork). Property can thus be underappraised or overappraised. For the sake of equity, property should be appraised regularly (for example, every five years). Otherwise, property that does not change ownership becomes increasingly undervalued.

Property tax systems are further criticized for exempting certain types of real estate and buildings. Government buildings such as hospitals and state offices are not taxed, even though they utilize police and fire protection, trash collection, and other local government services. Churches, synagogues, mosques, and related property used for religious purposes are also exempted in the vast majority of jurisdictions.

circuit breaker
A limit on taxes applied to certain categories of people, such as the poor or the elderly.

In an effort to make property taxation more equitable and more in keeping with ability to pay, thirty-five states have enacted some form of **circuit breaker.** For instance, the property of low-income individuals is excluded from taxation in some states; others assign lower assessment ratios to the homes of senior citizens or set a top limit on the tax according to the owner's income (for example, 4 percent of net income). At least twenty-two states have "truth in taxation" laws. Most also offer homestead exemptions, in which owner-occupied homes are taxed at lower rates or assessed at lower values than rental homes or business property.[8] Massachusetts municipalities permit seniors to earn credits against their tax bills through public service activities.

Despite such attempts to make property tax fairer, differences in property values among cities, counties, and school districts still have important implications for the quality and distribution of services. Jurisdictions with many wealthy families, capital-intensive industries, or rapid construction growth can provide high levels of services with low tax rates, whereas areas with weak property tax bases must tax at high rates merely to yield enough revenues to maintain minimal services. Residential property tax rates vary widely in individual cities. For example, the rate is $4.55 per $100 of assessed value in Bridgeport, Connecticut, but only $0.67 in Denver, Colorado. Altering the unequal distribution of property values is essentially beyond the control of local governments. As a result, "wealthy suburbs remain wealthy, poor communities remain poor, and services remain unequal."[9] Inequity in school funding has been the target of a growing number of lawsuits. In Michigan, the legislature significantly reduced property taxes for public education and asked voters to substitute either sales tax increases or higher income taxes. Voters opted overwhelmingly for a 2¢ sales tax increase accompanied by a 50¢-per-pack cigarette tax hike. Dramatic property tax relief measures have also been adopted recently in South Dakota, Wisconsin, Idaho, Washington, and Texas. Because of a recent state supreme court ruling that its property tax–funded public-school system is unconstitutional, New Hampshire is probably next.

Sales Tax   Mississippi was the first state to adopt this form of taxation, in 1932. Others followed suit very rapidly, and states currently collect more of their revenues today from the general sales and gross receipts tax than from any other source. It accounts for about one-third of total own-source state taxes, just behind personal income taxes. (Again, see Figure 12.1.) Only five states do not levy a general sales tax: Alaska, Delaware, Montana, New Hampshire, and Oregon. State sales tax rates vary from 7 percent in Rhode Island and Mississippi, and 6.5% in Minnesota, Nevada, and Washington, to 3 percent in Colorado. The national average is 6.25 percent. Some states, particularly those that do not have personal income taxes, are exceptionally dependent on the sales tax: Florida, Washington, and Tennessee derive approximately 60 percent of their own-source revenues from the sales tax.

The sales tax has remained in favor for two major reasons. First, citizen surveys have consistently shown that when a tax must be raised, voters prefer the sales tax. Although the reasons are not entirely clear, this tax is perceived to be fairer than other forms of taxation. Second, there is an abiding belief that high state income taxes depress economic development.[10] Moreover, the property tax is widely detested.

Thirty-three states authorize at least some of their municipalities and counties to levy local sales taxes.[11] When state and local sales taxes are combined, the total tax bite can be painful. In Baton Rouge, the purchase of a $1 item requires 10¢ in sales tax. The rate on the dollar is 9.75¢ in Nashville, and 9¢ in New Orleans and in Mobile, Alabama. Sales taxes are almost always optional for the local jurisdiction, requiring majority approval by the city or county legislative body. Typically, states impose ceilings on how many pennies the localities can attach to the state sales tax; states also specify which sizes and types of local governments are permitted to exercise this option.

When applied to all merchandise, the sales tax is clearly regressive. Poor folks must spend a larger portion of their incomes than rich people on basics such as food and clothing. Therefore, the sales tax places a much heavier burden on low-income people. Most of the forty-five states with a sales tax alleviate its regressivity by excluding certain "necessities." Thirty-one states do not tax food, only five tax prescription drugs, thirty-one exempt consumer electric and gas utilities, and six exclude clothing.[12] New Jersey excludes paper products. When the sales tax was extended to paper products in 1990, enraged Jerseyites mailed wads of toilet paper—some of it used—to legislators, who quickly rescinded the tax.

States can improve the yield of the sales tax by broadening the base to include services. In this way, more of the burden is passed on to upper-income individuals, who are heavier users of services. More than half of the states tax services such as household, automobile, and appliance repairs, barber and beauty shops, printing, rentals, dry cleaning, and interior decorating. Hawaii, New Mexico, and South Dakota tax virtually all professional and personal services. However, two states moved too far and too fast with taxes on services. Florida and Massachusetts both broadened the base of their sales tax to services, only to have it repealed shortly afterward, the result of successful lobbying efforts by the business community.

These setbacks are likely to be temporary. Services are the largest and fastest-growing segment of the U.S. economy. Eighty-five percent of new jobs are in services. As political journalist Neil Peirce asked, "How can one rationalize taxing autos, videocassettes, and toothpaste, but not piped-in music, cable TV, parking lot services, or $100 beauty salon treatments?"[13] Pet grooming services, legal and financial services, and many others from landscaping to septic-tank cleaning are likely to lose their tax-favored status in years to come, as states extend sales taxes to services incrementally, fighting industry and lobbyists one at a time.

In recent years, a big fight has erupted over state and local governments' right to tax an enormously promising revenue stream—electronic commerce on the Internet. Twenty-one states were levying taxes or fees on Internet access, data downloads, or goods purchased on the Internet. Pressures from Internet interests, including servers (for example, America Online), media companies, and retail businesses, led Congress to pass the Internet Tax Freedom Act, which imposes a three-year moratorium on taxation of online sales until November 2003. State and local officials have strongly opposed such limitations, estimating that it has cost them $13 billion in taxes in 2001 alone, as more and more goods were bought electronically.[14] Already states estimate that they forfeit $5 billion a year in uncollected taxes from interstate catalog sales. (Only catalog sales to citizens living in a state in which the mail-order firm has a physical presence are now taxed. A rapidly growing number of states require citizens to declare and pay such sales taxes in their annual state income tax returns, usually to no avail because of difficulty of enforcement).

Internet taxation is both complicated and controversial, and it has become a compelling issue for the states. A 1992 U.S. Supreme Court ruling blocked taxation of catalog sales on the grounds that it violated the interstate commerce clause. a ruling that has obvious applicability to taxing Internet commerce today.[15] Congress has been tied in knots over the issue, as have the governors. No less than the fiscal integrity of state revenue systems is at stake. If states lose billions of dollars to a tax-free Internet, how will the gaping budget holes be filled? What about Main Street retailers whose prices are made less competitive by the amount of the sales tax? Yet it would be a heavy burden indeed for vendors to comply with the tax laws of 7,600 taxing jurisdictions in the United States. A compromise under active consideration (adopted by 31 states as of mid-2002) is the streamlined sales tax, wherein each state would collapse all its local sales tax rates into one statewide rate, resulting in only 50 Internet tax jurisdictions.[16] This approach would have the added value of laying the foundation for taxing mail-order catalog sales.

Elasticity is not a strong point of the sales tax—although its productivity falls when consumer purchases slow—but broadening the base helps. A few states have attempted to make the sales tax more responsive to short-term economic conditions by increasing it on a temporary basis, to make up lower-than-anticipated revenues, then reducing it when needed monies are collected. A problem with these tactics, however, is that consumers tend to postpone major purchases until the tax rate falls.

The sales tax is relatively simple for governments to administer. Sellers of merchandise and services are required to collect it and remit it to the state on a regular basis. Political accountability is also an advantage, since legislative bodies must enact laws or ordinances to increase the sales tax rate. And, as we have observed, the sales tax is the least unpopular of the major taxes.

Income Tax   Most states tax personal and corporate income. Wisconsin was the first, in 1911, two years before the national government enacted its own personal income tax. Forty-one states have broad-based taxes on personal income, whereas two (Tennessee and New Hampshire) limit theirs to capital gains, interest, and dividends. Only Alaska, South Dakota, Florida, Texas, Nevada, Washington, and Wyoming leave all personal income untaxed. The last three of these also refuse to tax corporate income. Personal income taxes garner 34.5 percent of all state own-source taxes (see Figure 12.1), and the corporate tax brings in 6.1 percent. Eleven states permit designated cities, counties, or school districts to levy taxes on personal income.

State and local income taxes are equitable when they are progressive. This contingency normally entails a sliding scale, such that high-income filers pay a greater percentage of their income in taxes than low-income filers do. Almost half of the states do not levy a personal income tax on people whose earnings fall below a certain floor—say, $10,000. Overall, personal income taxes in the states are moderately progressive and are gradually becoming more so.

Personal and corporate income taxes are superior to other taxes on the criteria of yield and elasticity. By tapping virtually all sources of income, they draw in large sums of money and respond fairly well to short-term economic conditions. Through payroll withholding, income taxes are fairly simple to collect. Also, many states periodically adjust income tax rates in response to annual revenue needs.

As mentioned earlier, political accountability can be problematic with respect to income taxes during periods of rising prices. Unless income tax rates are indexed to inflation, cost-of-living increases push salaries and corporate earnings into higher tax brackets. At least seventeen states have adopted indexing.

Miscellaneous Taxes   A wide variety of miscellaneous taxes are assessed by state and local governments. "Sin taxes" raise about 5.5 percent of all state revenues.[17] All states tax cigarettes; the average tax per pack was 76¢ in 2002, rising quickly as nearly half the states hiked the cigarette tax to help balance their budgets in 2002. New York and New Jersey discourage smokers with a $1.50 per-pack tax. Kentucky charges only 3¢ per pack, and North Carolina 5¢; not surprisingly, both are tobacco-growing states. This startling disparity in prices has led to a flourishing trade in cigarette smuggling from low- to high-tax states. Recently the states experienced the equivalent of winning the lottery. A court settlement with tobacco companies is expected to send a total of $246 billion into state coffers. Few strings are attached. Some states are spending their share creatively, on smoking prevention, health care services, and education. Others used their 2002 allotments to balance the state budget.

Alcoholic beverages are also taxed in all fifty states, although rates vary according to classification: beer, wine, or spirits. Beer guzzlers steer clear of Hawaii, where the tax per gallon of beer is 92¢. Frequent imbibers are invited to visit Missouri and Wisconsin, where the tax is only 6¢ per gallon. Could such low rates be related, perhaps, to the fact that these states host the headquarters of two of the largest brewers in the country? (The eighteen states that hold monopolies on wholesale distribution of alcoholic beverages or that have their own state-run liquor stores are not accounted for in these figures.) Ironically, as drinking and smoking have declined during the past few years, so have their tax-based revenues. Clearly, raising alcohol and tobacco taxes helps to curtail these "sins." It has been suggested that marijuana and other "recreational" drugs be legalized so that they, too, can be taxed.

Though not a "sin," gasoline falls under the taxman's shadow as well. The highest state tax on driving in 2002 was in Wisconsin (27.3¢ per gallon). The lowest was in Georgia (7.5¢). All states also tax vehicles and vehicle licenses.

Most states tax death in one form or another. Estate taxes must be paid on the money and property of a deceased person before the remainder is disbursed to the survivors; the rate is as high as 21 percent in Mississippi, Ohio, and Oklahoma. Eighteen states tax those who inherit assets valued at more than $675,000. Rates are generally staggered according to the value of the estate and the relationship to the deceased. As noted above, however, abolition of the federal estate tax has foretold a slow death knell for such state taxes as well.

Other miscellaneous sources of revenue include hunting and fishing licenses, business licenses, auto license fees, parking tickets, and traffic violation fines. One of the newest devices is the "jock tax." Some twenty states and several cities require professional athletes to pay a prorated income tax for games played in their jurisdiction. For highly paid baseball, basketball, and football players, the jock tax burns. Toronto Blue Jays' star Carlos Delgado is charged $3,080 for every game he plays in Boston against the Red Sox.[18]

User Fees

Setting specific prices on goods and services provided by state and local governments is one method that clearly pursues the *benefit principle:* Only those who use the goods and services should pay. User fees have been in existence for many years. Examples include college tuition, water and sewer charges, and garbage collection assessments. Toll roads and bridges are coming back in fashion as well. Today, user fees are being applied broadly as state and especially local officials attempt to tie services to their true costs. Such fees are increasingly being levied on "nonessential" local government services, such as parks and recreation, libraries, airports, and public transit. The average American pays more than $1,243 a year in user fees,[19] accounting for about 20 percent of all state and local revenues.

User fees offer several advantages. If priced accurately, they are perfectly fair under the benefit principle and they enjoy a relatively high level of political acceptability. But those people who do not have enough money to purchase the goods and services may have to do without—a circumstance that violates the ability-to-pay principle. A good case in point is higher education, which is shifting increasingly from state funding to tuition funding. (Fortunately, rebates, scholarships, fee waivers, and reduced-fee schedules mitigate ability-to-pay difficulties among low-income residents.) User fees are structured to yield whatever is needed to finance a particular service. An added benefit is that service users who do not live in the taxing jurisdiction must also pay the price, say, for a day in the state park. Elasticity may be achieved if the amount of the charge is varied so that it always covers service costs. In many instances user fees can be levied without the specific permission of the state.

Because service users must be identified and charged, some user fees can be difficult to administer. Political accountability is low because the charges can be increased without legislative action. However, a special advantage of user fees is that they can be employed to ration certain goods or services. For instance, entrance charges can be increased to reduce attendance at an overcrowded public facility, or varied according to the day of the week in order to encourage more efficient utilization. If the municipal zoo has few visitors on Mondays, it can cut the entrance fee on that day of the week by one-half.

An increasingly popular and specialized form of user charge is the local impact fee, or "exaction" requiring private land developers to contribute roads, sewers, and other infrastructure as a price for local regulatory approval for development projects, such as subdivisions or factories. In this manner, the cost of infrastructure is shifted to private firms and, ultimately, to those who purchase or use their buildings or facilities.[20] A related concept applied through a special sales tax on travel-related services is the travel tax. Here, taxes on lodging, rental cars, and other services paid largely by out-of-towners are imposed at rates averaging 12 percent. Table 12.2 rates major taxes and fees based on the six criteria discussed at the beginning of this section.

TABLE 12.2	Rating State and Local Taxes According to Six Criteria					
TAX	EQUITY	YIELD	ELASTICITY	EASE OF ADMIN-ISTRATION	POLITICAL ACCOUNTABILITY	ACCEPT-ABILITY
Property	C	B	C	D	D	D
Sales	D	B	B	B	A	B
Personal and corporate income	B	A	B	B	C	C
User fees	C	B	A	C	C	B

A = Excellent   B = Good   C = Fair   D = Poor

Severance Tax

States blessed with petroleum, coal, natural gas, and minerals have for many years taxed these natural resources as they are taken from the land and sold. A fortunate few are able to "export" a substantial portion of their tax bite to people living in other states. However, in-staters must pay the same tax rate as out-of-staters. A large majority of states (thirty-nine) place a severance tax on some form of natural resources, but just ten states collect 90 percent of all severance tax revenues. Taxes on oil and natural gas account for 85 percent of total state revenues in Alaska. Wyoming brings in about 35 percent of its revenues from severance taxes on coal, oil, and gas. (Perhaps this is why these states are able to forgo personal income taxes.) Several states are rather creative in applying the severance tax. Virginia levies the tax on pilings and poles; Washington, on oysters and on salmon and other game fish;[21] and Louisiana, on mussels.

Severance taxes are popular in states rich in natural resources, because they help keep income, property, and sales taxes relatively low. Severance tax revenues also help to pay for environmental damage resulting from resource extraction operations, such as strip mining. The major disadvantage is that a state economy too dependent on severance taxes can be damaged badly if the price of its natural resources declines, as Alaska experienced in 1999 with depressed crude oil prices. Even so, natural resources have been individually enriching for Alaskans. For more than twenty years every man, woman, and child resident of Alaska has received a rebate from the state's Permanent Fund. Checks totaled $1,850.28 per person in 2001. Established primarily with severance taxes on petroleum, the $25 billion Permanent Fund's reserves are now diversified through investments in office buildings, industrial complexes, stocks, and bonds.[22]

Gambling: Lotteries and Casinos

The lottery is an old American tradition; initially established in the 1600s, it was popular from the colonial days until the late 1800s. Lotteries flourished throughout the country as a means of raising money for such good causes as new schools, highways, canals, and bridges. But scandals and mismanagement led every state and the national government to ban "looteries." From 1895 to 1963, no legal lotteries were operated. Then New Hampshire established a new one, followed in 1967 by New York. Since then thirty-eight states have created lotteries. Other states are seriously considering them.

Several factors account for the rebirth of "bettor government." First, lotteries can bring in large sums of money—more than 7 percent of all state tax revenues in South Dakota in one recent year, for example. Second, they are popular and entertaining. And they are voluntary—you do not have to participate. In addition, lotteries help relieve pressure on major taxes. In some states, net lottery earnings take the place of a 1¢ increase in the sales tax. Finally, state ownership of a game of chance offers a legal and fair alternative to illegal gambling operations such as neighborhood numbers games or betting (parlay) cards.

But there are disadvantages as well. First of all, lotteries are costly to administer and have low yields. Prize awards must be great enough to encourage future ticket sales. The higher the payout, the more people play. New games must be created to retain enthusiasm. Ticket vendors must be paid commissions. And tight (as well as expensive) security precautions are required to guarantee the game's integrity. As a result, lotteries generate only a small percentage of most states' total revenues, usually less than 3 percent of own-source income.[23] The average yield for players is low as well: About 50 percent of the total revenues is returned to players in prize money. This is far below the returns of other games of chance, such as slot machines, roulette, or craps. Although many states earmark lottery proceeds for popular programs, especially education, parks and recreation, and economic development, the result is often a shell game. For instance, Florida's lottery officially benefits schools and colleges, but in reality lottery money simply *replaces* general-fund revenues, rather than actually enhancing education funding.[24]

Lotteries can also be attacked on the grounds of equity and elasticity. Although the purchase of a ticket is voluntary and thus seemingly fair, studies indicate that low-income individuals are more likely to play. Participation is also higher among blacks, males, older people, and those with low levels of education.[25] The lottery, then, is a regressive way to raise revenues. Furthermore, lotteries tend to encourage compulsive gambling. In recognition of this problem, some states earmark a portion of lottery proceeds for treatment programs. Lotteries are considered inelastic because earnings are cyclical and generally unstable. Sales depend on such factors as the legalized gambling activities in neighboring states, the size of jackpots, and the effectiveness of marketing efforts.

As interstate lottery competition depresses profits, states are increasingly adopting other forms of legalized gambling, such as pari-mutuel betting on horse and dog races, as well as gambling on riverboats, on Indian reservations, and at Old West historical sites like mining towns. In a frantic quest for more revenues, eleven states have legalized casino gambling. Once restricted to Atlantic City and Las Vegas, casino gambling actually now occurs in twenty-two states, when some 220 Native American casinos are taken into account. Gambling establishments virtually blanket Minnesota and Mississippi. Touted as producers of jobs and tourist dollars, casinos share many of the same disadvantages as lotteries, including diminishing returns as new casinos open monthly across the country. And little, if any, state revenue is derived from tribal casinos. What's next? Interactive systems permit couch potatoes to place bets over the Internet with their personal computers. There are hundreds of illegal Internet gaming sites, most of them from Caribbean Islands so as to skirt U.S. prohibition and taxing authority.[26] Revenues may increase, but the net human costs are yet to be determined.

The Political Economy of Taxation

Spending

Taxes lead to spending. The principle of diversity in state and local finance is evident given what nonnational governments choose to do with their revenues. First, the governments spend a great deal of money. State and local spending has long been rising faster than the gross national product and the level of inflation. The functional distribution of spending varies from state to state. As indicated in Figure 12.2, education consumes the largest proportion of total state spending (29.1 percent), followed by social services (21.8 percent), which includes public assistance, medical services, and health care.

Within each of these functional categories lies a wide range of financial commitments. For instance, higher-education expenditures in a recent year ran from 14.5 percent of total state and local spending in Utah to only 4.5 percent in

FIGURE 12.2   **Total State and Local Government Spending by Area**

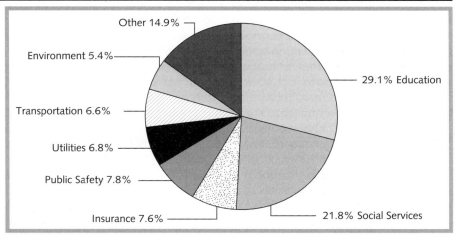

SOURCE: U.S. Census Bureau.

New York. Alabama dedicated 18 percent of its spending to health care and hospitals, whereas Vermont set aside just 2.5 percent for the same purpose.[27] Such differences represent historical trends, local economic circumstances, and citizens' willingness to incur debt to pay for services. Demographic factors also play a role. For instance, states with high populations of children invest more money in schools than do states with large proportions of senior citizens. Overall size of the state population also drives up expenditures for such services as law enforcement, water and sewer systems, and street maintenance. The largest expenditure gains in recent years have been registered in corrections and Medicaid as populations of prisoners and the medically indigent have ballooned.

One of the most difficult decisions for an elected official is to go on record in favor of raising taxes. The political heat can scorch even the coolest incumbent. But when revenues do not equal service costs and citizens do not want to cut services, raising taxes may be the only answer. However, most people do not want higher taxes. This is the familiar **tax-service paradox:** People demand new, improved, or at least the same level of government services but do not want to pay for them through higher taxes. For instance, the people of Washington State, in their collective wisdom, voted in a 1999 constitutional referendum to slice taxes. But the very next year they passed another initiative to reduce class size and hike teachers' pay—without providing any new money. Is it any wonder that user charges have become a popular option?

The tax-service paradox reflects a growing alienation between government and its citizens. The widespread belief that government at all levels—and particularly the federal government—has become too big and wasteful undoubtedly has some basis in fact. The size and responsibilities of state and local governments have grown dramatically, and waste and inefficiency have sometimes accompanied this growth. But the unwillingness of citizens to accept the inevitable reductions in services that follow tax cuts borders on mass schizophrenia.

Helping promote the tax-service paradox are the news media, which "commonly paint government with the broad brush of incompetence."[28] Prime-time television news capsules on "how government wastes your money" and typical reporting on actions of states and localities search for and emphasize the negative while ignoring the positive. Meanwhile, state and local government functions have become much more complex and technical, tending to make government more difficult to understand or to interact and communicate with.

State and local governments have begun responding to this inconsistency with outreach efforts designed to educate citizens about what their governments are doing for them and where their tax dollars are going. New York City's website provides personalized tax receipts, showing what each citizen's tax dollars paid for. Everywhere, local governments are striving to write their annual budgets in reader-friendly formats.[29]

Thus, the **political economy**—the set of political choices that frames economic policy—has become enormously perplexing for state and local officials. Other aspects of the political economy include the tax revolt, fiscal stress, and limited discretion in raising new revenues.

tax-service paradox
A situation in which people demand more government services but do not want to pay for them through higher taxes.

political economy
Political choices that have economic outcomes.

Texas citizens denouce proposed tax increase by Texas legislature. (© Bob Daemmrich/ The Image Works)

Tax Revolt

Taxpayer resentment of property taxes, and the general perception of government as too big, too costly, and too wasteful, first took on a tangible form in 1978 with the passage of Proposition 13 in California. Between 1978 and 1980, eighteen states enacted statutory or constitutional limitations on taxing and spending by slashing personal or corporate income taxes, indexing their income taxes to the cost of living, and cutting the sales tax. In some instances, citizens took tax matters into their own hands through the initiative process. In other cases, state legislators jumped in front of the parade and cut taxes and spending themselves. The taxpayer revolt continued at a much slower pace during the 1980s and 1990s. Its legacy, however, remains enormously important. Public officials must work hard to justify tax increases; otherwise, they risk a citizen uprising and perhaps political death. Indeed, the stirrings of new tax revolts are constantly in evidence. The prairie fire of tax revolt is not dead—only smoldering.

Most state and local jurisdictions managed the fallout of the tax revolt reasonably well. Many of them held large budget surpluses that they utilized to ameliorate the immediate effects of **taxation and expenditure limitations (TELs).** These are restrictions on government taxing and spending, such as limiting the growth in spending to no more than the latest year's growth in per capita income. For example, California had a $3 billion surplus with which it temporarily replaced property tax revenues forgone by local governments. Only a handful of states followed California's stringent TELs, which cut property taxes by 60 percent. Massachusetts was one such state; approved on the general-

taxation and expenditure limitations (TELs) Restrictions on state and/or local government taxing and spending.

election ballot in 1980, Proposition 2½ limited local property tax revenues to 2.5 percent of the total value of taxable property. Tax bills for Massachusetts home owners soon dropped by $1.3 billion.[30] Forty-one states have some sort of property tax restriction in effect, and many place limitations on other forms of taxation as well.[31] Raising taxes now requires a constitutional amendment, voter approval, or an extraordinary legislative majority in quite a few states. States and localities have resisted reducing service levels, opting instead to shift tax burdens or to find new sources of revenues, such as user charges.

Political and economic consequences of the tax revolt have been much studied. In many cases, TELs have made state and local finance an extraordinarily difficult undertaking: Voters insist on passing spending mandates for education, law enforcement, or other popular programs while at the same time tying the hands of legislatures with restrictions on new revenue raising. So far, TELs have not significantly reduced the size and cost of government as advertised.[32] Political and electoral influences are apparently more important in determining expenditures and size of government.[33] However, TELs have led local governments to depend more on the states and to greater recognition by public officials of the continuing need to consult with the taxpaying public on tax issues.[34]

Fiscal Stress

fiscal stress

Financial pressure on a government from such factors as revenue shortfalls and taxing and spending limitations.

During national and regional economic downturns, many state and local jurisdictions experience severe **fiscal stress:** They struggle to pay for programs and provide services that citizens want and need without taxing the citizens at unacceptably high levels. Many factors contribute to fiscal stress. Typically, adverse social and economic conditions, mostly beyond state and local government control, establish an environment conducive to financial problems. Older industrial cities are particularly vulnerable. Many jobs and manufacturing industries have been lost because of the gradual but compelling shift to a service-based economy and to states and countries with lower labor costs. In cities such as Detroit, Philadelphia, and New York, the exodus of jobs and firms has eroded the value of taxable resources (mostly property); yet citizens left behind have growing service demands.

Concentration of the poor and minorities in deteriorating housing, the shortage of jobs, high levels of crime, the illegal drug trade, homelessness, and related factors have produced crisis-level situations. Declining infrastructure also plagues older cities: water and sewer lines, treatment plants, streets, sidewalks, and other components of the urban physical landscape are in dire need of restoration or replacement. The estimated amount needed to replace the Detroit metropolitan area's crumbling sewer system alone is an astounding $52 billion. Most of these problems, it should be noted, will require national government attention if they are to be addressed effectively. Special factors contributing to state fiscal stress include weak real-estate markets, declines in natural resource prices, unfunded federal mandates, and court- and congressionally mandated spending increases in corrections, education, and other areas. The terrorist actions of 9/11 erased travel and tourism income and cost states millions in police overtime pay and new security measures in 2002.

Political sources of fiscal stress typically compound the economic problems of older cities. Mismanagement of resources and inefficient procedures and activities are common complaints. Pressures from city workers and their unions have also driven up service provision costs in some localities. Thus, service demands and the costs of providing services grow while taxes and intergovernmental revenues decline. This is a well-tested recipe for fiscal stress, evoking fears of bond defaults and even bankruptcy.

New York City offers a thirty-year case study of fiscal stress. People, jobs, and industry fled the city for the suburbs and the Sunbelt in the early 1970s, thereby reducing fiscal capacity. Yet public employees' pay and pensions grew to some of the highest levels in the United States, and welfare payments to the poor and a growing number of unemployed were generous. The tuition-free City University of New York (CUNY) had an enrollment of 265,000 students.

As revenues increasingly lagged behind expenditures, the city government played fiscal roulette with the budget and borrowed huge sums through municipal notes and bonds. Eventually it was poised on the brink of bankruptcy. Defaults on the city's bonds, notes, and other debt instruments seemed imminent. City officials cried out to the national government and New York State for help, but some people had little sympathy for a city that had lived beyond its means for too long.

Aided by national guarantees of new long-term loans, New York State and other large holders of New York City debt finally agreed to a bailout. Had this immense urban financial edifice collapsed, the fiscal shocks would have threatened New York State's economic stability and even resulted in serious fiscal repercussions for other states and localities throughout the United States.

Unfortunately, the Big Apple in 1992 once again risked being reduced to a seedy core. It faced a budget deficit of $3.5 billion, a mass exodus of jobs (100,000 within just three years), and the enormous cost of thousands of AIDS and crack babies. Seventy percent of the city's more than 2,000 bridges desperately needed expensive repairs, and water and sewer lines were rupturing regularly. Mayor David Dinkins responded with a variety of actions, including massive layoffs of city employees, closure of libraries and clinics, and shutdown of 25 percent of the city's streetlights. New York City's fiscal problems cannot be solved overnight. Its 235,000 employees and $30 billion operating budget serve 7 million people spread throughout five counties. The city itself is the area's biggest landlord. It owns television and radio stations, a huge higher-education system, and four hospitals. When Mayor Rudolph Giuliani took office in 1994, the operating deficit was pegged at $2.3 billion, even as most of the country was enjoying economic growth. Giuliani, too, cut city employment and targeted various services for budget reductions.[35] New York City continues today to struggle with its vast fiscal problems, with no relief in sight. As the ashes of the Twin Towers cooled in late 2001, the new mayor, Michael Bloomberg, wrestling with a deficit of approximately $4 billion in his $43 billion budget, entertained the idea of a state takeover of city finances.[36]

Most jurisdictions have not experienced the misfortune faced by New York City. Taxpayer revolt and fiscal stress notwithstanding, budgets have been balanced, payrolls met, and most services maintained. When necessary, state officials have swallowed hard, held their noses, and raised taxes. A national economic recovery beginning in 1992 spawned a nine-year period of nearly unprecedented economic growth, causing the state-local picture to improve rapidly. In 2000, state tax revenues had spurted beyond revenue estimates for seven years running in most states. Year-end treasury balances leaped, and everything seemed to be going right for most states, which were able to cut billions of dollars in taxes and fees and also shore up rainy day funds (see below).

The fiscal tides then took a dramatic turn. Forty-eight states were wrestling with budget deficits in late 2002 as the national economy struggled to emerge from recession. California's sea of red ink was estimated at $23.6 billion. Governors laid off state workers, delayed prison construction and released prisoners early, cut agency spending, hiked college tuition, raided rainy day funds, and asked their legislatures for tax increases. For many states, the budget shortfall was projected to be even worse in 2003.

Recession notwithstanding, some states and localities face chronic fiscal shortfalls because of structural problems deeply embedded in their revenue systems. Structural imbalances result from tax systems developed for radically different state economies of fifty years past. E-commerce and globalization have altered how people work and spend their money; TELs have hampered revenue raising; and anti-tax dogma pervades politics. Bold decisions must be made if state leaders are to accommodate their revenue systems to the characteristics of the "new economy."[37]

Limited Discretion

TELs have placed ceilings on rates and amounts of taxation and spending, thus limiting the discretion of the nonnational governments. Other constraining factors, too, keep state and local governments from falling prey to the temptation of taxing and spending orgies. One important factor is interstate competition for jobs and economic development. High-tax states run a serious risk of having jobs, firms, and investments "stolen" by low-tax states.

Earmarking taxes for popular programs also limits state and local taxing and spending discretion. Earmarking is well established: Gasoline taxes have been set aside for road and highway programs ever since automobiles first left ruts in muddy cow pastures. What differs at present are the levels of specificity and creativity in earmarking. Nearly 25 percent of state tax revenues are earmarked today, a proportion much lower than that of thirty years ago; but the number of dedicated purposes has grown markedly. Surpluses may accumulate in some dedicated funds, such as highways, while other important needs such as education or law enforcement are not sufficiently met. The hands of government officials are tied, however, because they cannot move the funds around. Cigarette buyers in Washington cough up millions of dollars each year to help clean up Puget Sound. Several states earmark penny increases in the sales tax for public education.

Financial discretion is partly determined by one's position on the fiscal food chain. The national government can essentially tax and spend as it wishes, subject only to its underdeveloped capacity for self-discipline. States must meet federal spending mandates for Medicaid, corrections, and other functions while somehow balancing their budgets each year. And even though their legal authority to raise revenues remains severely circumscribed in most states, local governments in this game of "shift and shaft federalism" must comply with an ever-increasing number of state spending mandates. Some would say that local governments are not masters of their own fiscal fate.[38]

Borrowing and Debt

Every state except Indiana and Vermont is constitutionally or statutorily mandated to balance its budget each fiscal year. In turn, the states require their local governments to balance *their* budgets. However, these requirements apply only to *operating budgets,* which are used for daily financial receipts and disbursements. Capital budgets, used for big purchases that must be paid for over time (for example, a new bridge or school building), typically run substantial deficits. Operating budgets may also run in the red during the fiscal year, so long as expenditures equal revenues at the end of the year.

Temporary cash-flow deficits in the operating budget are alleviated through tax-anticipation or revenue-anticipation notes, whereby investors such as banks lend money to a government on a short-term basis (typically thirty to ninety days). In such cases, the loan is backed up by anticipated revenues from income, sales, and property taxes or from other specified sources and is paid off as soon as the funds become available.

Estimating Revenues

Until fairly recently, state and local governments estimated their annual revenues simply by extrapolating from past trends. This approach works well during periods of steady economic growth, but it fails miserably during years of boom or bust. The finance officers of states and most larger cities and counties are much more sophisticated today. Using computer technology, they employ econometric modeling to derive mathematical estimates of future revenues. Increasingly, economic forecasting firms and/or academics assist or provide independent projections.

Econometric modeling places key variables in equations to predict the fiscal-year yield of each major tax. A wide variety of variables are used, including employment levels, food prices, housing costs, oil and gas prices, consumer savings levels, interest rates, intergovernmental aid projections, and state and local debt obligations. Because state and local economies are increasingly linked to national and international factors, estimates often include measures for the value of the dollar, international trade and investment, and national fiscal policy.

Two critical factors determine the accuracy of revenue estimates: the quality of the data and the validity of the economic assumptions. Indeed, econometric modeling of state and local economies can be a voyage into the unknown. Data problems include difficulty in measuring key variables; periodic revisions of historical economic data, which require new calculations; and modifications in tax laws or fee schedules. But the major sources of error are the economic assumptions built into the models.[39] Examples are legion. The national economy may not perform as expected; energy prices may plummet or soar; natural or human disasters may disrupt state or local economic growth. Recessions are particularly damaging to fiscal stability, since state and local taxes are highly sensitive to economic downturns.

Rainy Day Funds

Because a balanced budget is mandatory but estimation errors are inevitable, forty-seven states and many localities establish contingency or reserve funds. Popularly known as "rainy day funds," these savings accounts help insulate budgets from fiscal distortions caused by inaccurate data or faulty economic assumptions; they are also available for emergencies. In years of economic health, the funds accumulate principal and interest. When the economy falls ill, governments can tap their "fiscal shock absorbers" to balance the budget and avoid imposing tax and fee increases.[40] During the sunny days of the 1990s, the states filled up their contingency funds to 7.7 percent of total spending. Amidst the recessionary clouds of 2002, they were forced to dip into them.[41] The task of balancing the budget is especially daunting in local governments, given their lack of economic diversity, dependency on state taxes and financial aid, and sensitivity to economic dislocations. The departure of a single large employer can disrupt a local economy for years. So the potential advantages of such funds are numerous in the fragile fiscal context of cities and counties.

Other Financial Management Practices

State and local governments, of necessity, are becoming more knowledgeable about how to manage cash and investments. Cash reserves that once sat idly in non-interest-bearing accounts or a desk drawer are now invested in money market accounts, U.S. Treasury bills, certificates of deposit, and other financial instruments in order to maximize interest earnings. Most states have local government investment pools that manage billions of dollars in short-term assets. The process of spending and collecting monies is also manipulated to advantage. For example, large checks are deposited on the day they are received; conversely, payable checks are drawn on the latest date possible. In general, state and local financial management today resembles that of a large corporation instead of the mom-and-pop approach of years ago. After all, the nonnational governments spend and invest more than $1.5 trillion annually.

The most important state or local investment is usually the public-employee pension fund. These retirement accounts comprise about $1.8 trillion in assets. In the past, they were conservatively managed and politically untouchable. Today, however, they tend to be invested in more aggressive instruments such as corporate stock. They also represent a tempting honey pot for financially suffering states whose governors have dipped their hands in the funds and pulled out billions to balance the budget.

State and local investments must not be managed too aggressively, as the case of Orange County, California, demonstrates. One of the nation's largest and wealthiest local jurisdictions, Orange County became the largest in history to file for federal bankruptcy in 1994. The county's financial nightmare commenced when its investment pool manager, Robert L. Citron, placed millions of dollars in financial instruments called derivatives. These instruments "derive" their value from underlying assets such as stocks, bonds, or mortgages. The derivatives' value changes when the price of the underlying assets changes. Orange County lost $1.5 billion when its derivatives, which were tied to interest rates, declined precipitously in value. In effect, Citron was borrowing money from stocks, bonds, and other assets to bet on the direction of interest rates. He lost, and so did Orange County's taxpayers.[42] Citron pleaded guilty to six felonies, more than eight hundred county employees were laid off, and $52 million was cut from social services. Moreover, citizens lost faith in their local government.[43]

Long-Term Borrowing   Like corporations, state and local governments issue long-term debt obligations, typically for five to twenty-five years. Bonds are the most common form of long-term borrowing. Because of federal and state tax breaks for investors, the nonnational governments are able to finance bonded indebtedness at significantly lower rates than corporations. Selling bonds directly to investors on the Internet saves even more money. There are three conventional types of bonds: general obligation bonds, revenue bonds, and industrial development bonds.

general obligation bond
A debt instrument supported by the full financial resources of the issuing jurisdiction.

The principal and interest payments on **general obligation bonds** are secured by the "full faith, credit, and taxing power" of the state or local jurisdiction issuing them. General obligation bonds are used to finance public projects such as highways, schools, and hospitals. Lenders are guaranteed repayment so long as the bond-issuing government is solvent; defaults are nearly nonexistent, Orange County notwithstanding.

revenue bond
A bond that is paid off from income derived from the facility built with the bond proceeds.

Revenue bonds are backed up by expected income from a specific project or service; examples include a toll bridge, a municipal sewer system, or mortgage loans. Revenue bonds are payable only from the revenues derived from the specified source, not from general tax revenues. Because they typically represent a riskier investment than general obligation bonds, they command a higher rate of interest.

industrial development bond (IDB)
A bond issued to fund the construction of a facility to be used by a private firm.

The **industrial development bond (IDB)** is a type of revenue bond. The payment of principal and interest on IDBs depends solely on the ability of the industry using the facilities financed by the bond to meet its financial obligation. If the user fails to make payments, creditors can seize and sell any real or personal property associated with the facility. Private interests, such as shopping malls or firms, are the primary beneficiaries of IDBs. Conventionally, these private-purpose bonds are issued by local governments to attract economic activity and investments; in fact, they are frequently used to furnish loans at highly favorable interest rates to small- or medium-size firms.

Limits on Borrowing   Almost all states place constitutional or statutory restrictions on their own and local government borrowing. Some have set maximum levels of indebtedness; others require popular referenda to create debt or to exceed specified debt limits. They tightly restrict local government debt, especially general obligation bonds. (State-imposed constraints normally do not apply to revenue bonds.) The impetus for these restrictions came from a series of bond defaults and bankruptcies in the 1860s and 1870s, and again during the Great Depression.

The bond market places its own informal limitations on debt by assessing the quality of bonds, notes, and other debt instruments. Investors in government bonds rely on Moody's Investors Service, Standard and Poor's Corporation, and other investment services for ratings of a jurisdiction's capacity to repay its obligations. Criteria taken into consideration in bond ratings include existing debt levels, rainy day funds, market value of real estate, population growth, per capita income, employment levels, and other measures of overall financial health and solvency. Highly rated bond issues receive ratings of *Aaa, Aa,* and *A*. Variations of *B* indicate medium to high risk. A rating of *C* is reserved for bonds in danger of default. The average interest rate on risky low-rated bonds usually exceeds that of top-rated ones by one and a half to two percentage points; this translates into a considerable difference in interest payments. Bond ratings tend to rise during periods of economic growth but can drop rapidly during recessions, driving up borrowing costs.

bond bank
A state-administered fund that aggregates local government debt instruments and sells them as a package at a reduced interest rate.

States can consolidate the bond sales of smaller municipalities and counties through a **bond bank.** These banks help provide increased management capacity to less-experienced local governments and, through economies of scale, save them significant sums of money.

Where All the Money Goes: State and Local Spending

What do state and local governments choose to do with their revenues? First of all, they spend a great deal of money. To provide a closer look at how governments spend their (and your) money, we now examine three policy areas: economic development, education, and health and welfare.

Economic Development

In 2003, sport utility vehicles began rolling off the assembly line at a new Nissan plan—not in Japan, but in Mississippi. Luring the automaker to the Magnolia State was an incentive package that included $295 million in job training, infrastructure improvements, and tax breaks. Why was the state willing to pay the big bucks? There are four related reasons. First is Nissan's four thousand jobs, which will generate a $160 million annual payroll. Second, the state hopes that Nissan will have a ripple effect and attract other industries to the area. Third, the state believes that winning Nissan's business adds some much-needed luster to Mississippi's tarnished image. And, last but not least: If Mississippi had not come through with an attractive incentive package, its neighbor to the east, Alabama, would have.[44] The motto for state economic development may well be "You've got to pay to play."

Economic development strategies vary greatly. Some states still engage in a form of smokestack chasing by dangling tax breaks, subsidies, and other financial inducements before firms, hoping to recruit them from other locations. Travel and tourism are also big business. States publicize their natural resources, cultural amenities, cuisine, and casinos—whatever it takes to attract tourism dollars. Advertising campaigns are developed around catchy slogans, such as "You Could Use a Little Indiana" and "Kansas Secrets."

Dance, theater, and opera are used as development strategies in some metropolitan areas. These performing arts not only attract tourism dollars; they also appeal to high-technology firms and their ranks of well-paid, culturally-sensitive "knowledge workers." Arts-led downtown economic revivals are occurring today in cities as diverse as Providence, Rhode Island; Beaumont, Texas; and Newark, New Jersey.

The professional sports realm is another economic development tool, although its economic advantages for beneficiaries other than the owners are greatly disputed. Professional sports and big-league cities go hand-in-hand. Hosting a professional sports team is a sign that a city has "arrived." Still, acquiring a professional baseball, basketball, hockey, or football team is not inexpensive. Cities and states compete against one another frantically, offering to build hugely expensive playing facilities and to invest millions of dollars in new highways and other infrastructure. Eight U.S. cities have launched expensive bids for the 2012 Olympic Games.

Increasingly, state and local governments are casting their acquisitive eyes beyond national borders, looking abroad for international trade and development opportunities. Foreign markets are often important for manufacturers of state products, and foreign investors can provide new jobs and tax revenues. States actively market themselves and their local governments, often sending the governor and other high-ranking officials on trade missions overseas. For in-state firms, the state may arrange financing and technical support to help them initiate new international opportunities.

Economic development remains a high priority for all of the states, but critics are asking troubling questions: Do subsidies, tax breaks, and other giveaways really pay off? Does government spend too much in pursuit of more economic growth? Does more economic growth come at the cost of environmental problems and lower quality of life? And has interstate competition for firms become dysfunctional and damaging, as firms play one state off another in a greedy game designed to extort the taxpayer?

Education Policy

Education consumes more of state and local budgets than any other function. More than $483 *billion* is spent on elementary and secondary education by states and localities each year. That comes to around $7,000 per pupil. Citizens have high—but largely unrealized—expectations for the public schools. The schools, it is said, are in crisis and failing to make the grade.

The case against public education involves four major charges. First, standards have declined. Students are being taught how to feel good about themselves instead of how to read, write, calculate, and think. Second, too little is expected of students, many of whom are functionally illiterate upon graduating and poorly prepared for either work or higher education. (Students are also alleged to be poorly motivated and lazy, and more concerned with the latest TV show, computer game, or sports contest than with their schoolwork.) Third, critics claim that the quality of teachers has declined. University programs for training teachers are weak and misdirected, and the teachers themselves are underprepared for their classroom duties. Finally, critics blame the education bureaucracy: There are too many administrators and too few teachers. The result is red tape, excessive paperwork, and inefficiency.

Who answers these charges? The president and Congress regularly fuss about the problems of K–12 education and take assorted symbolic actions. The national government also contributes a significant sum of money for public education. And the federal courts have thrown entire education-financing systems into disarray over issues of funding fairness across school districts. But the primary policy and financial responsibilities for education reside with the state and local governments, which actually have been actively engaged in education innovation and reform for more than two decades. Pay is being hiked to attract and keep more capable classroom teachers. Standards are being raised through strengthened curricula and stricter promotion and graduation requirements. Student-teacher ratios are being reduced. Outcomes-based education, an innovation that strives to hold students, teachers, and administrators accountable for student performance, is becoming a key policy innovation. And various techniques for "school choice" are being assessed, including magnet schools, charter schools, voucher plans, and virtual schools.

Progress *is* taking place, but public education remains perhaps the most perplexing—and important—policy challenge for state and local governments. The quality of public schools is clearly related to economic development, social and behavioral conditions, and the overall quality of life in the United States. But progress does not come cheaply or easily. Smaller classrooms mean more teachers and classroom space. Attracting and retaining qualified teachers requires competitive pay and benefits. Simply wiring classrooms for Internet access has cost hundreds of millions of dollars.

Social Welfare and Health Care Policy

Poverty in the United States has many faces, affecting immigrants, illegal aliens, unwed mothers and their children, the physically and mentally disabled, the unemployed, and countless others. Their needs are many and diverse. Numerous public assistance and health care programs have been established to help ease their problems and pains.

Social welfare and health care policies include national programs such as Medicare (medical care for the aged) and Food Stamps, as well as state-developed programs like General Assistance. State and local governments also administer several programs, such as Medicaid (medical care for the poor), various employment and housing programs, and the "social insurance" programs included under Social Security and Unemployment Compensation.

Any search for innovative policymaking in social welfare and health care leads directly to the states. Two major policy initiatives have dominated the states' agenda during the past several years: saving the children and turning welfare checks into paychecks.

The plight of the nation's children is both sad and perplexing. Divorce rates are high (almost one-half of all children experience a family divorce), about one in four of all infants are born to unwed mothers, and the number of irresponsible fathers who refuse to support their offspring is disheartening (the child support rate is only about 50 percent). Single mothers who work often find it difficult to secure affordable, high-quality daycare for their kids. Finally, many children are born not only into poverty but also into illness. Lack of prenatal care, parental drug abuse, inadequate diets, and related factors cause many mothers to give birth to premature, sickly, and underweight infants.

Several programs seek to help such unfortunate children. Head Start, a federally funded program that many states augment with their own efforts, provides preschool education, medical and dental care, and social services for more than 800,000 three- to five-year-olds. The federal Family Support Act of 1988 requires the states to withhold court-ordered child support payments from the wages of absentee parents. And through DNA techniques, states are often able to establish paternity for children born out of wedlock.

Daycare for children of working and single parents is garnering much attention as states and localities subsidize daycare programs through tax breaks and experiment with various child-care arrangements. Several states guarantee child-care assistance to poor families.

Welfare checks are being turned into paychecks under the 1996 federal Welfare Reform Act's Temporary Assistance for Needy Families (TANF) program, which relies heavily on state innovation and creativity. Instead of simply handing over welfare checks to recipients, states are requiring them to prepare for and find gainful employment. The goal, of course, is to help welfare recipients leave the welfare rolls altogether. Wisconsin, for example, offers transportation assistance, generous child-care benefits, health care subsidies, and drug counseling for unemployed welfare recipients. Those who cannot find jobs must perform community service or pursue further job training or education. Like all other states, Wisconsin has recorded a substantial drop in its welfare rolls since implementing TANF.

Given Congress's inability to address the matter of health care effectively, health care reform has become largely a state-driven policy. Although the quality of health care technology in the United States is unsurpassed, the "system" is inordinately expensive and, for many, dysfunctional. Some 44 million Americans remain uninsured and, therefore, largely dependent on government for medical services. The costs for these services have soared to more than $1 trillion annually—14 percent of the national economy and the highest of any country in the world. Medicaid alone, funded by the states at a rate varying from 21 to 50 percent of total program costs, consumes more than 20 percent of the typical state budget. These expenses reflect the care of millions of elderly people in nursing homes, public hospitals, and other health-related services.

In the national policy vacuum, states have aimed at expanding health care coverage to the uninsured, containing escalating costs, and maintaining the quality of health care. All states are involved in reforming health care, but their approaches vary markedly. For example, Florida and several other states subsidize health care programs for poor children. Hawaii operates an extensive health care program for those unable to afford health care insurance, which has resulted in an effective insurance coverage rate of 89 percent and excellent health statistics for state residents. Tennessee has replaced Medicaid with its own health care program for the poor and extended coverage to many uninsured residents through managed-care organizations. And Oregon has established a health care rationing system that ranks illnesses and conditions according to their priority for state Medicaid expenditures. Under this system, child immunization, birth control, and maternal health care receive high priority; terminal AIDS and the common cold come last.

Unless and until Congress and the president agree on a national health care approach, the states will take the lead and reform will continue at a lively pace. The principal concerns continue to be rising costs (particularly for Medicaid) and gaps in insurance coverage, problems that the national government could help resolve through courageous action.

State and Local Finance in the 2000s

Common miseries afflict the great majority of large U.S. cities during bad economic times. In the past, the federal and state governments would have ridden to the fiscal rescue with economic assistance. But today their own financial problems rival those of the local governments. The national government, finally determined to keep its own budget in balance, and having invested billions in a war on terrorism, has cut aid to the states, which in turn contribute less to city and county coffers.

The keys to surviving financial crisis are intergovernmental cooperation, burden sharing, capacity building, and citizen comprehension of the basic tax-service relationship. The national and state economies are strong but encountered serious financial dislocations in 2002 due to a national recession.

Long-term taxing and spending trends are being reconsidered by states and localities. They hope that the national government will join them in facing up to the spiraling costs of Medicaid, corrections, and public education—burdens that should not be laid on the back of a single level of government. Mandates without money should be abolished in most instances. When mandates and program responsibilities are pushed to a different rung of the federal ladder, funds should follow. Local governments, particularly, need more revenue-raising authority and broader tax bases to pay for the services they deliver. They also need more authority to consolidate services on a regional basis. And they must do a better job of mobilizing resources for public services.[45] Most states have been receptive to these principles; the federal government requires further education.

The call for increasing state and local capability and responsiveness by reinventing and reinvigorating government is being heard loud and clear. According to this approach, the structures and processes of state and local governments must be made more appropriate to the social and economic environment in which they operate, which includes a service-based economy, global markets, aging baby boomers (the "gray peril"), and the changing gender, racial, and ethnic composition of the labor force. Special challenges are being posed to state and local governments that are not being sufficiently met by present revenue systems.

Education is also needed for taxpayers, who seldom grasp the relationship between taxes paid and services rendered. Resistance to new or existing taxes is to be expected, but citizens must be made to understand through "truth in taxation" campaigns that the result may be fewer services. Elected officials have the primary responsibility for taxpayer education, but often politics intrudes.

Chapter Recap

➤ The two basic principles of state and local financial systems are interdependence of the three levels of government and diversity of revenue sources.

➤ Among the criteria for evaluating taxes are equity, yield, elasticity, ease of administration, political accountability, and acceptability.

➤ The major state and local taxes are those that are assessed on property, sales, and income. A variety of other taxes and fees are also imposed.

➤ Legalized gambling and gaming also raise money.

➤ Taxpayer resistance has produced tax and expenditure limitations in many states; increased sensitivity of state and local officials to taxpayer preferences; and, in some cases, fiscal stress for governments.

➤ State and local governments estimate annual revenues and set aside money in rainy day funds for emergencies and contingencies.

➤ State and local financial relationships are characterized by sharing and cooperation, but also by conflict over mandates and limited local discretion.

Key Terms

own-source revenue (*p. 274*)
intergovernmental transfers
  (*p. 274*)
tax capacity (*p. 276*)
tax effort (*p. 276*)
regressive tax (*p. 278*)
progressive tax (*p. 278*)
proportional (flat) tax (*p. 278*)
benefit principle (*p. 278*)
indexing (*p. 280*)

circuit breaker (*p. 281*)
tax-service paradox (*p. 290*)
political economy (*p. 290*)
taxation and expenditure limitations
  (TELs) (*p. 291*)
fiscal stress (*p. 292*)
general obligation bond (*p. 297*)
revenue bond (*p. 297*)
industrial development bond (IDB) (*p. 297*)
bond bank (*p. 298*)

Surfing the Net

There are a variety of interesting state and local budget sites. Those interested in playing governor by attempting to balance a state budget should go to **http://216.110.169.143/Budget%20Game/BUDGAME.HTM.** One of the best individual sites on state tax and budget information is that of the Texas State Comptroller at **www.window.state.tx.us.** For reports in developments, trends, and policy changes in state government finances, see the website of the Center for the Study of the States at SUNY–Albany: **www.rockinst.org.** Comparative state and local revenue, tax, and expenditure data may be found at the U.S. Census Bureau's website, **www.census.gov,** and at the Tax Foundation's web address, **www.taxfoundation.org.**

REFERENCES

Chapter 1 **NEW DIRECTIONS FOR STATE AND LOCAL GOVERNMENT** pp. 1–19

1. Governor Scott McCallum, "2002 State of the State Address," *Governors' Speeches,* www.nga.org.
2. Bruce Wallin, "State and Local Governments Are American, Too," *The Political Science Teacher* 1 (Fall 1988): 1–3.
3. Mike Sullivan, as quoted in "Wyoming's Governor Signs Law to Restructure State Government," *Denver Post* (March 5, 1989), p. 8B.
4. "2001 Innovations in American Government Award Winners," *Governing* 15 (January 2002): A4–A6.
5. Beth Walter Honadle, "Defining and Doing Capacity Building: Perspective and Experiences," in Beth Walter Honadle and Arnold M. Howitt, eds., *Perspectives on Management Capacity Building* (Albany: State University of New York Press, 1986), pp. 9–23.
6. "How We Grade Them," *Governing* 14 (February 2001): 34.
7. Julie Bund and Gene M. Lutz, "Connecting State Government Reform with Public Priorities: The Iowa Test," *State and Local Government Review* 31 (Spring 1999): 73–90.
8. David M. Hedge, *Governance and the Changing American States* (Boulder, Colo.: Westview, 1998).
9. Terry Sanford, *The Storm Over the States* (New York: McGraw-Hill, 1967), p. 21.
10. Quoted in ibid.
11. John Herbers, "The New Federalism: Unplanned, Innovative and Here to Stay," *Governing* 1 (October 1987), p. 28.
12. William A. Galston and Geoffrey L. Tibbetts, "Reinventing Federalism," *Publius: The Journal of Federalism* 24 (Summer 1994): 23–48.
13. Ann O'M. Bowman and Richard C. Kearney, *The Resurgence of the States* (Englewood Cliffs, N.J.: Prentice-Hall, 1986).
14. Sanford, *Storm Over the States.*
15. Ann O'M. Bowman and Richard C. Kearney, "Dimensions of State Government Capability," *Western Political Quarterly* 41 (June 1988): 341–62.
16. Larry Sabato, *Goodbye to Good-time Charlie: The American Governor Transformed,* 2d ed. (Washington, D.C.: Congressional Quarterly Press, 1983).
17. Deil S. Wright, *Understanding Intergovernmental Relations,* 3d ed. (Pacific Grove, Calif.: Brooks-Cole, 1988).
18. James L. Garnett, *Reorganizing State Government: The Executive Branch* (Boulder, Colo.: Westview, 1981).
19. Alan Rosenthal, *Legislative Life: People, Process, and Performance in the States* (New York: Harper & Row, 1981).
20. Robert A. Kagan et al., "The Evolution of State Supreme Courts," *Michigan Law Review* 76 (1978): 961–1005.
21. Jacqueline Calmes, "444 North Capitol Street: Where State Lobbyists Are Learning Coalition Politics," *Governing* 1 (February 1988): 17–21.
22. Charles Strum, "Vanity for a Cause: States Expand Special Plates," *New York Times* (February 22, 1993), p. A8.
23. Penelope Lemov, "Balancing the Budget with Billboards and Souvenirs," *Governing* 8 (October 1994): 46–50.
24. Seth Mydans, "From Signs to Pistols, Cash-Short Cities Sell Past," *New York Times* (September 6, 1993), p. 6.
25. Tamar Lewin, "Battle for Family Leave Will Be Fought in States," *New York Times* (July 27, 1991), p. A6.
26. Russell L. Hanson, "Health Care Reform, Managed Competition, and Subnational Politics," *Publius: The Journal of Federalism* 24 (Summer 1994): 4–68.
27. Donald P. Haider-Markel, "Policy Diffusion as a Geographical Expansion of the Scope of Political Conflict: Same Sex Marriage Bans in the 1990s," *State Politics and Policy Quarterly* 1 (Winter 2001): 5–26.
28. Penelope Lemov, "The Workers' Comp Tug of War," *Governing* 10 (January 1997): 24–25.
29. Craig Savoye, "States Spare Residents from Telemarketers," *Christian Science Monitor* (December 22, 2000), p. 8.
30. William Celis III, "Unusual Public School Aiming to Turn a Profit," *New York Times* (November 6, 1991), p. B8.
31. Charles Mahtesian, "Charter Schools Learn a Few Lessons," *Governing* 11 (January 1998): 24–27.
63. David Winder, James T. LaPlant, and Larry E. Carter, "State Lawsuits Against Big Tobacco," paper presented at the annual meeting of the Southwestern Political Science Association, San Antonio, April 1999.
33. Derek Cane, "States Sue Music Labels for Price Fixing," http://dailynews.yahoo.com (August 8, 2000).
34. Jim DuPlessis, "S.C. Wants Its Slice of Out-of-State Sales," *The State* (March 24, 2002), pp. F1, F3.
35. Ann O'M. Bowman, "Interstate Interactions," paper presented at the annual meeting of the Midwest Political Science Association, Chicago, April 2000.
36. Ann O'M. Bowman and Michael A. Pagano, "The State of American Federalism, 1993–1994," *Publius: The Journal of Federalism* 24 (Summer 1994): 1–21.
37. Governor George Voinovich, as quoted in "Reassessing Mandates," *State Policy Reports* 11 (October 1993): 16.

38. Gary Enos, "Court-Ordered Tax Hikes Upheld," *City & State* 7 (April 23, 1990): 49.

39. Richard C. Kearney and Reginald S. Sheehan, "Supreme Court Decision Making," *Journal of Politics* 54 (November 1992): 1008–25.

40. John Kincaid, "The State of U.S. Federalism, 2000–2001," *Publius: The Journal of Federalism* 31 (Summer 2001): 1–69.

41. Richard Nathan, as quoted in Mary B. W. Tabor, "State Worker's Fiscal Coup: Windfall for Massachusetts," *New York Times* (June 8, 1991), p. 5.

42. Todd Sloane, "Governors Face Mounting Deficits," *City & State* 8 (November 4, 1991): 1, 20.

43. "Is the Party Over? Report Shows State Revenue Growth Slowing," www.stateline.org (December 20, 2000).

44. Bowman, "Interstate Interactions," p. 17.

45. Thomas J. Lueck, "New York Vengeful Over Neighbor's 'Raid,'" *New York Times* (October 11, 1994), p. C20.

46. Rodney E. Hero and Caroline J. Tolbert, "A Racial/Ethnic Diversity Interpretation of Politics and Policy in the States of the U.S.," *American Journal of Political Science* 40 (August 1996): 851–71.

47. Christopher Conte, "North of the Border," *Governing* 15 (January 2002): 29–33.

48. "Resident Population of the 50 States, the District of Columbia, and Puerto Rico," www.census.gov.

49. Warren Richey, "In Court: Fight Over House Seat," *Christian Science Monitor* (March 27, 2002), pp. 1, 4.

50. Daniel B. Wood, "California's New Exit Strategy – Driving by Number," *Christian Science Monitor* (February 21, 2002), p. 2.

51. Daniel J. Elazar, *American Federalism: A View from the States,* 3d ed. (New York: Harper & Row, 1984).

52. David R. Morgan and Sheilah S. Watson, "Political Culture, Political System Characteristics, and Public Policies Among the American States," *Publius: The Journal of Federalism* 21 (Spring 1991): 31–48.

53. Jody L. Fitzpatrick and Rodney E. Hero, "Political Culture and Political Characteristics of the American States: A Consideration of Some Old and New Questions," *Western Political Quarterly* 41 (March 1988): 145–53.

54. Keith Boeckelman, "Political Culture and State Development Policy," *Publius: The Journal of Federalism* 21 (Spring 1991): 49–62; Russell L. Hanson, "Political Culture Variations in State Economic Development Policy," *Publius: The Journal of Federalism* 21 (Spring 1991): 63–81.

55. James P. Lester, "A New Federalism: Environmental Policy in the States," in Norman Vig and Michael Kraft, eds., *Environmental Policy in the 1990s* (Washington, D.C.: Congressional Quarterly Press, 1994), pp. 51–68; Steven A. Peterson and James N. Schubert, "Predicting State Aids Policy Spending," paper pre-sented at the annual meeting of the American Political Science Association, New York City, September 1994.

56. Joel Lieske, "Regional Subcultures of the United States," *Journal of Politics* 55 (November 1993): 888–913.

57. Frederick M. Wirt, "'Soft' Concepts and 'Hard' Data: A Research Review of Elazar's Political Culture," *Publius: The Journal of Federalism* 21 (Spring 1991): 1–13.

58. Emily Van Dunk, "Public Opinion, Gender and Handgun Safety Policy Across the States," paper presented at the annual meeting of the Midwest Political Science Association, Chicago, April 2000.

59. John Shannon, "The Return to Fend-for-Yourself Federalism: The Reagan Mark," *Intergovernmental Perspective* 13 (Spring 1987): 34–37; David R. Morgan and Kenneth Kickham, "Modernization among the U.S. States: Change and Continuity from 1960 to 1990," *Publius: The Journal of Federalism* 27 (Summer 1997): 23–39.

60. Alan Ehrenhalt, "The Increasing Irrelevance of Congress," *Governing* 11 (January 1998): 6–7.

61. Richard Morin, "In State Government We Trust," *Washington Post,* national weekly edition (February 3, 1997), p. 35.

Chapter 2   FEDERALISM AND THE STATES   pp. 20–46

1. David B. Walker, *Toward a Functioning Federalism* (Cambridge, Mass.: Winthrop, 1981), p. 25.

2. James Madison, *The Federalist,* No. 45, 1788.

3. Quoted in Richard Hofstadter, *The American Political Tradition* (New York: Vintage Books, 1948), p. 9.

4. Quoted in Richard H. Leach, *American Federalism,* No. 45 (New York: W.W. Norton, 1970), p. 1.

5. Forrest McDonald, *States' Rights and The Union: Imporium in Imperio, 1776–1876* (Lawrence: University Press of Kansas, 2000).

6. Quoted in ibid., p. 1788.

7. Walter Berns, "The Meaning of the Tenth Amendment," in Robert A. Goldwin, ed., *A Nation of States* (Chicago: Rand McNally, 1961), p. 130.

8. Walker, *Functioning Federalism,* pp. 47–48.

9. Hofstadter, *American Political Tradition,* p. 72.

10. *McCulloch v. Maryland,* 4 Wheaton 316 (1819).

11. *Gibbons v. Ogden,* 9 Wheaton 316 (1819).

12. *National League of Cities v. Usery,* 426 U.S. 833 (1976).

13. *Garcia v. San Antonio Metropolitan Transit Authority,* 105 S.Ct. 1007, 1011 (1985).

14. Ibid. (O'Connor, dissenting).

15. John C. Pittenger, "Garcia and the Political Safeguards of Federalism: Is There a Better Solution to the Conundrum of the Tenth Amendment?" *Publius: The Journal of Federalism* 22 (Winter 1992).

16. *U.S. v. Lopez,* 115 S.Ct. 1424 (1995). See Kenneth T. Palmer and Edward B. Laverty, "The Impact of *U.S. v.*

Lopez on Intergovernmental Relations," *Publius: The Journal of Federalism* 26 (Summer 1996): 109–26.

17. *Alden* v. *Maine,* 527 S.Ct. 706 (1999).

18. *Kansas* v. *Hendricks,* 117 S. Ct.2072 (1997).

19. *Printz* v. *United States,* No. 95–1478 (1997).

20. *Coalition for Economic Equity* v. *Wilson,* No. 96–50605 (1997).

21. *Lee* v. *Harcleroad,* No. 96–1824 (1997).

22. *Hill* v. *Colorado,* No. 98–1856 (2000).

23. *Seminole Tribe of Florida* v. *Florida,* 116 S.Ct. 1114 (1996).

24. *College Savings Bank* v. *Florida Prepaid Postsecondary Education Expense Board et al.,* 98 S.Ct. 149 (1999).

25. *Kimel* v. *Florida Board of Regents,* 120 S.Ct. 631 (2000).

26. *Federal Maritime Commission* v. *South Carolina Ports Authority,* no. 01-46 (2002).

27. *Crosby* v. *National Foreign Trade Council,* 2000 US. LEXIS 4134.

28. *Sternberg* v. *Carhart,* 2000 U.S. LEXIS 4484.

29. *Lorillard Tobacco* v. *Reilly,* No. 00–596 (2000).

30. Timothy J. Conlan and Francos Vergniolle de Chantal, "The Rehnquist Court and Contemporary American Federalism," *Political Science Quarterly* 116 (Summer 2001): 253–75.

31. Bill McGarigle, "The Battle Over Ellis Island," www.govtech.net (January 2000): 44–45; Neil MacFarquhar, "Ruling Like Solomon's Favoring New Jersey Splits Ellis Island in Two," *New York Times* (April 2, 1997), p. A21.

32. Glenn Beamer, *Creative Politics: Taxes and Public Goods in a Federal System* (Ann Arbor: University of Michigan Press, 1999).

33. Wright, *Understanding Intergovernmental Relations,* pp. 40–42; McDonald, op. cit. (2002).

34. Timothy J. Conlon "Federalism and Competing Values in the Reagan Administration," *Publius: The Journal of Federalism* 16 (Winter 1986): 29–47.

35. Ann O'M. Bowman and Michael A. Pagano, "The State of American Federalism 1989–1990," *Publius: The Journal of Federalism* 20 (Summer 1990): 1–25.

36. Art Hamilton, as quoted in Carol Tubbesing, "As the Twig Is Bent," *State Legislatures* 19 (October 1993): 24.

37. John Kincaid and Richard L. Cole, "Changing Public Attitudes on Power and Taxation in the American Federal System," *Publius: The Journal of Federalism* 31 (Summer 2001): 205–14.

38. Jonathan Walters, "'Save Us from the States.'" *Governing* (June 2001): 20–21.

39. See Marcella Ridlen Ray and T. J. Conlon, "At What Price? Costs of Federal Mandates Since the 1980s," *State and Local Government Review* 28 (Winter 1996): 7–16.

40. Donald F. Kettl, "10th Amendment Turf War," *Governing* (October 1998): 13.

41. Quoted in U.S. Advisory Commission on Integovernmental Relations, *State Constitutions in the Federal System* (Washington, D.C.: ACIR, 1989), p. 37.

42. Cheryl Arvidson, "As the Reagan Era Fades, It's Discretion vs. Earmarking in the Struggle Over Funds," *Governing* 3 (March 1990): 21–27.

43. Marcia L. Godwin, "Innovations Across American States," paper presented at the 2001 annual meeting of the American Political Science Association, August 30–September 2, 2002, San Francisco.

44. See Lamar Alexander, "Breaking Up the Arrogant Empire," *Madison Review* 1 (Fall 1995): 16.

45. See David B. Walker, "The Advent of Ambiguous Federalism and the Emergence of New Federalism III," *Public Administration Review* 56 (May/June 1996): 271–80.

46. Samuel H. Beer, "The Future of the States in the Federal System," in Peter Woll, ed., *American Government: Readings and Cases* (Boston: Little, Brown, 1981), p. 92.

Chapter 3 **STATE CONSTITUTIONS** pp. 47–67

1. See Nat Frothingham and Jake Brown, "Gay Rights 'Civil Unions' Nearing Reality in Vermont," www. stateline.org (March 27, 2000); Alan Ehrenhart, "Vermont's Judicial Distillery," *Governing* 13 (February 2000): 7

2. G. Alan Tarr, *Understanding State Constitutions* (Princeton, N.J.: Princeton University Press, 1999).

3. U.S. Advisory Commission on Intergovernmental Relations (ACIR), *State Constitutions in the Federal System,* A-113 (Washington, D.C.: ACIR, 1989), p. 2.

4. Donald S. Lutz, "The United States Constitution as an Incomplete Text," *Annals of the American Academy of Political and Social Science* 496 (March 1989): 23–32.

5. G. Alan Tarr and Mary Cornelia Porter, "Introduction: State Constitutionalism and State Constitutional Law," *Publius: The Journal of Federalism* 17 (Winter 1987): 5.

6. Donald S. Lutz, "Toward a Theory of Constitutional Amendment," *American Political Science Review* 88 (June 1994): 356; G. Alan Tarr, ed., *Constitutional Politics in the States* (Westport, Conn.: Greenwood Press, 1996), p. xv.

7. Donald S. Lutz, "The Iroquois Confederation Constitution: An Analysis," *Publius: The Journal of Federalism* 28 (Spring 1998): 99–127.

8. Daniel J. Elazar, "The Principles and Traditions Underlying State Constitutions," *Publius: The Journal of Federalism* 12 (Winter 1982): 11.

9. Quoted in Perry Gilbert Miller, "Thomas Hooker and the Democracy of Early Connecticut," *New England Quarterly* 4 (1931): 695.

10. Bruce Fraser, *The Land of Steady Habits: A Brief History of Connecticut* (Hartford: Connecticut Historical Commission, 1986), p. 10.

11. John Estill Reeves, *Kentucky Government* (Lexington: University of Kentucky, 1966), p. 7. As quoted in Penny M. Miller, *Kentucky Government and Politics* (Lincoln: University of Nebraska Press, 1994), p. 82.

12. Albert L. Sturm, "The Development of American State Constitutions," *Publius: The Journal of Federalism* 12 (Winter 1982): 61.

13. Ibid., pp. 62–63.

14. Paul G. Reardon, "The Massachusetts Constitution Makes a Milestone," *Publius: The Journal of Federalism* 12 (Winter 1982): 45–55.

15. Quoted in Thomas Parrish, "Kentucky's Fourth Constitution Is a Product of Its 1980 Times," in Thad L. Beyle, ed., *State Government: CQ's Guide to Current Issues and Activities* 1991–92 (Washington, D.C.: Congressional Quarterly Press, 1991), p. 46.

16. U.S. Advisory Commission on Intergovernmental Relations (ACIR), *The Question of State Government Capability* (Washington, D.C.: ACIR, 1985), p. 36.

17. David Fellman, "What Should a State Constitution Contain?" in W. Brooke Graves, ed., *Major Problems in State Constitutional Revision* (Chicago: Public Administration Service, 1960), p. 146.

18. Sturm, "American State Constitutions," p. 64.

19. David C. Nice, "Interest Groups and State Constitutions: Another Look," *State and Local Government Review* 20 (Winter 1988): 22.

20. Donald S. Lutz, "Patterns in the Amending of American State Constitutions," in G. Alan Tarr, ed., *Constitutional Politics in the States* (Westport, Conn.: Greenwood Press, 1996), pp. 24–27.

21. U.S. Advisory Commission on Intergovernmental Relations (ACIR), *A Report to the President for Transmittal to the Congress* (Washington, D.C.: U.S. Government Printing Office, 1955).

22. National Municipal League, *Model State Constitution*, 6th ed., rev. (New York: National Municipal League, 1968).

23. John J. Carroll and Arthur English, "Traditions of State Constitution Making," *State and Local Government Review* 23 (Fall 1991): 103–109.

24. Thomas C. Marks, Jr., and John F. Cooper, *State Constitutional Law* (St. Paul: West, 1988).

25. Ibid., p. 38.

26. Ibid., pp. 38–42.

27. Council of State Governments, *The Book of the States*, 34 (Lexington, Ky.: Council of State Governments, 2002), Table 1.4.

28. Albert L. Sturm, *Thirty Years of State Constitution-Making: 1938–1968* (New York: National Municipal League, 1970), pp. 27–28.

29. Ibid., p. 62.

30. Sturm, *Thirty Years*, p. 69.

31. Jay S. Goodman et al., "Public Responses to State Constitutional Revision," *American Journal of Political Science* 17 (August 1973): 571–96.

32. Elmer E. Cornwell Jr., Jay S. Goodman, and Wayne R. Swanson, *State Constitutional Conventions* (New York: Praeger, 1975), p. 81.

33. Janice C. May, "Texas Constitutional Revision: Lessons and Laments," *National Civic Review* 66 (February 1977): 64–69.

34. Robert F. Williams, "Are State Constitutional Conventions Things of the Past? The Increasing Role of the Constitutional Commission in State Constitutional Change," *The Hofstra Law and Policy Symposium*, Vol. 1 (1996): 1–26.

35. Janice C. May, "State Constitutions and Constitutional Revision: 1988–89 and the 1980s," *The Book of the States, 1990–91* (Washington, D.C.: Council of State Governments, 1991), p. 25.

36. Quoted in U.S. Advisory Commission on Intergovernmental Relations, *State Constitutions in the Federal System* (Washington, D.C.: ACIR, 1989), p. 37.

37. Sturm, "American State Constitutions," p. 104.

38. W. Brooke Graves, "State Constitutional Law: A Twenty-Five Year Summary," *William and Mary Law Review* 8 (Fall 1966): 12.

39. ACIR, *State Government Capability*, p. 60.

40. Richard H. Leach, "A Quiet Revolution: 1933–1976," in *The Book of the States, 1975–76* (Lexington, Ky.: Council of State Governments, 1976), p. 25.

Chapter 4   CITIZEN PARTICIPATION AND ELECTIONS
pp. 68–90

1. "Local Innovators," *National Civic Review* 89 (Summer 2000): 1–5.

2. William E. Lyons and David Lowery, *The Politics of Dissatisfaction* (Armonk, N.Y.: M. E. Sharpe, 1992).

3. Henry E. Brady, Sidney Verba, and Kay Lehman Schlozman, "Beyond SES: A Resource Model of Political Participation," *American Political Science Review* 89 (June 1995): 271–94.

4. See also Richard Murray and Arnold Vedlitz, "Race, Socioeconomic Status, and Voting Participation in Large Southern Cities," *Journal of Politics* 39 (November 1977): 1064–72.

5. Virginia Sapiro, *The Political Integration of Women* (Urbana: University of Illinois Press, 1983).

6. "Voters and Nonvoters Compared," *New York Times* (November 9, 1994), p. A8.

7. Amy Linomon and Mark R. Joslyn, "Trickle Up Political Socialization: The Impact of Kids Voting USA on Voter Turnout in Kansas," *State Politics and Policy Quarterly* 2 (Spring 2002): 24–36.

8. Jan E. Leighley and Arnold Vedlitz, "Race, Ethnicity, and Political Participation," *Journal of Politics* 61 (November 1999): 1092–1114; Debra Horner, "Critiquing Measures of Political Interest," paper presented at the annual meeting of the Midwest Political Science Association, Chicago, 2000.

9. Earl Black and Merle Black, *Politics and Society in the South* (Cambridge, Mass.: Harvard University Press, 1987).

10. "Voter Turnout in Nonpresidential Years," The Learning Network, www. infoplease.com.

11. Kim Quaile Hill and Jan E. Leighley, "Party Ideology, Organization, and Competitiveness as Mobilizing Forces in Gubernatorial Elections," *American Journal of Political Science* 37 (November 1993): 1158–78.

12. "Voter Registration and Turnout, 2000," www.fec.gov/ pages/turnout.

13. "Muslim Group Starts an Effort to Increase Voter Registration," *New York Times* (February 23, 2002), www.nytimes.com.

14. "Ventura to Enjoy a Lobster à la Voter Turnout," *Minneapolis Star-Tribune* (December 21, 2000), p. 1.

15. Robert A. Jackson, Robert D. Brown, and Gerald C. Wright, "Registration, Turnout and the Electoral Representativeness of State Electorates," *American Politics Quarterly* 26 (July 1998): 259–87.

16. "Voter Registration Information," *The Book of the States 1996–97* (Lexington, Ky.: Council of State Governments, 1996), p. 162.

17. David Foster, "States Get Creative to Raise Voter Turnout," *Nation's Cities Weekly* (October 31, 1994), p. 10.

18. Margaret Rosenfield, "All-Mail Ballot Elections," Federal Election Commission (September 1995).

19. Priscilla Southwell and Justin Burchett, "The Effect of Vote-by-Mail on Turnout," paper presented at the annual meeting of the American Political Science Association, San Francisco, 1996.

20. "Methods of Nominating Candidates for State Offices," *The Book of the States, 1996–97,* pp. 157–58.

21. Malcolm E. Jewell and Sarah M. Morehouse, *Political Parties and Elections in American States,* 4th ed. (Washington, D.C.: Congressional Quarterly Press, 2001).

22. Steven H. Haeberle, "Rundown on the Runoff: Party Runway Run Amok," paper presented at the annual meeting of the Southern Political Science Association, Charlotte, N.C., 1987.

23. Stephen A. Salmore and Barbara G. Salmore, "The Transformation of State Electoral Politics," in Carl E. Van Horn, ed., *The State of the States,* 2d ed. (Washington, D.C.: Congressional Quarterly Press, 1993), pp. 51–78.

24. Dennis M. Anderson, "One Way to Run a Legislative Body: The End of an Era in Ohio," *Comparative State Politics* 15 (April 1994): 34–37.

25. Randall W. Partin, "Economic Conditions and Gubernatorial Elections," *American Politics Quarterly* 23 (January 1995): 81–95.

26. Alan Greenblatt, "The Politics of Parity," *Governing* 15 (January 2002): 18–22.

27. Tari Renner, "Municipal Election Processes: The Impact on Minority Representation," in International City Management Association, *The Municipal Year Book 1988* (Washington, D.C.: ICMA, 1988), pp. 13–21.

28. Brian F. Schaffner, Gerald Wright, and Matthew Streb, "Teams Without Uniforms: The Nonpartisan Ballot in State and Local Elections," *Political Research Quarterly* 54 (March 2001): 7–30.

29. Arnold Fleischmann and Lana Stein, "Campaign Contributions in Local Elections," *Political Research Quarterly* 51 (September 1998): 673–89.

30. Luis Ricardo Fraga, "Domination Through Democratic Means: Nonpartisan Slating Groups in City Electoral Politics," *Urban Affairs Quarterly* 23 (June 1988): 528–55.

31. David B. Magleby, "Taking the Initiative: Direct Legislation and Direct Democracy in the 1980s," *PS: Political Science and Politics* 21 (Summer 1988): 600.

32. Council of State Governments, *The Book of the States, 2000–2001.*

33. Elisabeth R. Gerber, et al,. *Stealing the Initiative* (Upper Saddle River, N.J.: Prentice-Hall, 2001).

34. Ibid.

35. Shaun Bowler and Todd Donovan, "Economic Conditions and Voting on Ballot Propositions," *American Politics Quarterly* 22 (January 1994): 27–40.

36. Michael B. Magleby, as quoted in Robert Pear, "Debate on Whose Voice Is Heard on Initiatives," *New York Times* (November 7, 1994), p. A11.

37. Gerber, *Stealing the Initiative.*

38. Shaun Bowler, Todd Donovan, Max Neiman, and Johnny Peel, "Institutional Threat and Partisan Outcomes: Legislative Candidates' Attitudes Toward Direct Democracy," *State Politics and Policy Quarterly* 1 (Winter 2001): 364–79.

39. Paula D. McClain, "Arizona 'High Noon': The Recall and Impeachment of Evan Mecham," *PS: Political Science and Politics* 21 (Summer 1988): 628–38.

40. James P. Melcher, "Do They Recall?" *Comparative State Politics* 17 (August 1996): 16–25.

41. Joseph F. Zimmerman, *Participatory Democracy: Populism Revived* (New York: Praeger, 1986).

42. Jim Cleary, as quoted in "Fighting City Hall—and Winning," *The State* (May 26, 1987), p. 7A.

43. Thomas E. Cronin, "Public Opinion and Direct Democracy," *PS: Political Science and Politics* 21 (Summer 1988): 612–19.

44. U.S. Advisory Commission on Intergovernmental Relations, *Citizen Participation in the American Federal System* (Washington, D.C.: ACIR, 1979).

45. Ibid.

46. Charles Mahtesian, "The Endless Struggle over Open Meetings," *Governing* 11 (December 1997): 48–51.

47. Neal Peirce, "Oregon's Rx for Mistrusted Government," *National Journal* 24 (February 29, 1992): 529.

48. Thomas I. Miller, "How to Really Get in Touch with Your Constituents," *Governing* 5 (June 1992): 12–13.

49. Ellen Perlman, "The Call-In Connection," *Governing* 15 (June 2002): 50, 52.

50. Anya Sostek, "The Immortal Chad," *Governing* 15 (January 2002): 26–28.

51. Shane Harris, "Bridging the Divide," *Governing* 13 (September 2000): 36.

52. Steve Millard, "Voluntary Action and the States: The Other Alternative," *National Civic Review* 72 (May 1983): 262–69.

53. Harry P. Hatry and Carl F. Valente, "Alternative Service Delivery Approaches Involving Increased Use of the Private Sector," in International City Management Association, *The Municipal Year Book 1983* (Washington, D.C.: ICMA, 1983), pp. 199–216.

54. Mary A. Culp, "Volunteering as Helping," *National Civic Review* 77 (May/June 1988): 224–30.

55. Evan J. Ringquist, Kim Quaile Hill, Jan E. Leighley, and Angela Hinton-Andersson, "Lower-Class Mobilization and Policy Linkage in the U.S. States: A Correction," *American Journal of Political Science* 41 (January 1997): 339–44.

56. Rob Gurwitt, "A Government That Runs on Citizen Power," *Governing* 6 (December 1992): 48.

57. Tom W. Rice and Alexander F. Sumberg, "Civic Culture and Government Performance in the American States," *Publius: The Journal of Federalism* 27 (Winter 1997): 99–114.

58. Ibid., p. 113.

Chapter 5 **POLITICAL PARTIES, INTEREST GROUPS, AND CAMPAIGNS** pp. 91–114

1. "Mississippi Legislators Name Musgrove New Governor," http://dailynews.yahoo.com, January 4, 2000.

2. Larry J. Sabato, *The Party's Just Begun* (Glenview, Ill.: Scott, Foresman, 1987).

3. Kenneth Janda, Jeffrey M. Berry, and Jerry Goldman, *The Challenge of Democracy: Government in America,* 2d ed. (Boston: Houghton Mifflin, 1989), p. 304.

4. Robert S. Erikson, Gerald C. Wright, and John P. McIver, *Statehouse Democracy* (New York: Cambridge University Press, 1993).

5. Denise L. Baer, "Interest Intermediation and Political Party Reform: A Comparative Study of State Party Charters," paper presented at the annual meeting of the American Political Science Association, Washington, D.C., 1988.

6. Malcolm E. Jewell and Sarah M. Morehouse, *Political Parties and Elections in American States,* 4th ed. (Washington, D.C.: Congressional Quarterly Press, 2001).

7. John H. Aldrich, "Southern Parties in State and Nation," *Journal of Politics* 62 (August 2000): 643–70.

8. Malcolm E. Jewell and David M. Olson, *Political Parties and Elections in American States,* 3d ed. (Chicago: Dorsey Press, 1988).

9. James L. Gibson et al., "Whither the Local Parties? A Cross Sectional and Longitudinal Analysis of the Strength of Party Organizations," *American Journal of Political Science* 29 (February 1985): 139–60.

10. Christopher P. Gilbert and David A. Peterson, "Minnesota: Christians and Quistians in the GOP," in Mark J. Ruzell and Clyde Wilcox, eds., *God at the Grassroots* (Lanham, Mo.: Rowman & Littlefield, 1995).

11. Scott Pendleton, "GOP Religious Right Flexes Muscle in Texas," *Christian Science Monitor* (March 28, 1994), p. 2.

12. John F. Persinos, "Has the Christian Right Taken Over the Republican Party?" *Campaigns & Elections* 15 (September 1994): 21–24.

13. Frank J. Sorauf and Paul Allen Beck, *Party Politics in America,* 6th ed. (Glenview, Ill.: Scott, Foresman, 1988).

14. Jewell and Morehouse, *Political Parties and Elections,* pp. 224–25.

15. Scott Lasley, "Explaining Third Party Support in American States," paper presented at the annual meeting of the American Political Science Association, Washington, D.C., 1997.

16. Richard L. Berke, "U.S. Voters Focus on Selves, Poll Says," *New York Times* (September 21, 1994), p. A12.

17. Stephen C. Craig, "The Decay of Mass Partisanship," *Polity* 20 (Summer 1988): 705–13.

18. Larry M. Bartels, "Partisanship and Voting Behavior, 1952–1996," *American Journal of Political Science* 44 (2000): 35–50.

19. Cornelius P. Cotter et al., *Party Organizations in American Politics* (New York: Praeger, 1984).

20. Paul S. Hernnson, "The Importance of Party Campaigning," *Polity* 20 (Summer 1988): 714–19.

21. L. Harmon Zeigler, "Interest Groups in the States," in Virginia Gray, Herbert Jacob, and Kenneth N. Vines, eds., *Politics in the American States,* 4th ed. (Boston: Little, Brown, 1983), pp. 97–131.

22. Clive S. Thomas and Ronald J. Hrebenar, "Interest Groups in the Fifty States," *Comparative State Politics* 20 (August 1999): 3–16.

23. Ibid.

24. Ibid.

25. Zeigler, "Interest Groups in the States," pp. 111–19.

26. Sarah M. Morehouse, "Interest Groups, Parties, and Policies in the American States," paper presented at the annual meeting of the American Political Science Association, Washington, D.C., 1997.

27. Clive S. Thomas and Ronald J. Hrebenar, "Toward a Comprehensive Understanding of the Political Party–Interest Group Relationship in the American States," paper presented at the annual meeting of the Western Political Association, Seattle, 1999.

28. Ibid.

29. Virginia Gray and David Lowery, "A Niche Theory of Interest Representation," *Journal of Politics* 58 (February 1996): 91–111.

30. Donald P. Haider-Markel, "Interest Group Survival: Shared Interests versus Competition for Resources," *Journal of Politics* 59 (August 1997): 903–12.

31. Thomas and Hrebenar, "Interest Groups in the States," in Virginia Gray, Herbert Jacob, and Robert B. Albritton, eds., *Politics in the American States,* 5th ed. (Glenview, Ill: Scott, Foresman/Little, Brown, 1990), p. 143.

32. Ellen Perlman, "The Art of Persuasion," *City & State* 9 (May 18, 1992): 3, 29.

33. "Lobbyists: Registration and Reporting," in *The Book of the States, 1996–97* (Lexington, Ky: Council of State Governments, 1996), p. 486.

34. Alan Rosenthal, *The Third House* (Washington, D.C.: Congressional Quarterly Press, 1993).

35. Ibid.

36. Clive S. Thomas and Ronald J. Hrebenar, "Comparative Interest Group Politics in the American West," *State Government* 59 (September/October 1986): 130.

37. William P. Browne, "Variations in the Behavior and Style of State Lobbyists and Interest Groups," *Journal of Politics* 47 (May 1985): 450–68; Charles W. Wiggins, Keith E. Hamm, and Charles G. Bell, "Interest Group and Party Influence Agents in the Legislative Process: A Comparative State Analysis," *Journal of Politics* 54 (February 1992): 82–100.

38. Ron Faucheux, "The Grassroots Explosion," *Campaigns & Elections* (December/January 1995): 20.

39. Anthony J. Nownes and Patricia Freeman, "Interest Group Activity in the States," paper presented at the annual meeting of the American Political Science Association, San Francisco, 1996.

40. "Our Gang," *Campaigns & Elections* 15 (December 1994/January 1995): 9.

41. William P. Browne and Delbert J. Ringquist, "Michigan Interests: The Politics of Diversification," paper presented at the annual meeting of the Midwest Political Science Association, Chicago, 1987, p. 24.

42. Fred Monardi and Stanton A. Glantz, "Tobacco Industry Campaign Contributions and Legislative Behavior at the State Level," paper presented at the annual meeting of the American Political Science Association, San Francisco, 1996, p. 8.

43. Frederick M. Herrmann and Ronald D. Michaelson, "Financing State and Local Elections: Recent Developments," in *The Book of the States, 1994–95* (Lexington, Ky: Council of State Governments, 1994), pp. 228–30.

44. Howard A. Faye, Allan Cigler, and Paul Schumaker, "The Municipal Group Universe: Changes in Agency Penetration by Political Groups," paper presented at the annual meeting of the American Political Science Association, Washington, D.C., 1986.

45. Glenn Abney and Thomas P. Lauth, *The Politics of State and City Administration* (Albany: State University of New York Press, 1986).

46. Jeffrey M. Berry et al., *The Rebirth of Urban Democracy* (Washington, D.C.: Brookings Institution, 1993).

47. *Campaigns & Elections* 9 (May/June 1988): 1.

48. Kris Axtman, "Que Es Esto? A Texas Debate in Spanish?" *Christian Science Monitor* (March 1, 2002), pp. 1, 4, 5.

49. Jerry Hagstrom and Robert Guskind, "Selling the Candidate," *National Journal* 18 (November 1, 1986): 2619–26.

50. Robert G. Berger, "The Homemade Home Video," *Campaigns & Elections* 12 (October/November 1991): 44–46.

51. Cleveland Ferguson III, "The Politics of Ethics and Elections," *Florida State University Law Review* 25 (Fall 1997): 463–503.

52. Dan Balz, "Hispanic Executive Wins Tex. Democratic Gubernatorial Bid," *Washington Post* (March 13, 2002), p. A2.

53. Alan Greenblatt, "The Mapmaking Mess," *Governing* 14 (January 2001): 20–23.

54. Sarah M. Morehouse, "Money Versus Party Effort: Nominating for Governor," paper presented at the annual meeting of the American Political Science Association, Chicago, 1987.

55. Donald A. Gross and Robert K. Goidel, "The Impact of State Campaign Finance Laws," *State Politics and Policy Quarterly* 1 (Summer 2001): 80–195.

56. William E. Cassie and Joel A. Thompson, "Patterns of PAC Contributions to State Legislative Candidates," in Joel A. Thompson and Gary F. Moncrief, eds., *Campaign Finance in State Legislative Elections* (Washington, D.C.: Congressional Quarterly Press, 1998).

57. Robert J. Huckshorn, "Who Gave It? Who Got It? The Enforcement of Campaign Finance Laws in the States," *Journal of Politics* 48 (August 1985): 773.

58. "Campaign Finance Laws," *The Book of the States 2000–01* (Lexington, Ky: Council of State Government, 2000), pp. 187–98.

59. "Funding of State Elections: Tax Provisions and Public Financing," in *The Book of the States, 1994–95,* pp. 276–78.

60. Ruth S. Jones, "State Public Financing and the State Parties," in Michael J. Malbin, ed., *Parties, Interest Groups, and Campaign Finance Laws* (Washington, D.C.: American Enterprise Institute, 1980), pp. 283–303.

61. Elizabeth G. King and David G. Wegge, "The Rules Are Never Neutral: Public Funds in Minnesota and Wisconsin Legislative Elections," paper presented at the annual meeting of the Midwest Political Science Association, Chicago, 1984.

62. John J. Mountjoy, "The Buck Stops Where?" *State Government News* 42 (March 1999): 29–31.
63. Gross and Goidel, "The Impact of State Campaign Finance Laws."

Chapter 6 **STATE LEGISLATURES** pp. 115–140

 1. Denny Heck, "Couch Potatoes Are Watching You," *State Legislatures* 24 (January 1998): 40–41.
 2. Mark C. Ellickson and Donald E. Whistler, "Explaining State Legislators' Casework and Public Resource Allocations," *Political Research Quarterly* 54 (September 2001): 553–69.
 3. Ellen Perlman, "The 'Gold-Plated' Legislature," *Governing* 11 (February 1998): 36–40.
 4. Rich Jones, "State Legislatures," in *The Book of the States, 1994–95* (Lexington, Ky.: Council of State Governments, 1994), p. 99.
 5. National Municipal League, *Apportionment in the 1960s*, rev. ed. (New York: National Municipal League, 1970).
 6. *Baker* v. *Carr,* 369 U.S. 186, 82 S.Ct. 691 (1962).
 7. *Reynolds* v. *Sims,* 84 S.Ct. 1362 (1964).
 8. Timothy G. O'Rourke, *The Impact of Reapportionment* (New Brunswick, N.J.: Transaction Books, 1980).
 9. David C. Saffell, "Reapportionment and Public Policy: State Legislators' Perspectives," in Bernard Grofman et al., eds., *Representation and Redistricting Issues* (Lexington, Mass.: D. C. Heath, 1982), pp. 203–19.
10. Jeremy Buchman, "Save Me a Seat," paper presented at the annual meeting of the American Political Science Association, Washington, D.C., 1997.
11. Quoted in Alan Greenblatt, "The Mapmaking Mess," *Governing* 14 (May 2001): 21.
12. Sam Roberts, "Where Will Mappers of New Districts Draw the Line?" *New York Times* (March 23, 1992), p. B12.
13. Ronald E. Weber, "Emerging Trends in State Legislative Redistricting," *Spectrum* 75 (Winter 2002): 13–15.
14. Ibid, p. 13.
15. *The Book of the States, 1998–99,* p. 78.
16. "Legislative Compensation: Regular," in *The Book of the States, 2002–03* (Lexington, Ky: Council of State Government, 2002), pp. 86–87.
17. Ellen Perlman, "The Gold-Plated Legislature," *Governing* 11 (February 1998): 40.
18. Peverill Squire, "Member Career Opportunities and the Internal Organization of Legislatures," *Journal of Politics* 50 (August 1988): 726–44.
19. Thomas H. Little, "A Systematic Analysis of Members' Environments and Their Expectations of Elected Leaders," *Political Research Quarterly* 47 (September 1994): 733–47.
20. Keith E. Hamm and Robert Harmel, "Legislative Party Development and the Speaker System: The Case of the

Texas House," *Journal of Politics* 55 (November 1993): 1140–51.
21. Keith E. Hamm, Ronald D. Hedlund, and Stephanie S. Post, "Committee Specialization in State Legislatures During the Twentieth Century," paper presented at the annual meeting of the American Political Science Association, Washington, D.C., 1997.
22. Alan Rosenthal, *Legislative Life: People, Processes, and Performance in the States* (New York: Harper & Row, 1981).
23. Squire, "Member Career Opportunities."
24. Ibid.
25. Eric M. Uslaner and Ronald E. Weber, "U.S. State Legislators' Opinions and Perceptions of Constituency Attitudes," *Legislative Studies Quarterly* 4 (November 1979): 563–85.
26. Donald R. Songer et al., "The Influence of Issues on Choice of Voting Cues Utilized by State Legislators," *Western Political Quarterly* 39 (March 1986): 118–25.
27. Uslaner and Weber, "U.S. State Legislators' Opinions," p. 582.
28. Rosenthal, *Legislative Life.*
29. "Bill and Resolution Introductions and Enactments," in *The Book of the States, 2002–03,* p. 111.
30. Alan Rosenthal, "The Legislature as Sausage Factory," *State Legislatures* 27 (September 2001): 12–15.
31. Tom Loftus, *The Art of Legislative Politics* (Washington, D.C.: Congressional Quarterly Press, 1994), p. 76.
32. Ibid., p. 77.
33. Dawn Duplantier, "An Insider's View of the Legislative Process," *Texas Banking* (August 1997): 5–6.
34. David C. Saffell, "School Funding in Ohio: Courts, Politicians, and Newspapers," *Comparative State Politics* 18 (October 1997): 9–25.
35. "Getting from No to a Little Yes," *State Legislatures* 24 (January 1998): 18.
36. James N. Miller, "Hamstrung Legislatures," *National Civic Review* 54 (June 1989): 28–33.
37. Citizens' Conference on State Legislatures, *The Sometimes Governments: A Critical Study of the 50 American Legislatures,* 2d ed. (Kansas City, Mo.: CCSL, 1973), pp. 41–42.
38. John Grumm, "The Effects of Legislative Structure on Legislative Performance," in Richard Hofferbert and Ira Sharkansky, eds., *State and Urban Politics: Readings in Comparative Public Policy* (Boston: Little, Brown, 1971), pp. 298–322.
39. Albert K. Karning and Lee Sigelman, "State Legislative Reform and Public Policy: Another Look," *Western Political Quarterly* 28 (September 1975): 548–52.
40. Philip W. Roeder, "State Legislative Reform: Determinants and Policy Consequences," *American Politics Quarterly* 7 (January 1979): 51–70.
41. Ann O'M. Bowman and Richard C. Kearney, "Dimensions of State Government Capability," *Western Political Quarterly* 41 (June 1988): 341–62.

42. Alan Rosenthal, "The New Legislature: Better or Worse and for Whom?" *State Legislatures* 12 (July 1986): 5.

43. Charles Mahtesian, "The Sick Legislature Syndrome," *Governing* 10 (February 1997): 16–20.

44. Andrea Paterson, "Is the Citizen Legislator Becoming Extinct?" *State Legislatures* 12 (July 1986): 22–25.

45. Charles W. Wiggins, as quoted in ibid., p. 24.

46. Representative Vic Krouse, as quoted in ibid., p. 24.

47. Alan Rosenthal, "The State Legislature," paper presented at the Vanderbilt Institute for Public Policy Studies, November 1987.

48. Jones, "State Legislatures," p. 99.

49. Richard Nathan, as cited in Kathe Callahan and Marc Holzer, "Rethinking Governmental Change," *Public Productivity Management & Review* 17 (Spring 1994): 202.

50. Stuart Rothenberg, "How Term Limits Became a National Phenomenon," *State Legislatures* 18 (January 1992): 35–39.

51. Thad Beyle and Rich Jones, "Term Limits in the States," in *The Book of the States, 1994–95*.

52. Joel A. Thompson and Gary F. Moncrief, "The Implications of Term Limits for Women and Minorities: Some Evidence from the States," *Social Science Quarterly* 74 (June 1993): 300–309.

53. John M. Carey, Richard G. Niemi, and Lyuda W. Powell, "The Effects of Term Limits in State Legislatures," *Spectrum* 74 (Fall 2001):16–18.

54. Jim Brunelle, "The Reign in Maine," *State Legislatures* 23 (September 1997): 28–29; Gary Moncrief and Joel A. Thompson, " Lobbyists' Views on Term Limits," *Spectrum* 74 (Fall 2001): 13–15.

55. Karen Hansen, "The Third Revolution," *State Legislatures* 23 (September 1997): 20–26.

56. Ibid.

57. "Idaho Makes Term Limits History," http://www.ncsl.org/programs (February 1, 2002).

58. Lucinda Simon, "Legislatures and Governors: The Wrestling Match," *State Government* 59 (Spring 1986): 1.

59. Ted Strickland, as quoted in ibid., p. 5. See also, Cynthia J. Bowling and Margaret R. Ferguson, "Divided Government, Interest Representation, and Policy Differences: Competing Explanations of Gridlock in the Fifty States," *Journal of Politics* 63 (February 2001): 182–206.

60. Peter Eichstaedt, "No, No, Two Hundred Times No," *State Legislatures* 21 (July/August 1995): 46–49.

61. Madeleine Kunin, as quoted in Sharon Randall, "From Big Shot to Boss," *State Legislatures* 14 (June 1988): 348.

62. Simon, "Legislatures and Governors."

63. Samuel K. Gove, "State Management and Legislative-Executive Relations," *State Government* 54, no. 3 (1981): 99–101.

64. Rosenthal, *Legislative Life.*

65. Dianna Gordon, "Virginia's JLARC: A Standard of Excellence," *State Legislatures* 20 (May 1994): 13–16.

66. Jerry Brekke, "Supreme Court of Missouri Rules Legislative Veto Unconstitutional," *Comparative State Politics* 19 (February 1997): 32–34.

67. Kathleen M. Simon and Dennis O. Grady, "Overseeing Rulemaking Discretion in the Resurgent American States," paper presented at the annual meeting of the American Political Science Association, San Francisco, 1996.

68. As quoted in Dave McNeely, "Is the Sun Setting on the Texas Sunset Law?" *State Legislatures* 20 (May 1994): 17–20.

69. Ibid.

70. William M. Pearson and Van A. Wigginton, "Effectiveness of Administrative Controls: Some Perceptions of State Legislators," *Public Administration Review* 46 (July/ August 1986): 328–31.

71. Rosenthal, "The New Legislature," p. 5.

72. Rosenthal, *The Decline of Representative Democracy,* p. 85.

73. Alan Ehrenhalt, "An Embattled Institution," *Governing* 5 (January 1992): 28–33.

Chapter 7 **GOVERNORS** pp. 141–171

1. David Broder, "Governors Tackling Real-World Problems," *The News and Observer* (August 12, 2001): D3

2. Eileen Shanahan, "The Sudden Rise in Statehouse Status," *Governing* 9 (September 1996): 15.

3. Ann O'M. Bowman and Richard C. Kearney, *The Resurgence of the States* (Englewood Cliffs, N.J.: Prentice-Hall, 1986), p. 52.

4. For a more detailed discussion of the processes and results of the state government reform movement, see Bowman and Kearney, *Resurgence,* pp. 47–54.

5. Larry Sabato, *Goodbye to Goodtime Charlie: The American Governorship Transformed* (Lexington, Mass.: Lexington Books, 1978), p. 13.

6. Ibid.

7. Ibid., p. xi.

8. Ibid., pp. 27–31.

9. As quoted in George F. Will, "Ashcroft in 2000? He's Playing the Part," *Hartford Courant* (September 9, 1997), p. A24.

10. Greg Lucas and Lynda Gledhill, "Governor Race Spending Clobbered 1994 Record," *San Francisco Chronicle* (February 5, 1999), p. A19.

11. Thad L. Beyle, "The Governors, 1992–93," in *The Book of the States, 1994–95* (Lexington, Ky.: Council of State Governments, 1994), p. 39.

12. *State Trends Bulletin* (Lexington, Ky.: Council of State Governments): 7.

13. Randall W. Partin, "Assessing the Impact of Campaign Spending in Governor's Races," *Political Research Quarterly* 55 (March 2002): 213–25.

14. Beyle, "The Governors," p. 95.

15. Malcolm E. Jewell and David M. Olson, *Political Parties and Elections in the American States,* 3d ed. (Chicago: Dorsey Press, 1988).

16. Peverill Squire, "Challenger Profile and Gubernatorial Elections," *Western Politics Quarterly* 45 (1992): 125–42.

17. Richard G. Niemi, Harold W. Stanley, and Ronald J. Vogel, "State Economies and State Taxes: Do Voters Hold Governors Accountable?" *American Journal of Political Science* 39 (November 1995): 936–57; Robert C. Lowry, James E. Alt, and Karen E. Feree, "Fiscal Policy Outcomes and Accountability in American States," *American Political Science Review* 92 (December 1998): 759–72.; Jason A. MacDonald and Lee Sigelman, "Public Assessments of Gubernatorial Performance: A Comparative State Analysis," *American Politics Quarterly* 27 (April 1999): 201–15.

18. Elizabeth Adell Cook, Ted G. Jelen, and Clyde Wilcox, "Issue Voting in Gubernatorial Elections: Abortion and Post-Webster Politics," *Journal of Politics* 56 (February 1994): 187–99; John Nagy, "Govs Upbeat, Wordy in Setting 'Quality of Life' Agendas," www.stateline.org (February 14, 2001): p. 2.

19. Alan Rosenthal, *Governors and Legislators: Contending Powers* (Washington, D.C.: Congressional Quarterly Press, 1990), pp. 52–54.

20. Sharon Sherman, "Powersplit: When Legislatures and Governors Are of Opposing Parties," *State Legislatures* 10 (May/June 1984): 9–12.

21. Sander M. Polster, "Maine's King Makes Independence a Virtue," www.stateline.org (November 30, 1999).

22. As quoted in Alan Ehrenhart, "The Debilitating Search for a Flabby Consensus," *Governing* 9 (October 1996): 8.

23. As quoted in Thad L. Beyle and Lynn R. Muchmore, *Reflections on Being Governor* (Washington, D.C.: National Governors Association, 1978), p. 45.

24. John Nagy, "Governors Batted Just Under .500 in 2001," www.stateline.org (January 29, 2002): 1–4.

25. Deborah D. Roberts, "The Governor as Leader: Strengthening Public Service Through Executive Leadership," in Frank J. Thompson, ed., *Revitalizing State and Local Public Service* (San Francisco: Jossey-Bass, 1993), pp. 41–67.

26. *Book of the States, 2000–2001,* Vol. 33, Table 2.3.

27. Rochelle L. Stanfield, "Just Do It," *National Journal* 28 (March 30, 1996): 693–94.

28. Thad L. Beyle and Lynn R. Muchmore, "The Governor and the Public," in Beyle and Muchmore, eds., *Being Governor,* p. 24.

29. Don F. Hadwiger, "State Governors and American Indian Casino Gambling: Defining State-Tribal Relationships," *Spectrum: The Journal of State Government* (Fall 1996): 16–25.

30. Thad L. Beyle and Lynn R. Muchmore, "Governors and Intergovernmental Relations: Middleman in the Federal System," in Beyle and Muchmore, eds., *Being Governor,* p. 193.

31. Cathilea Robinett, "Few Governors Grasp Digital Revolution," *Government Technology* (May 1999): 6.

32. Jonathan Walters, "Full Speed Ahead: Remaking a State Through Ideology and Determination," *Governing* (November 2001): 23.

33. Thad L. Beyle and Lynn R. Muchmore, "The Governor as Party Lader," in Beyle and Muchmore, eds., *Being Governor,* pp. 44–51.

34. Charles N. Wheeler III, "Gov. James R. Thompson, 1977–1991: The Complete Campaigner, The Pragmatic Centrist," *Illinois Issues* 16 (December 1990): 12–16; John Wagner, "Hunt," *The News and Observer* (April 1, 2000): pp. 1A, 18A.

35. As quoted in Samuel R. Soloman, "Governors: 1960–1970," *National Civic Review* (March 1971): 126–46.

36. Diane Kincaid Blair, "The Gubernatorial Appointment Power: Too Much of a Good Thing?" in Beyle and Muchmore, eds., *Being Governor,* p. 117.

37. As quoted in Coleman B. Ransome, Jr., *The American Governorship* (Westport, Conn.: Greenwood Press, 1982), p. 121.

38. *Rutan et al.* v. *Republican Party of Illinois,* 1110 S.Ct. 2229, 1990.

39. Charles W. Wiggins, "Executive Vetoes and Legislative Overrides in the American States," *Journal of Politics* 42 (November 1980): 1110–17.

40. Rosenthal, *Governors and Legislators,* pp. 11–12.

41. Beyle, "Governor as Chief Legislator."

42. David Osborne, *Laboratories of Democracy* (Boston: Harvard Business School Press, 1988), pp. 138–39.

43. Dan Durning, "Governors and Administrative Reform in the 1990s," *State and Local Government Review* 27 (Winter 1995): 36–54.

44. James Conant, "Executive Branch Reorganization: Can It Be an Antidote for Fiscal Stress in the States?" *State and Local Government Review* 24 (Winter 1992): 3–11.

45. Ibid.

46. Ibid.

47. As quoted in Flentje, "Governor as Manager," p. 70. For a description of failure in reorganization in Florida, see also Less Garner, "Managing Change Through Organization Structure," *State Government* 60 (July/August 1987): 191–95.

48. Norma M. Riccucci and Judith R. Saidel, "The Demographics of Gubernatorial Appointees: Toward an Explanation of Variation," *Policy Studies Journal* 29, no. 1 (2000): 11–22.

49. H. Edward Flentje, "Clarifying Purpose and Achieving Balance in Gubernatorial Administration," *Journal of State Government* 62 (July/August 1989): 161–67.

50. Richard C. Kearney, "How a 'Weak' Governor Can Be Strong: Dick Riley and Education Reform in South Carolina," *State Government* 60 (July/August 1987): 150–56.

51. Dan Durning, "Change Masters for the States," *State Government* 60 (July/August 1987): 145–49.

52. Matt Bai, "The Taming of Jesse," *Newsweek* (October 15, 1999): p. 38; Jesse Ventura, *I Ain't Got Time to Bleed: Reworking the Body Politic from the Bottom Up* (New York: Villard, 1999).

53. Rochelle L. Stanfield, "Just Do It," *National Journal* (March 30, 1996): 694–95.

54. Rosenthal, *Governors and Legislators,* p. 27.

55. Ransome, *The American Governorship,* p. 156.

56. See Thad L. Beyle, "Enhancing Executive Leadership in the States," *State and Local Government Review* 27 (Winter 1995): 18–35.

57. Jonathan Walters, "The Taming of Texas," *Governing* 11 (July 1998): 18–22.

58. Lee Sigelman and Roland Smith, "Personal, Office, and State Characteristics as Predictors of Gubernatorial Performance," *Journal of Politics* 43 (February 1981): 169–80.

59. Scott M. Matheson, with James Edwin Kee, *Out of Balance* (Salt Lake City: Peregrine Smith Books, 1986), p. 186.

60. See Paul West, "They're Everywhere! For Today's Governors, Life Is a Never-Ending Campaign," *Governing* 3 (March 1990): 51–55.

61. Beyle, "Enhancing Executive Leadership," p. 33.

62. Jack van Der Slik, "Jim Edgar's Dilemma, or the Perils of 'Third Way' Leadership," in Thad L. Beyle, *State Government: CQ's Guide to Current Issues and Activities 1997–98* (Washington, D.C.: Congressional Quarterly Press, 1997), pp. 107–8.

63. David L. Martin, "Alabama's Governor Removed on Ethics Conviction: Implications for Other American States," *Comparative State Politics* 14, no. 3 (1994): 1–4.

64. Alan Greenblatt, "Seizing the Initiative," *Governing* (July 2002): 76.

65. As quoted in Alice Chasan Edelman, "Is There Room at the Top?" in Beyle and Muchmore, eds., *Being Governor,* p. 107.

66. Thad L. Beyle, "The Governors, 1992–93," *The Book of the States, 1994–95* (Lexington, Ky.: Council of State Governments, 1996), p. 47.

Chapter 8 **BUDGETING, BUREAUCRACY, AND SERVICE DELIVERY** pp. 172–201

1. Beverly A. Cigler and Heidi L. Neiswender, " 'Bureaucracy' in the Introductory American Government Textbook," *Public Administration Review* 51 (September/October 1991): 442–50.

2. H. George Frederickson, "Can Bureaucracy Be Beautiful?" *Public Administration Review* 60 (January/February 2000): 47–53.

3. J. Norman Baldwin, "Public versus Private Employees: Debunking Stereotypes," *Review of Public Personnel Administration* 11 (Fall 1990–Spring 1991): 1–27.

4. See, for example, Theodore H. Poister and Gary T. Henry, "Citizen Ratings of Public and Private Service Quality: A Comparative Perspective," *Public Administration Review* 54 (March/April 1994): 155–59.

5. Harold D. Laswell, *Politics: Who Gets What, When, Where, How?* (Cleveland: World, 1958).

6. Robert D. Lee, Jr., "The Use of Executive Guidance in State Budget Preparation," *Public Budgeting and Finance* 12 (Fall 1992): 19–21.

7. See Irene S. Rubin, *The Politics of Public Budgeting* (Chatham, N.J.: Chatham House Publishers, 1990): 167–80; and U.S. General Accounting Office, *Balanced Budget Requirements: State Experiences and Implications for the Federal Government* (Washington, D.C.: USGAO, March 1993).

8. Aaron Wildavsky, "Toward a Radical Incrementalism," in Alfred De Grazia, ed., *Congress: The First Branch of Government* (Washington, D.C.: American Enterprise Institute, 1966).

9. Aaron Wildavsky, *The Politics of the Budgetary Process* (Boston: Little, Brown, 1964), pp. 1–13.

10. Glenn Abney and Thomas P. Lauth, *The Politics of State and City Administration* (Albany: State University of New York Press, 1986), pp. 110–11, 115, 142–43.

11. Charles E. Lindblom, "The Science of Muddling Through," *Public Administrative Review* 19 (Spring 1959): 79–88.

12. Jay Shafrtiz, "The Cancer Eroding Public Personnel Professionalism," *Public Personnel Management* 3 (November/December 1974): 486–92; David K. Hamilton, "The Staffing Function in Illinois State Government After Rutan," *Public Administration Review* 53 (July/August 1993): 381–86.

13. H. George Frederickson, "The Airport That Reforms Forgot," *PA Times* (January 2000): 11.

14. Jonathan Walters, "Untangling Albany," *Governing* 11 (December 1998): 18–22.

15. Steven W. Hays and Richard C. Kearney, "Anticipated Changes in Human Resource Management: Surveying the Field," *Public Administration Review* 61 (September/October, 2001).

16. See, for example, Kenneth J. Meier, "Representative Bureaucracy: An Empirical Analysis," *American Political Science Review* 69 (June 1975): 526–42; and Samuel Krislow and David H. Rosenbloom, *Representative Bureaucracy and the American Political System* (New York: Praeger, 1981), pp. 31–73, 75–107. But see also Kenneth J. Meier, "Latinos and Representative

Bureaucracy: Testing the Thompson and Henderson Hypotheses," *Journal of Public Administration Research and Theory* 3 (October 1993): 393–414.

17. U.S. Equal Employment Opportunity Commission, *Affirmative Action and Equal Employment: A Guidebook for Employers* (Washington, D.C.: U.S. Government Printing Office, 1974).

18. J. Edward Kellough, "Equal Employment Opportunity and Affirmative Action in the Public Sector," in Steven W. Hays and Richard C. Kearney, eds., *Public Personnel Administration: Problems and Prospects,* 4th ed. (Upper Saddle River, N.J.: Prentice Hall, 2003), pp. 209–24.

19. *Hopwood v. Texas* (1996). 78 F.3d 932 (5th Cir; 1990) cert denied, 1996 WL 227009.

20. Mary E. Guy, "Three Steps Forward, Two Steps Backward: The Status of Women's Integration into Public Management," *Public Administration Review* 53 (July/August 1993): 285–91; Norma Riccucci and Judith R. Seidel, "The Representativeness of State-Level Bureaucratic Leaders: A Missing Piece of the Representative Bureaucracy Puzzle," *Public Administration Review* 57 (September/October 1997): 423–30; Norma M. Riccucci, *Managing Diversity in Public Sector Workforces* (Boulder, Colo.: Westview Press, 2002).

21. See, for example, Lois R. Wise, "Social Equity in Civil Service Systems," *Public Administration Review* 50 (September/October 1990): 567–75; and Antonio Sisneros, "Hispanics in the Public Service in the Late Twentieth Century," *Public Administration Review* 53 (January/February 1993): 1–7; Riccucci, *Managing Diversity,* 2002.

22. *Meritor Savings Bank* v. *Vinson,* 1986, 477 U.S. 57; *Teresa Haris* v. *Forklift Systems, Inc.,* U.S. Supreme Court, 92–1168 (November 9, 1993).

23. *Clark County School District* v. *Breeden,* No. 00–866 (2001).

24. James S. Bowman and Christopher J. Zigmond, "Peering into the Fishbowl of Public Employment," *Spectrum* (Summer 1996): 24–36.

25. Richard C. Kearney, *Labor Relations in the Public Sector,* 3d ed. (New York: Marcel Dekker, 2001), pp. 23–43.

26. Ibid, pp. 139–76.

27. Joel M. Douglas, "State Civil Service Systems and Collective Bargaining: Systems in Conflict," *Public Administration Review* 52 (January/February 1992): 162–71.

28. Jeffrey S. Banks and Barry R. Weingast, "The Political Control of Bureaucracies Under Asymmetric Information," *American Journal of Political Science* 36 (May 1992): 509–24.

29. Kenneth J. Meier, Joseph Stewart, Jr., and Robert E. England, "The Politics of Bureaucratic Discretion: Educational Access as an Urban Service," *American Journal of Political Science* 35 (February 1991): 155–77.

30. See Frederick C. Mosher, *Democracy and the Public Service,* 2d ed. (New York: Oxford University Press,

1982); and James A. Gazell and Darrell L. Pugh, eds., "Professionalization in Public Administration," Symposium in *International Journal of Public Administration* 16, no. 12 (1993).

31. Kearney and Sinha, "Professionalism and Bureaucratic Responsiveness," pp. 571–79.

32. Ibid.

33. Charles T. Goodsell, *The Case for Bureaucracy: A Public Administration Polemic* (Chatham, N.J.: Chatham House, 1983), pp. 44–48; see also Abney and Lauth, *Politics of State and City Administration,* pp. 209–10.

34. David Osborne and Ted Gaebler, *Reinventing Government* (New York: Penguin Books, 1993).

35. James E. Swiss, "Adapting Total Quality Management (TQM) to Government," *Public Administration Review* 52 (July/August 1992): 356–62.

36. Robert Jay Dilger, Randolph R. Moffett, and Linda Struyk, "Privatization of Municipal Services in America's Largest Cities," *Public Administration Review* 57 (January/February 1997): 21–26.

37. Bruce A. Wallin, "The Need for a Privatization Process: Lessons from Development and Implementation," *Public Administration Review* 57 (January/February 1997): 11–20.

38. Eliott D. Sclar, *You Don't Always Get What You Pay For: The Economics of Privatization* (Ithaca, N.Y.: Cornell University Press, 2000).

39. J. D. Greene, "Does Privatization Make a Difference? The Impact of Private Contracting on Municipal Efficiency," *International Journal of Public Administration* 17 (July 1994): 1299–325; George A. Boyne, "Bureaucratic Theory Meets Reality: Public Choice and Service Contracting in U.S. Local Government," *Public Administration Review* 58 (November/December 1998): 474–84.

40. John Rehfuss, "Contracting Out and Accountability in State and Local Governments—The Importance of Contract Monitoring," *State and Local Government Review* 22 (Winter 1990): 44–48; Jonas Prager, "Contracting Out Government Services: Lessons from the Private Sector," *Public Administration Review* 54 (March/April 1994): 176–84.

41. Sclar, *You Don't Always Get…;* Gary Enos, "We May Go Private," *Governing* 9 (November 1996): 40–41.

42. See "Infrastructure Conference Report," *Governing* 9 (October 1996): 73; Lawrence L. Martin, "Public-Private Competition: A Public Employee Alternative to Privatization," *Review of Public Personnel Administration* 19 (Winter 1999): 59–70; Dilger et al., "Privatization of Municipal Services," pp. 23–24; Boyne, "Bureaucratic Theory," pp. 475–80.

43. Polly Forster, "Internet Gives Friendlier Face to State Government," www.stateline.org (August 30, 2000): 1–3.

44. H. Brinton Milward and Louise Ogilvie Snyder, "Electronic Government: Linking Citizens to Public Organizations Through Technology," *Journal of Public Administration Research and Theory* 6 (April 1996): 261–75.

45. Jeffrey L. Brudney, F. Ted Hebert, and Deil S. Wright, "Reinventing Government in the American States: Measuring and Explaining Administrative Reform," *Public Administration Review* 59 (January/February 1999): 19–30.

Chapter 9 **THE JUDICIARY**   pp. 202–228

1. W. John Moore, "In Whose Court?" *National Journal* (October 15, 1991): 2396.

2. Henry Robert Glick and Kenneth N. Vines, *State Court Systems* (Englewood Cliffs, N.J.: Prentice-Hall, 1973), p. 19.

3. Ibid., p. 21.

4. Erick B. Low, "Accessing the Judicial System: The States' Response," in *The Book of the States, 1994–95* (Lexington, Ky.: Council of State Governments, 1994), pp. 186–87.

5. Kenneth G. Pankey, Jr., "The State of the Judiciary," in *The Book of the States, 1992–93* (Lexington, Ky.: Council of State Governments, 1992), p. 211.

6. See Larry Berkson and Susan Carbon, *Court Unification: History, Politics and Implementation* (Washington, D.C.: U.S. Department of Justice, National Institute for Law Enforcement and Criminal Justice, 1978).

7. Doug Lemov, "Bringing Order to the Courts," *Governing* 10 (February 1997): 58–59.

8. Tom Carlson, "Courts Ride the Information Superhighway," *Judicature* 80 (September/October 1996): 98–100.

9. American Bar Association, *Standards Relating to Court Organization* (New York: ABA, 1974), pp. 43–44.

10. *Republican Party of Minnesota* v. *White,* U.S. Sup.Ct. No. 01-521 (June 27, 2002).

11. See Traciel V. Reid, "PAC Participation in North Carolina Supreme Court Elections," *Judicature* 80 (July/August 1996): 21–22.

12. Francis Graham Lee, "Party Representation of State Supreme Courts: 'Unequal Representation' Revisited," *State and Local Government Review* 11 (May 1979): 48–52. See also Herbert Jacob, *Justice in America* (Boston: Little, Brown, 1965), p. 98.

13. Sheila Kaplan, "Justice for Sale," in Thad Beyle, *State Government: CQ's Guide to Current Issues and Activities, 1986–87* (Washington, D.C.: Congressional Quarterly Press, 1987), pp. 151–57.

14. As quoted in ibid., p. 152.

15. William Glaberson, "States Take Steps to Rein In Excesses of Judicial Politicking," *New York Times* (June 15, 2001), pp. 1–4.

16. See, for example, Richard A. Watson and Ronald C. Downing, *The Politics of the Bench and Bar* (New York: John Wiley and Sons, 1969), pp. 43–48, 136–38.

17. Ibid.

18. Susan Carbon, "Judicial Retention Elections: Are They Serving Their Intended Purpose?" *Judicature* 64 (November 1980): 210–33.

19. Melinda Gann Hall, "State Supreme Courts in American Democracy: Probing the Myths of Judicial Reform," *American Political Science Review* 95 (June 2001): 315–30.

20. See, for example, Carbon, "Judicial Retention Elections," p. 221.

21. John Culver, "California Supreme Court Election: 'Rose Bird and the Supremes,'" *Comparative State Politics Newsletter* (February 1987), p. 13.

22. Steven D. Williams, "The 1996 Retention Election of Justice White," *Comparative State Politics* 17 (October 1996): 28–30.

23. Bradley C. Canon, "The Impact of Formal Selection Processes on the Characteristics of Judges—Reconsidered," *Law and Society Review* 6 (1972): 575–93; Burton M. Atkins and Henry R. Glick, "Formal Judicial Recruitment and State Supreme Court Decisions," *American Politics Quarterly* 2 (October 1974): 427–49.

24. John Paul Ryan et al., *American Trial Judges* (New York: Free Press, 1980), pp. 125–30.

25. Philip L. Dubois, *From Ballot to Bench: Judicial Elections and the Quest for Accountability* (Austin: University of Texas Press, 1980), ch. 4.

26. Hall, p. 319.

27. Kathleen A. Bratton and Rorie L. Spill, "Existing Diversity and Judicial Selection: The Role of the Appointment Method in Establishing Gender Diversity in State Supreme Courts," *Social Science Quarterly* 83 (June 2002): 508–18.

28. Melinda Gann Hall, "Electoral Politics and Strategic Voting in State Supreme Courts," *Journal of Politics* 54 (1992): 427–46; Melinda Gann Hall, "Toward an Integrated Model of Judicial Voting Behavior," *American Politics Quarterly* 20 (1992): 147–68.

29. James P. Wenzel, Shaun Bowler, and David J. Lanoue, "Legislating from the State Bench: A Comparative Analysis of Judicial Activism," *American Politics Quarterly* 25 (July 1997): 363–79.

30. *Gregory* v. *Ashcroft,* 111 S.Ct. 2395 (1991).

31. ACIR, "State Court Systems," p. 190.

32. "New Questions About Rhode Island Chief Justice," *New York Times* (October 3, 1993), sec. 1, p. 22; "Ex-Top Judge Ends Rhode Island Appeal with a Guilty Plea," *New York Times* (April 30, 1994), sec. 1, p. 12; "Justice in Impeachment Inquiry Quits in Rhode Island," *New York Times* (May 29, 1986), p. A14.

33. Harry Kalven, Jr., and Hans Zeisel, *The American Jury* (Boston: Little, Brown, 1966), pp. 502–503.

34. Paul Brace, Laura Langer, and Melinda Gann Hall, "Measuring the Preferences of State Supreme Court Judges," *Journal of Politics* 62 (May 2000): 387–414.

35. Glick and Vines, *State Court Systems,* p. 78; Kenyon D. Bunch and Gregory Casey, "Political Controversy on Missouri's Supreme Court: The Case of Merit versus Politics," *State and Local Government Review* 22 (Winter 1990): 5–16.

36. Glick and Vines, *State Court Systems,* pp. 81–82.

37. Bunch and Casey, "Political Controversy," p. 12.

38. Hall, "Electoral Politics and Strategic Voting."

39. Melinda Gann Hall, "Justices as Representatives: Elections and Judicial Politics in the American States," *American Politics Quarterly* 23 (October 1995).

40. James W. Douglas and Roger E. Hartley, "State Court Budgeting and Judicial Independence: Clues from Oklahoma and Virginia," *Administration and Society* 33 (March 2001): 54–78.

41. See John C. Kilwein and Richard A. Brisbin, Jr., "Policy Convergence in a Federal Judicial System: The Application of Intensified Scrutiny Doctrines by State Supreme Courts," *American Journal of Political Science* 41 (January 1997): 145.

42. Gregory A. Caldeira, "The Transmission of Legal Precedent: A Study of State Supreme Courts," *American Political Science Review* 79 (March 1985): 178–93.

43. Gregory A. Caldeira, "Legal Precedent: Structures of Communication Between State Supreme Courts," *Social Network* 10 (1988): 29–55.

44. Low, "Accessing the Judicial System," pp. 168–80.

45. Stuart Nagel, "Political Party Affiliation and Judges' Decisions," *American Political Science Review* 55 (December 1961): 843–60.

46. See Beverly Cook, "Women Judges and Public Policy in Sex Integration," in Debra Stewart, ed., *Women in Local Politics* (London: Scarecrow Press, 1980); Gerald S. Gryski, Eleanor C. Main, and William J. Dixon, "Models of State High Court Decision Making in Sex Discrimination Cases," *Journal of Politics* 48 (February 1986): 143–55; Melinda Gann Hall and Paul Brace, "Justices' Responses to Case Facts: An Interactive Model," *American Politics Quarterly* 24 (April 1996); Donald R. Songer and Kelley A. Crews-Meyer, "Does Judge Gender Matter? Decision Making in State Supreme Courts," *Social Science Quarterly* 81 (September 2000): 750–62.

47. Malcolm D. Holmes et al., "Judges' Ethnicity and Minority Sentencing: Evidence Concerning Hispanics," *Social Science Quarterly* 74 (September 1993): 496–505.

48. Darrell Steffernsmeier and Chester L. Britt, "Judges' Race and Judicial Decision Making: Do Black Judges Sentence Differently?" *Social Science Quarterly* 82 (December 2001): 749–64.

49. Richard C. Kearney and Reginald Sheehan, "Supreme Court Decision Making: The Impact of Court Composition on State and Local Government Litigation," *Journal of Politics* 54 (November 1992): 1008–25.

50. Bradley C. Canon, "Defining the Dimensions of Judicial Activism," *Judicature* 66 (December/January 1983): 236–47.

51. John J. Scheb III, Terry Bowen, and Gary Anderson, "Ideology, Role Orientations, and Behavior in the State Courts of Last Resort," *American Politics Quarterly* 19 (July 1991): 324–35.

52. Canon, "Defining the Dimensions," pp. 238–39.

53. As quoted in Stanley M. Mosk, "The Emerging Agenda in State Constitutional Law," *Intergovernmental Perspective* 13 (Spring 1987): 21.

54. Mark L. Glasser and John Kincaid, "Selected Rights Enumerated in State Constitutions," *Intergovernmental Perspective* 17 (Fall 1991): 35–44.

55. See John Patrick Hagan, "Patterns of Activism on State Supreme Courts," *Publius: The Journal of Federalism* 18 (Winter 1988): 97–115.

56. Canon, "Defining the Dimensions," pp. 246–47.

57. American Bar Association, *Standards,* pp. 97–104.

58. Charles G. Douglas III, "Innovative Appellate Court Processing: New Hampshire's Experience with Summary Affirmance," *Judicature* 69 (October/November 1985): 147–52.

59. Marcia J. Lim, "State of the Judiciary," in *The Book of the States, 1985–86.*

60. Alan Greenblatt, "Docket Science," *Governing* (June 2001): 40–42.

61. George F. Cole, "Performance Measures for the Trial Courts, Prosecution, and Public Defense," in U.S. Department of Justice, *Performance Measures for the Criminal Justice System* (October 1993), pp. 87–108.

62. Council of State Governments, *Book of the States,* Vol. 34 (Lexington Ky: Council of State Governments, 2002): 220–21.

63. Edward B. McConnell, "State Judicial Salaries: A National Perspective," *State Government* 61 (September/October 1988): 179–82.

64. Eric Slater, "Four Men Wrongly Jailed Get $36 Million Settlement," *The News and Observer* (March 6, 1999), p. 9A.

Chapter 10 **STATE-LOCAL RELATIONS** pp. 229–247

1. Charles Rabin, " Cities Can't Ban Use of Cellphones," *Miami Herald,* April 26, 2002, www. miami.com.

2. Steven D. Gold, "NCSL State-Local Task Force: The First Year," *Intergovernmental Perspective* 13 (Winter 1987): 11.

3. *Merriam* v. *Moody's Executors,* 25 Iowa 163, 170 (1868). Dillon's rule was first written in the case of

City of Clinton v. *Cedar Rapids and Missouri Railroad Co.* (1868).

4. U.S. Advisory Commission on Intergovernmental Relations, *The Organization of Local Public Economies* (Washington, D.C.: ACIR, December 1987), p. 54.

5. Joseph F. Zimmerman, *State-Local Relations* (New York: Praeger, 1983).

6. Peter J. May, "Policy Design and Discretion: State Oversight of Local Building Regulation," paper presented at the annual meeting of the American Political Science Association, San Francisco, 1996.

7. David R. Berman and Lawrence L. Martin, "State-Local Relations: An Examination of Local Discretion," *Public Administration Review* 48 (March/April 1988): 637–41.

8. Dale Krane, Platon N. Rigos, and Melvin B. Hill, Jr., *Home Rule in America: A Fifty State Handbook* (Washington, D.C.: Congressional Quarterly Press, 2001).

9. R. G. Downing, "Urban County Fiscal Stress," *Urban Affairs Quarterly* 27 (December 1991): 314–25.

10. U.S. Advisory Commission on Intergovernmental Relations, *State Laws Governing Local Government Structure and Administration* (Washington, D.C.: ACIR, 1993); Alan Greenblatt, "Enemies of the State," *Governing* 15 (June 2002): 26–31.

11. Renu Khator, "Coping with Coercion: Florida Counties and the State's Recycling Law," *State and Local Government Review* 26 (Fall 1994): 181–91.

12. Jane Massey and Edwin Thomas, *State-Mandated Local Government Expenditures and Revenue Limitations in South Carolina*, part 4 (Columbia: Bureau of Governmental Research and Service, University of South Carolina, March 1988).

13. David R. Berman, "State-Local Relations: Devolution, Mandates, and Money," in International City Management Association, *The Municipal Year Book 1997* (Washington, D.C.: ICMA, 1997).

14. Joseph F. Zimmerman, "State Mandate Relief: A Quick Look," *Intergovernmental Perspective* 20 (Spring 1994): 28–36.

15. George Pataki, as quoted in Alison Mitchell, "Governor Takes Message to New York City Council," *New York Times* (January 20, 1995), p. A16.

16. Gold, "NCSL State-Local Task Force," p. 12.

17. www.census.gov/govs/estimate/96stlus.txt (October 26, 2000).

18. See David R. Morgan and Robert E. England, "State Aid to Cities: A Causal Inquiry," *Publius: The Journal of Federalism* 14 (Spring 1984): 67–82; Keith J. Mueller, "Explaining Variation in State Assistance Programs to Local Communities: What to Expect and Why," *State and Local Government Review* 19 (Fall 1987): 101–7.

19. See Samuel Nunn and Mark S. Rosentraub, "Metropolitan Fiscal Equalization: Distilling Lessons from Four U.S. Programs," *State and Local Government Review* 28 (Spring 1996): 9–102.

20. Andree E. Reeves, "State ACIRs: Elements of Success," *Intergovernmental Perspective* 17 (Summer 1991): 13.

21. www. acir.state.va.us.

22. U.S. Advisory Commission on Intergovernmental Relations, *State-Local Relations Bodies: State ACIRs and Other Approaches* (Washington, D.C.: ACIR, 1981).

23. Ibid., pp. 38–40.

24. Anthony Downs, as cited in Joel Garreau, "From Suburbs, Cities Are Springing Up in Our Back Yards," *Washington Post* (March 8, 1987), p. A26.

25. Myron Orfield, *American Metropolitics: The New Suburban Reality* (Washington, D.C.: Brookings, 2002).

26. Jack Meltzner, *Metropolis to Metroplex* (Baltimore: Johns Hopkins University Press, 1984), p. 17.

27. Joel Garreau, *Edge City* (New York: Doubleday, 1991).

28. "Denver," Sierra Club, www.sierraclub.org/sprawl/report98.

29. William Fulton and Paul Shigley, "Operation Desert Sprawl," *Governing* 12 (August 1999): 16.

30. Ibid., p. 17.

31. Jayson T. Blair, "Maryland Draws Line Against Sprawl," *Boston Globe* (December 7, 1997), p. A26.

32. "Land Use Planning," Sierra Club, www.sierraclub.org/sprawl/report99.

33. U.S. General Accounting Office, *Local Growth Issues— Federal Opportunities and Challenges* (Washington, D.C.: U.S. GAO, September 2000).

34. Christopher R. Conte, "The Boys of Sprawl," *Governing* 13 (May 2000): 28–33; Peter Gordon and Harry W. Richardson, "The Sprawl Debate: Let Markets Plan," *Publius: The Journal of Federalism* 31 (Summer 2001): 131–49.

35. J. Edwin Benton and Darwin Gamble, "City/County Consolidation and Economics of Scale: Evidence from a Time Series Analysis in Jacksonville, Florida," *Social Science Quarterly* 65 (March 1984): 190–98.

36. Gary Alan Johnson and Suzanne Leland, "Stealing Back Home: How One City and County Beat the Odds and Successfully Consolidated Their Governments," paper presented at the annual meeting of the Midwest Political Science Association, Chicago, 2000.

37. David Rusk, *Cities Without Suburbs* (Washington, D.C.: Woodrow Wilson Center Press, 1993), p. 5.

38. Daniel Kemmis, as quoted in Neal R. Peirce, "Missoula's 'Citistate' Claim Marks a New Way to Define Regions," *The News & Observer* (July 1, 1993), p. 14A.

39. Sam Walker, "U.S. Cities Making Allies of the 'Burbs,'" *Christian Science Monitor* (September 4, 1997), p. 16.

40. Larry N. Gerston and Peter J. Haas, "Political Support for Regional Government in the 1990s," *Urban Affairs Quarterly* 29 (September 1993): 162–63.

41. Randolph P. Smith, "Region Idea Works, Oregon City Says," *Richmond Times-Dispatch* (October 30, 1994), pp. Al, A18.

42. Mark Baldassare, "Regional Variations in Support for Regional Governance," *Urban Affairs Quarterly* 30 (December 1994): 275–84.

43. Orfield, *American Metropolitics.*

44. DeWitt John, as cited in William K. Stevens, "Struggle for Recovery Altering Rural America," *New York Times* (February 5, 1988), p. 8.

45. Seroka, "Community Growth and Administrative Capacity," p. 45.

46. Beryl A. Radin et al., *New Governance for Rural America* (Lawrence: University Press of Kansas, 1996).

47. Joseph F. Zimmerman, "Partnership Government: State-Local Relations," *Spectrum* 74 (Summer 2001): 9–13.

48. George Pataki, "Governor Pataki Offers $1 Billion Plan to Help Local Governments," Press Release, January 10, 1997.

49. John Lawton, as quoted in "Preparing for a New Century," *Missoulian* (September 8, 1994), p. 10.

Chapter 11 **LOCAL GOVERNMENT: STRUCTURE AND LEADERSHIP** pp. 248–272

1. William Fulton and Paul Shigley, "Putting Los Angeles Together," *Governing* 13 (June 2000): 20–26; John H. Culver, "Reforming Los Angeles Government," *Comparative State Politics* 20 (October 1999): 41–44.

2. *1997 Census of Governments*, Vol. 1, *Government Organization* (Washington, D.C.: U.S. Census Bureau, 1999).

3. Council for Excellence in Government 2000, www. excelgov.org.

4. Victor S. DeSantis and Tari Renner, "Governing the County: Authority, Structure, and Elections," in David R. Berman, ed., *County Governments in an Era of Change* (Westport, Conn.: Greenwood, 1993), pp. 15–28.

5. J. Edwin Benton and Donald C. Menzel, "County Services: The Emergence of Full-Service Government," in Berman, ed., *County Governments in an Era of Change,* pp. 53–69.

6. Dale Kraue, Platon N. Rigos, and Melvin B. Hill, Jr., *Home Rule in America: A Fifty State Handbook* (Washington, D.C.: Congressional Quarterly Press, 2001).

7. Barbara P. Greene, "Counties and the Fiscal Challenges of the 1980s," *Intergovernmental Perspective* 13 (Winter 1987): 14–19.

8. Beverly A. Cigler, "Revenue Diversification Among U.S. Counties," paper presented at the annual meeting of the American Political Science Association, New York City, September 1994.

9. "Counties Out of Date," *State Legislatures* 17 (March 1991): 17.

10. Jonathan Walters, "The Disappearing County," www. governing.com (July 5, 2000).

11. Joel Miller, "Boundary Changes 1990–1995," in International City/County Management Association, *The Municipal Year Book 1997* (Washington, D.C.: International City/County Management Association, 1997).

12. James H. Svara, *Official Leadership in the City* (New York: Oxford University Press, 1990).

13. David R. Morgan, *Managing Urban America,* 2d ed. (Belmont, Calif.: Wadsworth, 1984).

14. Heywood T. Sanders, "The Government of American Cities: Continuity and Change in Structure," in International City Management Association, *The Municipal Year Book 1982* (Washington, D.C.: International City Management Association, 1982), pp. 178–86.

15. Melissa Conradi, "But Definitely Not St. Ventura," *Governing* 14 (January 2001): 16.

16. Gary A. Mattson, "Municipal Services and Economic Policy Priorities Among Florida's Smaller Cities," *National Civic Review* 79 (September/October 1990): 436–45.

17. Frank Bryan and John McClaughry, *The Vermont Papers* (Post Mills, Vt.: Chelsea Green, 1989).

18. Kathryn A. Foster, *The Political Economy of Special Purpose Government* (Washington, D.C.: Georgetown University Press, 1997).

19. U.S. Advisory Commission on Intergovernmental Relations, *State and Local Roles in the Federal System* (Washington, D.C.: ACIR, 1982), p. 154.

20. John C. Bollens, *Special District Governments in the United States* (Berkeley: University of California Press, 1957).

21. Charlie B. Tyer, "The Special Purpose District in South Carolina," in Charlie B. Tyer and Cole Blease Graham, Jr., eds., *Local Government in South Carolina* (Columbia, S.C.: Bureau of Governmental Research and Series, 1984), pp. 75–89.

22. Nancy Burns, *The Formation of American Local Governments* (New York: Oxford University Press, 1994).

23. Michael A. Molloy, " Local Special Districts and Public Accountability," paper presented at the annual meeting of the Midwest Political Science Association, Chicago, 2000.

24. Robert D. Thomas, Suphapong Boonyapratuang, and Renee Gilliam, "Local Government Complexity: Consequences for Counties," paper presented at the annual meeting of the American Political Science Association, Washington, August 1991.

25. Foster, *The Political Economy of Special Purpose Government.*

26. Scott Bollens, "Examining the Link Between State Policy and the Creation of Local Special Districts," *State and Local Government Review* 18 (Fall 1986): 117–24.

27. Jeffrey Henig et al., "Restructuring School Governance: Reform Ideas and Their Implementation," paper

presented at the annual meeting of the American Political Science Association, New York City, September 1994.

28. Gail Russell Chaddock, "Mayors, States Push School Boards Aside," *Christian Science Monitor* (February 26, 2002), pp. 1, 4.

29. Rob Gurwitt, "The Case of the Missing Schools," *Governing* 12 (September 1999): 21–26.

30. Jameson W. Doig and Erwin C. Hargrove, eds., *Leadership and Innovation* (Baltimore: Johns Hopkins University Press, 1987).

31. Floyd Hunter, *Community Power Structure* (Chapel Hill: University of North Carolina Press, 1953); and *Community Power Succession* (Chapel Hill: University of North Carolina Press, 1980).

32. Robert Dahl, *Who Governs?* (New Haven, Conn.: Yale University Press, 1961).

33. Clarence N. Stone, *Regime Politics: Governing Atlanta, 1948–1988* (Lawrence: University Press of Kansas, 1989).

34. Tom Lassetter, "Rock Group Takes on Ga. Town's Political Network," *The State* (July 25, 1999), p. A15.

35. George J. Gordon, *Public Administration in America,* 3d ed. (New York: St. Martin's, 1986).

36. Rob Gurwitt, "The Lure of the Strong Mayor," *Governing* 6 (July 1993): 36–41; Terrell Blodgett, "Beware the Lure of the 'Strong' Mayor," *Public Management* 76 (January 1994): 6–11.

37. David R. Morgan and Sheilah S. Watson, "The Effects of Mayoral Power on Urban Fiscal Policy," paper presented at the annual meeting of the American Political Science Association, New York City, September 1994.

38. Thomas P. Ryan, Jr., as quoted in Jane Mobley, "Politician or Professional? The Debate Over Who Should Run Our Cities Continues," *Governing* 1 (February 1988): 42–48.

39. Rob Gurwitt, " Black, White and Blurred," *Governing* 14 (September 2001): 20–14.

40. Huey L. Perry, "Deracialization as an Analytical Construct in American Urban Politics," *Urban Affairs Quarterly* 27 (December 1991): 181–91.

41. Mary E. Summers and Philip A. Klinkner, "The Daniels Election in New Haven and the Failure of the Deracialization Hypothesis," *Urban Affairs Quarterly* 27 (December 1991): 202–15.

42. Several of these studies are summarized in Susan A. MacManus and Charles S. Bullock III, "Women and Racial/Ethnic Minorities in Mayoral and Council Positions," in International City/County Management Association, *The Municipal Year Book 1993* (Washington, D.C.: International City/County Management Association, 1993), pp. 70–84.

43. Jon Jeter, "In Minnesota, Political Views Change with Minority Influx," *Washington Post* (March 3, 1998), p. A1.

44. Rob Gurwitt, "Mysteries of Urban Momentum," *Governing* 15 (April 2002): 26–29.

45. Clifford J. Wirth and Michael L. Vasu, "Ideology and Decision Making for American City Managers," *Urban Affairs Quarterly* 22 (March 1987): 454–74.

46. This subject is debated in H. George Frederickson, *Ideal & Practice in Council-Manager Government* (Washington, D.C.: International City Management Association, 1989).

47. Wayne F. Anderson, Chester A. Newland, and Richard J. Stillman II, *The Effective Local Government Manager* (Washington, D.C.: International City Management Association, 1983), pp. 45–73.

48. Ibid., p. 48.

49. Timothy Bledsoe, *Careers in City Politics: The Case for Urban Democracy* (Pittsburgh: University of Pittsburgh Press, 1993), p. 50.

50. Larry Azevedo, as quoted in Alan Ehrenhalt, "How a Liberal Government Came to Power in a Conservative Suburb," *Governing* 1 (March 1988): 51–56.

51. Kenneth Prewitt, *The Recruitment of Political Leaders: A Study of Citizen-Politicians* (Indianapolis: Bobbs-Merrill, 1970).

52. MacManus and Bullock, "Women and Racial/Ethnic Minorities in Mayoral and Council Positions," pp. 70–84.

53. Bari Anhalt, "Minority Representation and the Substantive Representation of Interests," paper presented at the annual meeting of the American Political Science Association, San Francisco, 1996.

54. Kenneth E. Yeager, *Trailblazers: Profiles of America's Gay and Lesbian Elected Officials* (Binghamton, N.Y.: Haworth, 1999).

55. Susan Welch and Timothy Bledsoe, *Urban Reform and Its Consequences* (Chicago: University of Chicago Press, 1988).

56. James Svara, "Council Profile: More Diversity, Demands, Frustration," *Nation's Cities Weekly* 14 (November 18, 1991): 4.

57. Dick Simpson et al., "City Council Coalitions and Mayoral Regimes in Chicago from 1955–1995," paper presented at the annual meeting of the American Political Science Association, Washington, D.C., 1997.

58. National Municipal League, "All-America Cities 1985–1986 Continue a Heritage of Achievement," *National Civic Review* 75 (May/June 1986): 130–37.

59. Harry P. Hatry, "Would We Know a Well-Governed City If We Saw One?" *National Civic Review* 75 (May/June 1986): 142–46.

Chapter 12 **TAXING AND SPENDING** pp. 273–304

1. David Firestone, "Fiscal Stature of Tennessee Slips in War Over Taxes," *New York Times* (August 23, 2001), pp. 1–3.

2. American Council on Intergovernmental Relations, *Significant Features of Fiscal Federalism,* Vol. 2 (Washington: D.C.: ACIR, 1998), Table 14.

3. Ibid., pp. 182–83.

4. Ivan Sciupac, "Federal Estate Tax Repeal Would Affect States," www.stateline.org (March 16, 2001).

5. U.S Bureau of the Census, October 2000, www.census.gov.

6. Robert Tannenwald and Jonathan Cowan, "Fiscal Capacity, Fiscal Need, and Fiscal Comfort Among U.S. States: New Evidence," *Publius: The Journal of Federalism* 27 (Summer 1997): 113–25.

7. ACIR, *Significant Features of Fiscal Federalism,* Vol. 2 (1998), Table 54.

8. ACIR, *Significant Features of Fiscal Federalism,* Vol. 1 (1993), pp. 149–54.

9. Mark Schneider, "Local Budgets and the Maximization of Local Property Wealth in the System of Suburban Government," *Journal of Politics* 49 (November 1987): 1114.

10. Thomas R. Dye and Richard C. Feiock, "State Income Tax Adoption and Economic Growth," *Social Science Quarterly* 76 (September 1995): 648–54.

11. Edward T. Howe and Donald J. Reeb, "The Historical Evolution of State and Local Tax Systems," *Social Science Quarterly* 78 (March 1997): 116.

12. ACIR, *Significant Features of Fiscal Federalism,* Vol. 2 (1994), pp. 96–97; "Exemptions on Edibles," *Governing* 9 (February 1996): 43; Council of State Governments, *Book of the States* 34 (Lexington, Ky: CSG, 2002), p. 289.

13. Neal R. Peirce, "Service Tax May Rise Again," *Public Administration Times* 11 (August 12, 1988): 2.

14. Laura Wilbert, "Taxing Times in Cyberspace," *New England Financial Journal* 3 (Summer 2000): 14–16; David C. Powell, "Internet Taxation and U.S. Intergovernmental Relations: From *Quill* to the Present," *Publius* 30 (Winter 2000): 39–51; Penelope Lemor, "The Untaxables," *Governing* (July 2002): 36–37.

15. *Quill* v. *North Dakota* 504 U.S. 298 (1992).

16. Powell, "Internet Taxation and U.S. Intergovernmental Relations,"

17. On "sin taxes," see Cathy M. Johnson and Kenneth J. Meier, "The Wages of Sin: Taxing America's Legal Vices," *Western Political Quarterly* 43 (September 1990): 577–96.

18. Steve Marantz, "Tax Targets Sox Foes," www.bostonherald.com, April 2, 2002.

19. *State and Local Sourcebook.* 2002, p.138.

20. Jerry Kolo and Todd J. Dicker, "Practical Issues in Adopting Local Impact Fees," *State and Local Government Review* 25 (Fall 1993): 197–206.

21. Council of State Governments, 2002: Table 7.13.

22. www.apfc.org/alaska/dividendprgrm.cfm (March 28, 2002).

23. John L. Mikesell, "Lotteries in State Revenue Systems: Gauging a Popular Revenue Source After 35 Years," *State and Local Government Review* 33 (Spring 2001): 86–100.

24. Ibid.; see also Donald E. Miller and Patrick A. Pierce, "Lotteries for Education: Windfall or Hoax?" *State and Local Government Review* 29 (Winter 1997): 43–52.

25. See, for example, Mary Herring and Timothy Bledsoe, "A Model of Lottery Participation: Demographics, Context, and Attitudes," *Policy Studies Journal* 22, no. 2 (1994): 245–57.

26. Matt Richtel, "U.S. Companies Profit from Surge in Internet Gambling," *New York Times* (July 6, 2001), pp. 1–4; Reuters, "Gambling's Future on the Net Is Risky Bet," *Miami Herald,* international edition (March 4, 1998), pp. C1, C2.

27. Hovey and Hovey, p. 236.

28. Mark A. Glaser and W. Bartley Hildreth, "A Profile of Discontinuity Between Citizen Demand and Willingness to Pay Taxes: Comprehensive Planning for Park and Recreation Investment," *Public Budgeting and Finance* 16 (Winter 1996): 97.

29. Penelope Lemov, "Educating the Elusive Taxpayer," *Governing* 10 (September 1997): 68–69.

30. See Sherry Tvedt, "Enough Is Enough! Proposition 2½ in Massachusetts," *National Civic Review* 70 (November 1981): 527–33.

31. ACIR, *Significant Features of Fiscal Federalism,* Vol. 2, pp. 102–3.

32. Tyson King-Meadows and David Lowery, "The Impact of the Tax Revolt Era State Fiscal Caps: A Research Update," *Public Budgeting and Finance* 16 (Spring 1996): 102–12; James C. Clingermayer and B. Dan Wood, "Disentangling Patterns of State Debt Financing," *American Political Science Review* 89 (March 1995): 108–20; Daniel E. O'Toole and Brian Stipak, "Coping with State Tax and Expenditure Limitation: The Oregon Experience," *State and Local Government Review* 30 (Winter 1998): 9–16.

33. James W. Endersby and Michael J. Towle, "Effects of Constitutional and Political Controls on State Expenditures," *Publius: The Journal of Federalism* 27 (Winter 1997): 83–98.

34. Alan Sokolow, "The Changing Property Tax and State-Local Relations," *Publius: The Journal of Federalism* 28 (Winter 1998): 165–87.

35. Rob Gurwitt, "The Job of Rudy Giuliani," *Governing* 8 (June 1995): 23–27.

36. "Losing Control," *New York Times* (November 13, 2001), pp. 1–2.

37. David Brunori, *State Tax Policy: A Political Perspective* (Washington, D.C.: The Urban Institute, 2001).

38. Michael A. Pagano and Jocelyn Johnston, "Life at the Bottom of the Fiscal Food Chain: Examining City and

Council Revenue Decisions," *Publius: The Journal of Federalism* 30 (Winter 2000): 159–70.

39. Kirk Jonas, Gregory J. Rest, and Terry Atkinson, "Virginia's Revenue Forecasting Process and Models," *Public Budgeting and Finance* 12 (Summer 1992): 70–81.

40. John E. Petersen, "Don't Forget Your Umbrella," *Governing* 11 (October 1998): 70.

41. "Budget Shortfalls Lead States to Dip Into Rainy Day Funds," *The Washington Times* (February 5, 2002), www.washtimes.com.

42. Sallie Hofmeister, "Fund Head Resigns in California" and "Many Questions, But Too Late," *New York Times* (December 6, 1994), pp. D1, D2.

43. Adam Pertman, "Orange County Officials Reap Bitter Fruit," *Boston Globe* (July 16, 1995), p. A6; Kevin P. Kearns, "Accountability and Entrepreneurial Public Management: The Case of the Orange County Investment Fund," *Public Budgeting and Finance* 15 (Fall 1995): 3–21.

44. Christopher Swope, "Mississippi Signs on the Assembly Line," *Governing* 14 (January 2001): 62.

45. John H. Bowman, Susan MacManus, and John L. Mikesell, "Mobilizing Resources for Public Services Financing," *Urban Affairs* 14 (March 4, 1992): 311–35.

INDEX

Abortion, 32, 53, 62, 83, 96, 127, 129, 147, 218, 221
Accountable legislatures, 130
ACIR, 56, 66, 230, 231–32, 236–37
Adams, John, 27, 50
Administrative agencies and departments. *See* Bureaucracy
Administrative case, 203
Administrative efficiency, 23
Administrative procedure acts, 85
Administrative rules and regulations review, 137–38
"Adopt a Highway" program, 87
Advertising in campaigns, 108–10
Advisory commissions on intergovernmental relations, 236–37
Advisory committee, 85
Affirmative action, 185–87
AFL-CIO, 99
African Americans, 13–14, 24, 56, 71, 118, 120, 121, 145, 186, 214, 263–65, 267, 270
AIDS, 9, 17, 43, 293, 302
AIDS Institute, 9
Aiken, George A., 151
Air Quality Act, 31
Alabama, 12, 44, 53, 55, 57, 76, 97, 118, 131, 152, 154, 167, 176, 205, 290, 299
    Mobile, 282
Alaska, 41, 60, 64, 76, 87, 118, 122, 145–46, 207, 234, 250, 276, 282, 284, 287
Alcohol, Drug Abuse, and Mental Health Block Grant, 43
America Online, 283
American Bar Association, 208–9, 211
American Civil Liberties Union, 186–87
American Red Cross, 8
Americans with Disabilities Act, 43
Anaya, Tony, 145
Annexation, 259
Anti-Federalists, 20
Appalachian Regional Commission (ARC), 33
Appellate courts, 205, 218
    jurisdiction, 204, 205
Appointment power of governors, 155–57

Apportionment of legislative districts, 119–21
Arkansas, 76–77, 101, 103, 117, 131, 134, 177, 207
    Little Rock, 197
Argentina, 22
Arizona, 14, 34, 44, 56, 62, 75, 76, 87, 104, 112, 136, 145, 160, 168–69, 189, 196–97, 217, 219, 224, 233, 260, 280
    Flagstaff, 98
    Phoenix, 3, 196–97, 237, 256
    Scottsdale, 197
Articles of Confederation, 25–27
Ashcroft, John, 21–22, 145
Asian Americans, 13–14, 145
Association of State Highway and Transportation Officials, 7
Astroturfing, 106
At-large elections, 267
Attorney general, 168
Auditing function of legislatures, 139
Audits and budget cycles, 176–79

Babbitt, Bruce, 160
Back-door strategies, 226
Baker v. Carr (1962), 119
Baker v. Vermont, 47
Barnes v. Glen Theatre Inc. (1991), 202
Beer, Samuel H., 45
Belton, Sharon Sayles, 264–65
Bench trial, 216
Benefit principal, 278, 286
Bennett, Robert F., 162
Berns, Walter, 27
Bevilacqua, Joseph A., 215
Bill of Rights, 57–58
Bills, legislative, 127–30
Bird, Rose, 213
Blacks. *See* African Americans
Blanket primary, 76
Block grants, 35, 41
Board of commissioners (or supervisors), 251
Bloomberg, Michael, 261, 293–94
Bond bank, 298
Bonds, 182, 297–98
    general obligation, 182, 297–98
    industrial development, 297–98

ratings, 298
revenue, 182, 297–98
Borrowing and debt, 295–98
Boston Gazette, 120
Boutique courts, 224
Brady Handgun Violence Protection Act, 11
Brown, Jerry, 167
Brown, Willie, 134
Buckley v. Valeo (1976), 112
Budgets (budgeting), 176–82
    balanced, 178, 295
    capital, 182, 295
    centralized (unified court), 222–23
    cycle, 176–79
    deficits, 295
    governors' power, 160–61, 179
    incrementalism, 181, 194
    line-item, 181, 182
    management and planning, 182
    operating, 182, 295
    participants (actors), 179–80
    performance, 182
    tax- or revenue-anticipation notes, 295
    types, 181
Bumper-sticker policy spot, 109
Bureau of the Census, U.S., 13, 15–16, 258
Bureaucracy (administrative agencies and departments), 172–201
    employees, 172–76
    governors, 149–51
    legislative oversight, 135–39
    personnel policy, 183–91
        affirmative action, 185–87
        equal employment opportunity (EEO), 185
        merit system, 183–91
        neutral competence, 183
        representative bureaucracy, 185, 187
        reverse discrimination, 186
        sexual harassment, 187–88
        unions and collective bargaining, 188–91, 195, 196
    politics, 192–94
        bureaucratic discretion, 192
        clientele groups, 192–94
        professionalism, 193–94
    quality, 198–200

Bureaucracy (administrative agencies and departments) (*cont.*)
  reinventing government, 194–98
    e-government, 197–98
    privatization, 196–97
    total quality management, 195–96, 198
  reorganization power of governors, 161–62
  representative, 185
  Web sites, 201
Bureaucratic discretion, 192
Burger, Warren, 220–21
Burns, Nancy, 260
Bush, George, 38, 145
Bush, George W., 39, 142, 145, 165, 166–67, 206
Bush, John E. (Jeb), 145, 187, 229

Calhoun, John, C., 27–28
California, 2, 3, 8, 9, 11, 12, 14, 16, 44, 53, 57, 62–63, 75, 79, 98, 105, 106, 111, 115, 122, 123, 125–26, 133, 134, 143, 145, 146, 150, 159, 162, 167, 178, 212, 213, 217, 221, 223, 227, 244, 252, 253, 274, 275, 280–81, 282, 294
  Concord, 267
  Indian Gaming Initiative, 83
  Los Angeles, 15, 83, 107, 150, 280
  Los Angeles County, 8, 167, 191, 206–7, 222, 248, 250, 259
  Oakland, 167, 194, 257
  Orange County, 297
  Proposition 13, 81, 280–81, 291
  Proposition 209, 32, 186–87
  Riverside, 196
  San Diego, 256
  San Fernando Valley, 248
  San Francisco, 134, 242, 250, 267
  San Francisco Bay area, 267, 280–81
  San Jose, 244
  Santa Monica, 98
California Plan for selecting judges, 212
Campaign finance, 110–13
Campaign reform, 111–12
Campaigns, 107–13
  consultants, 110
  financing, 107, 110–13
  gubernatorial, 145–46
  mass media, 108–9
  negative, 109–10
  public funding, 112–13
  Web sites, 114

Campaigns & Elections (magazine), 96, 108–9
Canada, 22, 24
Capacity enhancement, 227
Capacity of state and local governments, 3–11, 18, 235
  increase in, 6–11
  presence in Washington, D.C., 7
  state reform, 6–7
Capital budgets, 182, 295
Caribbean Islands, 289
Carter, Jimmy, 167
Caseloads, court, 219, 223–24
Categorical grants, 35–36
Cellucci, Paul, 81
Centralized budgeting (unified court budgeting), 222–23
Charter, 253
Charter schools, 9, 261
Checchi, Al, 146
Chesapeake Bay, 8
Christian right, 96
Circuit breaker, 281
Cities, 253–57
  councils, 266–70
  managers, 263–66
  mayors, 253–55
  structures, 253–56
Citizen access to government, 84–87
  advisory committee, 85–86
  participation, 80–84, 87–88
  surveys, 86
Citizens' Conference on State Legislatures (CCSL), 130–31
Citizen Voice, 68–69
Citron, Robert L., 297
City commission form of government, 256–57
City councils, 266–70
City-county consolidation, 242–43
Civil cases, 203, 205
Civil Rights Act of 1964, 72, 187
Civil rights and liberties, 58
Civil service, 58, 157–58, 183–84
Civil Service Reform Act of 1978, 183
Civil War and Reconstruction, 52, 183
Clientele groups, 192
Clinton, Bill, 167, 195
Closed primary, 76
Coattail effect, 78
Collective bargaining, 188–191
Colorado, 62, 72, 75, 82, 85, 106, 112, 117, 130, 133, 136, 167, 204–5, 227, 260, 280, 282
  Denver, 238, 264, 282

Comiskey Park, Chicago, 8
Commerce clause, 29
Common law, 203
Commonwealths, 51
Compact theory, 27, 36
Compensation
  judges, 224–25
  legislators, 121–22
Conant, James K., 161
Confederacy, 22
Confederate States of America, 28, 52
Conference committees, 123
Conflict
  federal system, 23
  interjurisdictional, 12–13
  national-state, 10–11
Congress, U.S., 2, 7, 8, 10, 15, 18, 20, 23, 25–26, 30, 34–35, 38, 41–43, 44, 60, 84, 119, 132, 142, 152, 186, 275, 283, 300, 302
Connecticut, 12–13, 26, 49, 75, 111, 112, 125–26, 127, 130, 169–70, 198, 221, 231, 250, 257, 285
  Bridgeport, 282
  Charter Oak, 49
  Constitution of 1818, 49
  Fundamental Orders of 1639, 49
  Hartford, 145, 257
Constitution, U.S., 11, 24–26, 28–30, 33, 36, 48, 50, 52–53, 56–58, 60, 66, 84, 109
  Amendments, 27, 30–33, 72, 119, 158, 185, 202, 205
Constitutional commission, 65–66
Constitutional conventions, 64–65
Constitutional initiative, 62–64
Constitutions, state, 47–67
  changing (amending or revising), 56–66
  dual constitutionalism, 48
  evolution, 49
  excessive length, 52–55
  executive powers, 51–52
  first, 49–51
  fundamental law, 48
  higher-law tradition, 57
  initiative, 52, 62–64
  judicial review, 61
  legislative supremacy, 51
  Model State Constitution, 56–60
  positive-law tradition, 57
  recall, 52
  referendum, 52

reform, 48–49, 56–60, 66–67
weaknesses, 52–56
Cooperative federalism, 36–39
Correctional Corporation of American, 227
Council-administrator plan, 252
Council-manager, 263, 265–66
Council of American-Islamic Relations, 73
Council of State Governments, 7
Counties, 250–52
council-administrator plan, 252
council-elected executive plan, 252
County commission, 251
County party organizations, 94–95
Courts, state (court systems). *See also* Judges
appellate, 217
criminal justice, 225–27
intermediate appellate, 205, 225
reform, 206–7, 222–25
structure, 204–7
supreme, 217
trends, 221–22
trial, 217
Web sites, 228
Criminal case, 203, 205
Crises management, governor's role, 150

Dairy Queen, 245
Davis, Gray, 145, 146
Dealignment, 98
Dean, Howard, 47
Declaration of Independence, 25
Delegates, legislative, 126
Delaware, 64, 131, 145, 231, 282
Deming, W. Edwards, 195
Democratic party, 92–98. *See also* Political parties
recent state elections, 78–79
runoff primaries, 77–78
"yellow dog," 93
Departments of community affairs, 236–37
Deracialization, 263–64
Determinate sentencing, 226
Devolution, 38
Digital divide, 87
Dillon, John F., 230
Dillon's rule, 230, 249
Direct action, 107
Direct initiative, 62

Districts
school, 260–62
special, 258–60
Diversity, 18
Divided government, 97
Doctrinal diversity, 218
Downsizing, 12
Drug Enforcement Administration, U.S., 21
Dual constitutionalism, 48
Dual court system, 206
Dual federalism, 36
Due process, 30

E-commerce, 294
E-Government, 86, 161
Earmarking, 294
Easley v. Cromartie, 121
Eastman Kodak Company, 12
Economic development, 152, 298–99
Edgar, Jim, 167
Edge cities, 237
Egypt, 22
Elazar, Daniel, 16–17
Elections, 68–84. *See also* Voting
2002, 79, 118
at-large, 267
district (ward), 267
general, 77–78
gubernatorial, 145–46
judicial, 208–11
non-partisan, 78–79, 210–11
primaries, 77–78
recent, 78–79, 118
referendum, 80–81
run-offs, 77–78
Electoral College, 15
Elite theory, 262
Ellis Island, 34
Employees of states and localities, 175–76
Engler, John, 152
Enumerated (delegated) powers, 27
Equal Employment Opportunity Commission (EEOC), 185
Equal protection of the laws, 30
Equal rights amendments, 57
Equalization formula, 261–62
Equity of taxation, 277–79
Erikson, Robert, 93
Estate tax, 275, 285
Ethnic groups (ethnicity), 13–14, 118
Executive amendment, 159
Executive boards and commissions, 56

Executive branch, 25, 51–52, 143
legislatures, 135–39
Model State Constitution, 58–59
officials, 168–70. *See also* Governors
Executive orders, 161, 188
Expenditures, 35, 289–90, 298–302
economic development, 298–300
education policy, 300
social welfare and health care policy, 300–2

Factions, 24, 25, 95–96, 148
FAIIR, 130–132
Fair Labor Standards Act (FLSA), 31
Family Support Act of 1988, 300
Fay, Thomas F., 215
Federal Emergency Management Agency (FEMA), 151
Federal funds, 30, 39–43, 152, 235, 275
Federal mandates, 10, 41–43, 194, 233
Federal preemption, 30, 42–43
Federal revenue transfers, 274–75
Federalism (federal system), 4, 20, 22–45, 152
advantages and disadvantages of, 23–24
compact theory of, 27
concept of, 22–24
cooperative (1933–1964), 36–37
creative, 37
defined, 4
dual (1787–1932), 36
federal funds and, 30
future of, 43–45
history of, 24–33
early history of, 24–26
growth of national power, 28–32
state-centered, 27–28
judicial, 47–48, 206
models of, 36–39
nation-centered, 30–32
new, 37–39
Web sites, 46
Federalists, 20, 27
Feel-good spot, 109
Financial World (magazine), 151
Fifth Circuit Court, 186
Finance, 273–76, 302–3. *See also* Expenditure; Revenues; Taxes
limited discretion, 294–95
Model State Constitution, 59
principals, 273–76
diversity, 275–76
interdependence, 274–75
state and local, 302–3

Financial relations, intergovernmental, 35–36
Fines against lawyers and litigants, 223
Fiscal stress, 292–94
Fiscal years, 176
Five Nations of the Iroquois, 49
Flat tax, 278
Florida, 8, 9, 11, 12, 14, 17, 32–33, 65–66, 74, 75, 76–77, 84, 87, 105, 111, 112, 119, 133, 145, 168, 178, 184, 187, 206, 219, 229, 231, 232–33, 235, 243, 260, 264, 282, 283, 284, 288, 302
    Dade County, 9
    Miami, 197, 229
    Jacksonville-Duval County, 242–43
    Tampa, 8
Ford Foundation, 2
Formula grants, 35
France, 22, 274
Freedom, individual, 23–24
Front-door strategies, 226–27
Frostbelt, 14–15, 245
Full faith and credit clause, 33
Functional legislatures, 130
Fundamental Orders of 1639, 49
Fund-raising by legislative leaders, 123
Fusion, 78

Gaebler, Ted, 195
Gambling, 287–89
Garcia v. San Antonio Metropolitan Transit Authority, 31–32
Garfield, James, 183
Garreau, Joel, 237
Gasoline tax, 285
Germany, 152
General Agreement on Tariffs and Trade (GATT), 43
General elections, 77–78
General jurisdiction, 204
General obligation bonds, 297
General-purpose local governments, 230, 249, 257, 259–60
General revenue sharing, 38
General welfare clause, 29
Georgia, 12, 14, 53, 56, 76–77, 97, 122, 142, 159, 166–67, 184, 207, 285
    Athens, 262
    Atlanta, 80, 237
Gerry, Elbridge, 120
Gerrymander, 120
Gerston, Larry, 244

Gibbons v. Ogden (1824), 29
Giuliani, Rudolph, 95, 293
Glendening, Parris, 240–41
Gore, Al, 195
Government Performance Project, 198–200
Governors, 140–71. *See also* Executive branch
    campaigns, 145–46
    ceremonial leader, 151
    chief administrator, 149–51
    chief legislator, 147–49
    economic development promoter, 152
    executive branch officials, 168–70
        Attorney General, 168
        Lieutenant Governor, 168–69
        Secretary of State, 170
        Treasurer, 169–70
    formal powers, 154–64
        appointments, 155–58, 213–14
        budgetary, 160–61
        relevance, 163–64
        reorganization, 161–62
        staffing, 162–63
        tenure, 154–55
        veto, 149, 158–60
    history, 142–45
    informal powers, 154, 164–67
        characteristics, 166–67
        tools, 164–66
    intergovernmental coordinator, 151–52
    legislative process, 129
    party leader, 153–54
    personal characteristics, 166–67
    policymaker, 146–47
    removal from office, 167–68
    state constitutions, 51–52
    Web sites, 171
Grant, Ulysses S., 183
Grassroots lobbying, 106
Graves, W. Brooke, 66
Great Binding Law, 49
Great Compromise, 26
Great Depression, 29, 36, 237, 298
Great Plains, 245
Green party, 265
Gibbons v. Ogden (1824), 29
Gulick, Luther, 5
Gun Free School Zones Act of 1990, 32

HIV, 41
Haas, Peter, 244
Hall, Melinda Gann, 218

Hamilton, Alexander, 28–29
Hawaii, 8, 60, 73, 112, 113, 115, 122, 145, 159, 207, 217, 234, 276, 283, 285, 302
Head Start, 300
Health-care expenditures, 300–302
Hedge, David, 3
Higher-law tradition, 57, 66
Hispanic, 13–14, 186–187, 214, 219, 220, 267, 270
Hobbes, Thomas, 24
Home rule, 231, 249, 250, 253
Homestead exemption, 281
Hooker, Thomas, 49
Hopwood v. Texas, 186
Hrebenar, Ronald, 101, 103–4
Hull, Jane, 145
Hunt, Guy, 167
Hunt, Jim, 151, 155, 166–67
Hyperpluralism, 103

Idaho, 74, 76, 134, 282
    Boise, 116, 145
Illinois, 63, 112, 155, 167, 184, 225, 233, 257
    Chicago, 79, 106, 184, 194, 196, 204, 259, 269–70
Immigration, 13–14
Impact fee, 240
Impeachment, 167, 214–15
Implied powers, 29
Income tax, 112–13, 275, 278. *See also* Taxes
Income tax bracket, 278–79
Incorporation, 253
Incremental budgeting, 181, 194
Independent legislatures, 130
Indexing, 280
Indiana, 76, 113, 117, 176, 178, 202, 231, 257, 295, 299
    Indianapolis, 118, 197
    Indianapolis-Marion County, 242
Indirect initiative, 62
Individual freedom, 23–24
Individualistic political culture, 17
Industrial development bond (IDB), 297–98
Industrial Revolution, 29, 51, 152
Informal powers of governors, 154, 164–67
Informed legislatures, 130
Initiatives, 62–64, 81–84
Innovations, 8–9, 23
"Innovations in American Government" award, 2

Interest groups, 98–107, 127, 159, 160, 163, 165, 176–77, 179, 190, 193, 219
  local-level, 107
  public interest research groups (PIRGs), 101
  state-level, 101–3
  techniques, 103–7
  types, 99–101
Intergovernmental relations, 4
Intergovernmental transfers, 274–75
Intermediate appellate court, 205, 225
Intermodal Surface Transportation Efficiency Act (ISTEA), 243–44
Internal Revenue Service, 172
International City/County Management Association, 7, 265
Internet, 283, 289
Internet Tax Freedom Act, 283
Interstate commerce clause, 29, 283
Interstate compact clause, 33
Interstate relations, 9–11, 33–34
Interstate rendition clause, 33
Investment pools, 296
Iowa, 3, 14, 64, 75, 76, 104, 167, 217, 231, 242

Jackson, Andrew, 28, 183
Jefferson, Thomas, 27, 28, 56, 64
Jock tax, 285
Johnson, Gary, 148
Johnson, Lyndon B., 37
Joint committees, 123
Joint Legislative Audit and Review Commission (JLARC), 137
Judges, 208–221. *See also* Judiciary (judicial system)
  caseload management, 223–24
  compensation, 224–25
  decision-making, 215–20
    appellate court, 217
    legal system, 217–19
    personal, 219–20
    trial court, 215–17
  new federalism, 206, 220–21
    judicial activism, 220–21
  selection, 208–15
    gubernatorial appointment, 213
    legislative, 208
    merit plan, 211–13
    nonpartisan popular election, 210–11
    partisan popular election, 208–9
    removal, 214–15

Judicial activism, 220–21
Judicial federalism, 220–21
Judicial review, 61
Judiciary (judicial system), 202–28. *See also* Courts, state; Judges
  growth of national power, 28–30
  Model State Constitution, 58
  New Judicial Federalism, 220–21
Judiciary Act of 1789, 28
Jurisdiction, 3, 204–6
Jury trials, 216
Justice, U.S. Department of, 31

Kansas, 75, 83, 93, 111, 115, 126, 162, 217, 248–49, 257, 299
Kentucky, 50–51, 66, 77, 104, 106, 112, 117, 120, 176, 218, 231, 236, 262, 285
Kestnbaum Commission, 56, 66
Kids Voting USA, 71
King, Angus, 148, 153–54
Korea, 152
Kunin, Madeleine, 136

La Follette, Robert, 97
Lasswell, Harold, 176
Leach, Richard, 66
Leadership skills, of governors, 166–67
Leavitt, Mike, 151, 165
Legislative branch, 25. *See also* Legislatures, state
  Model State Constitution, 58
Legislative districts, 58, 119–21
  redistricting, 120–21
Legislative oversight, 137–39
Legislative process, 126–30, 137–39
Legislative proposals, 61–62
Legislative supremacy, 51
Legislative veto, 129, 136–37
Legislatures, state, 115–40
  bicameral, 118
  capacity, 130–35, 139
  caucuses, 123
  committees, 123–25, 128
  compensation, 121–22
  composition, 118–19
  executive branch (governors), 135–39, 147–49
  functions, 116, 123, 138–39
  fundraising, 123
  informal norms, 125–26
  ideal, 130–31
  issues, 116

  leadership, 122–23
  oversight, 116, 137–39
  public opinion, 126
  reform, 130–35
    effects, 131–32
    ideal characteristics, 130–31
    term limits, 132–35
  rules and procedures, 127–30
  sessions, 117–18
  term limits, 58, 132–35, 139
  terms of office, 118
  unwritten policies, 125–26
  Web sites, 140
Libertarian party, 97–98
License plates, specialty, 8
Lieske, Joel, 17
Lieutenant governors, 168–69
Limited jurisdiction, 205
Line-item veto, 58–59, 159, 160
Lobbying, 104–106, 149, 177, 190, 283
  grassroots, 106
Local government(s), 248–271. *See also* State-local relations
  capacity. *See* capacity of state and local governments
  functions, 2–3
  governance, 270–71
  leadership, 262–70
    mayors and managers, 263–66
    city councils, 266–70
  Model State Constitution, 59
  types, 249–62
    county, 250–52
    municipalities, 253–57
    school districts, 260–62
    special districts, 258–60
    towns and townships, 257–58
  Web sites, 271–72
Local party organizations, 94–96
Locke, Gary, 145
Locke, John, 51
Loftus, Tom, 127
Long, Russell, 280
Lopez, Alfonso, 31–32
Lotteries, 287–89
Louisiana, 53, 56, 76, 88, 118, 132, 136, 186, 218, 226, 250, 280, 287
  Baton Rouge, 282
  New Orleans, 242, 282
Lungren, Dan, 145

Madison, James, 23–24, 25, 27
Magna Carta, 49, 51

Maine, 8, 73, 74, 104, 113, 134, 148, 154, 156, 159, 168–69, 224, 226, 241
Major trial court, 205
Malapportionment, 119
Manchin, A. James, 169
Mandate-reimbursement requirements, 233
Mandates
    federal, 10, 41–43, 194, 233
    state, 235, 293, 295
Marshall, John, 28–29
Martinez, Bob, 145
Martz, Judy, 145
Maryland, 8, 12, 28, 53, 64–65, 109, 113, 118, 120, 163, 217, 234, 240–41
    Baltimore, 9, 53, 250
Massachusetts, 3, 9, 18, 26, 32, 44, 49–51, 57, 62, 81, 88, 93, 106, 113, 117, 120, 134, 158, 169–70, 184, 196, 202, 218–19, 221, 252, 257, 281, 283, 291–92
    Boston, 197, 202, 261
    Proposition 2½, 291–92
Matching requirements, 36
Matheson, Scott, 166
May, Peter, 231
Mayflower, 12
Mayor-council form of government, 253–55
Mayors, 253–57
    Web sites, 272
McCall, Tom, 156
McCallum, Scott, 1, 18
McCulloch v. Maryland (1819), 28–29
McIver, John, 93
Media, 17, 71, 72, 101, 104, 126, 136, 163, 165, 283, 290
Medicaid, 301–2
Merit plan for selecting judges, 211–13
Merit system, 59, 150, 157
Mexico, 152
Michigan, 3, 75, 101, 106, 112, 117, 132, 133, 152, 176, 187–88, 217, 231, 257, 262, 282
    Detroit, 194, 244, 261, 292
Microsoft Corporation, 10
Migration, 14–16
Miller, Zell, 166–67
Minner, Ruth Ann, 145

Minnesota, 4, 8, 9, 44, 73, 74, 87, 96, 98, 101, 111, 113, 115, 131, 143, 148, 154, 164, 198, 209, 221, 226, 244, 257, 258, 289
    Minneapolis, 9, 244, 264–65
    St. Paul, 107, 244
    Travis County, 96
Mississippi, 9–10, 18, 44, 62, 74, 76–77, 80, 88, 91, 93, 97, 118, 136, 160, 168, 177, 186, 189, 217, 221, 245, 282, 285, 288–89, 298–99
Missouri, 112, 138, 145, 211, 217, 257, 285
    Jefferson City, 116
    Kansas City, 11
    St. Louis, 80, 250
Missouri Plan, 211–12
Model State Constitution, 56–59
Mofford, Rose, 56
Montana, 43, 81, 101, 118, 145, 161, 204–5, 211, 224, 231, 244, 246, 262, 282
    Missoula, 246
Montesquieu, Baron de, 51
Moody's Investors Service, 298
Morales, Dan, 186
Moralistic political culture, 17
Morgan, David, 263
Morrison case, 11
Municipalities (cities), 253–57
    creation, 253
    population trends, 14–16
    structure, 253–56
    Web sites, 271–72
Musgrove, Ronnie, 91
Muslims, 73
Myanmar, 32

Nathan, Richard, 132
National Association of Counties, 7
National Association of State Development Agencies, 7
National Association of Towns and Townships, 258
National Center for Small Communities, 258
National Center for State Courts, 224
National Conference of State Legislatures, 7, 229–30, 233
National government, 5, 8–9, 26, 27. *See also* Federalism (federal system)
National Governors Association, 7, 38, 142, 147, 151–52, 155

National League of Cities, 7, 38
National League of Cities v. Usery, 31
National Municipal League, 56–58, 270
National Performance Review, 195
National supremacy clause, 28
National Voter Registration Act of 1993, 74
Nation-centered federalism, 27
Native American, 13, 32, 34, 49, 101, 118, 151, 249, 267, 288–89
Navajo Nation, 34
Nebraska, 3, 32, 43, 58, 73, 78, 81, 118, 119, 122, 150, 231, 257, 260
Necessary and proper clause, 28–29
Negative campaigning, 109–10
Nelson, Ben, 43
Neutral competence, 183
Nevada, 10, 14, 73, 75, 104, 115, 117, 134, 145, 159, 169, 240, 249, 284
    Las Vegas, 11, 238, 240, 288
New Deal, 29, 36
New Federalism, 39
New Hampshire, 17, 57, 74, 78, 97, 98, 104, 117, 122, 145, 154, 156, 168–69, 217, 224, 253, 276, 280, 282, 284, 288
New Jersey, 12, 29, 77, 79, 104, 106, 111, 115, 117, 119, 145, 156, 163, 164, 168–70, 194, 198, 233, 257, 262, 283, 285
    Atlantic City, 288
    Newark, 299
New Jersey Plan, 26
New judicial federalism, 220
New Mexico, 14, 34, 122, 136, 137, 145, 148, 212, 280, 283
    Albuquerque, 243
    Santa Fe, 122
New York, 3, 9, 11, 29, 41, 43, 57, 64, 78, 93, 95, 97, 101–2, 112, 122, 125–26, 145, 154, 158, 159, 162, 168, 169, 184, 196, 217, 218–19, 221, 224, 233, 234, 246, 257, 276, 285, 288, 289–90, 293
    Albany, 184
    Buffalo, 256
    New York City, 8, 12–13, 21, 79, 87, 95, 173, 178, 197, 237, 246, 261, 290, 292–94
Nigeria, 24

Ninth Circuit Court of Appeals, 186
Nissan, 298–99
Nixon, Richard M., 37
Nonparticipation, 70–71
Nonpartisan elections, 79–80
North Carolina, 5, 15, 76–77, 113,
    131, 136, 151, 155, 158,
    166–67, 189, 211, 218, 221,
    226
  Chapel Hill, 98
  Charlotte, 256
North Dakota, 4, 14, 74, 85, 104, 112,
    117, 132, 156, 226, 257
Nullification, doctrine of, 27, 36

Offices of court administration, 206
Ohio, 10, 78, 97, 113, 115, 122, 128,
    134, 161, 211, 231, 236, 257,
    285
  Cincinnati, 256
  Cleveland, 261
  Dayton, 88
Ojibway tribe, 101
Oklahoma, 2, 53, 76–77, 81, 93, 113,
    126, 132, 133, 143, 154, 164,
    205, 208, 226, 231, 285
Open meeting laws, 84
Open primary, 76
Ordinance, 232, 251
Oregon, 8, 44, 73, 75, 80, 81–82, 85,
    101, 115, 118, 133, 134, 156,
    167, 168–69, 176, 205, 221,
    241, 280, 282, 302
  Death with Dignity Act, 21–22, 32,
    44
  Portland, 8, 107, 244, 256
Original jurisdiction, 204, 205
Osborne, David, 195
Oversight, legislative, 137–39
Own-source revenue, 274

Package veto, 158
Paine, Thomas, 66
Participation, 59–64, 68–90. *See also*
    Voting
  citizen, 59, 60, 84–88
  direct action, 107
  election-day lawmaking, 80–84
  nonparticipation, 70–71
  volunteerism, 87
  Web sites, 90
Pataki, George, 9, 78, 169, 233,
    246
Patronage, 157, 165, 183
Peirce, Neil, 283

Pendleton Act of 1883, 183–84
Pennsylvania, 9, 12, 17, 50, 76, 86, 97,
    98, 101, 106, 109, 112, 132,
    142, 152, 154, 205, 220, 221,
    257
  Harrisburg, 116, 145
  Philadelphia, 24–25, 60, 68–69, 242,
    250, 292
  Pittsburgh, 256
Pennzoil, 209
Performance, 3, 7
Performance budgeting, 182
Performance standards, for state trial
    courts, 224
Personal Responsibility and Work
    Opportunity Reconciliation Act,
    39
Personnel policy, 183–91. *See also* Merit
    system
Petak, George, 83
Petition, 80
Plea bargaining, 216
Plural executive, 156
Pluralist theory, 262
Plurality, 78
Pocket veto, 159
Policy entrepreneurs, 127
Policy and program evaluation, 137
Political accountability of tax increases,
    279–80
Political action committees (PACs), 98,
    106–7, 111, 113, 209
Political campaigns. *See* Campaigns
Political conflict. *See* Conflict
Political culture, 16–17, 73
Political economy, 290
Political parties, 91–98, 153. *See also*
    Democratic party; Republican
    party
  dealignment, 98
  leadership, 95
  organization, 94–96
  responsible party model, 92–94
  third parties, 97–98
  ticket-splitting, 92
  two-party system, 96–98
  Web sites, 114
Politicos, legislative, 127
Poll taxes, 72
Popular referendum, 80
Population growth, 14–16
Populists, 52
Pork barrel, 136, 149, 166
Port Authority of New York and
    New Jersey, 259

Positive-law tradition, 57
Precedent, 218
Pre-emption, federal, 30–31, 41–43
Primaries, 75–79, 153
Primary system, 75
Privacy, right of, 57
Privatization, 196–197
Privileges and immunities clause, 33
Proactive, 6
Professionalism, 131–32, 193–94
Program evaluations, 137
Progressive reforms, 48, 52, 62, 75,
    80, 142–43, 265
Progressive tax, 278, 284
Project grants, 35
Property tax, 261, 276, 278, 279,
    280–82
Proportional (flat) tax, 278
Proposition 13 and 209. *See* California
Providence Journal-Bulletin, 101
Public authorities, 258–59
Public campaign financing, 112–13
Public-employee pension fund, 297
Public employees (civil servants),
    175–76, 188–91
Public-private partnerships, 195

R.E.M., 262
Racial minorities. *See* African
    Americans; Ethnic groups
    (ethnicity)
Racicot, Marc, 161
Rainy day funds, 3, 274, 296
Ransome, Coleman B., Jr., 165
Ray, Robert, 167
Reagan, Ronald (Reagan
    administration), 37–38, 136,
    167, 189–90, 234
Reapportionment, 119–21, 147, 220,
    234
Recalls, 80–81
Red River Valley, 4
Redistricting, 120–21
Referendum, 80–81, 83–84, 258, 262
Regime analysis, 262
Regional governments, 242, 244
Regressive tax, 278, 282–83
Rehnquist Court, 32, 202–3
Reinventing government, 161, 194–98,
    303
Representative bureaucracy, 185
Republican party, 92, 94–97. *See also*
    Political parties
  Christian right, 96
  recent state elections, 78–79

Republican party (*cont.*)
  runoff primaries, 77–78
  state legislatures, 118
Reserved powers, 27
Responsible party model, 92
Restructuring, 2
Revenue bonds, 297
Revenue sharing, 35, 275
Revenues (revenue systems), 7, 35,
    178. *See also* Taxes
  diversity, 275–76
  estimating, 178, 295
  gambling sources, 287–89
  increased capacity, 7–8
  own-source, 274
  user-fees, 286
  Web sites, 304
Reynolds v. Sims (1964), 119
Rhode Island, 85, 93, 101, 112, 119,
    122, 163, 215, 217, 231, 250,
    282
  Providence, 101, 299
Rice, Tom, 88
Ridge, Tom, 142, 152
Riffe, Vern, 78, 122
Roberts, Barbara, 85
Romer, Roy, 167
Roosevelt, Franklin D., 29, 36
Rosenthal, Alan, 131, 139
Ross, Betsy McCaughey, 169
Rousseau, Jean-Jacques, 51
Runoff elections, 76–77
Rural Development Councils, 245
Rusk, David, 243
Russia, 226
*Ruten et al. v. Republican Party of
    Illinois* (1990), 158
Rybak, R. T., 265

Sabato, Larry, 143
Sainthood spot, 109
Sales tax, 282–84
Salvation Army, 8
Sanchez, Tony, 110–11
Sanford, Terry, 5
School choice, 261, 300
School districts, 260–62
Secretary of state, 170
September 11, 2001, 4, 8, 21, 39, 78,
    142, 178, 184, 292–93
Set-asides, 41
Severance tax, 287
Sexual harassment, 187–88
Shaheen, Jeanne, 145
Shays, Daniel, 26

Shays's Rebellion, 26
Sierra Club, 241
Sin taxes, 285
Single-purpose local government,
    249–50, 260
Sioux tribe, 101
Slating groups, 79–80
Small-claims courts, 205
Smart growth, 240–41
Smith v. Allwright (1944), 72
Social Security Act of 1935, 184
Social Security system, 41
Social welfare expenditures, 300–302
Soft money, 112
South, the (southern states), 52, 72
South Carolina, 7, 27–28, 44, 53,
    76–77, 104, 105, 136, 152,
    177, 189, 208, 234, 262
South Dakota, 77, 80, 97, 134, 245,
    257, 276, 282, 283, 284, 288
Spending. *See* Expenditures
Spitzer, Eliot, 168
Standard and Poor's Corporation, 298
Standing committees, 123–25
State and Local Legal Center, 7
State government(s). *See also* State-local
    relations
  capacity of, 3–11, 18
  functions of, 2–3
  improvements, 7–8
  jurisdiction, 3, 5, 9–12
  presence in Washington, D.C., 7
  problems facing, 11–13
  reform, 6–7
  study of, 2–3
State-centered federalism, 27
State legislatures. *See* Legislatures, state
State-local relations, 12–13, 229–47
  distribution of authority, 230–35
    amount and type, 230–31
    financial relations, 233–34
    local wants, 234–35
    state mandates, 232–33
    tug of war, 231–32
  interaction, 246
  metropolitics, 237–44
    regional governance, 242–44
    smart growth, 239–41
  organizations, 235–37
  rural communities, 245
  Web sites, 247
State party organizations, 94–96
States' powers, 27, 56–59
States' rankings on three indicators, 4
States' sovereignty, 32

Strong-mayor, 253, 256–57
Study commission, 65–66
Sumberg, Alexander, 88
Sunbelt, 14–15, 293
Sunset laws, 138–139
Sunshine laws, 84
Supreme Court, U.S., 2, 11, 20, 26,
    28, 32–33, 38, 57–58, 72, 112,
    119, 121, 158, 185, 186,
    188–89, 202–3, 206, 209, 218,
    220–22, 283
Supreme courts, state, 205
Surveys, citizen, 86
Synergism, 154

Task forces, 236
Tax capacity, 276
Tax effort, 276
Tax equity, 277–79
Tax revolts, 291–92
Taxation and expenditure limitations
    (TELs), 291–92, 294
Taxes (taxation). *See also* Revenues
    (revenue systems)
  evaluating, 276–80
  gambling, 275, 287–89
  income, 112–13, 235, 278, 279,
    284–85, 291
  miscellaneous, 285
  Model State Constitution, 59
  political economy, 289–95
  progressive, 278
  property, 261, 276, 278, 279,
    280–82
  proportional (flat), 278
  regressive, 278
  sales, 235, 278, 279, 282–84, 291
  severance, 287
  travel, 286
  user fees, 279, 286
Taxing and spending power, 30
Tax-service paradox, 290
Technology, 3, 86–87, 224, 302
Temporary Assistance for Needy
    Families (TANF) program,
    301
Tennessee, 75, 119, 168–69, 205, 213,
    241, 242, 273, 276, 282, 284,
    302
  Memphis, 15
  Nashville-Davidson County, 242,
    256, 282
Term limits, 58, 139
Terms of office, 132–35, 154–55
Terrorist acts, 4, 147, 292–93

Testimonial spot, 109
Texaco, 209
Texas, 11, 23, 53, 57, 65, 75, 76–77, 96, 110–11, 118, 121, 123, 128, 133, 136, 142, 145, 159, 160, 165, 168, 169, 176, 186, 194, 198, 205, 209, 218, 226, 227, 262, 276, 282, 284
  Austin, 3, 5
  Beaumont, 299
  Dallas, 256
  Galveston, 256
  Houston, 267
  Loving County, 250
  San Antonio, 31, 194
Third parties, 97–98
Thomas, Clive, 101, 103–4
Thompson, Jim, 155
Thompson, Tommy, 148, 160
Ticket splitting, 92
Tobacco companies, 10, 106, 168
Total quality management (TQM), 195–96
Town meeting, 126
Towns and townships, 257–58
Traditionalistic political culture, 17
Treasurer, 169–70
Trial by jury, 216
Trial courts, 204–6
Trustees, legislators, 126
2040 Plan, 244
Two-party system, 96–98

U.S. Advisory Commission on Intergovernmental Relations (Kestnbaum Commission), 56, 66, 230, 231–32, 236–37
U.S. v. Lopez, 11, 31–32
U.S. Conference of Mayors, 7
U.S. Department of Education, 186
U.S. Department of Justice, 72
U.S. Energy Department, 10–11

U.S. Equal Employment Opportunity Commission (EEOC), 185, 186
U.S. Treasury bills, 296
Underwood, Cecil H., 155
Unfounded Mandate Reform Act of 1995, 41–42
Unified court budgeting, 222–23
Unified court system, 206
Unified government, 97
Unions, 112, 188–91
Unitary system, 22
United Kingdom, 22
Urban sprawl, 238–39
Urbanization, 237
User fees,
Utah, 3, 15, 17, 34, 111, 112, 136, 151, 159, 165, 166, 189, 280

Van Dunk, Emily, 17
Ventura, Jesse, 143, 148, 154, 164
Vermont, 17, 47, 78, 88, 98, 109, 136, 145–46, 151, 154, 163, 178, 231, 241, 258, 295
Veto, 129, 136, 142, 158–60, 169
Violence Against Women Act, 32
Virginia, 41, 50, 77, 79, 137, 145, 159, 160, 189, 208, 221, 236, 250, 285, 287
Virginia Plan, 26
Voinovich, George, 10, 161
Volunteerism, 87, 195
Voting, 71–73
Voting Rights Act of 1965, 72, 121
Voucher plans, 195

Wallace, George, 97
War of Independence, 49
Warner, Mark, 160
Warren, Earl (Warren Court), 57, 119, 202–3, 220
Washington, 3, 76, 81–82, 87, 104, 106–7, 123, 133, 134, 197,

223, 242, 245, 282, 284, 287, 290, 295
  Puget Sound, 295
  Seattle, 8, 197
Washington, D.C., 7, 30, 38, 41, 43, 44, 141, 152, 178, 250, 258, 274–75
Washington, George, 27
Washington, Harold, 270
Washington Post, 237
Watson, Sheila, 263
Weak mayor, 254, 256
Web sites, 19, 46, 67, 90, 114, 140, 171, 201, 228, 247, 271–72, 304
Webb, Wellington, 264
Weber, Ronald, 121
Welfare reform, 8
Welfare Reform Act's Temporary Assistance for Needy Families (TANF), 300
West Virginia, 9–10, 14, 98, 155, 163, 168–69, 234
White, Penny, 213
Whitman, Christine Todd, 145
Wildavsky, Aaron, 179
Wilder, Douglas, 145
Wilson, Pete, 150
Wisconsin, 1, 44, 74, 76, 83, 97, 104, 105, 113, 127–28, 132, 133, 148, 160, 189, 198, 211, 221, 234, 241, 257, 282, 284, 285
World Trade Center, 21
World War II, 56, 237, 260
Wright, Gerald, 93
Wyoming, 2, 74, 76, 131, 136, 168–69, 231, 276, 284, 287
  Cheyenne, 237

Yield of taxes, 279
Yugoslavia, 24